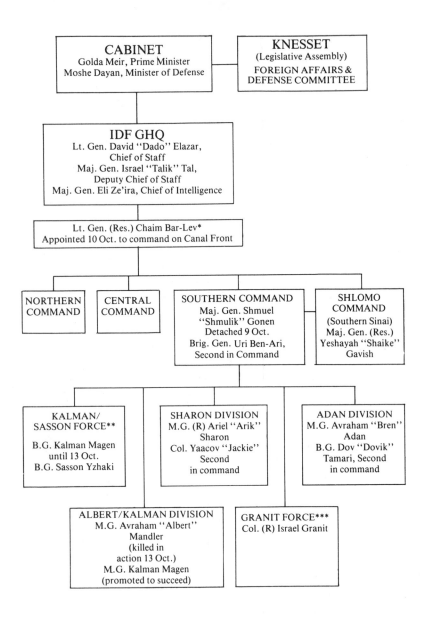

CABINET
Golda Meir, Prime Minister
Moshe Dayan, Minister of Defense

KNESSET
(Legislative Assembly)
FOREIGN AFFAIRS &
DEFENSE COMMITTEE

IDF GHQ
Lt. Gen. David "Dado" Elazar,
Chief of Staff
Maj. Gen. Israel "Talik" Tal,
Deputy Chief of Staff
Maj. Gen. Eli Ze'ira, Chief of Intelligence

Lt. Gen. (Res.) Chaim Bar-Lev*
Appointed 10 Oct. to command on Canal Front

NORTHERN
COMMAND

CENTRAL
COMMAND

SOUTHERN COMMAND
Maj. Gen. Shmuel
"Shmulik" Gonen
Detached 9 Oct.
Brig. Gen. Uri Ben-Ari,
Second in Command

**SHLOMO
COMMAND**
(Southern Sinai)
Maj. Gen. (Res.)
Yeshayah "Shaike"
Gavish

**KALMAN/
SASSON FORCE****

B.G. Kalman Magen
until 13 Oct.
B.G. Sasson Yzhaki

SHARON DIVISION
M.G. (R) Ariel "Arik"
Sharon
Col. Yaacov "Jackie"
Second
in command

ADAN DIVISION
M.G. Avraham "Bren"
Adan
B.G. Dov "Dovik"
Tamari, Second
in command

ALBERT/KALMAN DIVISION
M.G. Avraham "Albert"
Mandler
(killed in
action 13 Oct.)
M.G. Kalman Magen
(promoted to succeed)

GRANIT FORCE***
Col. (R) Israel Granit

*Ex-Chief of Staff, then Minister of Industry & Commerce
**Detached from Adan's Division, morning of 8 October
***Detached from Kalman's Division, morning of 18 October (when Kalman's Division crossed)

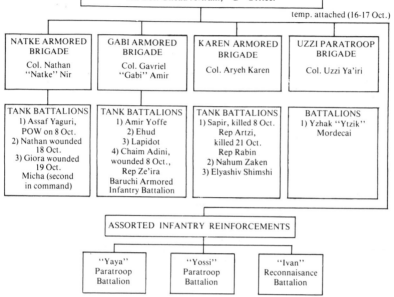

ADAN DIVISION
Maj. Gen. Avraham "Bren" Adan
Brig. Gen. Dov "Dovik" Tamari, Second in Command
Lt. Col. Gilead Aviram, "G" Officer

temp. attached (16-17 Oct.)

NATKE ARMORED BRIGADE Col. Nathan "Natke" Nir	GABI ARMORED BRIGADE Col. Gavriel "Gabi" Amir	KAREN ARMORED BRIGADE Col. Aryeh Karen	UZZI PARATROOP BRIGADE Col. Uzzi Ya'iri
TANK BATTALIONS 1) Assaf Yaguri, POW on 8 Oct. 2) Nathan wounded 18 Oct. 3) Giora wounded 19 Oct. Micha (second in command)	TANK BATTALIONS 1) Amir Yoffe 2) Ehud 3) Lapidot 4) Chaim Adini, wounded 8 Oct., Rep Ze'ira Baruchi Armored Infantry Battalion	TANK BATTALIONS 1) Sapir, killed 8 Oct. Rep Artzi, killed 21 Oct. Rep Rabin 2) Nahum Zaken 3) Elyashiv Shimshi	BATTALIONS 1) Yzhak "Ytzik" Mordecai

ASSORTED INFANTRY REINFORCEMENTS

"Yaya" Paratroop Battalion	"Yossi" Paratroop Battalion	"Ivan" Reconnaisance Battalion

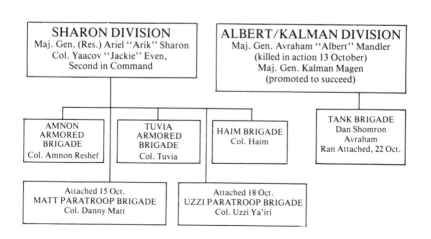

SHARON DIVISION
Maj. Gen. (Res.) Ariel "Arik" Sharon
Col. Yaacov "Jackie" Even, Second in Command

ALBERT/KALMAN DIVISION
Maj. Gen. Avraham "Albert" Mandler
(killed in action 13 October)
Maj. Gen. Kalman Magen
(promoted to succeed)

AMNON ARMORED BRIGADE Col. Amnon Reshef	TUVIA ARMORED BRIGADE Col. Tuvia	HAIM BRIGADE Col. Haim	TANK BRIGADE Dan Shomron Avraham Ran Attached, 22 Oct.

Attached 15 Oct. MATT PARATROOP BRIGADE Col. Danny Matt	Attached 18 Oct. UZZI PARATROOP BRIGADE Col. Uzzi Ya'iri

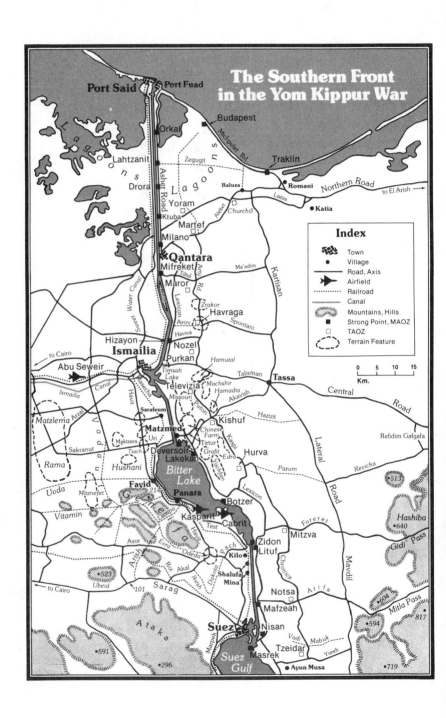

The Southern Front in the Yom Kippur War

Index

- 🏘️ Town
- ● Village
- Road, Axis
- ✈ Airfield
- ···· Railroad
- — Canal
- 〰 Mountains, Hills
- ■ Strong Point, MAOZ
- ☐ TAOZ
- ⬭ Terrain Feature

0   5   10   15
Km.

Port Said · Port Fuad
Budapest
Orkal
Michpelet Rd.
Lahtzanit
Zegugit
Traklin
Drora
Baluza
Romani
Northern Road
to El Arish
Yoram
Aleket
Listim
Katia
Ktuba
Churchill
Martef
Milano
Qantara
Mifreket
Ariy Rd.
Ma'adim
Maror
Tiltul
Kartisan
Zrakor
Havraga
Lexicon
Arov
Spontani
Haviva
Hizayon
Nozel
Ismailia
Purkan
Hamutal
Abu Seweir
Timsah Lake
Talisman
Tassa
Ismailia Canal
Televizia
Machshir
Hamadia
Central Road
Missouri
Akavish
Sarafeum
Hazizit
Matzlema
Arzal
Kishuf
Refidim Gafgafa
Maktzera
Uri
Chinese Farm
Lateral Road
Sakranut
Tsach
Matzmed
Tirtur
Kaspi
Tsach
Deversoir
Grafit
Revicha
Rama
Hushani
Lakekan
Edra
Hurva
Pazum
513
Uuda
Mitznefet
Bitter Lake
Lexicon
Hashiba
640
Vitamin
Fayid
214
Panara
Botzer
Gidi Pass
Lampo
Kasparit
Cabrit
Foreret
Mitzva
Asor
Euro
Odeda
Zidon
Lituf
Kilo
Chronca
Mavdii
523
Ubeid
101
Dakota
Shalufa
Mina
Notsa
Atifa
504
Mitla Pass
to Cairo
Sarag
Mafzeah
594
817
Suez
Nisan
Marpek
Vadi
Mabuk
Yoreh
591
Tzeidar
Masrek
719
296
Suez Gulf
Ayun Musa

THE YOM KIPPUR WAR

GENERAL AVRAHAM ADAN

A DRUM BOOK
1986

THE YOM KIPPUR WAR

Originally published in Hebrew as *On Both Sides of the Suez*
Copyright © 1979 by Edanim Publishers, Jerusalem

Published in English as *On the Banks of the Suez*
Copyright © 1980, 1986 by Presidio Press

Published by arrangement with Presidio Press

ISBN: 0-931933-34-X

Cover design by Joe Curcio

Cartography by Bill Yenne Studios

Drum Books are published by
Richardson & Steirman
246 Fifth Avenue
New York, N.Y. 10001

PRINTED IN CANADA

CONTENTS

INTRODUCTION

During the Yom Kippur War, I commanded an armored division that fought on the Egyptian front. At the outset of this war we were taken by surprise, and the mistakes we made cost us dearly. We lost many of our soldiers early in the battle. In spite of these unfortunate conditions at the start, we managed to hold our own; we were able to recover quickly and launch a counterattack. When we were finally stopped, eighteen days later, our forces were 40 km from Damascus, Syria, and 100 km from Cairo, Egypt. It was understandable, therefore, that at the end of the fighting, I felt our army had excelled in this war. I sensed that the morale among the rank and file was also high.

The response of the people in the rear, however, was quite different. The gap between the expectations of the Israeli Defense Forces (IDF) and the way in which the war was actually conducted — being prolonged and with many casualties — caused a deep crisis. Resentment grew and as time went on, I could see that a paradox had developed: the Yom Kippur War, which was exceptionally hard, full of extensive and heroic battles, and not comparable to the 1956 War and the 1967 War, was being described inappropriately.

Partial and incomplete information leaked out to the public from different sources. A national crisis of confidence developed. The people became concerned with what had or had not been done to find those personally responsible for the *Machdal* — a term which refers to the failure of the government and the army to avoid the initial surprise attack and its consequences.

The division under my command actively fought with all three brigades during eighteen successive combat days. We were engaged in heavy fighting, covering the entire zone of operations on both sides of the Suez, from Romani in the north to Suez City in the south. But in the atmosphere of the *Machdal*, the participation of the soldiers was underrated and their impressive role was obscured, at least in the material published since the war.

I want to tell of the outstanding capability, heroism, and strong spirit I saw on the battlefields but which were lost sight of in the cry of the *Machdal*. I felt I had to describe the path of the fighting and the experiences I witnessed in the division I commanded.

Augmenting the detailed story of my own division, I will describe the fighting of other divisions on the Egyptian front, as well as the assessments and considerations that influenced the various decision-making echelons: within the division, in the Southern Command, at General Headquarters (GHQ), and at the cabinet level.

My story is essentially personal and subjective, and primarily about the events and the people with whom I was in close contact. These are, of course, only part of the total events and people in this war. In working on this book I made an effort to use authentic sources: decoded radio messages; war logs; stenograms from briefings; after-action reports, which were written immediately after the war; and even information from enemy logs, which we had captured at the end of the war. I was supported in my research by the Department of History of the IDF and by the notes of Colonel (Ret.) Elhannan Orren, Ph.D., who headed a team from the history department that covered the battles of my division. I am grateful to the head of the history department, to his aides, and particularly to Dr. Orren. I am also grateful to my brigade commanders and friends who read my manuscript and gave me their encouragement.

Although I was assisted by many, everything I have written is my responsibility, particularly my reflections and reassessments that are scattered throughout the book. These paragraphs are my own criticisms of events and strategic moves, as well as of people, myself included.

It is quite understandable that human weakness, such as fear, exhaustion, and prolonged stress, will reduce effectiveness. Further, the many considerations and decisions made by commanders are strongly influenced by their own personalities and motivations; this, too, can lead to mistakes. I am aware that some readers will find the workings of the Israeli Army difficult to understand, but it is my belief that I must present the truth as I have seen it. It seems about time that we Israelis got rid of our myths and became acquainted with all aspects of the 1973 War.

Criticism should not diminish the trust of the nation in the IDF. In fact, quite the opposite. The results of this very difficult war are the best evidence we have that the IDF is not only strong and efficient but also that it is able to overcome the most problematic situations even granted some mistakes.

I am convinced that knowing the truth is essential to our future trials in war as well as in peace.

HISTORICAL NOTE

The Yom Kippur War was the fifth war of the Arab-Israeli conflict. The first war broke out in May 1948 on the same day the state of Israel was born. Our forces were few, short in manpower and equipment, and just emerging from the underground. Five Arab armies invaded Israel together with local Palestinian forces. They cut off and besieged the Negev, Jerusalem, and the Western Galilee region.

Under these conditions Israel had to build up the IDF (Israel Defense Forces) to the point of being able to counterattack and ultimately defeat the Arab armies. The casualties Israel suffered were very heavy — one percent of the population — but the state survived. Israel (Palestine) stopped its advance and signed a truce agreement when it believed that a peace treaty was sure to follow. However, the Arabs didn't recognize the state of Israel.

During the fifties Israel absorbed masses of Jewish immigrants while it built and developed the country under constant terrorist attacks supported by the neighboring Arab governments. The reprisal strategy Israel adopted against these terrorist attacks — retaliation — didn't bring about the expected results. As soon as the British evacuated Egypt, President Nasser closed the Straits of Firan and the Suez Canal for maritime traffic into and out of Israel. The siege became severe.

In October 1956 Israel went to war against Egypt in an attempt to break the siege. The offense was planned in collaboration with France and England on a loose basis of cooperation, which stated that the IDF was to fight the Egyptian army in the Sinai desert alone, while England and France would present both sides with an ultimatum as the IDF got closer to the Canal. Subsequently, the two powers were to intervene to regain the Suez Canal, hopefully toppling Nasser's regime.

The IDF fought alone for six days and crushed the Egyptian army in the Sinai and reached the Suez Canal within 100 hours, but was forced to retreat by the United States and UN. The only gains Israel achieved were the reopening of the Straits of Firan for maritime use to and from Eilat, and the positioning of UN observers between the Egyptian and Israeli forces, which resulted in a period of quiet along the southern border.

The situation along Israel's eastern border with Jordan and Syria was quite different. The Arabs resumed their fighting in the form of Fedayeen terrorist attacks. They also tried to shift Israel's water sources to their territory by digging a new canal and thus preventing the water which originated on their territory from flowing into the Jordan River, which Israel relied on as its main water source. The IDF managed to prevent this by effective tank fire in border clashes with the Syrian forces which grew in number and in scope. Then, information given by the Soviets to the Syrians and Egyptians concerning alleged mass IDF concentrations in the North led to the Six Days War.

President Nasser acted quickly. He drove the UN out of Sinai and concentrated his army along the Israelis' southern border. He also blocked the Straits of Firan. The Arab world enthusiastically followed Nasser's lead. Crowds demonstrated ecstatically in the streets of the Arab capitals and demanded a war of annihilation against Israel. King Hussein flew from Jordan to Cairo to sign a military alliance with Egypt and Syria. The United States and other countries which were committed to obtain free maritime traffic in the Straits of Firan were hesitant and did not take any measures against Egypt.

The Israeli Reserve Army, which consisted of practically all the labor force, was mobilized for three weeks and the economy was paralyzed. There was no telling what the next morning would bring.

On June 6, 1967 the Israeli army set out on a campaign to lift the blockade and break the siege. The IDF enjoyed a tactical surprise in time and method. In three hours the Israeli air force destroyed the Egyptian air force while the latter was still on the ground. The IDF ground forces broke through the Egyptian lines into Sinai and conquered the whole peninsula within four days. The Egyptian army, equipped with the best Soviet arms was defeated and destroyed. King Hussein ordered his army to open fire in Jerusalem although he was urged by the Israeli cabinet not to participate in the war. Consequently, he lost most of his air force and army as well as the entire west bank of the Jordan river including Jerusalem.

The Syrians who shelled the Israeli settlements in the Northern region were pushed behind the city of Kuneitra on the Golan Heights.

Immediately following the war, Israel hoped to begin peace negotiations, but the Arabs rejected this. They announced the Khartoum conference proclamation: No peace, No negotiation, No recognition. The Arabs held to the idea of destroying Israel, but Israel had won new defensible borders which made future attacks more difficult. The Arabs fought with whatever means they had. Terrorism from within the occupied territories, and from the Jordan and Lebanese borders, expanded into the European arena. In the war against terrorism, Israel succeeded in reducing the number and scope of the terrorist raids to the point where the state could live with it and continue to develop.

The Israelis realized that the Arab countries were getting ready for the next round, but they also perceived that the gap between the IDF and the Arab armies was widening and that the Arabs wouldn't attack until they succeeded in narrowing that gap. The dazzling victory in the '67 war and Israel's ability to suppress the terror, as well as her success in the War of Attrition, contributed to the building of a myth around the IDF and its personnel. The common expectations from the IDF were that any future war would be short with few casualties.

In October '73, Israel was taken by surprise. The charging Egyptian and Syrian armies were met by the Israel regular army alone, while Israel's main force, the Reserve army, was just beginning to mobilize and move to the front. Israel paid dearly for this surprise, which affected the conduct of the entire war and its consequences.

PART I

TAKEN BY SURPRISE

CHAPTER ONE

6 October: THE RUSH TO THE FRONT

At 0600 on 6 October, 1973, the Jewish Day of Atonement (Yom Kippur), my home telephone rang. A duty officer from General Headquarters (GHQ) was on the line. Having ascertained that he was indeed talking to the commander of the Armored Corps, he informed me that I was requested to attend a meeting at GHQ as soon as possible.

For the past ten days there had been tension in the air. GHQ had been concerned over the buildup of equipment and of forces along our borders with the Egyptians and the Syrians. Senior commanders had been summoned frequently for briefing, evaluation of the enemy situations, and discussions of measures to be taken.

The 6 October briefing began at 0700. The director of Military Intelligence (DMI), Maj. Gen. Eli Ze'ira, asserted that he expected war to break out that very evening. His statement was based on new information received only a few hours before from a reliable source.

My colleagues and I were certainly surprised. The underlying assessment of Israeli Intelligence was that the armed forces of the Arab nations were still unprepared for war; hence the probability of war seemed very low. For the past ten days, the director of Military Intelligence had stuck to this evaluation, offering reasonable explanations about the buildup of forces. Moreover, the evening before, when he had briefed us about the evacuation of families of the Soviet technicians from Egypt and Syria, he explained it as just the result of the widening gap between the Arabs and the Soviets. Now suddenly, without any signs of emotion or embarrassment, the DMI was predicting that war would erupt within hours.

That the Egyptians and Syrians would dare to launch a war against Israel seemed incredible. I couldn't believe they were unaware that the Israel Defense Forces (IDF) were far superior to theirs, and they would be risking a painful defeat.

I first noticed the general tension on 24 September when I attended a routine conference at GHQ in Tel Aviv. The commander of Northern Command, Maj. Gen. Yitzak Hofi, was concerned that the Syrian forces were concentrating too near our borders. Normally at this time of the year — the onset of winter in the Middle East — Syria reduced its troops. But this year they had moved many units to the front and were now deployed there in unusual strength. General Hofi also warned and stressed that in this situation, unlike in the Sinai where there was a natural obstacle of the Suez Canal, Syria's troops were so close to Israel's borders that they could advance abruptly and very rapidly.

Hofi asked for immediate reinforcement of his front. But the chief of staff, Lt. Gen. David ("Dado") Elazar, agreed with the assessment of the DMI, which was that the Syrians were preparing only to retaliate for an air-to-air engagement on 13 September, when they lost thirteen MIGs to the Israeli Air Force. Therefore to forestall further escalation they were increasing their front-line forces.

Also attending the conference was the minister of defense, Moshe Dayan. Impressed by Hofi's concern, he asked General Elazar what he intended to do about the uncertain situation. Elazar decided to move an active IDF battalion from the 7th Tank Brigade to the Golan Heights.

On 1 October, the eve of Rosh Hashanah (Jewish New Year), Dayan and Elazar toured the northern front, and the minister of defense addressed Israeli settlers on the Golan Heights. This was intended as a warning to the Syrians that Israel was alert and concerned about their buildup so close to its border. He declared that Israel would react to any hostile Syrian act with a painful blow.

In the south, too, there had been stepped-up activity all along the Egyptian side of the Suez Canal. Israel's Intelligence reported that the Egyptians would hold a large-scale exercise between the first and seventh of October. Like the Syrians, they were massing troops and equipment and had moved artillery up, along with a great deal of bridging gear. While this was accepted as logical for this kind of exercise, it still caused us concern.

Israel responded to the Arabs' military movements by beginning to deploy regular forces closer to the border and placing troops on a high alert level. On 5 October, the 7th Tank Brigade was dispatched to the Golan Heights and Colonel Gabi's armored brigade to Sinai. Preliminary steps were taken to call the reserves up. This was a serious contingency measure, but using only regular troops was a precaution Israel had tailored for a low- or no-war situation.

Now, on 6 October, after the DMI completed his briefing, Dado briefly summed up: he differed with the minister of defense on what steps should now be taken. The two of them would meet with the prime minister, Mrs. Golda Meir, and Dado intended to ask her permission for general mobilization and authority to launch a preemptive air strike. The defense minister, however, was against the air strike, favoring only a limited call-up.

Elazar ordered us to move to our command posts and await directives for mobilizing the reserves.

"I assume that in the coming three days we will be engaged in containment battles and in mobilization and getting the forces to the front; afterwards we will be able to move to the counteroffensive," the chief of staff concluded.

Nonetheless, the fact that even at this stage Dado was not permitted to call up the reserves made me even more skeptical that we really were on the verge of another war. It seemed that most of my colleagues shared my opinion since we had received this kind of information in the past. Still, the atmosphere was strained, and we were all tense — so many things to do, and at once. I was impatient, but the entire meeting lasted only about ten minutes, and then we hurried off. I alerted my staff and subordinate commanders to await my arrival and left quickly for my headquarters in the south.

Israel's highways, roads, and streets were empty. As we sped south,

I fell into deep thought. If war were indeed to break out today, our situation would be precarious. The schedule and time needed for mobilizing the reserves, equipping them, and moving them to the front was clear to me. I thought about the difficult period the few available front-line forces would face until the reserves arrived.

Considerable improvisation would be needed; for instance, one of my jobs would be to form a division from the reserve brigades I would be allocated. I made a mental list of the steps I would have to take to prepare for war in the most effective way. I decided to split my headquarters into two sections: one to deal with the problems of the Armored Corps, and the other with my new division, which would probably be given an urgent task in the Sinai.

Again and again, I found myself wondering about the unbelievable surprise. Just two weeks earlier, I recalled, I had been in my office, working with my aide on my October schedule. This was a special working plan, for in the month ahead I was to make a farewell visit to each of the Armored Corps units, hand over command of the Armored Corps, and retire from the IDF after thirty years of active military service.

My retirement in 1973 was natural; but I had mixed feelings about it. I had discussed my retirement date with the chief of staff about six months before. In October, I would have completed five years as commander of the Armored Corps, long by Israeli standards since none of my predecessors had such tenure. Although rotation and promotion policies were never put on paper, they were well known and accepted in the IDF. I knew that I had to make room for the next generation, but I loved my job and wasn't anxious for it to terminate. I felt that I had been able to apply all my experience and military knowledge as I played a part in strengthening the Armored Corps. Its spirit was now high, and it was a vital and influential part of the Israeli Army, the strongest element of the ground forces. It had grown by about two and a half times over the past five years. Now as we seemed to be on the verge of war, I knew that the bulk of the burden would fall on the Armored Corps, the same troops I had formed and trained.

I had full confidence in our capability. We were well trained, adequately equipped, and professionally prepared. Considering the growth of armored forces on both sides of the border, we had emphasized large armored formations for the previous two years. Our doctrine for mobile warfare had been well developed and assimilated.

When I took over the Armored Corps, its organization was quite different. In order to enhance the capacity of all commanders to exploit the potential of their units, I carried out a reorganization. Platoon, company, and battalion levels were reduced in size, while brigade and division levels were strengthened. I was also responsible for military doctrine and training all of Israel's armored divisions; now they would be tested on the battlefield.

I recalled having been in a similar situation in 1956. I had just finished reorganizing and training my tank battalion when war broke out and my "product" was to be tested in the field. We took part in a lengthy series of actions for one hundred hours nonstop. We fought in the celebrated battle at Abu-Agheila, regarded as one of the most successful armor engagements of that war.* In 1956, as a result of good training and adequate preparations, I enjoyed a common language and understanding with my staff and men, and the battalion moved quickly and fought smoothly. This time I feared our task would be far more complex because of the element of surprise which would cause us many difficulties.

My thoughts were interrupted by our arrival at my headquarters. It was 0900 hours. As I scanned the room, my eyes fell on the photographs on the wall: burned-out Stalin and T-55 tanks, their turrets severed from the hulls, on the ground beside them — mute testimony of our last war, in 1967. I recalled our feelings after that striking victory. Who would have believed then that within six years we would be at war again.

Looking around the conference table at my staff officers, I was satisfied. I had been privileged to work with them for a long period. A well-trained team, they reported on the progress of the mobilization. Then I briefed them, stressing that the most important thing at this stage was to mobilize the reserves and issue their equipment quickly so that we could get to the front as soon as possible, even if we had to finish up organizing the formations as we moved south.

Next I met with the commanders of the reserve armored brigades

---

*For full details on this battle, see S. L. A. Marshall, *Sinai Victory* (Morrow, 1958).

that GHQ had allocated to my division: Colonels Nathan "Natke" Nir, Aryeh Keren, Rami, and Fedale. These were officers I had worked with for a long time, and we instinctively understood each other. In briefing them about the situation, I again stressed the necessity of speeding to the front while organizing on the move.

The meeting with the staff officers and brigade commanders was brief and to the point. None of them stopped to discuss the issue of the surprise; their questions and remarks showed that they understood the gravity of the situation and were anxious to get moving.

As soon as I had time, I went out to visit the neighboring brigade camps to follow the process of equipping them closely. About noon, the first of the reserve soldiers belonging to Natke's brigade began to arrive. Along with the regular troops, they were working feverishly at organizing piles of equipment next to their tanks. But since the tanks were not yet ready for action and the same situation existed in the neighboring camps, I used the time before departing for the south to go to GHQ and update myself on the overall situation. En route to Tel Aviv I found that the usual Yom Kippur rest and silence had been broken. Some vehicles were already traveling on the highways and roads. As I entered the city, I saw many people still carrying their prayer books but walking quickly and purposefully; mobilization was in full progress.

When I entered the GHQ bunker at 1420 hours on 6 October, I had no idea that we had already been at war for twenty minutes. I was dumbfounded to learn that fighting had begun.

It was strange to find myself in Tel Aviv while a war was being fought on our borders. The corridors and bunker rooms were packed with officers clustered in small groups. They seemed almost embarrassed since they did not yet have any real work to do. Their preoccupation for the moment was to listen to the constant humming of the receiver sets and pass the news on to others nearby.

I was told that Maj. Gen. Shmuel ("Shmulik") Gonen, the commander of Southern Command, had asked me to contact him. I phoned him at once. He asked me to speed up my division's movement to the northern Sinai sector and prepare an attack on the enemy in accordance with a plan that called for the capture of Port Fuad.

His instructions seemed very odd to me, particularly the part about preparing an attack. Gonen knew as well as I did that it would take many hours for my division to arrive in the area. Moreover, it was premature to speak of an attack according to a plan that had been drawn up for completely different conditions. That plan was not based on the element of surprise which now confronted us, nor did it consider that first we would have to contain an enemy attack before we could take the offensive. I told Gonen that I would expedite the division's movement south and that I had ordered my units to move in incomplete, unorganized formations, improvising their organizing while on the approach march.

Then I met with the chief of staff, Dado Elazar, who seemed both calm and in full control, though he had to deal with a growing number of problems. I obtained his approval for some emergency assignments. Brig. Gen. Kalman Magen, for example, had been scheduled to assume control of the Sinai Division on 3 October, replacing Maj. Gen. Avraham (Albert) Mandler. Mandler, however, refused to leave his troops in view of the deteriorating situation, so Magen now had no assignment. Dado and I agreed that Magen would be placed under Mandler's command. Elazar also approved the assignment of Brig. Gen. Mordechai Zippori (lately my deputy), to the post of chief Armored Corps officer at GHQ, with the task of dealing with corps problems on all fronts. This enabled my present deputy, Brig. Gen. Dov ("Dovik") Tamari, to serve as my deputy armored division commander.

Tall and handsome, Dovik had served with us only a short time. He joined the Armored Corps after long service in the paratroops, after which he commanded a special elite unit. A precise planner and a natural leader, he was selected as my deputy after completing a tour as an armored brigade commander. I followed his absorption into the Armored Corps closely. What I liked most about him was his self-discipline in learning his new tasks. He did not push his way through but preferred to invest time and effort in learning, even if that might slow promotion possibilities. He wanted to be a professional among his new colleagues, not basing his new career on past achievements in the paratroops.

Impatient now, I rushed to join my units in the south. On the way, however, I received instructions to proceed to Southern Command Headquarters in Beersheba. As I passed my headquarters, I stopped long enough to insure that my staff had issued written orders to facilitate movement on the roads to El Arish and Baluza. A rendezvous point was set for an advance party made up of representatives of all my formations. The advance party was to organize an assembly area near Baluza. This would enable our division to concentrate near the front line. To save time, and stress the urgency of our move south, I arranged a second meeting with the brigade commanders for 2300 hours at Rafiah.

I then sped to Beersheba. A few buses crowded with soldiers were already on the highway. I reached Southern Command at about 1730 and met Gonen. It was clear now that the Egyptians were crossing the Suez Canal in mass along its entire length, the most difficult situation being in the northern sector. Mandler's formations, we were told, were moving westward. I realized that our plans were in a state of flux; the deployment of the regular Sinai Division called for in our *Shovach Yonim* Plan had not materialized. Nevertheless, Gonen again ordered me to prepare to attack toward Port Said. He added that something different might occur, in which case I would cross the canal south of Ismailia. These notions were consistent with plans drawn up before the war, but I now found them irrelevant to a situation in which the enemy was already attacking our few front-line forces, with our main forces still far from the front. Therefore, I took his guidelines as a kind of declaration of intent for a swift shift from defense to counterattack. In any case my main concern at the moment was to get my division to the front as fast as possible.

How soon we could reach the front, however, depended on the availability of tank transporters now being mobilized. Most of my divisional units were concentrated in the coastal plain north of the Negev Desert with only a few in the Negev itself. On the other hand, most of Maj. Gen. Ariel ("Arik") Sharon's forces were actually in the Negev. Since only a limited number of transporters were available, I requested Gonen to give my units priority while the forces in the Negev, Sharon's and mine, would proceed from there on their own tracks. Gonen agreed.

Activity was feverish at Southern Command, with officers coming and going all the time. Having obtained the tank transporters, I wanted to get to the front with my division as quickly as possible.

As I left, I found myself thinking about the two division commanders who would be my colleagues on the battlefield, Mandler and Sharon. I knew Albert Mandler well because he had served twice as my deputy, once when I commanded the 7th Armored Brigade and later in the Armored Corps. He knew how to impose order and discipline in his units, doing it with a fair approach and showing full appreciation for his subordinates.

Mandler was an able officer, with organizational capacity, good knowledge and understanding of how staffs function, and fine tactical perception. I knew that Mandler had a cool disposition, but I didn't envy his present situation. It would take many hours before my reserve division and Arik Sharon's could reach the zone of operation. Until then, Albert Mandler would have to bear the full brunt of the surprise enemy attack alone.

The third divisional commander, Arik Sharon, was well known throughout the IDF and no less famous throughout all of Israel. As a platoon leader in the 1948 War of Independence, he was wounded in the Battle of Latrun against the Jordanians. During the first years after Israel gained its independence, around 1948, the Arabs raided and terrorized the country. This was not an auspicious period for the regular army, which was unable to prevent or halt the raids, so Sharon set up a volunteer unit to conduct reprisal raids into the enemy's territory. Because of this success, he was given command of the paratroops whom he merged into his own unit, quickly converting them into a splendid fighting team. With the support of the then chief of staff, Moshe Dayan, he enlarged his battalion to brigade strength and continued to attack Egyptian, Jordanian, and Syrian troops and military positions. His objective was to make them understand that if they continued to give support to raids against Israel, they would be punished — hopefully making them conclude that their best interest was to prevent, not support, raids into Israeli territory.

Those retaliatory operations gradually increased in frequency and scope. Although they always attained their immediate military aim, they never achieved their strategic objective: putting an end to infiltration and raids into Israel. The war of 1956 finally stopped the raids, producing a period of quiet. Sharon gradually advanced through positions of increased responsibility until in 1970, shortly before the end of the War of Attrition, he was put in charge of Southern Command. In that post, he was totally successful in suppressing terrorists in the Gaza Strip.

Arik wanted to be chief of staff, but when that did not come about, he had retired from the army and entered politics. He was a candidate to the Israel Knesset (parliament). All of this was three months before the Yom Kippur War.

I knew Sharon from his service in the Armored Corps and from his participation in frequent discussions with senior corps commanders. At those times, he often reflected more of his infantry experience than any special insight about armored operations. Compared with other officers transferred from infantry to armor, my impression was that he did not seem cut out to be an Armored Corps soldier.

When I was given command of the Armored Corps in 1969 and thus joined the General Staff forum, I had further opportunities to hear his ideas. During the War of Attrition, Arik expressed many extreme notions, which sounded simplistic to me, especially those concerning strategic-political issues. He criticized the chief of staff, and his views leaked to the press.

When he was the head of Southern Command and I was at Armored Corps, we generally worked in cooperation. I concentrated on canal-crossing operations with respect to the development of means and methods and training of the troops. At the same time Arik devoted himself to plans and practical preparations on the ground for future operations. It was natural that we should have certain differences. He pressed for an increase in the number of regular armored forces to be employed in ongoing operational duties on the front line, while I urged that more troops undergo further training and basic preparation for war. As part of these preparations, we engaged in discussions, operative planning, and war games. I briefed Sharon on plans for employing my division in the south; there were no differences between us on this. From all I heard and saw, my impression was that General Sharon, while not one to show unswerving loyalty to his superiors, was an excellent combat commander who had unusual tactical perception and first-rate planning and execution ability.

At 2000 on 6 October, I made one more visit to Natke's brigade. I found great activity, along with many problems. Crew members were arriving steadily, but many crews were still incomplete, complicating preparation of the tanks. Nevertheless, many were already in an advanced state of readiness with weapons and ammunition removed from storage and in place on the vehicles, along with periscopes, optical sights, range finders, radio sets, food, and water. I instructed Natke to hurry the preparation of those tanks that were almost ready so he could get them on transporters as soon as they were available.

The first transporters arrived at 2200 hours, and the loading of tanks began. A half-hour later the first convoy left for the south. This was quite an achievement — a reserve armored force was able to move out just twelve hours after the mobilization order.

I reached Rafiah at 2300 hours that night and saw our checkpoint already in operation. Rafiah was a road junction on the border between Israel and Sinai, 200 km from the canal and 100 km from where Natke's and Fedale's brigades were stationed.

I urged Rami, whose mechanized brigade was the closest to Rafiah, to move his tank battalion under their own power to get through Rafiah ahead of Natke's transporters. Otherwise traffic would be disrupted. I knew that everyone understood the severity of the situation and was doing his utmost, but I couldn't help urging each commander to speed things up even more. I was content only after the tanks had left for the front, shortly before the big convoys arrived.

Meanwhile, the brigade commanders whom I had summoned to meet me arrived. From their reports I learned that getting Aryeh's brigade ready had become very complex. One of his battalions was supposed to be composed of regular troops, but it had been sent to the Golan Heights prior to the outbreak of the war. Thus he was now short almost a full battalion of tanks and men — nearly a third of his strength. Other tank crews belonging to his brigade were caught up in the so-called "operational employment." These were reserve crews who had been called up for a limited period to augment regular units along the borders and were now deployed in widely scattered locations, from Sharm el-Sheikh in the far south to Mount Hermon in the north. As a result, Aryeh now had to assemble tanks and crews from other sources that Armored Corps placed at his disposal. Nevertheless, I was pleased that while his deputy was remaining behind to complete the task of rebuilding the brigade, Aryeh himself intended to move to the front at midnight with about half a brigade.

After midnight I watched for a while at the Rafiah junction as the tank convoys moved south. It was an impressive sight. The dozens of tank-carrying transporters looked like gigantic monsters as they lumbered along at a steady pace. In contrast, the crewmen seemed the size of fleas as they sat huddled in the small vans of the transporters. Here and there a few hands could be seen waving *shalom,* and some crewmen stood up to identify their location. Next I met my deputy, Dovik, with the division advance party en route to prepare the assembly area. At this point I felt that in spite of all the difficulties caused by the surprise, we would enter action organized.

I was wrong.

At about 0200 on 7 October, I headed south. With me in the car were my operations officer, the division artillery commander, my aide, and the driver. We passed several tank convoys. The narrow road ran between high dunes, and the wide transporters took up its entire width. Along the hair-raising drive, we were barely able to pass the transporters even after lengthy signaling to let us through.

Later we encountered transporters that had broken down, blocking the road. To make the road passable again they had to be pushed into the dunes, a far from easy task. Overall though, while traffic had been badly disrupted here and there, it was still moving. We could also see that some tanks had lost their tracks as they moved the stalled transporters off into the dunes. I was worried because I knew how complicated, difficult, and time consuming it was to repair a tank that had lost a track in heavy dunes. Soon we saw vehicles moving in the opposite direction, too, and this gave rise to fresh concern, because two-way traffic on such a narrow road could cause grave problems.

Despite these difficulties, I was encouraged by the fact that ahead of us my tanks were moving forward not too far from the front; while somewhere in the rear, at the Rafiah junction, Natke's tanks were coming via transporters from the coastal plain; and Aryeh's were coming on their own tracks from the Negev. Rami's battalion was ahead, on tracks. One of his companies remained in El-Arish to guard against an enemy raid from the sea.

At dawn on 7 October, about 0530, I arrived in the vicinity of Romani, 35 km from the canal. There I met my deputy and the division advance party who were completing preparations for moving the division into its assembly area. From them I learned of the division's first casualty in this war. Maj. Oded Hermony, my cultural officer, had been killed in an accident on the overcrowded road while on his way to the front. I was shocked; we hadn't even reached the front line, and already we had our first casualty.

Oded, a talented volunteer, and I had worked together for about two years. Respected and well liked, he was the youngest officer at my HQ with whom I had a direct working relationship. I had developed a special fondness for him.

I left Dovik and continued on my way to the front. A thousand and one thoughts kept me busy, but Oded's image came to mind time and again. Dark haired and bespectacled, his facial expression reflected his intelligence, and his ever-present somewhat impish smile seemed to say, "There is no problem we cannot overcome." A year ago he had married, and in a few days his child would be born. I thought of Mira, his young wife, who had never had an opportunity to spend much time with Oded at home. How many similar tragedies were now coming to pass on the front lines?

We drove on to Baluza. Though many hours would pass until the whole division was in the area, I was satisfied that in spite of the haste, the inevitable improvisations and organizational difficulties, and the narrow congested roads, we had managed to arrive less than twenty-four hours after the mobilization was ordered. Within seventeen hours of the outbreak of war, we had succeeded in getting the lead elements of the division close to the front. I was confident that the rest would soon follow and that the morning hours would see us ready to enter battle.

But other thoughts also kept assailing me. There is no place for such optimism, I told myself. After all, the arriving troops were hastily prepared — the men were showing up a few at a time — this, while the enemy was already fighting at full strength, exploiting his initial surprise.

Listening on the radio net, I found it difficult to understand what was going on at the front. But it was clear that we were in trouble. I could hear many calls for help and requests for evacuation of wounded men. I was glad that we were already nearby.

CHAPTER TWO

EGYPTIANS CROSS AND ATTACK

F irst light, 7 October. The road was empty and the white dunes nearby seemed aglow as I approached Baluza in my jeep, followed by my staff in armored personnel carriers (APCs). Here, some 20 km from the Suez Canal, there was a pastoral silence. One could hardly believe that a war was in the making. At Baluza, the huts looked gloomy, with vehicles parked around the command bunker. There was no movement in the vicinity of the hospital bunker, and the yard was quiet. I ordered my command vehicles to spread out and entered the bunker.

Inside things were different. The bunker was long and narrow and had several rooms. Communications equipment was in full operation; officers were so busy studying maps and making contact with various places simultaneously that they did not even notice my arrival. Suddenly, one of the signal officers identified me and showed me the way to the commander's room. When I entered, Colonel Alush, the sector commander, approached. Next to him, to my surprise, was Brig. Gen. Kalman Magen.

Only seventeen hours earlier Kalman had been at the GHQ bunker in Tel Aviv, looking for an assignment. There it was decided that he should proceed to the Sinai Division. Upon arriving at

Refidim, in the late afternoon of 6 October, Kalman was ordered by Gen. Albert Mandler to take command of the northern sector of the Sinai front.

Since I had known Kalman for many years, it was enough just to look at him now to see how grave the situation was. He had served under me in several assignments. I liked him, considered him an excellent officer, and admired his character. A talented man possessed of initiative and organizational capability, he accomplished much, always quietly and modestly. In any army, commanders can become selfish, concerned only about their own units, but in Kalman's case, the opposite was true. He was ready to cooperate, disliked friction, and solved the problems he encountered constructively. His leadership was self-evident, and he was liked not only by the men who served under him but also by other commanders and civilians who worked with him.

Kalman told me that General Gonen had phoned for me to contact him immediately upon my arrival. When I contacted Gonen, he sounded tired and told me, "Bren, it's good you have arrived. The situation along the canal is rough. Albert is having trouble controlling such a broad sector. Take command of the northern part. The Egyptians have crossed the canal en masse, and our casualties are heavy. Move your forces to contain the enemy and prevent a breakthrough eastward in your sector. Let me know as soon as you have a plan."

"Okay, Shmulik," I answered, and hung up.

I looked at the map, with which I had become very familiar. As the first commander of the Sinai Armored Division, I had built the so-called Bar-Lev Line in 1968.

The Suez Canal is a water-obstacle 12 meters deep, 160–180 meters wide, and 160 km in length. Along its west bank, Egyptian infantry were deployed in trenches and firing positions. Opposite them, on the east bank, we defended from seventeen *maozim* (small strongpoints), situated at intervals of 10–30 kms. On the banks of the canal both sides had erected sand barriers to prevent observation, provide concealment, and protect from direct hits by flat-trajectory weapons. The barriers also provided fields of fire over the water and the opposite bank, and they served as obstacles to prevent vehicle disembarkments after a canal crossing.

The Israeli sand barriers were 3–10 meters high, while the Egyptians had not long before raised their ramparts to a height of 15–30 meters, thus improving observation and the ability to employ flat-trajectory fire.

Extending 2–10 km eastward on our side of the canal was a negotiable level area which, however, included impassable swamps and lagoons. Just beyond this flat strip, sandy hills rose gently, reaching to the first dune ridge, some 10–12 kms from the canal. This ridge line was of great topographical importance, as it afforded clear observation of most of the level strip right to the canal. It was just behind this ridge that the IDF had constructed its north-south Artillery Road, allowing artillery units to deploy and shift positions. The section of this road that ran through my sector was code-named Hazizit.

Between the first and second — higher — ridge line lay some 30 km of virtually impenetrable dunes. On the second ridge line we constructed our Lateral Road (code-named Kartisan, Mavdil on Israeli maps), designed to enable maneuvering and shifting of forces from one sector to another. The natural barrier of sand dunes extended eastward to the area of the mountains and passes, some 70 km from the canal. Beyond this zone lay sandy terrain and corridors between the mountains. Longitudinal roads, generally running east-west — most of them of Egyptian construction — led to the canal. In the southern sector was the Sharm el-Sheikh-Suez Road and the roads traversing the Mitla and Gidi passes. In the central sector lay the Abu Agheila-Refidim-Tasa-Ismailia Road (code-named Talisman), with a branch-off (code-named Akavish) from Tassa to Deversoir. The northern sector had a road (Aleket) running from Rafiah to El Arish to Qantara. In addition, many short approach roads had been paved from the Artillery Road (Hazizit) to the canal strongpoints.

I now considered the northern sector, over which I had just been given command. My front line ran along 45 km of the canal, from the Mediterranean Sea in the north to Balah Island in the Suez Canal to the south. The terrain itself was a problem, largely inaccessible to traffic. Its continuity was broken by the Tinah Lake lagoons and swamps, which formed a large triangle in the sector's most northerly corner, and by the 10 km of the canal's eastern bank, south of Port Fuad, which we had not occupied in the 1967 War and was still held by the Egyptians.

To counteract this, the IDF had created a separate subsector in the northernmost zone, between Tinah Lake and the Mediterranean, where there was a narrow strip of land, 30–100 meters wide. There were two Israeli strongpoints in this subsector on the Mediterranean coast: Budapest, 10 km east of Port Fuad, and Traklin, 25 km east of Budapest. Between them a road had been constructed, code-named Michpelet, which turned south near Traklin and joined with the main northern road, Aleket, near Romani.

Terrain near the canal in my sector was divided into two sections. The southern part ran from Strongpoint Mifreket near Balah Island to 5 km north of Qantara. There were many swamps in this section, covered by a thin layer of sand. This posed a danger to tanks and other vehicles. The other part of the sector ran from 5 km north of Qantara up to the Orkal Strongpoint, 10 km south of Port Fuad. It was here that Tinah Lake, actually a large lagoon which extended up to the Mediterranean, was situated. Between the lagoon and the canal there was a narrow strip of terrain, 100–800 meters wide. The Asher Road, which had been built on it, could be easily blocked.

With this kind of terrain, it would be easy to cut off the three northern strongpoints, Drora, Lahtzanit, and Orkal. To reduce that risk during the War of Attrition, we had connected this subsector to the rear by the Zegugit Road, building it in the middle of the lagoon from west to east, from Strongpoint Lahtzanit to the Aleket Road near Baluza.

Construction of that road was a unique feat. It was designed and built by Dan Zaslavski, a young professor from the Haifa Technion. A plastic sheet was laid on the bottom of the shallow lagoon with tons of soil piled on it to form a roadbed. From the Zegugit Road another branch led to Strongpoint Drora. Concerned that the enemy could easily block this road near the strongpoints and that we might then have to fight our way to link up with them, we constructed small sandbanks — nicknamed "the fins" — to the right and left of the road 800 meters from Drora and Lahtzanit.

It really is a tough sector, I thought, lacking continuity from either north to south or from east to west.

My thoughts were interrupted by Kalman Magen, who told me that when he had arrived at the Sinai Division, the situation in the northern sector was so grave that Albert had ordered him to take command there. He had asked Colonel Alush to describe how the war had begun. Alush said he had been called by Mandler at 1000 hours on 6 October and ordered to ready his forces and deploy them according to *Shovach Yonim,* the plan designed to deploy our regular forces — with minor reserve reinforcement — well forward. He was to begin to move the tanks forward at 1600 to be prepared at 1700. Alush returned to his headquarters at 1230 hours, called in the battalion commanders, and issued his orders. At 1315 hours Alush received an alert order to deploy immediately according to *Shovach Yonim,* but this was canceled within minutes. At 1350 hours, Egyptian artillery opened fire, and their planes attacked the strongpoints as well as Alush's artillery batteries. The troops manning our strongpoints were caught by surprise.

The report from the higher levels of command concerning a general war commencing that evening on both fronts was understood at lower command levels in the strongpoints to mean that the Egyptians planned to commence an artillery barrage at 1800 hours, causing them to think that a War of Attrition was about to resume. This impression was reinforced when at 1315 hours a "shelling alert" was promulgated, calling for countermeasures against a possible artillery bombardment. As soon as this alert was ordered, observation posts outside the strongpoints folded up operations, and the men entered the strongpoints. Here and there some of these observation points did not comply, and the soldiers later made their way to the strongpoints or to the rear. Alush's report painted the following fragmented picture: from all the strongpoints excited reports began coming in, first via telephone link and then, when the lines were cut, by radio. The network was loaded, and the picture that emerged was that the Egyptians, under cover of the artillery shelling, were carrying out a canal-crossing operation on the flanks of the strongpoints and at several places opposite them.

Lieutenant Colonel Yomtov was a tank battalion commander in the northern sector. In periods of tension, two or three tanks were usually kept at each of the strongpoints that could easily be cut off. But when the war broke out, the situation was different. Only at the northernmost strongpoint, Orkal, was there a tank platoon. The rest of the battalion was camped in two waiting areas in the rear, intending to operate against enemy forces crossing the canal. Two companies, Uri's and Noam's, were at Katia, 40 km from the canal. The third company, Yonatan's, was at the "Churchill" waiting area, about 20 km from the canal.

When at 1400 hours, forty Russian-built Sukhoi fighter planes attacked various targets near Baluza, Yomtov's tanks started to move toward the canal. Uri's company at Katia regrouped into pairs of tanks and hurried to the three strongpoints on the northern strip — Drora, Lahtzanit, and Orkal — and to Budapest on the Mediterranean. Noam's company from Katia was sent to Qantara, while Yonatan's company advanced from Churchill toward Mifreket, just north of Balah Island. Yomtov advanced with Yonatan's company. One platoon was immediately deployed near Qantara; and Yomtov, with the other two platoons of Yonatan's company, headed for Mifreket. As they approached, they saw hundreds of Egyptian infantry soldiers who suddenly fired a barrage of missiles at them. The small company of seven tanks split into two, one platoon to the left and one to the right of the Tiltul Road, opening fire on Egyptian tanks across the canal as well as at enemy infantry in their own area. As they moved closer, Egyptian RPG-7 and Sagger missiles hit some tanks. Other tanks got stuck in the sand-covered marshes as they maneuvered to avoid the missiles.

At this stage, Noam's company arrived from Katia and joined the force. Yomtov deployed it south of the Tiltul Road, with the remnants of Yonatan's company north of the axis. Heavy Egyptian artillery fire made the operation difficult. Some tanks had to be used to pick up wounded soldiers and others to recover damaged tanks. Fewer and fewer tanks remained operable. At this stage, Mifreket called for help. Egyptian forces using flame throwers were advancing, and there were dead and wounded soldiers in the strongpoint.

Uri's company, in the northern part of the sector, reported that it was having trouble reaching the strongpoints because of ambushes. Radio communication with Lahtzanit was soon cut off, and Alush's headquarters ordered Yomtov to dispatch tanks there. Before Yomtov ordered tanks to Lahtzanit, he directed Yonatan to break through to Mifreket under the cover of all the able tanks. But the attempt failed, and Yonatan was killed. Other attempts to approach from the southern flank also failed. Alush, concerned over the absence of communication with Lahtzanit, told Yomtov that an armored infantry company under Yaron would arrive in his sector from Refidim, and he urged Yomtov to have additional tanks join the Yaron company and then move to help Lahtzanit.

Yomtov dispatched the deputy commander of Noam's company with a tank platoon to join Yaron's armored infantry company. The platoon set out through the rear marshes to Lahtzanit, which was 40 km to the north. However, not far from Qantara they were ambushed and suffered heavy casualties. They were now left with only one tank. The few men left from the armored infantry platoon worked to recover the wounded and evacuate them to the rear.

By now, all three tank commanders from the platoon of Yonatan's company that had been left opposite Qantara were wounded. Two tanks were recovered, and the third was busy evacuating injured personnel. At this stage, Yomtov succeeded in penetrating Mifreket with one tank and half-track to evacuate the wounded. As darkness approached, Yomtov had only three operable tanks left of the twenty he had deployed near Qantara and Mifreket. These were engaged in pulling out stuck tanks.

The situation of Uri's company, split into pairs of tanks and operating in the north of the sector, was no better. The company commander accompanied by an additional tank had arrived at the barrier near Drora when he heard that the platoon moving north towards Lahtzanit was in trouble. An Egyptian infantry team equipped with antitank weapons had set up an ambush in the "fins." The platoon leader and tank commander were killed while exposed in their turrets. Nevertheless, the two tanks continued towards Lahtzanit. Near this strongpoint, one of these tanks was destroyed, while the other sped northward and reached Orkal, the dead platoon commander still bent over in the turret. Alush's headquarters pressured Uri to link up with Lahtzanit, whose radio channel was still silent.

South of Uri, opposite the Ktuba strongpoint, the deputy company commander and another tank scored hits on two Egyptian tanks on the ramps of the opposite bank. Uri decided to move north to help Lahtzanit and instructed his deputy to do the same. The two pairs of tanks approached Lahtzanit from different directions and at different times. Uri's two tanks came under missile fire as they approached from east to west, and both were damaged as they tried to back off. The deputy, moving on the Asher Road along the canal from south to north, lost another tank. He pressed on alone, but his tank was also hit near Lahtzanit.

Of all of Uri's company, only the platoon under Lieutenant Saul reached its destination, the Budapest strongpoint on the Mediterranean, on time. This was at 1450 hours when Budapest was being heavily shelled, following an air attack in which napalm had been dropped. A column of Egyptian tanks and armored personnel carriers (APCs) was advancing toward Budapest from the direction of Port Fuad. Fortunately, most troops were in their shelters, and the gunners were firing from fortified positions in support of Strongpoint Orkal.

When he saw that an Egyptian armored attack was about to be launched in his direction, the strongpoint commander ordered his artillery to stop firing its long-range guns temporarily and use 120mm mortars against the enemy. However, after they had fired six mortar shells, their position took a direct hit. The artillery men who survived returned to fire their long-range guns from the fortified bunker.

Saul, accompanied by two tanks, arrived just in time. He noted that Egyptian tanks were just 900 meters in front of him. He opened fire and caused such damage to the advancing column that the Egyptians withdrew quickly, leaving their tanks and APCs behind. But this was not the final attack on Budapest. Thirty hours later, early on 8 October, Saul's two tanks would again play a decisive role in stopping a bold Egyptian attack there. Just before sunrise that day, Egyptian infantry was spotted at the barbed wire around Budapest's western slope. Saul's tanks scored direct hits on four amphibious APCs advancing from the sea and killed scores of Egyptians who had been lying in wait by the barbed-wire fence. The job was finished by the men of the strongpoint in a mopping-up operation. Saul's tanks then moved to help in wiping out the Egyptian infantry who had fled into the marshes.

While the tanks fought to reach the strongpoints, all the *maozim* came under heavy artillery fire and infantry assault. All were reporting that Egyptian infantry was continuing to cross the canal. They managed to sink some of the boats and repel attacks, but they suffered heavy casualties in the process.

Soldiers in the strongpoints were beginning to get used to their grim situation. They gradually recovered from the shock of the surprise attack, and in almost every strongpoint, they managed to direct our artillery fire effectively. But our small number of guns was reduced even further because of excessive wear and breakdowns caused by sustained heavy firing. Ammunition was also running out. Eventually only a single gun remained in action, firing bursts in the air over the strongpoints to try to repel the Egyptian infantry while our soldiers huddled in their bunkers and shelters. The character of the fighting in each strongpoint depended to a large degree on its commander, but as the fighting wore on, more and more commanders were killed, and the ability of the strongpoints to resist declined.

The commander of the infantry battalion whose men were manning the strongpoints in the sector moved about in the area with a forward command group in two vehicles, receiving reports from the strongpoints. Suddenly he spotted six Egyptian helicopters flying low from the direction of Port Fuad toward the marshes and then landing by Tel Farma, 6 km northwest of Baluza. He contacted sector HQ in order to ask for the help of the air force. At about that same time another forty-four Egyptian helicopters took off from the southern canal sector in order to land commando forces deep into the sector near the Gidi and Mitla passes and in the hills along the Gulf of Suez.

To the battalion commander's surprise, his report was received with incredulity. Sector HQ replied that according to the air force, they knew of the helicopters and had in fact shot them down. And, indeed, of the fifty commando-filled Egyptian helicopters, Israeli planes had shot down twenty. The air force's reply was received just as the battalion commander saw Egyptian soldiers leaping from the helicopters with his own eyes. His insistence led to the appearance of a pair of Mystere aircraft overhead, but they saw nothing and flew off. The Egyptian helicopters took off and headed back westward, and one of them was shot down by fire from Strongpoint Drora. The battalion commander's attempts to call in the sector's reconnaissance force were unsuccessful, because the force experienced so many traffic difficulties in the dunes that its movement was delayed. As dark approached, new reports were received of more landings by Egyptian commandos in our rear. We were to encounter them that night and the next morning.

Cut-off of the strongpoints was of grave concern to the senior command. The soldiers in them were unaware of how grave the situation actually was and did not even imagine that our forces would not link up with them. But Yomtov knew that his tank battalion had been virtually annihilated in only a few hours, with only four operative tanks remaining in the entire northern sector. The sector commander, Colonel Alush, knew that the strongpoints were surrounded and crying for help and waiting at least for their wounded to be evacuated, but he was unable to get reinforcements to them.

The division commander, General Mandler, received similar reports from all sectors along the entire canal front. It was a heavy burden to command a sector of 160 km coming under massive attack along its whole length. The hundreds of grim fragmentary reports from what was left of his own units and from the strongpoints themselves made it difficult to piece the real situation together. They were sufficient, of course, to cast a pall of imminent disaster over our headquarters.

The northern sector was in the most difficult situation. Albert, therefore, diverted Gabi's tank brigade, as well as another armored battalion from his division (Lapidot's battalion), and sent them to that hard-pressed sector. They set out from Refidim at 1400 and had to move 100 km to reach the sector that was so anxiously awaiting them. By 1600, division headquarters believed that Lahtzanit and Mifreket had fallen and that Orkal and Budapest were under heavy enemy tank attack. They asked for and got air strikes, but these had little effect. In fact, however, the strongpoints had withstood the enemy attacks. There was now nothing to do except wait for reinforcements.

As dusk began to fall, Brig. Gen. Kalman Magen arrived at the northern sector to take over command. Establishing communications, he learned from Yomtov that his tank battalion had been annihilated. From division headquarters he learned that two armored units were moving to reinforce his command. These were Col. Gavriel ("Gabi") Amir's reduced brigade — by now, just one battalion of four tank companies — and the Lapidot task force, made up of two tank companies. The other two battalions of Gabi's brigade had been diverted to other sectors while on their way to Baluza.

Pressure from the strongpoints to evacuate the wounded was intense. In accordance with the orders he received, Kalman planned to split Gabi's brigade (which had started with forty-four tanks but arrived with only thirty-six because some got stuck in the dunes), sending two companies to Mifreket and two to Qantara. He intended to dispatch the Lapidot force to the sandbar on the Mediterranean and split it into two, one company to the Traklin sector and the other to the Budapest sector.

At 1900 Yomtov met Gabi at Ma'adim-Hazizit crossroads. Yomtov gave a precise report on what had happened to his battalion. In accordance with the orders he received, Gabi split Amir Yoffe's battalion into two "mini-battalions." Yomtov, who knew the sector, guided Amir, with two companies, to Mifreket. Yomtov returned later to Gabi's brigade headquarters. Gabi's other two companies were now organized into a battalion that was placed under the deputy brigade commander Lieutenant Colonel Shilo. They moved, via Lexicon and Aleket, toward Qantara. But before they got there Amir's battalion was already engaged in battle.

Amir was the only one in his battalion acquainted with the area, but he was unaware that the Egyptians had laid mines there. He deployed Raviv's company south of Mifreket and Erez's company to the north of Mifreket. Two tanks from Raviv's company were damaged by mines before the rest arrived at the sand barriers and began firing at Egyptian tanks on the opposite bank. Meanwhile, Erez reported that he had spotted an Egyptian bridge almost completed and had opened fire at the bridge and at the infantry next to it. Amir decided to move personally to the Erez sector. En route there, his tank hit a mine, so he called for another tank and used it as his command vehicle. But this tank stalled in the marshes, so Amir asked for another tank to pull him out. Meanwhile, other tanks also got stuck, and still more tanks had to be used to try to free them.

Amir decided to concentrate the remnants of his battalion opposite the bridge. At the same time a communications link was established with Strongpoint Mifreket, which now reported that Egyptian infantry was inside the strongpoint and that only five unwounded soldiers out of twenty remained inside the bunkers. Lt. Michael Vardi, a platoon leader from Erez company, was ordered to break through into the strongpoint. He did so, and at 2100 he asked for permission to evacuate the fighters and the wounded from the strongpoint. Baluza headquarters, however, refused his request.

While Amir's tanks were busy recovering other bogged-down tanks, the first Egyptian tanks crossed the bridge and opened fire. By now, Erez's tank was stuck too. The Vardi platoon was ordered to leave Mifreket and move to the north toward the bridge. Two of our tanks were hit during the firing, but the Egyptians also had two tanks hit as well as a bulldozer. As a result, the Egyptians around the bridge were stunned, giving the Israeli forces time to recover. Vardi went by the tanks that had taken hits and evacuated wounded crewmen from them. Only a few tanks were recovered. Those that were disabled were towed to the rear near the junction of Tiltul-Lexicon. The wounded men were evacuated to a battalion medical station at the same point. But as dawn was about to break, many tanks were still in the marshes.

Amir ordered Michael Vardi to penetrate Mifreket again, since reports now indicated that the Egyptians had once again entered the strongpoint. But Vardi's tank threw one of its tracks, and soon after, the other tank under Choder also lost a track. Both commanders went on foot to look for other tanks to carry out the mission. Choder found and joined Mike's tank, and together they penetrated the strongpoint. Choder's request for permission to evacuate the strongpoint was again turned down, so he proceeded to take out only the wounded. On his way he met a tank en route to the medical aid station. Transferring the wounded to that tank, Choder then returned toward Mifreket. Meanwhile Vardi had also found a tank and penetrated Mifreket with it. Near the strongpoint he again met Choder. Vardi continued his effort to break into the Mifreket Strongpoint.

But daybreak brought with it doom for Amir's battalion, as Egyptian tank fire and Sagger missiles began to hit our tanks. Lieutenants Vardi and Erez (the company commanders) were killed. Michael Vardi was twenty-two years old at his death. His father, Raphael, was a major general in the IDF and my friend. Michael Vardi was a close friend of my son, Omer. He had been accepted for a pilot's course in the Israeli Air Force, and whenever they had leave they would spend it either in our home or in Vardi's. When Michael did not complete the pilot's course, he volunteered for armor and graduated first in his class. He proved himself in battle and was posthumously awarded a medal for valor. I learned of his fighting and his death only near the end of the war.

At 0600 Amir was able to establish communications with the

brigade commander, Gabi, who ordered him to evacuate Strongpoint Mifreket and then to withdraw with the remnants of his battalion to the rear. But Amir's attempts to link up with the strongpoint in daylight failed, leading to additional casualties. In a short time, only two of the twenty tanks in Amir's sector remained in action. At about 0800 hours two Patton tanks that had managed to move out of Qantara and two of Amir's own Centurion tanks that had been repaired arrived to join him. That was considered real reinforcement.

At one point Amir, scanning the area to his left, suddenly saw his younger brother, Eyal, next to him in another tank. A few moments later that tank was hit, and Eyal was wounded. Amir bit his lip but continued his maneuvering. The few tanks moved from one position to another, engaging the Egyptians near the bridge and trying to delay the enemy crossing. It is doubtful whether they had any concrete effect on this.

The fate of Gabi's Shilo task force was not much different. Its mission was to break through into Qantara and link up with the Milano Strongpoint. As the tanks neared Qantara, Shilo arranged the force to create a "fire box" so fire could be directed to his front and to both flanks. At 2000 hours, just as they started to advance, flares lit up the sky and the tanks came under heavy artillery, small-arms, and machine-gun fire, and salvos of missiles. The tanks advanced toward the streets where they were forced to change formation to a column and came under more automatic-weapons fire and grenade attack from the windows. The combination of our own and enemy fire created a scene like hell itself.

Zapko, the brigade operations officer, was ordered to take command of one of Shilo's two companies, and Yomtov was sent to replace him. Zapko was killed in the attack, and control of his company was lost as his tanks scattered in Qantara's streets and alleys. Some of the tanks were destroyed, and others had to be left behind as their crews tried to make their way to the rear even though surrounded by Egyptian infantry. They were joined by remnants of crews from Yomtov's former battalion whose tanks had been hit hours before. The last few functioning tanks of Zapko's company tried repeatedly to return and link up as instructed by Gabi's brigade headquarters.

The other company, with the brigade commander Gabi and his deputy Shilo, managed to advance to the sand barrier at the entrance of Strongpoint Milano, only 200 meters from the Suez water line. There the force stopped to recover dispersed tanks, renew communications, and brief the crews and officers who replaced those killed. But it was a difficult job; communications were cut off, and Shilo had to walk from tank to tank to organize the force. When Shilo's task force finally entered the strongpoint, it moved quickly to the sand barriers and opened fire on the western bank. Throughout this time Gabi continued his efforts to brief straying and stuck tanks and to guide them to the strongpoint.

By about 0430 hours Gabi concluded that his presence in the Milano Strongpoint was ineffectual and, after contacting General Magen, he was ordered to move north and try to reach Yoram, about 15 km northeast of Qantara. I can imagine what the feelings were of the infantrymen in the strongpoint when the tanks left. But Yankele, the commander there, never lost heart. He continued to direct his men as well as those tank crewmen who had managed to get into the strongpoint after their tanks had been hit.

Gabi's extrication from the trap of Qantara was as difficult as the penetration. By dawn, after encountering many difficulties and suffering more casualties, only five tanks of the twenty-two that had been dispatched to Milano and Qantara succeeded in breaking out. They regrouped in the Yoram sector, later leaving for Martef. Nine tanks were lost at Qantara. Four were hit during the penetration into Qantara but managed to get to Baluza. Two tanks from Zapko's company, which went astray in Qantara, succeeded in moving south and reached Amir's battalion at 0800 hours. Many crewmen from Gabi's brigade made their way on foot and joined the Milano Strongpoint. Others remained in the stuck tanks, continuing the fighting on the next day as well until they were hit. Then they, too, linked up by foot in the strongpoint.

The Lapidot task force moved to the northern sector along the same 100-km route over which Gabi's brigade had traveled. They saw tanks from Gabi's brigade stuck in the dunes, and soon understood why — firsthand. By 2130 hours on 6 October, twenty-one out of twenty-four tanks from the Lapidot force had arrived at Baluza. The others were stuck en route. At Baluza they were delayed for two hours until it was decided to move them out to reinforce the strong-points in the northern corner of the sector.

Lapidot divided his force into three units. Five tanks, command-ed by a deputy company commander, were sent via Zegugit — the marshy road — to Lahtzanit in order to make contact with the strongpoint and block the route of a deeper enemy advance. The sec-ond force, a reduced company of eight tanks, was rushed through Romani in the direction of Traklin in order to prevent a possible enemy landing from the Mediterranean. Lapidot, with eight tanks, advanced along the Michpelet axis, then along the Mediterranean sand bank to link up with Budapest, which that afternoon had re-pulsed an armored attack.

At about midnight, as Lapidot's force advanced to within 4 km of Budapest, one of his tanks was damaged by a mine. Suddenly the skies were lit by illuminating shells. Missiles were fired, and two more tanks were hit. Lapidot moved to the rear and evacuated one dead and five wounded soldiers to Baluza. Lapidot did not know that a reinforced Egyptian commando company had landed from the sea on the sand bank earlier that night. So his first thought was that he had been fired upon mistakenly by two Israeli tanks, which he knew had arrived at Budapest some time before. But he soon realized that he had been ambushed by Egyptian infantry troops firing Sagger missiles.

General Magen ordered him to wait for first daylight and then link up with Budapest. Lapidot summoned three of the tanks that had arrived safely at Traklin. First light found him advancing cautiously along both sides of the road when he noticed mines block-ing the entire width of the sand bank. He stopped, but suddenly a salvo of missiles was fired at him from only 500 meters away. One tank was hit. Magen, who was monitoring Lapidot's radio net and was aware of the situation, ordered the force to withdraw and await help. Later Lapidot was notified that he would be reinforced by a battery of 120mm mortars and an infantry company from the sector reconnaissance force. Magen instructed him to launch another at-tack, this time with a balanced force of tanks, infantry, and mortars. Of the twenty-one tanks with which Lapidot had arrived in the sector, only seventeen were left — five of them on Zegugit and twelve with him awaiting reinforcements.

During these first hours of desperate fighting along the canal, the commanding officer of Southern Command, General Gonen, tried to control the situation by giving suggestions and orders. Until 0200 hours he commanded from his headquarters in Beersheba. Then he flew by helicopter to his forward command post in Sinai, from where he began commanding by 0300 hours. He spent the first night of the fighting trying to get an'overview of the situation by piecing together the dozens of fragmented reports picked up from the radio nets. But the picture he formed was at variance with reality.

His knowledge of the situation in the canal sector came from reports by Mandler, who was responsible for the area opposite the canal as commander of the Sinai Division, and from the commander of Southern Sinai, who was responsible for the Gulf of Suez and Sinai's mountainous area. Gonen received some additional information by monitoring the radio nets of brigades fighting on the canal itself. At times he was in direct communication with the commanders of Ras Sudar and of Abu Rudeis, on the Israeli-held side of the Gulf of Suez. From time to time he spoke with the chief of staff or his deputy, General Tal, in Tel Aviv. At 2124 hours he was contacted by Defense Minister Moshe Dayan from Tel Aviv. Gonen updated him on the overall military situation on his front as he knew it.

At 1753 hours on 6 October, just four hours after hostilities had started, Gonen had a brief phone conversation with the chief of staff and gave his opinion that the Egyptian 4th Armored Division would try to cross the canal in one or two hours. The crossing, he said, would take place between Great Bitter Lake and Suez. The basis for Gonen's assumption is unclear. In that same conversation, the chief told Gonen that in order not to split Israeli forces he would not oppose evacuating any of the strongpoints. As things turned out, it would appear that Gonen did not take his advice. At 1818 hours Gonen briefed his staff officers, reiterating his assessment that the 4th Armored Division would cross the canal and expressing confidence that Gabi would take Qantara and then move north to relieve Strongpoint Orkal.

By then Gabi's brigade had been reduced to the size of only one operative battalion, consisting of four reduced companies, which was on its way to a sector that was already in a grave situation. At 2000 hours Gonen told General Mandler that when Gabi reached Orkal, 10 km south of Port Fuad, he should go on and take an Egyptian stronghold 900 meters north of Orkal. Yet at that very time the road from Qantara to Orkal was crawling with Egyptians, as Yomtov's battalion in that sector had been virtually annihilated.

At about 2200 hours information was received at Southern Command to the effect that an Egyptian infantry brigade was crossing the canal at Gessar El-Harash, 10 km north of Qantara. Gonen instructed his operations officer to direct Mandler to get Gabi to make contact with the crossing force. This, of course, was just two hours after Gabi had penetrated Qantara, where the remnants of his two companies were fighting for survival.

At 2356 hours Gonen reported to the Chief of Staff Dado Elazar that the Egyptians had raided Baluza and had carried out a landing from the sea opposite Traklin. Neither, in fact, had occurred. Gonen added that at several points in the central sector enemy penetrations had taken place, in some places even accompanied by tanks. Only in the southern sector was the situation stable, he said. Gonen added that there were no more tanks in reserve and went on to recommend a raid at Jabbel (Mount) Ataka to destroy an Egyptian radar installation there and another raid on the opposite bank of the Suez Gulf to destroy a radar station at Ras Zafrani. The chief of staff replied that no plans or preparations existed for such operations, and he could see no chance for improvisations of this kind.

Fifty minutes later, Gonen reported to Dado that in the central sector Amnon's tanks were widely dispersed, but that if trouble should occur, he would send Gabi there from the north and Col. Dan Shomrom from the south.* Gonen went on to ask for authority to capture the strongpoint 900 meters north of Orkal. Elazar told Gonen that approval from supreme headquarters should be the least of his worries, and that he should concentrate on blocking the Egyptian crossing. Gonen's proposal in fact came at a time when Gabi's

---

*Amnon and Dan were tank-brigade commanders in Mandler's division. When the war broke out, only Amnon had been deployed in the canal zone. Gabi and Dan rushed from Refidim and Bir Teimada, reached the canal zone at about 1800 hours, and were assigned the north and south sectors, respectively.

forces were virtually nonexistent, since they were fighting for their lives in the trap at Qantara.

Gonen's departure from reality was compounded by a tendency to see the situation overoptimistically. For example, he told his officers at 0130 hours that in his opinion the Egyptian crossing was a failure because they had been unable to move an armored brigade to the Israeli side of the canal. Gonen arrived at conclusions without taking counsel with his subordinate commanders or staff. Instead of having his staff officers take part in the process of assessing situations, he relied on his intuition, based on his previous experience with the Egyptians, whom he held in deep contempt.

At 0356 hours Southern Command tried to make a count of the number of tanks still in action. It was found that only 110 tanks remained operative in the entire canal zone.

At 0530 hours it became clear to Gonen that the two companies of Lapidot's task force (one of which had advanced toward Lahtzanit and the other moving on the sand bank toward Budapest) had been stopped by antitank ambushes. He found, moreover, that the force dispatched to evacuate the wounded and the damaged tanks had also sustained losses. Only then, in the early morning hours of 7 October, did Gonen seem to think realistically for the first time. He ordered the tanks to keep their distance from the enemy and not risk additional losses.

CHAPTER THREE

RESERVES ARRIVE IN THE BALUZA SECTOR

About an hour later, at 0630 hours, Gonen received more heartening news. I contacted him to report: "Shmulik, I'm at Baluza. The division is following — its head is nearing the sector, but its tail is still far north. The division is entering the sector." When I arrived at the bunker in Baluza to take command of the northern sector, Gonen's order was to refrain from sending tanks ahead but to concentrate them as a reserve force near Baluza and to come up with a plan to block an Egyptian breakthrough eastward.

Upon hearing what happened the night before in this sector, I felt that I had to see Gabi personally. Gabi was a well-balanced commander. Under any normal mobilization, he would have commanded a brigade in my division, but because of the surprise attack, he was operating within the Sinai Division. I thought Gabi could clarify why our losses were so heavy and our failure so grave. I told Kalman to inform me by radio of any changes in the sector, and I set out for Martef. En route I called Gabi on the radio, identified myself, and asked for his location.

After what he had been through the night before, Gabi was happy to hear of my arrival. He knew that my division was on the move but was undoubtedly surprised to find that we had already started to arrive. It was natural for him to ask immediately how many tanks I had. But with the hardness of a commander who had not yet had a bullet fired at him and who was still concerned about radio security, I replied, with a hint of anger, "I have 100 divisions!" In spite of the exaggeration, everybody was relieved that the reserves were at last arriving.

On my way to meet Gabi, I heard my brigade commander, Colonel Natke, reporting by radio his arrival at Romani with Assaf's battalion ready for action. But Natke cautioned that en route west, his second battalion, under Lieutenant Colonel Natan, had been ambushed near Romani while disembarking from the transporters. Two of his tanks and one half-track had been set afire. I heard Natke order Assaf to turn his battalion to the rear and wipe out the Egyptian ambush.

Natke's decision seemed a mistake to me. After all, I thought, that was exactly what the Egyptians hoped to accomplish, i.e., block the axis to prevent our forces from reaching the front. I thought it best to open the axis with newly arriving forces rather than turn Assaf's battalion to the rear. Natke clarified his position, saying that the Egyptian blocking force was large, dispersed and lying in ambush from the dunes near the road to hills 500 meters away. He also reported seven dead and twenty-one wounded. I then approved Natke's decision and ordered my deputy not to wait for him to break the roadblock but to continue pouring forces to the front through a bypass of Romani via the Listim axis.

Moving on the Aleket Road, I saw only two vehicles, but on a sandy area to the right were five tanks and an armored infantry carrier. Could this be all that was left of Gabi's brigade, I wondered. Is Gabi around? From experience in many maneuvers and exercises, I could usually find the brigade commander after quickly scanning the area and looking near its center for the antennae of his command vehicles. However, all I saw now were several tanks in the middle of a vast, empty, and sandy flat area.

It was a gloomy picture and made me realize at once that the situation was really grim. Inwardly I had refused to believe the reports I had received at Baluza, thinking them inaccurate because of "the fog of battle." I soon recognized Gabi by his bald and tanned head. He and Yomtov were together in their armored command vehicle. Their expressions told in a way no words could the story of commanders whose units had been hit hard and had virtually ceased to exist.

I had known and liked Gabi for many years. Senior officers of his kind are very rare. He was sensitive and had made his way in the army through hard work and natural talent. He hated friction or quarrels and was willing to work harder so as not to waste energy on futile matters. His leadership was such that his soldiers respected him. He tackled problems directly, analyzed matters logically, and did his best to improve things instead of complaining or blaming others.

Gabi, a short fellow, stood tiredly in the armored command carrier, took off his headset, and was ready to jump from the vehicle to greet me. I told him to stay where he was and climbed up to him. We shook hands and I asked him to tell his story. Again I heard the details: surprise attack — running — arrival with one battalion — splitting into two — entering hell — desperate attempts to recover personnel and vehicles calling for assistance. I continued to interrogate him on the impact of the enemy operations on our forces. The overall picture remained vague, but two things were clear. We had lost many tanks because of the marshes, and our forces were split and dispersed after encountering infantry equipped with antitank missiles and tanks, which they could do little to oppose.

I concluded that we had fought bravely but ineffectively and had suffered many losses against only light casualties for the enemy. From Gabi, I learned that even now he was trying to raise the morale of the teams in his area and to establish better communications. He reported that besides the five tanks remaining from Shilo's force (the five tanks with Gabi now), Amir had four tanks in the Mifreket sector.

As Gabi finished his report, I realized that all the troops were waiting for my orders. I felt very badly about what had happened and thought that even in our worst dreams, nobody could have anticipated such a grim situation. I knew that things were too grave to be changed by some magic word. I also knew my forces would arrive soon, but I wasn't sure what to expect from the enemy. Would he attack the strongpoints? Would he move with caution because of our tanks stuck in the marshes — which nevertheless continued to fire at him? Or would he advance rapidly? Would my approaching forces have time to deploy into blocking positions? Should I stop Gabi's brigade from functioning as a unit — for they were badly beaten, with only nine tanks left — and attach his tanks to another brigade?

I knew that the morale of Gabi's few survivors must be low. On the other hand, I felt that disbanding them would destroy the fighting spirit they still had, despite their cruel experiences. Moreover, they were still fighting hard, and even after my arrival Gabi had not asked to be moved to the rear in order to reorganize.

I decided to let them operate as a unit and assigned them the task of recovering as many tanks and personnel as possible. It might have been more profitable, I thought, to send them to the rear and replace them with one of my brigades, but I felt it was vital not to cut them off from operational responsibility. It might affect their morale even more to take them completely out of action. Thus I decided to reduce their sector of responsibility, move them a little to the rear, and keep them on alert in case the enemy penetrated more deeply in our direction.

I had no way of knowing then how important that decision would prove to be. In the coming days, we were to confront a new reality. Crushing blows were to be directed at many of my divisional units — blows that would quickly reduce the size of our companies, battalions, and brigades. My decision to keep Gabi's battered brigade intact was consistent with the spirit of Israel's Defense Forces, that no matter how badly units are decimated, companies, battalions, and brigades must continue to function and fight.

I told Gabi that the division was on its way, that Natke had been attacked while disembarking from the transporters and was now engaged in battle near Romani, and that additional forces were bypassing the blocked road and moving to stabilize the situation. I informed Gabi of my decision that he was to deal mainly with the recovery of tanks and personnel. He was also to reactivate Amir's remaining vehicles and move them to the Ma'adim-Hazizit junction, there to reorganize, refuel, take on ammunition, and be on the alert for new orders to confront the enemy.

At that moment I received a radio message: Gonen told me of indications that Egyptian armor was crossing the canal south of my sector, over the Firdan Bridge (at Strongpoint Hizayon), probably with the mission of penetrating deep into our area. Gonen told me to assemble a force on the Lateral Road at the Reactia junction. That order had serious implications, since part of my forces would have to withdraw to 30 km from the canal. I noted that if there were a breakthrough in the adjacent sector, the Egyptians would certainly try to penetrate my sector as well. It was vital, then, to take precautions and deploy my forces quickly.

I left for Baluza, listening to the division radio net. Natke was fighting the commandos in the Romani area, while Dovik was directing forces arriving toward the front through the Listim axis. I decided to order Rami, the newly arrived mechanized brigade commander, to move a tank battalion to Reactia. I instructed him to dig in with the armored infantry battalions in a wide belt as soon as they arrived, to protect the Baluza-Romani sector.

One serious problem remained. I had to deploy armor to the south to replace Gabi's forces in order to block the possible advance of Egyptian armor from the direction of Qantara and Mifreket (i.e., from west to east deep into our territory). Natke now reported that he had overcome the Egyptian commandos. I ordered him to deploy his brigade at Martef and at Yoram, 8 km east of the canal, as a second line to give us some in-depth defense.

When I returned to the Baluza bunker I found, to my astonishment, that the commandos had renewed their action and destroyed additional vehicles. Natke asked for infantry reinforcement because the advance of our tanks in the dunes was too slow, and the commandos were fighting fiercely.

It was a sticky situation, for the division's infantry elements had not yet arrived, and I didn't know where I would get infantry troops. Next to the Baluza bunker were four APCs, two of them manned by soldiers from the sector reconnaissance unit. I sent them to Natke and pressed him to move some of his forces to the south in order to seal the sector and at the same time to annihilate the commandos.

An hour and a half later, Natke reported that the commandos had been wiped out. He praised the tank crews and the reconnaissance-unit troops for excellent fighting and described at length the fierceness with which the Egyptians had fought. We had taken more casualties in the fighting, but one hundred Egyptian commandos had been killed, and we now held their commanding officer captive. I had mixed feelings about the engagement with the commandos. I was happy with the results but frustrated that it had taken a full three hours to overcome the Egyptians. By my evaluation, the commandos' fighting had been impressive. Natke reported that the captured commanding officer was cursing. He felt neglected for not having been reinforced and frustrated because he was unable to complete his mission despite the heavy price he paid in men.

When I returned to the bunker at 0930 hours, Kalman reported that the strongpoints were still sustaining many casualties and were continuing to plead for help. Lapidot, he said, was to begin a new attack to wipe out the ambush still blocking the road to Budapest. This time the attack was to be carried out with a balanced force. Infantry of the sector reconnaissance unit were able to attack under cover of tanks and 120mm mortars.

But that attack also failed. It would be difficult enough to deal with an entrenched ambush on the narrow sand bank between the sea and the lagoon, but the position was also on a plateau, and a mine belt made it difficult for tanks to storm it. It was difficult to detect the enemy infantry, who were proving an ineffective target for our tank fire. The mortars started shelling, and infantry encircled the enemy from the right along the shore of the Mediterranean. The area there was relatively low and sloping. This enabled our infantry to advance and find new positions. But as they drew near, the enemy's effective automatic-weapons fire killed fifteen soldiers and wounded thirty others, including the company commander and his three platoon leaders. Lapidot, therefore, halted the attack to evacuate his casualties. Under fire, this took three hours. Budapest remained cut off.

Our efforts to reach the other strongpoints also failed, and by midday these attempts were halted too. Clearly we had failed to prevent the enemy crossing, and the results of the battle had been grave. Most of our regular tank units had been lost, and the strongpoints that were still holding out were calling for help that we could not provide. Enemy intentions were unclear, but we feared that the Egyptians would break out eastward. The only question was when; would it be before or after our deployment had provided enough forces to contain them?

In order to simplify command and control, I decided that Rami would concentrate on defense around Baluza-Romani with the two armored infantry battalions and attach his tank battalion — which he had sent to Reactia — to Gabi, who was reorganizing there. Dovik was moving from place to place to expedite and supervise these activities.

In the afternoon, Gabi reported on his reorganization. Who would have believed that Gabi, whom I had met that morning with only nine tanks, would now report that he had a brigade — albeit reduced — consisting of two tank battalions, with twenty-five tanks in each of them? One battalion was the reserve force that had been detached from Rami; another was Amir's battalion.

When Amir got the order to disengage from the Mifreket zone, he called Raviv's company and found that the five tanks remaining in the company deployed south of the strongpoint were fighting but unable to move, some because of mines, others beause they were stuck in swamps. Amir ordered the men to leave their tanks and move eastward. He established a rendezvous point where everyone would meet, took personnel on his own tanks, and moved his troops slightly to the rear.

By now Amir had split his thirty men into three units. One unit would evacuate the wounded, another remove the weapons and communications equipment from the disabled tanks, and the third secure the area. At noon he moved to the Kartisan-Ma'adim road junction, a further 30 km to the east, and began regrouping. He obtained fuel and ammunition and assembled all the tanks from Yomtov's battalion and Shilo's force that had survived the fighting in the Qantara-Mifreket sector. By evening he had eighteen Centurions and seven Pattons, of which only seven had originally gone into action with him. He had had to abandon thirteen tanks near Mifreket. Of his eighty soldiers, ten were dead and eighteen wounded.

Gabi reported that he had collected the surviving crew members of the abandoned tanks, helped them with their equipment and spoken with them to boost their morale. He was, he said, sending them to Baluza to serve as reinforcements should more tanks be repaired.

Meanwhile, IDF traffic along the shore road from northern Israel to Sinai was moving laboriously. Tank transporters were on their way back after unloading tanks at Romani, 20 km from the canal, but they frequently ran into obstacles and traffic jams. The road was narrow with deep dunes along the sides. All along one could see disabled tank transporters, stalled vehicles, and disabled tanks. GHQ issued an order to the Nahal Yam sector, 70 km from the canal, and later to El Arish, 150 km from the canal, to have the tanks removed from their transporters and let them proceed on their tracks alongside the blocked road. It was a slow way to move, causing unnecessary wear and tear on the tanks, but it was the only way to make progress possible.

Fortunately the Israeli Air Force controlled the skies over Sinai and now, on the morning of 7 October, our planes were to attack Egyptian forces on the far side of the canal. According to plans prepared during the night between 6 and 7 October, the air force was to launch a massive attack to destroy the Egyptian surface-to-air missile batteries in the Suez Canal zone. But on 7 October at about 0700 hours, just as the first strike was being launched, the operation was canceled — this, after the defense minister called GHQ from Northern Command and told the air force commander that our front line in the southern sector on the Golan Heights had been breached and that the only way to salvage the situation was to attack at once with aircraft. The air operation on the canal was called off after the first sortie, and most of the planes were dispatched to the Syrian front. There is no telling what the results might have been had the operation along the canal continued. The air force might have succeeded in destroying the missiles, thus gaining freedom of action to support the ground forces. But it may be assumed that the one sortie we did manage to carry out on the morning of 7 October was instrumental in the decision by the Egyptian Air Force to keep its planes in reserve to defend Egyptian skies. After that, few Egyptian planes flew over Sinai, thus allowing our planes to be masters of the sky. Had the Egyptian Air Force attacked our stalled convoys on the Qantara-El Arish Road, I doubt that we would have escaped the same disastrous fate that befell the Egyptian forces from the Israeli air attacks on that same road in the 1956 and 1967 Wars.

As the hours went by our deployment continued, while the Egyptians seemed to be dragging their feet and holding back with any eastward advance. Would they continue to bide their time?

CHAPTER FOUR

PLANNING AND TESTING CANAL DEFENSES: 1967–1973

T his was not the way I had imagined war breaking out. I had believed that our intelligence services would give us advance warning, enabling us to deploy in time according to prepared plans. But that was not to be.

In order to understand the events of the first night the plans and preparations of both sides for the war must be considered. These preparations were made during the War of Attrition, a limited-but-protracted engagement that was difficult for both sides.

Immediately after the 1967 War, the Suez front was held by one of our reinforced tank brigades. In spite of a formal cease-fire, there were many skirmishes. The situation could be described as one of tense quiet shattered by occasional fire clashes.

Gradually, as the defeated Egyptian army received increased equipment and training from the Russians, Nasser broke the cease-fire. In April 1968, he proclaimed to his people: "We have reached the phase of the 'resolute stand'." That September his minister of war declared that this phase was over and that a new phase, of "the active deterrent," had begun.

We learned what this meant on 8 September 1968, when the Egyptians launched a massive artillery attack on the sector from Qantara northward. Our troops entered their defensive bunkers, but these had been prepared very amateurishly. Many were easily penetrated by the Egyptian artillery shells. So we suffered ten killed and eighteen wounded in one day, a heavy price by Israeli standards.

This artillery barrage came as a surprise and jolted IDF Head-quarters. We decided to allocate increased funds to fortify our canal defenses. Southern Command was placed in charge of planning and execution. Some forty-seven days later, on 26 October, there was another massive Egyptian artillery barrage, this time across the entire front line and over a period of nine hours. Fifteen of our men were killed and thirty-four wounded.

Nasser, then, meant what he said. It was also clear that our small artillery forces would have little substantial impact on the Egyptians. We shelled the refineries and the port near Suez, but that did not seem to be much of a deterrent. Nasser had evacuated the three cities of Suez, Ismailia, and Port Said, indicating that he was more than ready to continue exchanging artillery fire.

Anxiety on our side grew. We knew that it would take months to complete the fortifications needed to protect our troops. A decision was made to attack Egypt deep in its own territory to show Nasser that we had the ability to select where and how to fight and that we could not be forced into circumstances he was seeking to dictate.

Four days after the shelling, on the night of 31 October–1 November, we raided Upper Egypt. Arriving via helicopter, our paratroopers destroyed an electrical transformer station near Najeh-Hamadi and a bridge on the Nile. Nasser understood the hint, but he was firmly determined not to tolerate a situation in which his army would condone Israel's presence in Sinai. He ordered a militia to be established to defend Egyptian territory internally and postponed further shelling until the militia could be set up and organized.

On the night of our operation at Najeh-Hamadi, I was an observer, along with other high-ranking officers, in the command post from which the operation was controlled. Following the raid, I was called, together with my commander, Maj. Gen. Israel Tal, to the office of the chief of staff, Lieutenant General Bar-Lev. He told us that, having discussed the situation with Dayan, they had decided to reinforce Sinai with one more armored brigade. With that, they would have an armored force of division size in Sinai. He added that Dayan had directed that one of us go to Sinai to assume command of the force there. I gladly volunteered and soon found myself busy with two major tasks: first, forming — for the first time in the IDF — a regular armored division that would also serve as a model for our reserve divisions; and secondly, planning and executing the Sinai defense plan. We all realized that the shelling might be renewed at any moment, so we felt we were working with a stopwatch in one hand.

I formed a team to revise the Sinai defense plan. Fortifications called for in the existing plan were already being constructed by Southern Command Headquarters. The plan's basic assumption was that the Egyptians would cross the canal in those sectors where they had roads — at Qantara, Ismailia, Firdan, Deversoir, and opposite the roads leading to Suez and to the Mitla and Gidi passes.

The master plan for the defense of Israel's borders was code-named *Sela.* By this plan, specific forces, most of them reserve units, were allocated for deployment on each front. The Southern Command plan called for deployment of a great portion of its allotted forces close to the eastern bank of the Suez Canal, opposite each of the crossing sites mentioned above. At each of these potential landing sites, a huge compound two kilometers square was to be built, surrounded by earth barriers two to three meters high. Each compound was to hold an infantry brigade supported by tanks. The tanks were to move in the compound and take firing positions anywhere along the barriers. The infantry was to spread out in specially prepared firing positions.

This plan had two major shortcomings. First, it would deploy considerable forces in a "position defense" on the forward edge of the battle area. Second, until our reserve forces could arrive to take up their positions, the small available forces of the regular army would be lost in the huge compounds. Each command would have no more than ten to twenty soldiers, split up into units of two to three men each to hold the positions on the corners of the compound. The danger would be especially great at night when they would be least able to defend themselves against enemy attack. They were not strong enough to prevent the enemy from capturing the compounds should an attack be launched before our reserves could reach the area.

I sought solutions to complex problems: how to tie the minimum force to routine operational tasks in order to enable the maximum to train and prepare for war; how to maintain small elements in the line of contact, yet provide them with a high degree of protection from shelling and enemy raids; and how to construct the defensive line in successive phases to allow the unengaged to join in the defense in a simple and smooth way, either before or during battle.

There are two basic methods of defense: position (fixed) and mobile. In position defense, the defender holds terrain features which he has fortified and from which he repels the attacker. To gain more flexibility, he sets up two or three successive in-depth lines, maintaining mobile armored forces for counterattacking and reinforcing the fixed positions. The Egyptians employed this linear fixed-defense method along the canal.

In the mobile (some call it "flexible") defense, defenders maintain a light reconnaissance screen in front of the forward edge of the battle area. Their mission is to provide information about the enemy's movements and to some extent delay and channel the enemy into areas where he may be destroyed. Other forces can hold terrain to gain depth in the rear, but even they are supposed to withdraw after delaying. The bulk of the defending force consists of mobile armor waiting somewhere in the rear. Its task is to counterattack in one of several preselected "killing zones." In a mobile defense, the defender temporarily trades territory to delay the enemy and channel his forces into a preselected battlefield or killing zone. Only after the enemy has been destroyed does the defender retake the territory he gave up in order to gain time. Between these two basic patterns of defense there are, of course, many variations.

The main advantage of the position defense is that the defender protects all of his territory and does not give up any terrain. He fortifies in advance and fights from strong defense positions. The disadvantage is that the enemy knows in advance where he is going to fight. This becomes more of a disadvantage if the defense line is so close to the line of contact with the enemy that he can carry out long and special preparations on his own territory before launching his attack. Another disadvantage is that when the enemy masses against a narrow sector of the defensive line, the forces defending elsewhere along it contribute little to the decisive section. Similarly, once the enemy bypasses or breaches the line, its fortified terrain and the forces elsewhere along the defensive line lose their value. This is what happened with the French Maginot Line in the Second World War.

The opposite is true in mobile defense, where the defender can concentrate most of his forces in the critical sector. Another advantage is that the enemy does not know where and when the decisive battle is going to take place, and so is unable to make advance preparations. The main disadvantage of mobile defense is that the defender relinquishes territory and trades terrain to obtain the time needed to concentrate his forces and create the right circumstances for a counterattack. Usually, it is difficult to give up territory even temporarily, especially if this means abandoning populated settlements and resources. In the Sinai, however, where most of the territory is empty desert, this could be done easily. Furthermore, the basic structure of the Israeli Army called for a mobile defense because the bulk of our ground forces were armor, better suited to mobile warfare than to fighting from fixed positions.

We had one strong strategic-political consideration, however, for not adopting a purely mobile defense. We were apprehensive that the Egyptians might seize some of our territory from which we would have withdrawn as part of our time-gaining tactic and then consolidate themselves there, thus preventing creation of the conditions required for our counterattack. They might then wait for superpower intervention to freeze the situation. An imposed cease-fire might prevent us from launching any counterattack. Then the only outcome would be the loss of territory. We faced a dilemma: on the one hand, we had ideal conditions for a mobile defense and, on the other, the sensitive political-strategic considerations of a small nation for which "trading" territory was anathema.

The plan I finally proposed was a combination of the two systems of defense. The organization of the forces for battle and the method of fighting were adopted from the mobile defense concept. But since we could not use the tactic of relinquishing territory and preselecting the battle site, I recommended that the battle be conducted along and near the water line; that a warning screen be established there based on light forces. The bulk of the forces would be mobile armored forces deployed in the rear, close enough to reach the zone of battle upon call. The combination of the two systems was possible because of the major water obstacle, the Suez Canal, which constituted the front line. In the flexible defense system, the small screening or reconnaissance forces retreat and trade space for time until mobile armored reserves deploy for the decisive battle. But here the enemy would first have to overcome the Suez obstacle, build bridges, and breach our barriers. This, I thought, would give us time to move up our armored reserves and attack the enemy before he could move tanks to our bank, thus making it easier to destroy his infantry and prevent his engineering operations.

At my disposal was an ad hoc planning team made up of representatives of all the relevant branches and corps. In considering the problem of creating a screening force in a hostile front-line environment, we used terrain analyses. We concluded that the physical data of the Suez Canal provided a rare opportunity to set up an electronic early-warning system. I thought that since the Suez Canal ran along continuous straight lines for many kilometers, we could beam an electronic ray which when cut by even a small enemy force would trigger an alarm. I asked our research and development department if the scheme was feasible and received an affirmative answer. I therefore decided that we must hold the very bank of the canal and that warning stations should be positioned at intervals of 10 km. In daylight our troops could observe 5 km in any direction. Night observation would depend on the electronic devices. Until these could be installed, we would have to plan ambush sites, though we certainly did not have enough forces to cover the entire canal sector with ambushes.

The plan provided some twenty stations for early warning and for that purpose only. I thought that the fifteen to twenty soldiers in each post would be able to maintain an all-around defense against raids or attacks. Their defensive positions could be as small as 50 x 50 meters, made up of four interconnected fighting positions, each with an attached bunker covered with steel beams as protection against artillery. (The beams we eventually used were tracks from the old English railroad which ran from the Suez to El Arish.) Enough ammunition, food, water, and medical supplies would be stocked to enable the strongpoints to hold out for several days. Each would have a central bunker for the command post and an aid station, with trenches connecting firing positions, mine belts, and fences. Since they had to be built directly on the canal, they would be enclosed by sand barriers to prevent enemy observation and protect against direct fire.

The thinking behind the strongpoint idea was based on my experience in the War of Independence when, as a young infantry-company commander, I planned and supervised the fortification of the small settlements in the Negev. To differentiate this kind of position from the IDF's regular and much larger strongpoints, I called it *maoz* (the Hebrew word for the strongest part of a castle).

These strongpoints never were planned to prevent a canal crossing or serve as a defensive line. They were only a warning line. The defensive role would fall to the armored forces in reserve, reinforced by infantry, artillery, and air support.

To facilitate the arrival of that support, I also recommended that two lateral roads be constructed. The first was to be situated behind a line of sand hills about 10 km from the canal. This road would let us move our artillery around and resupply it with ammunition. Near it we would deploy our first echelon of tanks so they could reach the strongpoints within thirty to sixty minutes. The second road would lie 30 km from the canal and serve to shift larger armored units and supplies from one sector to another, so that forces could arrive en masse to repel the enemy's main crossing.

When I presented my plan to Maj. Gen. Yeshayahu Gavish, the commander of Southern Command, he approved it, adding a few more strongpoints in sectors he thought were particularly sensitive — opposite Qantara, Ismailia, the Firdan, and the Mitla and Gidi passes. The chief of staff also added a few more at the northern and southern ends of the canal.

When the plan was discussed at General Headquarters, no one rejected its underlying concept of combining the principles of a fixed and mobile defense. The only differences of opinion had to do with the strongpoints. Arik Sharon, head of the Training Branch, suggested that we man the barriers on the Suez bank with only one or two observers and deploy support infantry platoons in a bunker behind each barrier. As he saw it, the platoon would be in its bunker when the enemy began his assault. Once our observers on the barriers gave the alert that a crossing was in progress, the platoon could race through trenches connected to the bunker to assault the enemy.

In my opinion, Sharon's suggestion was too simplistic. The

bunker location, although in a rear slope, would surely become known to the enemy. They would take measures to neutralize it, preventing the platoon from moving to take up fire positions against the intruders. General Tal, who was sitting next to me, supported my plan.

With that, the plan was approved, and I was given the job of implementing it. It was a large-scale operation involving thousands of soldiers and civilians; they worked enthusiastically under the direction of the Engineering Corps. While this construction was under way, I also organized and built up the Israeli Army's first regular armored division, training it to be able to fight a mobile defensive battle.

All but three strongpoints were complete when Nasser declared that he would no longer recognize the cease-fire that had followed the Six Day War. On 3 March, 1969, Egyptian artillery fire began what would become known as the War of Attrition. The first few days of the shelling allowed us to test the strongpoint concept. The bunkers survived artillery hits, and our tanks were able to move forward according to plans and fire at Egyptian positions across the canal. Over a period of several days, we had only a few casualties, and these occurred mainly in the exposed artillery units, not in the strongpoints. The Egyptians suffered heavy damage and heavy casualties. One of those killed was their chief of staff, General Riad. That the Egyptian chief of staff was killed in action on the front line made a strong impression on me. It showed me that General Riad had an outstanding personality, and I understood the grief that prevailed in Egypt following his death.

On 10 March, a week after the War of Attrition began, General Tal resigned as commander of the Armored Corps (he joined the Defense Ministry to work on developing a new tank), and I was promoted to that post. I was not happy over leaving Sinai, but command of the Armored Corps was something I had aspired to since I joined it in 1949. Maj. Gen. Shlomo Lahat replaced me as commander of the Sinai forces.

The War of Attrition was long and difficult. The nature of a long war is that each side tries to find solutions to the problems with which the other side confronts it. The Egyptians sought to cause us as many casualties as possible. Our problem was to minimize our casualties and force the Egyptians to stop the War of Attrition. Circumstances favored the Egyptians. They were deployed shoulder-to-shoulder and could see that our line was thinly held. The three strongpoints that we had not had time to complete left sections of 30–40 km without observation. We also failed to develop the electronic warning system. Egypt not only shelled us heavily but often crossed the canal, mainly at night, to mine our roads and attack small supply convoys. At times, they tried to raid our strongpoints, but these withstood heavy shelling and, with artillery and tank support, were able to repel the enemy attacks.

One way to prevent raiders crossing to our bank was to deploy infantry ambushes along the canal. For limited periods in various sectors, we did set such ambushes and of course they helped. But this was done by calling up reserve battalions to reinforce the small regular army, and Israel couldn't afford to maintain that kind of mobilization for long periods. Had we done so, Egypt would have achieved its objective in the War of Attrition.

Our problem was how to put an end to the War of Attrition without disrupting either the country's economy or the army's preparations for a general war. In addition, we faced the problem of holding the line of contact with small forces so as to allow most of the armed forces to pursue their training uninterrupted. We also wanted to limit the use of tanks and artillery on the front line in order to reduce wear and tear and costs.

In January of 1970, Arik Sharon became the commander of Southern Command and immediately started to put his own notions into practice. When he was head of the Training Branch, he had criticized Chief of Staff Bar-Lev for not being aggressive enough, asking, "Why should the Egyptians make our life miserable by raiding our side while we let them live in peace on their bank? It is vital that we raid their side and put them on the defensive." But Sharon would soon find that things were not so simple.

Under pressure, Bar-Lev approved Sharon's Operation Victoria — a raid by a single infantry battalion across the canal against Egyptian lines in the northern sector. The operation commenced with a massive air strike against Egyptian positions, followed by our crossing with support from tanks and artillery. Our forces mopped up about 2–3 km of the Egyptian defensive line and killed nineteen

Egyptians. But the fighting was long and fierce, with three of our soldiers killed and fifteen wounded. By Israeli standards, this was another heavy toll. No one proposed continuing that kind of operation against the Egyptian line.

Both before and after that operation, we carried out devastating raids deep into Egyptian territory. On Green Island, a small island at the northern end of the Red Sea Gulf, a small entrenched Egyptian force operated shore guns against our forces. An Israeli commando force in rubber boats attacked the island, penetrated the fortification, and destroyed the enemy unit in a face-to-face battle. After blowing up the guns there, our troops returned to Sinai.

A larger raid was mounted against Shaduan Island, at the southern extremity of the Gulf of Suez. This island dominates the Straits of Jubal and could serve as a springboard to Africa. A battalion of paratroopers landed by helicopter in the south of the island and advanced, with air support, to capture the entire island. The Egyptians suffered heavy losses, and dozens of their soldiers surrendered and were taken prisoner. Our quitting the island within a few days helped the Egyptians hide the debacle from their people.

Since I initiated, planned, and ran the IDF's armored raid across the Gulf of Suez, I shall try to explain and describe the immense amount of preparation required for such a raid into the enemy's depth. We conducted landing exercises in cooperation with the Israeli Navy, sent reconnaissance patrols to locate landing sites, and trained the raiding force using a model, while readying them also to function according to alternative modes of operation. We developed special means of warfare and new methods of mopping up a site, with the aim of reducing the likelihood of casualties in the raiding force. And we developed means for extricating vessels from a sand bank. All these preparations engaged us intensively for some six weeks.

The raid was successful. The attacking force consisted of only four tanks and three armored personnel carriers. For eight hours we advanced in enemy territory, overcoming patrols, attacking military encampments, destroying radar installations, and mopping up outposts. The enemy sustained hundreds of casualties, including high-ranking Egyptian officers and Soviet advisers. Throughout the raid, the Israeli Air Force covered us, shooting down Egyptian planes that tried to operate in the sector. We returned to our territory, our only casualties being one pilot killed and one soldier wounded. An indirect result of the raid was that Nasser dismissed his chief of staff, the commander of the Egyptian Navy, and the commander of the Red Sea sector.

Insofar as these and other raids deep into enemy territory were successful, they not only lowered enemy morale but caused the Egyptian army to disperse its forces and take up defensive postures at many places, far from the front line. In this the raids achieved their goal. However, it is also important to recognize the limitations of these operations — not just that the preparations were long and complicated but mainly that they could not prevent the Egyptians from raiding, mining, and shelling our side of the canal.

When we were about halfway through the War of Attrition, Sharon again suggested that we evacuate the strongpoints and maintain control of the canal area by means of long-range observation posts and mobile armored patrols. Shortly after the cease-fire came into effect, General Tal, then working in the Ministry of Defense, wrote a plan outlining a different approach to maintaining Israeli control along the canal. While Tal was not pleased with the strongpoints, he did not propose vacating them because they were already there. His idea was to maintain in them a presence of armored infantry squads on armored personnel carriers and to rotate them every twenty-four hours. He also suggested that the IDF deploy two tank brigades of three battalions and one reconnaissance company each, to cover the area from Qantara southward to Suez City.

By Tal's plan, then, the area from Qantara south would be divided into six battalion sectors. Each battalion would deploy one company near battalion HQ on the Lateral Road, 30 km from the canal, a second company near the Artillery Road, 10 km from the canal, and the third company would deploy three platoons on the canal's eastern bank. According to the twenty-four hour rotation system, the company on the bank of the canal would shift to the Artillery Road, the Artillery Road force would move to the Lateral Road, and the company there would shift to the bank of the canal. At night, armored infantry, setting ambushes, would join and reinforce the forward companies.

There were advantages as well as disadvantages to this proposal. The main advantage was that Tal's warning screen would be deployed at intervals of 3 to 4 km, with smaller gaps than our static positions offered, thus enabling more effective observation and a better warning system. But there were several deficiencies also. For some reason, Tal's proposal made no mention of the sector north of Qantara. This was an area of 45 km that would require about one more mixed infantry-tank brigade.

To maintain the type of force structure advocated by Tal would have required more than double the number of tanks allocated for day-to-day operations. This would have depleted the number available for training or else necessitated the removal of more tanks from the armories to be placed on an operational basis. We simply didn't have that many regular tank units. Nor could we afford to call reserve units to active duty to make up the difference. My approach was to maintain the tanks in concentrations, ready for action, thus avoiding expensive day-to-day small operations. Tal's notion of rotating over two tank brigades every twenty-four hours would have meant a lot of wear and tear on the vehicles. Further, one of our achievements in the War of Attrition was that we were able to continue preparations for any future total war. We were able to conduct an intensive training program to increase the number of tank formations in the IDF. Because of this stepped-up training and the operations along our borders, the IDF was already engaged in unprecedented tank activity. To increase it further would have meant increasing the budget and changing current priorities, at the expense of preparations for future conflicts. Another shortcoming was the idea of using tanks for surveillance. Had we thought it necessary to step up our surveillance along the canal, we could have called up reserve infantry and reconnaissance units, as we had done for brief periods with successful results.

No less significant was another disadvantage of Tal's plan. In a prolonged war, there were many ways the Egyptians could make our tanks ineffective. Tal himself noted this point in his plan: "It is true that our tanks could be hit — for example, by means of antitank ambushes to be set on the canal's eastern bank after a crossing — but we, too, shall continue to develop and find countersolutions. The process is a dynamic one."

But we had already experienced that very dynamic situation. The Egyptians would lay mines along the road near the barrier, and our tanks often hit them. In our search for dynamic countermeasures, we tried reconnaissance patrols along the canal road close to the barrier. The enemy struck back with more mines, artillery fire, and antitank missiles. We had to reinforce our patrols with infantry and combat engineers to clear the scattered mines under supporting artillery fire; but it was tough going, and we took many casualties. We varied the times and places for patrol, but our tanks continued to hit mines. Finally we gave in. There were areas where we had no strongpoints — which were so covered with mines that we stopped sending tanks there. We thus saw Tal's suggestion as both too expensive and unworkable.

Information to the effect that Tal and Sharon were criticizing the defense system on what had come to be known as the "Bar-Lev Line" and that they favored a purely mobile defense leaked to the Israeli public. But just as the fact that the warning line of twenty miniature strongpoints situated at intervals of 20–30 km did not constitute a fortified defensive line — even though the media dubbed it the "Bar-Lev Line" (thus conjuring up images of something like the Maginot Line) — so, too, Tal's suggestion to deploy dozens of tanks along the canal would not have produced a wholly mobile defense system. Tal's or Sharon's plans did not call for waging the defensive battle on a killing ground somewhere in the rear but along and proximate to the water line. The main difference between Tal's proposal and the system in existence lay in the notion of a mobile, armored warning screen instead of the warning screen made up of the strongpoints.

Finally after a long period of trial and error, we began to employ the air force against the Egyptians, and it was the air force that finally succeeded in bringing the War of Attrition to an end. It gained dominance of the air above Egyptian territory, shot down many Egyptian planes in air-to-air combat, and destroyed so many antiaircraft guns and missile emplacements that it was able to attack Egyptian artillery and infantry freely. The Egyptian raids and shellings virtually ceased. Moreover, the use of the air force was a particularly good solution in our circumstances. Since most of the air force consists of regular personnel, we could carry the war into enemy territory day after day without the need to call up our reserves or to undertake long and complicated preparations. We were also able to cut our casualty figures considerably.

Nasser found himself in a desperate situation and so began pressuring the Russians for a direct involvement in defending Egypt's skies. More sophisticated antiaircraft missiles arrived, and the Egyptians attempted to move them forward under an umbrella of other missile sites, which were farther to the rear. Using thousands of workers, they tried to construct fortified bunkers to house the surface-to-air missile batteries. But the Israeli Air Force prevented them from bringing the missiles sufficiently close to enable Egypt to control the skies above the canal. We were able to continue to inflict heavy casualties on the Egyptian ground forces. The War of Attrition had turned to Egypt's disadvantage, and Nasser finally accepted a cease-fire.

But under cover of that cease-fire, he immediately moved the missile sites forward near the canal and fortified them. That we let him do so was a near-fatal mistake. We should have renewed the war, or been more obstinate politically, to prevent Nasser from achieving under the cease-fire what he had been unable to achieve in combat. The Yom Kippur War would demonstrate how effectively this Egyptian step crippled our combat capability along the canal.

Even after the cease-fire came into effect, Israeli preparations for any possible new war continued. At the same time, Sharon got Dado Elazar's consent to abandon a number of strongpoints. Some claim that this was one of the reasons for our failure to prevent the Egyptian crossing in 1973. I do not think so, however, since the abandoned strongpoints were among those constructed at the behest of General Gavish as additional emplacements situated close to other such sites. As an early-warning system they were unnecessary.

During the War of Attrition, Moshe Dayan proposed an interim agreement in which the IDF would pull back from the canal. The general staff held discussions on whether to withdraw and how far. These discussions were an impetus for constructing a second line of defense, farther from the canal. In fact, we had reason to build such a line without even considering the possibility that we might "voluntarily" withdraw from the canal. It was Sharon who built this new line which he called *taozim* (strongholds) to differentiate them from the *maozim* (strongpoints). They were built on the ridge near the Artillery Road, 8–10 km from the canal. These strongholds were to be manned by the reserves during a period of emergency.

The line of *taozim* gave concrete expression to Sharon's concept formed in the days of the debate over the strongpoints. He built large modernized bunkers, each capable of housing an infantry company, enabling those manning them to lead a self-contained existence. The bunkers were constructed on the ridge's rear slope and were connected by camouflaged trenches to the ridge line. This time, unfortunately and in contrast to the case of the strongpoints, no General Staff discussions in a broad professional forum were held concerning the *taozim* idea. Hundreds of millions of pounds were poured into the construction, and all for nought. As a fortified defensive unit for infantry on the ridge line, the strongholds had no tactical value. Nor do I know how their construction was compatible with Sharon's calls for a mobile defense. As things turned out, our main containment battle was fought for six days running on the ridge line close to the strongholds. The various divisions made no tactical use of them, as they could be of no aid in a mobile defensive battle. They remained deserted in the midst of an area of fierce combat.

To sum up, during the War of Attrition there were various developments, changes, and adaptations. Basically we acted according to the *Maoz* Plan — a plan aimed at providing answers to problems of ongoing security while enabling the building of an infrastructure and necessary deployment should a general war break out. The headquarters for the armored forces in Sinai took an active part in all this. It commanded all the forces in Sinai — the troops holding the strongpoints, a mobile force of armored division size, and logistics forces and infrastructure installations established in the region to provide logistical and operational freedom of action. These installations were built to provide support for the forces in the field as well as maintenance for additional forces dispatched there in case of war. Near these installations bunkers were constructed as command posts, medical stations, and workshops. A network of roads was paved to permit movement of troops and supplies. The Sinai forces functioned according to a regular routine that included operational duties, training, external courses, and leave.

Naturally the level of operational alertness and, accordingly, the size and location of the force assigned to ongoing operational duty would be altered in accordance with each specific situation assessment. A whole series of contingency plans for possible defensive and offensive situations was planned and exercised. Of these plans, two defensive types were implemented in the Yom Kippur War, *Shovach Yonim* and *Sela.* But neither was carried out as written. The deviations were considerable, mainly as a result of the surprise and blunders on our part.

Shovach Yonim (literally "dovecote") was an operational plan for defensive deployment based mainly on regular forces. It was designed to counter any Egyptian operation in our territory falling short of all-out war. This plan would first use the regular army, to which reserves would be added in the event of general war. To that end, it was planned to reinforce the Sinai Division with tanks, infantry, and artillery units. The infantry would reinforce the strongpoints and protect vital areas and installations in the tactical rear and on the line of the passes and the military camps. (The armored infantry companies organic to the tank battalions of the Sinai Division belonged to the reserves, not the national service troops, and were not included in the *Shovach Yonim* Plan.)

The forward deployment plan divided the 160-km canal line among three brigades who were each responsible for the protection of the strongpoints in their sectors. The plan called for the distant strongpoints and those difficult of access (fifteen to thirty minutes from the Artillery Road) to be reinforced by an attached tank platoon. In each brigade sector, two to three tank companies were stationed on the Artillery Road, some 10 km from the canal. Their task was to get to the canal within thirty minutes and block any crossing attempts. In each brigade sector on the Lateral Road, 30 km from the canal, a tank battalion was to be held in reserve, able to reach the water line within two hours of an alert order. Finally *Shovach Yonim* called for a fourth armored brigade to be concentrated in the center of the front near Tassa as a reserve force to react to the enemy's main effort.

But Israel's Defense Forces never planned to fight a major war with only regular units. Our war plans hinged on our getting intelligence information with enough advance warning to let Israel mobilize its reserves and move them to the front. There was a twofold logic to *Shovach Yonim.* First to deploy our thin, regular forces so that even if warning came too late to call up the reserves in time, the regulars could block effectively — inflict heavy casualties on the enemy and delay a crossing. And second, the regulars would serve as the forward element of the *Sela* Plan.

The idea behind *Sela,* which would be employed in case of an all-out war, was to deploy forces to defend the southern region, while preparing to move to the offensive as quickly as possible. In this plan, two reserve armored divisions would be deployed behind the standing forward division in Sinai, ready to join the defensive battle when needed and then cross the canal in a counterattack. That move, of course, would be carried out only after a sufficiently strong defensive line had been established. These two additional divisions were only a preliminary reinforcement, with Israel's GHQ retaining an option to bring in additional forces as required. The plan assumed that our air force could maintain clear skies over our ground forces, with its first priority to neutralize Egyptian antiaircraft defenses, allowing the air force to provide close support for our ground forces.

To sum up, we had plans for defense, had made preparations, established the infrastructure for employing and maintaining the forces, and trained our troops for foreseeable missions. We had accumulated military experience from the War of Attrition. The general perception, in view of the difficulties involved in a canal crossing, was that the IDF could break at its inception any Egyptian attempt to cross the canal.

Why, then, did events develop differently? To answer that question, one should first consider the Egyptians' plans and preparations and then consider what actually happened on the Israeli side when the war started.

CHAPTER FIVE

THE EGYPTIAN PLANS, 1967–1973

The defeat of 1967 deepened the Arabs' awareness of Israel's military superiority and caused the Egyptian military and political leadership to revise established ideas, as regards both objectives and the means for achieving them. The aim of "liberating Palestine," which involved the liquidation of Israel, was deferred from the area of the concrete and the immediate to a more remote future, even to a future generation. This was replaced by the so-called "phased doctrine," the first stage being to "eliminate the results of the aggression" — namely, a return to the boundary lines of 4 June 1967. Restoration of "the legitimate rights of the Palestinian people" was left for the second phase. As part of this general revision, the armed struggle was no longer seen as being at the center of the effort but was integrated into the political struggle as a catalyst aimed at breaking a political stalemate.

At first, Nasser thought he would be able to repeat his "exercise" of 1956-1957 — attaining Israeli withdrawal from all the occupied territories in return for a minuscule political quid pro quo in the form of a shaky arrangement based on "understandings." This was to come about without recognition of Israel, without peace, and, most important, without the Arabs closing off their options for obtaining "phase two" — resolution of the "Palestinian question," even if this had to be postponed until the next generation. Unlike 1957, however, this time the United States refused to join the USSR in pressuring Israel. The Americans were ready to support a demand for Israeli withdrawal from the occupied territories but only in return for a genuine political settlement. They understood that prolonging the conflict would lead to greater Soviet encroachment in the region.

Although there was deadlock in the political arena, in the military sphere the Egyptian and Syrian armed forces enjoyed a rapid process of reconstruction and growth with massive Soviet assistance. The Egyptian army was engaged in an intensified buildup and in planning and exercising offensive operational plans for "liberating the occupied lands," but it was unable to reduce the sense of frustration that pervaded its ranks. The prospect was a grim one. "Liberation of the lands" was deferred to a remote, unspecified future date when they would be capable of taking on the IDF in a general war. For the present, all they could do was train and watch as the Israelis consolidated their hold on the Suez Canal.

This, then, was the background to Nasser's decision to launch the War of Attrition. The Egyptian leader hoped to achieve three goals by this act: first, to enable the Egyptian army to confront the IDF in a limited war under favorable conditions; second, to wear down the IDF and erode Israel's staying power, thus increasing its dependence on the United States; and third, to embroil the United States, hopefully bring it to the brink of war with the USSR at a time when the United States was already involved in a war in Vietnam. In short, Nasser hoped to wear down Israel and get the Americans to pressure Israel to withdraw from the occupied territories without any meaningful shift in the military balance.

The War of Attrition began in March 1969. At first, because of quantitative inferiority in manpower and fireunits (artillery in particular) and due to its greater sensitivity to casualties, Israel found itself hard pressed. But in the end, Nasser's expectations did not materialize. The IDF stood its ground, adapted itself, employed its air force as a "flying artillery," and — after systematically eliminating the antiaircraft installations — inflicted heavy casualties on the Egyptians. By early 1970 the Egyptians' situation had become intolerable. Their losses were increasing, and their attempts to wear us down were flickering as the Israeli Air Force was penetrating deep into their territory. Nasser's demands grew and grew, and the USSR — albeit with a certain unwillingness — moved from arms supplier and adviser to direct involvement, assuming responsibility for defending the skies over the Egyptian rear. They operated antiaircraft batteries and even flew interceptor aircraft. Four of these were shot down by the Israeli Air Force in an air battle. Finally, Nasser accepted a cease-fire which went into effect on 8 August 1970. Diplomatic efforts commenced by Jarring and followed up by Rogers proved ineffectual. There was renewed deadlock, a situation convenient for Israel but hard to bear for Egypt. Nasser's declaration as he opened the War of Attrition — "What was taken by force will be returned by force" — was not borne out.

Nasser died in September 1970 and was succeeded by Anwar Sadat, who inherited the situation of political and military stalemate in the region. In contrast to Nasser, whose leadership had been firm and unquestioned, Sadat had to struggle to consolidate his position. Nasser, responsible for the 1967 debacle, understood that preparations for the "liberation of occupied territories" would take a long time. But Sadat felt that perpetuation of the deadlock could lead to his ouster. He felt compelled to act for a speedy change of the status quo.

From the very beginning, then, Sadat acted vigorously to complete his military preparations, setting a series of specified dates that were meant to be ultimatums. "1971 will be the year of decision!" he proclaimed, adding that failure to achieve a political solution would lead him to use force. His first step was to sign a "friendship and cooperation treaty" with the USSR. As far as Sadat was concerned, this aimed at obtaining massive Soviet equipment and aid, far beyond what Nasser had received. Sadat wanted to be prepared to go to war — soon. His excuse for not going to war that year was the "foggy situation" that came in the wake of the India-Pakistan War.

In 1972 Sadat stepped up his efforts to obtain weapons and other military equipment for the Egyptian Army. He visited Moscow twice, in February and April, but there was no satisfactory Soviet response to his requests. In June he dispatched his minister of war, Sadek, again to no avail. Mid-July saw a high-ranking Egyptian delegation, headed by Premier Aziz Sidki, in the USSR; but this mission, too, resulted in failure.

Sadat now suspected that it was the policy of détente, adopted following the Nixon-Brezhnev meeting in May 1972, that was behind the Soviet refusals to grant his requests. Feeling that the Soviet Union had reneged on its promises to build up the Egyptian Armed Forces, Sadat expelled the Soviet advisers from Egypt, though both sides refrained from bringing matters to total rift. In September 1972, Sadat made one last effort to obtain the arms he wanted, dispatching Premier Sidki to Moscow again. However, all that Sidki was able to achieve was a declaration to the effect that according to the United Nations Charter, the Arabs have the right "to liberate their lands by various means." Sidki got words but not the war materiel Egypt wanted. Meanwhile unrest within Egypt was growing. In student demonstrations Sadat came under attack for the contradictions between his words and his deeds.

In retrospect this would seem to have been the point when Sadat reached the conclusion that he had no chance of obtaining the equipment he desired from the Soviet Union and that the only way to break the deadlock was to go to war. He may have assumed that his move would compel the Soviets to come to the aid of Egypt and Syria because they would risk either losing their credibility in the Arab world or allowing armies trained and equipped by them to suffer a crushing defeat. Sadat hoped that a military action, even if its objectives were limited, would lead to the collapse of détente. He was counting on causing a "shock wave" that would break the political stalemate.

When Sadat asked his minister of war, Sadek, to implement the military option, a sharp debate ensued. The Egyptian General Staff had on file an operational plan, code-named Granite 1, for the "liberation" of Sinai. But Sadek contended that the Egyptian Army was not yet ready for that kind of war. Sadat countered by insisting that there could be no more waiting; if the main goals were unattainable, more limited objectives must be set. Sadek argued that the IDF would react to even a limited war with all its might and that this could well lead to a disastrous Egyptian debacle. Sadek refused to be responsible for leading his army to defeat, not grasping Sadat's notion that military action, although possibly resulting in immense losses, was intended as a means only aimed at breaking the political impasse. On 26 September, ten days after Sidki's return from

Moscow, the debate ended with Sadek's dismissal and the appointment of Ahmed Ismail-Ali in his place.

In Israel, the significance of this move was glossed over. We viewed this reshuffle as a renewed attempt by Sadat to improve relations with the USSR by firing a war minister known for his anti-Soviet stance and for his urgings to have Soviet advisers expelled from Egypt.

Sadat and Ismail-Ali saw eye to eye. Egypt's war aims were updated, and Granite 1 was replaced by an amended plan, Granite 2. Instead of the conquest of all of Sinai, the new territorial objective was taking an area extending 100 km from the Suez Canal to a line running from A-Tur on the Gulf of Suez through Refidim (Bir-Gafgafa), including the Mitla and Giddi passes, and up to Nahal Yam on the Mediterranean. The brunt of the Egyptian effort, however, would go into the detailed planning of and preparations for the canal-crossing phase of the operation.

The lessons of the Six Day War and the War of Attrition led the Egyptians to search for solutions against the two strongest components of the IDF, the Israeli Air Force and the Armored Corps. They knew that it was not enough to rely on their own large air and armored forces. The Egyptians realized that in offensive mobile warfare — in which aggressiveness, initiative, flexibility, and capacity for improvisation are of the essence — the Israelis were superior. The Egyptians, however, also had certain advantages, particularly their greater firepower and larger number of troops. Moreover since 1948 they had fought effectively in defensive, static battles in which initiative, improvisation, and flexibility are less vital. Their planners therefore decided to counter the IDF's main strengths by weapons that were defensive in nature.

With Soviet assistance, the Egyptians had built one of the strongest antiaircraft systems in the world. Their armed forces, and particularly their infantry, were equipped with an abundance of antitank weapons. They worked hard to improve the quality of the manpower at their disposal. All college graduates were called up until the victory could be achieved. Indoctrination in the army provided motivation for hatred of the enemy and for "liberation of the sacred lands." An intensive and goal-directed training program was instituted as units were trained in their specific tasks under Granite 2.

Large-scale exercises were conducted by GHQ for the Egyptian Second and Third Armies.

From the beginning of 1973, Ahmed Ismail pushed for completion of terrain preparations. Many "Irish bridges," below water level, were completed along the Sweet Water Canal to enable smooth traffic to the Suez Canal. Along the canal they erected eighty-six ramparts, each 30 meters high, to enable observation and direct fire across the canal. Dozens of approach roads to the canal were constructed.

In January 1973, preliminary planning of Granite 2 was completed. The advantages and deficiencies of both the IDF and of the Egyptian army were analyzed, and the plan reflected original strategic thinking. The strategic framework was determined in line with the decision to work secretly and only with Syria. This decision increased the prospects for attaining surprise and provided the elementary strategic advantage of forcing the small Israeli Army to be split and fight on two fronts simultaneously. The decision was also based on the assumption — proven correct — that other Arab countries and the USSR would be pushed into coming to the aid of Egypt and Syria, even if they had not been in on the secret.

Most of the senior Egyptian command, including War Minister Ismail, had been trained in the Soviet doctrine of war, so in Israel it was taken for granted that they would strictly adhere to it. For example, in water-crossing operations, Soviet doctrine counsels two operational stages: first, the crossing itself and the taking of the bridgehead; second, the breakout from the bridgehead to operational objectives. Emphasis is placed on the rapid shift from the first to the second stage as soon as sufficient forces have crossed the water obstacle.

But the Egyptian war plan consisted of three phases: first, crossing and establishing a bridgehead; second, securing an "operational hold"; and, finally, penetration to capture the operational objectives.

In the first stage, emphasis was placed on maintaining the integrity of the attacking forces instead of seeking a quick depth penetration. Usually an army will try to establish a deep bridgehead that will throw the enemy back, especially his artillery, to prevent the crossing sites from coming under fire. But the Egyptian plan gave priority to expanding towards the flanks in order to prevent a breach of the flanks and encirclement from the rear. The goal was to attain a compact, solid bridgehead whose skies would be protected by a missile "umbrella," its front line by a dense antiattack screen and its rear by the Suez Canal itself. Farther behind, the army would be supported by hundreds of tanks and antitank guns.

Phase one, then, included the crossing and the taking of a continuous bridgehead ten to twelve kilometers deep, this to be completed by D plus one day (by the morning of 8 October). Only at the end of this stage would they push Israeli artillery back from the Artillery Road and put the canal bridges out of range of Israeli guns. The canal-crossing mission was assigned to the first-echelon forces, consisting of five infantry divisions, each made up of two infantry and one mechanized brigade, reinforced by an independent tank brigade. Crossing the canal in five thrusts along its entire length was not only consistent with nonexposure of their flanks, but was also designed to disperse the small Israeli force. If achieved, this would give the Egyptians overall numerical superiority.

The second stage, the "operational hold," was intended to enable the Egyptians to engage the Israelis' armor and air power in a static defensive battle under circumstances favorable to the Egyptians. The Egyptians assumed that the IDF would act according to its own doctrine, which called for a quick end to the war and for shifting the fighting to enemy territory. They surmised, therefore, that Israeli armor would storm the bridgehead, with the air force providing close air support. They hoped to wear down the air force by their antiaircraft missile umbrella and pulverize Israeli armored forces with their antitank weapons.

It is still not clear whether this phase was fixed at seven to eight days (until 15 October), or whether its termination was left to a decision based on development of the situation on the ground. I believe that because of the so-called "fear barrier," no specific time was laid down for termination of this stage. Thus, commencement of the third stage would be contingent upon the visible attrition of Israeli armor and air power. In the course of phase two, the Egyptians planned to move their second-echelon forces to the east bank in preparation for the third stage. These forces consisted of two armored divisions, two mechanized divisions, artillery, and surface-to-air missile batteries.

Phase three — the eastward penetration of about 100 km — was to be achieved by two main thrusts, each by an armored division and a mechanized division, with the support of armor and infantry from first-echelon forces. One thrust would be made by the Third Army towards the Mitla and Gidi passes; the other, by the Second Army, was aimed at Tassa and Refidim (Bir-Gafgafa). Two secondary efforts, to be carried out on the flanks of the two major thrusts, were intended to reach A-Tur in the south and Nahal Yam in the north.

The first stage, that of crossing the canal and establishing a bridgehead, was planned in great detail, including substages. During the first three to four hours, each of the five infantry divisions was to seize a bridgehead 3 km deep and 6 km wide. The war would be launched fifteen minutes prior to H-hour (when the infantry crossing would begin) with an air strike by 190 planes, attacking Israeli command posts, communications installations, artillery units, and tank concentrations up to 100 km from the canal. At the same time, a preparatory artillery barrage by 1,300 guns would paralyze the strongpoints, neutralize the few Israeli artillery batteries, and disrupt the movement of nearby Israeli tanks seeking to reach the canal.

Under cover of the air strike and the concentrated artillery fire — and with the support of tanks firing from atop the ramparts — infantry battalions, supported by antitank teams, would start the crossing in rubber assault boats and quickly take the barriers, which were not being manned by Israeli forces. Capture of the strongpoints themselves was left to a later stage. Within thirty to sixty minutes, a mass of antitank weapons would be deployed in each divisional sector on the Israeli side of the canal: 140 RPG-7s (effective against tanks from a maximum range of 500 meters), 58 recoilless 106mm guns (effective from 1,600 meters), and 24 Sagger missile launchers (effective from 3,000 meters). Within the three hours allotted for this stage, more antitank units would cross, and a dense antitank "wall" would be formed to include 314 RPGs, 108 recoilless guns, and 48 Sagger launchers in each divisional sector. All this was in addition, of course, to the dozens of tanks and antitank guns that would provide support from the ramparts on the west bank of the canal — a very impressive antitank wall, indeed.

A commando battalion was assigned to each of the divisions to hold up and disrupt the arrival of Israeli tank units which the Egyptians estimated to be deployed about 30 to 50 km from the canal. These tank units were expected to reach the canal zone within a few hours. The commandos were to penetrate about 15 km into Israeli territory to mine roads, set ambushes, and raid Israeli command posts and artillery batteries.

The mission of the first infantry to cross was to protect Egyptian engineers who would breach our barriers so that amphibious vehicles and tanks carried by barges could reach the eastern bank quickly. At the same time, the Egyptian engineers were to set up heavy bridges for armor and light bridges for infantry.

It would be a tremendous engineering feat, involving sixty breaches in our earth barriers along the entire length of the canal, eleven to sixteen crossing points in each divisional sector, three for bridges and the others for barges and amphibious vehicles. The breaches were to be made by water jets and bulldozers. The Egyptians estimated that it should take about seven hours before their tanks would be able to cross, but since the plans indicated that the two infantry brigades could complete the crossing within three hours, they decided to transfer the infantry of the mechanized brigade to the east bank without their vehicles and deploy them as second tactical echelon behind the assaulting infantry brigades.

Three to four hours after H-hour, when darkness would be falling, commando battalions would land by helicopter to block Israeli reserve armored units arriving from the far north, from Israel. These commandos were to land on the western side of the Mitla and Gidi passes in the central sector, along the mountains that dominate the Suez Gulf on our side in the southern sector, and at various points on the Qantara-El Arish Road in the northern part of the zone of operations.

Between 1400 and darkness, the Egyptians also planned to employ their 130th Amphibious Brigade, equipped with Soviet-built PT-76 light amphibious tanks and BTR-50 amphibious armored personnel carriers. The brigade's mission was to cross the Bitter Lake at its narrow southern part and rush to block the Gidi and Mitla passes.

Seven hours after the offensive was under way, the transfer of the tanks and the APCs of the mechanized brigade, as well as the tank battalions of the infantry brigades to the east bank would begin. All told, there would be 120 tanks in each divisional sector. Immediately thereafter mortars and artillery would be moved across. Next, at H plus ten hours the tank battalions of the infantry brigade, together with the mechanized brigades, would prepare an attack to widen the bridgehead to 16 km and deepen it to 8 km. This attack would be completed by H plus seventeen hours. Meanwhile, at H plus eleven hours the five independent tank brigades assigned to reinforce the five infantry divisions would begin their crossing. When that stage was completed, each division would have 218 tanks on the Israeli side of the canal.

Beginning on the morning of 7 October and throughout that day, the tank and mechanized brigades would widen the bridgehead to 20 km and deepen it to 10–12 km. With those objectives attained, the first operational phase would be accomplished. By then the divisional bridgeheads would have been joined into two consolidated army bridgeheads reaching as far as the hilly ridge overlooking the entire canal plain.

The Israeli Artillery Road (Hazizit) and the so-called *taozim* (the prebuilt but unmanned second-echelon strongholds) were situated on this very ridge line, and their capture was therefore included in the first operational phase.

Only then would the second operational phase begin. This would be the "hold," as Egypt consolidated its bridgeheads, waiting for the Israeli counterattack so they could decimate our forces. At the same time, the transfer to the east bank of the two armored and two mechanized divisions from the second echelon, together with artillery and antiaircraft missiles, would prepare for the third operational phase.

On the sixth of October the war that put the plans and preparations of both sides to the test began.

CHAPTER SIX

WHY WE WERE CAUGHT
BY SURPRISE

The Egyptians deserve much praise for the secrecy, meticulous planning, and deception that helped them achieve surprise at the start of the Yom Kippur War. But their success in surprising the IDF was due less to Egyptian planning than to the attitude within the IDF, underestimating the enemy and discounting his declarations and actions. Most of all, the surprise of the IDF was a result of our exaggerated overconfidence, which had been building up over a long period.

In spite of the Arabs' efforts to mask their intentions, the IDF possessed enough information and had clear intelligence indicators to conclude that Egypt and Syria were in the final stages of war preparation. But we refused to recognize this possibility. The director of military intelligence (DMI) claimed that the "probability" of war was low, and no one on the General Staff — myself included — disputed him. The chief of staff, the minister of defense, and the prime minister all accepted his view.

What accounts for this blindness?

The Agranat Commission of Inquiry (so named because it was headed by Chief Justice Shimon Agranat), which investigated Israel's lack of readiness in the Yom Kippur War, placed the blame on the IDF — in particular on the DMI and the chief of staff. In the commission's view, the surprise resulted from the assumption of our Intelligence Corps that, "As long as the Arabs do not have enough air power to allow them to strike deep into Israel and challenge the Israeli Air Force and as long as they do not possess long-range ground-to-ground missiles to deter — by threat of retaliation — deep Israeli air strikes, then war is not to be expected."

The Agranat Commission commended Dayan for his words of warning in a speech to the General Staff on 21 May 1973. In that address he predicted the possibility of war in the second half of the summer and ordered preparations for it.

To my mind, however, the Agranat Commission erred in distinguishing between specific intelligence evaluation made in October and the overall mistaken attitudes (contempt for the enemy and exaggerated confidence in the IDF's ability) that were prevalent throughout Israel, accepted by all: the IDF, the government, the Knesset, and the various political parties. It is these attitudes that explain how, in spite of so many warning signs, the DMI arrived at his incorrect appraisal, and which further explain why the DMI's appraisal was accepted by his military and civilian superiors.

Nor do I believe the commission's praise of Dayan for his forecast and warning to be warranted. Any real significance attaching to Dayan's warning could lie not in his words alone but in the overall context of the actions and events that followed. What value could Dayan's remarks have when just a few months later we were told to prepare plans for shortening the compulsory service period, reducing the regular army, and cutting the defense budget?

Moreover what value can be placed on Dayan's prediction when, in the middle of that summer of 1973, so many generals were concluding their army careers as scheduled and being replaced? Promotion and reassignment of officers with the rank of general had to be approved by the defense minister, Moshe Dayan. One prime consideration for making changes at the senior command level has always been the existing level of tension or the probability of war. If these were high, new appointments would be postponed until it was clear that major operations were not imminent, even if the changes had been announced previously. The same practice applied to officers due to retire. There is no doubt in my mind that General Sharon would have postponed his retirement as the commander of

Southern Command had he believed that three months later his front would be involved in a war. Nor would General Gonen, new and inexperienced, have been given this command. The minister of defense would not have initiated or approved such an extensive shift of high-ranking officers had he really believed that war would break out soon.

On the contrary, there is no better indicator of the feeling in the country that war was not imminent than the series of changes in Israel's military leadership carried out so close to the start of the war. Maj. Gen. Rechavam Ze'evi, commander of Central Command, retired on 30 September and was replaced by Brigadier General Efrat, previously the assistant chief of operations. He in turn was replaced in mid-September by Brigadier General Levy, who moved from the post of chief artillery officer, replaced there at the end of August by Col. Nati Sharoni. As commander of the Armored Corps, I planned to retire at the end of October; my replacement, Major General Mandler, was already designated. Mandler, in turn, had begun transferring his command of the armored forces in Sinai to Brigadier General Magen. (As noted earlier, this hand-over was to be completed on 3 October, but when the state of emergency was proclaimed, Mandler decided to stay on until the situation was clarified.) What is evident in all these shifts of command is that few of the new appointees were being assigned after being deputies or even serving within the formations they would command. They came from different headquarters or units.

How did Israel come to mislead itself with so many erroneous perceptions? Before the Six Day War, when Israel lacked strategic depth, it was natural that any activity across its borders which posed the least threat to its security should bring an immediate step-up of readiness. I remember how in 1955, when the Egyptians reinforced their forces in Sinai, we immediately mobilized reserve armored units and deployed them in the Negev. This was an expensive process that occurred repeatedly. The reserves were called to emergency stores, supplied with uniforms, and given arms. They prepared their tanks and loaded them with ammunition. Transporters were mobilized and carried the tanks to the south.

When the threat did not materialize or when the enemy withdrew his forces, the tanks and equipment were returned to the armories but not before the crews disarmed, cleaned, and fixed everything that needed repairing. Some of the men were retained an extra few days to assist the quartermaster and ordnance personnel in preparing all the gear and equipment so that an even speedier future reequipment would be possible. This happened frequently, on occasion three or four times consecutively, with just a few days between the reservists' release and remobilization. Pre-1967 Israel knew tense periods when reserve units were called up many times, with each call-up causing personal, economic, and family problems.

So it was only natural that after the Six Day War, when Israel acquired better borders, that its sensitivity to potential threats from across the borders should diminish. Moreover the fact that the borders were now shorter and were to some extent based on natural obstacles — the Suez Canal with Egypt, the Jordan River with Jordan, and the Rukad wadi with Syria — only strengthened the feeling of security. But most important, the lines were now farther away from the country's civilian population centers. We had strategic depth.

Strategic depth reduced the threat of the country being cut in two quickly or of its cities being shelled at the outbreak of war. For the first time since the establishment of the state, Israel now had ample warning time in the event of attack by enemy planes. The option of conducting delaying operations, with the possibility of temporarily giving ground in certain places to gain time for mobilization of the reserves now existed.

All this meant that the enemy would encounter greater difficulties in attacking. Since the Arabs had not succeeded in the past under better conditions for them, we felt confident — too confident — that they could not succeed in the new situation. Conversely, this new border situation, with Israeli forces closer to the enemy's population centers and national capitals, presented an inherently greater danger to his civilian population and regime in the event of war.

Against this background, we reasoned that it was not likely the Arabs would wage war before there was a decisive shift in the balance of forces. If they did, we believed, it would be suicidal for them.

A confluence of circumstances complicated the military evaluation. The Arabs did not placidly accept their defeat in the Six Day War. After 1967, Israel's Defense Forces had to fight against terrorism *and* the neighboring countries in the War of Attrition. Both presented complex military problems. Combating terrorism or guerrilla activity is an involved task for any regular army, more so for a small army like the IDF. The Arabs had excellent conditions for their terrorist acts: a sympathetic Arab population in the territory we held, bases across Israel's borders, and the possibility of striking at Israeli targets in the international sphere, where the authorities treated them with kid gloves. When the IDF succeeded in blocking most of their infiltration attempts and pushing them away from our borders, the terrorists shifted their activity to the territory of other states — but there, too, we succeeded in deploying to protect Israeli targets. Terrorist operations gradually diminished. The situation never became a comfortable one, but we could live with it, and it did not impede the country's development.

In the War of Attrition, the nature of which was largely dictated by the Arabs, we also faced difficult circumstances. It was a form of warfare that optimized the Egyptians' quantitative advantages in manpower and firepower and revealed our own deficiencies in those areas. They were able to deploy densely along the entire line of contact and could call on massive artillery fire. Since we could not deploy our small regular army with sufficient density, they were able to raid into our territory. They exploited the fact that our regular artillery forces were meager and shelled our troops relentlessly.

Nonetheless we succeeded not only in holding out in this protracted war, but also in bringing it to an end. We felt then that the Arabs were doing all they were capable of militarily — and they were losing. That they fought us while employing strategic methods that afforded them extra advantages led Israel's military planners to draw far-reaching conclusions. It was our evaluation that the "quality gap" was not decreasing but actually was still growing; that while war was to be expected in the future, it would not come until this gap was substantially reduced — that is, not in the near future.

Thus the prevailing feeling of security, based on the assumption that the Arabs were incapable of mounting an overall war against us, distorted our view of the situation. But the main reason for this state of affairs was our failure to understand the Arab mentality. When Colonel Gonen wrote to his son from the Suez Canal soon after the Six Day War saying, "I hope that you will not have to fight. Your father has ended that this time, for good''; or when Dayan, just after the same war, declared that he was now "waiting for a phone call from the Arabs," these words seemed to have logic behind them. But Arab logic was different. At the Khartoum Conference, 29 August 1967, the Arabs proclaimed: "No Peace, No Negotiations, No Recognition." This should have been a warning that the Arab nations were prepared to pay a high price to continue the fight and were confident of their ability to sustain severe losses without collapsing.

We failed to perceive that even if it were not within the Arabs' power to wage a major war in the near future, neither did they intend to accept a standstill situation of "neither war nor peace." We did not grasp that, having lost the two limited wars of terrorism and of attrition, they would search for yet another kind.

It was, in fact, precisely around this that the controversy between Sadat and his war minister, Sadek, revolved, before the latter was replaced at the end of 1972 by Ahmed Ismail-Ali. Sadat wanted a minister of war who would understand that a deadlocked political situation was intolerable and who, in order to break the stalemate, would prepare a military operation — even though that could not end in unequivocal victory and could cost Egypt enormous casualties. This led the Arabs to plan a war of inherently limited aims. Knowing that the IDF would react powerfully to a limited war, too, they decided to limit their military objectives but to employ maximum force to attain those objectives.

We looked on as Egypt prepared hundreds of roads and underwater passes on the Sweet Water Canal, which runs close and parallel to the Suez Canal. We said, "That's good; now it will be easier for us to cross it." We saw them prepare graduated slopes along the Suez Canal and we thought, "Now it will be easier to ascend the opposite bank." We watched them build high ramparts on which they established observation posts and firing positions to cover areas on our side previously obscured to them because of the sand barriers we had erected. Our reaction was, "Excellent, now we will know where their tanks are and where to concentrate our fire." We observed them practising river crossing opposite Balah Island and breaching barriers with water jets, as they dropped amphibious equipment into the water to move armored vehicles, tanks, and other vehicles to the island. We noted: "They certainly have a lot of equipment —

modern gear!" And we thought: "But the fact that they are training in our presence shows that they have no serious intentions."

During the War of Attrition, Israeli planes were occasionally hit by surface-to-air missiles, and antitank missiles were fired at our tanks in the south and on the Golan Heights. The Israeli Air Force and the Armored Corps were in the process of preparing countermeasures, but not enough attention was paid to these incidents, and certainly not enough urgency was given to finding solutions.

The constant split in the Arab world led us to take their preparations even less seriously. Nasser's death and his replacement by Sadat — who announced new dates for launching war several times and who kept proclaiming, time after time, that the "year of decision" had arrived — was mockingly disregarded. And when Soviet advisers left Egypt, we concluded even more confidently that war had again been postponed.

I considered Sadat's proclamation that the Egyptians were ready to sacrifice even a million casualties more as irrational rhetoric for his internal needs than as a serious indication of his readiness for sacrifice. We forgot that a million casualties might hurt Egypt, but less than twenty-five hundred could affect Israel seriously, and we wondered how it was possible for an Arab leader to suggest any such slaughter to his people. Failure to understand the Arab mentality was also widespread outside Israeli military circles. Political leaders, and even Arabists in the universities who stressed that the Arabs would not acquiesce to our existence, did not assess or warn that war was imminent.

It is an eye-opening exercise that demonstrates how far the logical assessments of Israel's top military leaders were distorted by their erroneous conception to compare what the defense minister and the chief of staff said in April-May 1973 with what they were saying less than half a year later, in September-October of 1973, on the eve of the war. In an evaluation they gave the general staff in April, the two spoke almost prophetically. Dayan explained that the Arabs would not put up with the stalemate, and the situation was liable to lead to an explosion. He explained that when Sadat proclaimed "readiness" for a million victims, he meant that he was ready to pay a high price for even a limited military achievement to use as leverage in international politics in order to break the deadlock. It was Dado Elazar's view that the Arabs would not be satisfied with limited or sporadic actions but would wage total war with the hope of "achieving something" through a "half surprise."

But his remarks of April did not prevent Dayan from telling the defense ministry's senior staff in July that he did not expect another war for the next ten years. Nor did it preclude his acceptance of a cut in Israel's defense budget or of plans to shorten the period of compulsory military service. Dado, in spite of his April assessment, accepted the evaluation of his DMI in September-October although there were already many indicators of a general war to be launched through a "half surprise."

Moreover, in a conference at GHQ in September 1973, some of the generals raised strong objections to the idea of shortening the period of compulsory military service and reducing the size of the regular army. The then deputy chief of staff, Maj. Gen. Israel Tal, claimed angrily that those who opposed the cuts did not have a comprehensive grasp of Israel's true national security problems.

On the assumption that war was a remote contingency, Israel's military planners carried out moves that they would not have taken otherwise. For many years it had been the custom to build more and more armored formations even before all the necessary equipment was available in the hope that the gaps would be made good in time. Such shortages were aggravated by commanders who would draw on the emergency stores for half-tracks, binoculars, and weapons for units on routine security tasks. When the 1973 war broke out, we were in the process of forming many new units, but they lacked much of their equipment.

We were also in the midst of transferring some emergency stores to forward zones, something the IDF would not have undertaken had we believed war was near. We were caught with several such depots unfinished, without electricity, and with shelves missing and equipment still disarrayed. On the other hand, this step led to the armories being close to the front lines, a fact that contributed much to reducing the time necessary for reserve tanks to get to the front, but it made no contribution to their leaving for the front in an organized way.

We relied totally on the belief that our Intelligence Corps would provide a strategic warning of at least forty-eight hours. This assumption led to situations of preparedness based on the model of the regular army being stationed along the borders, using equipment from emergency depots of reserve formations with their own equipment left in the center of the country. The result was a chain reaction with six formations being equipped not from their own depots or centers. Hundreds of tank crews had to rush to depots that were not theirs.

Because there was, in fact, no early warning, we were caught with dozens of tank crews busy performing what are actually infantry duties along the borders from Sharm el-Sheikh in the south to Mount Hermon in the north. It took a long time after the war began until these soldiers were able to join their armored units.

All these moves required many improvisations. The critical situation at the outbreak of the Yom Kippur War exacerbated the problem. Tank crews rushed to the front, leaving in their depots — especially those crews which were in the process of reorganization — a great deal of equipment that was needed badly in the battle zones.

I relate these facts because many Israelis believe that basically we were less prepared for the Yom Kippur War than for the Six Day War. The truth is exactly the opposite. It would have been very sad had we been taken by surprise in the Six Day War. We had three weeks of warning then, and it was used for intensive preparation to procure equipment, repair armor, and organize and train units. The fact is that in 1973, in spite of the surprise, we were able to move many well-equipped formations to the front in record time. I do not mean to say that these explanations can console the crew members who left for the battlefield lacking equipment. What I must conclude is that the lack of equipment came more from surprise and other objective factors than from neglect.

Thought must be invested so that Israel will not be caught this way again, especially since the surprise of the Yom Kippur War need not have occurred. As a matter of fact, the possibility of another Arab surprise is very real. All Arab armies are based on regular forces permanently deployed along Israel's borders. Mobilization of their reserves, or reinforcement by Arab countries not bordering

Israel, is not necessary until after war breaks out. Egypt and Syria can look upon those forces as second-echelon forces who could reach the zone of operations within a few days.

Israel, by contrast, faces many inherent limitations. The majority of the country's land forces will continue to be made up of reserves. Along with steps to improve our intelligence and early-warning system, we must also try to improve our ability to move into a war situation efficiently, even in circumstances of surprise. Furthermore, to overcome the threat to our existence in the wake of a possible surprise attack in the future, Israel must retain defensible borders. We must have borders that afford us the space and time for the regular army to engage in delaying tactics and provide cover while the reserves are mobilized and moved to the front.

CHAPTER SEVEN

SUMMARY: STRATEGIC ERRORS RESULTING FROM THE SURPRISE

The Egyptians and Syrians opened the war with tremendous advantages. To the strategic advantages accruing from having split the IDF and compelling it to fight on two fronts, the strategic surprise itself was added. This caused a further split, at least in the initial phase, between the reserves and the small regular army, because the reserves were not mobilized early enough. The Egyptian and Syrian military leadership may, then, congratulate themselves for the secrecy and deception with which they carried through their plan. But their achievement in fact exceeded their most optimistic expectations because they did not imagine that we would simply ignore all the concrete physical evidence on the ground.

Even after we finally had concluded that war was imminent, our reaction was sluggish, with precious hours wasted. When, following receipt of a reliable report, the DMI at last reached the conclusion that war was about to break out and passed that information to the chief of staff, the time was 0400 on 6 October — ten hours before hostilities began. And the report received spoke of war due to break out that evening. The chief of staff wanted to carry out a general mobilization at once, although he knew that time was too short, and that when war began only the small regular army would be on the front line to cope with the massive enemy attack. Dado therefore sought to activate the sole powerful element of the armed forces that could take on the enemy at short notice and weaken his opening blow — the air force. General Elazar immediately called the commander of the air force, Major General Peled, and ordered him to prepare a preemptive strike to be launched at about noon.

When Dado met with the minister of defense, however, the latter rejected both a full call-up and a preemptive air strike. Dayan would approve a call-up of just two divisions. An hour after the General Staff conference the two men then put their conflicting views before Prime Minister Golda Meir for her decision. Dayan's reasoning was that full mobilization was liable to bring about escalation and that a preemptive strike would lead many nations — particularly the United States — to accuse Israel of being the actual aggressor. Mrs. Meir approved the mobilization but ruled out the preemptive air strike. By then, four precious hours had already been lost. The call-up process would begin at 0900 instead of at 0500. At 1000 hours, Mrs. Meir called the American ambassador to Israel, asking him to have his country warn Egypt and Syria against opening hostilities, because Israel knew of their preparations, was ready, and would react powerfully.

As this description of the differences of opinion and of the slow pace of decision making shows, neither the prime minister nor the defense minister was, even at this late hour, wholly certain that war was about to erupt. More serious still, there was a feeling of overconfidence that even if things came to the worst, the IDF could control the situation with the regular army alone, without a preemptive air strike. The chief of staff, as I knew him, had a "feel" for and understanding of politics and was surely aware of the political implications of his proposals that morning. But since he also grasped the military significance of entering a war so badly outnumbered, he urged the preemptive strike. Decisions at the political level prevented him from taking the only step that could have tilted, however little, the grave opening imbalance of forces.

Could a preemptive air strike have had a substantial effect on the events of the battlefield? This hypothetical question permits no simple answer. Certainly the Arabs were alert to and prepared for that possibility, so probably its results would have been limited. But it is also clear that interference and disruptions could delay, hurt, and reduce the effectiveness of the Arab armed forces, especially because of their mediocre improvisational capacity. It is possible that because of the Arabs' high state of alert, the Israeli Air Force would have suffered substantial losses. But it would have been able to operate deliberately and massively against its primary enemy, the missile sites, thus gaining increased freedom of action to support the ground forces later.

But the chief of staff was compelled to cancel the preemptive strike. So when the fighting began, most of our planes were in the process of changing their ordnance and had to take off for air-to-air combat not fully prepared and having to improvise. Nonetheless, they were able to engage the first wave of enemy planes within five minutes after the latter had begun their attacks on tactical Israeli targets in Sinai. Eighteen Egyptian planes were shot down, and the planned second attack wave did not materialize.

It is surprising how ineffective the Egyptian air strike was. At Bir-Tamada, an IDF rear installation, one hut was hit and ten persons were killed. There were some casualties in artillery batteries and in static installations. The runway at the Bir-Tamada airfield was heavily damaged, but that airfield was not planned for our use. The Refidim Airfield was slightly damaged but was still usable. The intelligence installations at Umm-Hashiba were bombed but not damaged.

The moment the Israeli Air Force appeared, it dominated the skies over Sinai and made a critical contribution to the protection of our convoys streaming to the front. The air force also played a considerable role in disrupting Egyptian commando activity by shooting down many enemy helicopters packed with men. It was precisely in its attempts to prevent the canal crossing, however, that the air force had only limited success. Because of disruptions in deploying Israeli land forces, with the bulk making their way to the front, the air force had to abandon its intention of operating against missile batteries and try to prevent the crossing by striking at Egyptian troops on the bridges. Four of our aircraft were lost in those first hours, and another ten on 7 October, but the impact our planes had on the ground was small.

On top of the strategic surprise and the decision not to launch a preemptive strike, there was a serious operational mistake: failure to deploy the active Sinai Division according to the *Shovach Yonim* Plan. The atmosphere of the deescalation attempts apparently affected General Gonen too. Instead of expediting the deployment of forces, he held things back, ordering General Mandler to commence deployment not before 1700 hours in order to be ready at 1800 hours. Mandler objected to this but had only limited success; Gonen agreed to advance the process by one hour.

The Egyptians enjoyed opening conditions beyond their rosiest dreams. When the war broke out, at 1400, the Egyptian artillery barrage from thirteen hundred guns was answered by only twenty-eight deployed Israeli artillery pieces. Against the five Egyptian divisions that were crossing the canal stood 460 Israeli soldiers in the strongpoints. Tanks earmarked for the strongpoints were in the rear. About one hundred tanks were deployed along the 160 km of the canal, with two hundred more tanks at a distance of about 100 km from the front.

Israel's initial mistake, of having only one hundred tanks along a 160 km defensive line, was compounded by tactical errors when those one hundred tanks moved forward. Employing the tanks as we did, we violated a basic armor lesson drawn from the Second World War. Battle needs tempt one to deploy and employ tanks everywhere, as the French used their forces for the defense of France, dispersing most of their three thousand tanks throughout their infantry divisions. The Germans, on the other hand, were actually inferior in tank numbers, able to field only 2,700 tanks on the western front. But they concentrated their tanks into ten armored divisions. Seven of these made up two massive thrusts, tanks bursting through the French defenses in a true *blitzkrieg*.

When reports indicated that an Egyptian crossing was under way and that our strongpoints urgently needed help, the tank units reacted instinctively — just as they had learned to do during the War of Attrition — by rushing to the strongpoints. But this time it was total war, not just an isolated raid. All the strongpoints were calling for help, and this led to the immediate dispersion of nearby first-echelon tanks into "penny pockets." The roads near the canal were few, surrounded by marshes, with traffic through the approach axes limited. Since the crossing was relatively unopposed and quickly executed, small Israeli units of two to eight tanks ran into antitank ambushes on the barriers and the "fins," 600 to 1,500 meters from the canal. The tanks were eliminated by missiles and RPG-7s. Had they artillery or infantry with them, they might have survived. Without them, they were an unbalanced team, ineffective against infantry.

The absence of infantry and artillery was a result of the inherent difficulties in the composition of our small regular army. Planning called for these supporting elements to supplement the regular forces before war erupted, but the surprise left no time for these supplementary forces to arrive. The second-echelon forces moved swiftly, but the grave situation along the canal and the call for help from so many points at once resulted in the main armored force being split into small units, so they, too, were vulnerable without infantry or artillery support.

Despite the inferior tactical circumstances and heavy casualties, some of the armor reached the canal strongpoints thanks to the spirit and courage of the soldiers. But their mission was not clear to them. Some evacuated wounded soldiers while others asked for authority to evacuate the strongpoints but were refused. In short, Israeli tank crews fought bravely, but because of the ineffectual way in which they were operated and the conditions of tactical inferiority in which they found themselves, they were decimated. As dawn of 7 October approached, Southern Command would find that only 110 of the 290 tanks of the Sinai Armored Division were still functioning.

These grave results were inevitable given the circumstances. One cannot but wonder, however, if things would have gone differently had the Israeli forces been deployed in time according to the *Shovach Yonim* plan, providing for forward deployment but only of the regular troops.

I believe that had we launched a preemptive air strike and not made the mistake of splitting and scattering our armored forces, even then we could not have prevented the Egyptians from seizing substantial areas on the eastern bank of the canal. Had the Israeli tanks been employed in masses instead of in small, dispersed units, there still would have been a lack of balance. They would probably have achieved some successes along parts of the canal where tank concentrations could have been employed. But the Egyptians attacked along a 160-km front, and they would have been able to consolidate themselves at various points on the canal. When Israeli tanks reached those places, they would have hit mines and come under artillery and missile fire. They still would have lacked necessary infantry, artillery, and engineering support to overcome that kind of entrenched defense. Tanks operating alone are of limited effectiveness against entrenched infantry; their sight is limited and their fire ineffectual. The tank's gun is most effective when employed against "hard" targets. When charging tanks close with the enemy, they rely on escorting infantry or armored infantry who can turn to observe and fire in all directions at once.

We were fully aware of the existence of the enemy's antitank missiles, but the war caught us unprepared, still developing new tactics to deal with them. In encounters between tanks and missiles in the Six Day War and in the War of Attrition, antitank missiles had been largely ineffective. Therefore we concluded that in battle, with artillery fire and smoke and dust, even a trained soldier would have difficulty tracking his target. Further he would be exposed to fire during the time it took him to aim and fire and for the missile to reach its target (as much as thirty seconds altogether). The Egyptians succeeded in concentrating a large number of antitank weapons along the expected routes of advance, places where it was very difficult to maneuver, and we had virtually no artillery support for the tanks. This brought about different results. Many missiles missed their target, but the firing of so many salvos had its effect. The absence of close Israeli artillery and infantry support also allowed the short-range RPG rockets to be used with relative ease.

I shall return to the question of the antitank missile and its effect on armored battle later. For now, I shall confine myself to noting that the scope and effectiveness of these weapons were greatly inflated immediately after the war, when various myths sprang up. Studies we carried out after the war showed that many hits on our tanks by other means were attributed at the time to these missiles. One should remember that these missiles were employed throughout the war but could not halt our offensive or prevent the IDF's canal crossing and its encirclement of the Egyptians' Third Army.

Had we not made the mistake of delaying the deployment of our regulars and of operating in piecemeal fashion, the Egyptian crossing could have been greatly hampered. The Egyptian army is weak at improvising. If the IDF had been functioning according to the *Shovach Yonim* Plan of forward deployment, the Egyptians would have taken more casualties, which in turn would have lowered their morale and made the time needed to overcome them shorter. But we still would not have been able to prevent them from seizing large areas on our side of the canal, since the IDF had never intended to confront the Egyptians in an all-out war with the *Shovach Yonim* forces only.

It was for a situation of total war that the *Sela* Plan had been formed. Not only did the *Sela* deployment call for far greater forces, it would also have given us a balanced disposition of tanks, infantry, artillery, engineers, and supplementary forces for logistical and control activities. Had we received an early warning and so been able to implement *Sela*, the course of events would have been entirely different. We made many mistakes and operated under wholly adverse circumstances; despite this, we managed to get to the canal and link up with many of the strongpoints. One can imagine what would have prevailed had we had the larger and more balanced forces called for by the *Sela* Plan at our disposal.

We made mistakes, but what of the Egyptians? Their strategists had developed a plan tailor-made for the Egyptian army's capabilities. The splitting and dispersion of our armed forces on the strategic level occurred because the IDF had to fight a two-front war, and the Egyptians managed to surprise and confront our small regular army only. The dispersion of our forces on the tactical level was achieved by their attacking on a broad front along the 160 km of the Suez Canal. The Egyptians wanted us to try to stop them everywhere at the same time. Their hope materialized.

The strategy they selected, of attacking in five "equal efforts" and then making an "operational pause" as soon as possible, violated the principles of warfare known as "concentration of force" and "resumption of the initiative." Classical military doctrine calls for the massing of forces at focal points in order to overwhelm the enemy, break through his defenses, and penetrate in depth. Then, the concept goes, exploit the initial success by attacking more vulnerable targets such as artillery, headquarters and communications installations, and armories. This series of moves — massing, penetrating, following up while the enemy is off balance, and capturing vital strategic terrain — is a classic, bold, decisive form of combat for terminating a war quickly. It calls for the attacker to retain his initiative and momentum, thus preventing the enemy's recovery.

To wage such a war would have required the Egyptians to advance rapidly beyond the cover of their air defense umbrella and risk engagements in mobile armored warfare, something they wanted to avoid. They therefore preferred to forego these principles of warfare and emphasize instead "integrity of force," advancing cautiously along a broad front, careful not to leave any open flanks. They knew that the ratio of forces would enable them to outnumber us, giving them superiority at every crossing site. This would help their troops overcome the so-called "barrier of fear" *vis-à-vis* the Israeli soldier. The Egyptian planners were also correct in their assumption that Israeli military doctrine, which called for a quick termination of a war and its transfer to enemy ground, would lead the IDF to carry out an immediate all-out assault.

The Egyptian execution of the plan was also good. A crossing operation is quite a complex feat. It is true that they were lucky, that we made many mistakes, and that they had near ideal conditions. Nevertheless, to breach the earth barriers at dozens of points, set up ten bridges, transfer tens of thousands of infantry troops, hundreds of tanks, artillery pieces and vehicles quickly, constitutes a great achievement. Despite these advantages, however, the relatively ineffectual Israeli resistance was enough to prevent them from completing their missions.

The Egyptians crossed the canal with less resistance and fewer losses than they had anticipated. On 6 October they succeeded in establishing almost two army bridgeheads. Although they failed to transfer all the tanks they had planned, they still had 250 tanks on the east bank by the morning of 7 October. By that evening, they had only 450 tanks, instead of the 1,100 they had planned for. The delay, however, was not crucial, and they managed to transfer the additional tanks within a few days. More surprising were the ineffectiveness of the Egyptian Air Force and the failure of Egyptian commandos to prevent our reserves from reaching the front. Moreover, two key objectives that Egypt planned to achieve on 7 October were not achieved. They failed to capture most of the strongpoints, and, just as significantly, they did not expand their bridgeheads to the planned depth of 10 km from the canal to the ridge line and the Artillery Road.

What explains the Egyptians' inability to take full advantage of their situation as the war began? We were heavily outnumbered and had made mistakes at the tactical, operational, and strategic levels. But our steadfastness and boldness of attack were enough, if not to prevent the heavy price we paid in blood, then at least to frustrate the Egyptian moves and prevent them, after all, from overcoming the "barrier of fear." Their advance was slow and cautious, as their attacks on the strongpoints took the form of one step forward and two steps backward.

Most of the ridge line and the Artillery Road remained in our hands. This compelled the Egyptians to dig in for their second phase in inferior positions that could be fully observed. Had the IDF lost the line of the Artillery Road and ridge, it would probably have had to retreat to positions close by the Lateral Road, 30 km from the canal. Holding the ridge near the canal and the road along it was of great help in the fighting to come. This area enabled us to deploy our artillery to cover the terrain up to the canal with its fire. It was a key area for the development of the battles and moves of the coming days.

But now the situation was still unclear, fluid. The Egyptians were still crossing, attacking the strongpoints, pushing eastward. On our side, the reserve formations continued to arrive at the front.

PART II

FAILURE OF THE COUNTERATTACK

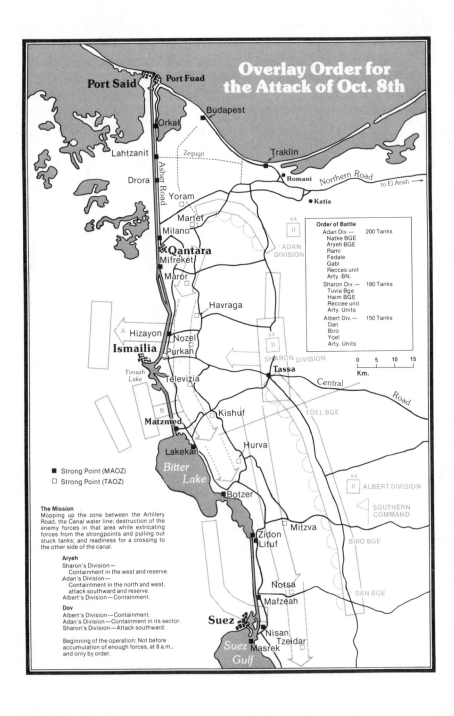

Overlay Order for the Attack of Oct. 8th

Port Said
Port Fuad
Orkal
Budapest
Lahtzanit
Zegugit
Traklin
Drora
Asher Road
Romani
Northern Road
to El Arish
Yoram
Katia
Martef
Milano
Qantara
Mifreket
Maror
Havraga
Hizayon
Nozel
Ismailia
Purkan
Timsah Lake
Televizia
Tassa
Central Road
Matzmed
Kishuf
YOEL BGE
Hurva
Lakekan
Bitter Lake
Botzer
Mitzva
ALBERT DIVISION
Zidon
Lituf
SOUTHERN COMMAND
BIRO BGE
Notsa
DAN BGE
Mafzeah
Suez
Nisan
Tzeidar
Suez Gulf
Masrek

Order of Battle

Adan Div.— 200 Tanks
Natke BGE
Aryeh BGE
Rami
Fedale
Gabi
Recces unit
Arty. BN.
Sharon Div.— 180 Tanks
Tuvia Bge
Haim BGE
Reccee unit
Arty. Units
Albert Div.— 150 Tanks
Dan
Biro
Yoel
Arty. Units

ADAN DIVISION

SHARON DIVISION

0   5   10   15
Km.

■ Strong Point (MAOZ)
□ Strong Point (TAOZ)

The Mission
Mopping up the zone between the Artillery
Road, the Canal water line; destruction of the
enemy forces in that area while extricating
forces from the strongpoints and pulling out
stuck tanks; and readiness for a crossing to
the other side of the canal.

Aryeh
Sharon's Division—
   Containment in the west and reserve.
Adan's Division—
   Containment in the north and west,
   attack southward and reserve.
Albert's Division—Containment.

Dov
Albert's Division—Containment.
Adan's Division—Containment in its sector.
Sharon's Division—Attack southward.

Beginning of the operation: Not before
accumulation of enough forces, at 8 a.m.,
and only by order.

CHAPTER EIGHT

DADO'S PLAN: 8 OCTOBER

At 1145 hours on 7 October, Defense Minister Moshe Dayan entered Southern Command Headquarters. General Gonen briefed him on the situation at the southern front. During the preceding hour, his headquarters had received several transmissions from the division commander, General Mandler, who reported that Egyptian armor was breaking through in several places along his lines, forcing him to retreat eastward to the Artillery Road. Gonen had also received information that an Egyptian armored attack eastward from the Firdan Bridge (Hizayon) was being launched. He had ordered me to rush an armored battalion to Reactia on the Lateral Road to engage enemy armor should they try to break through into our rear. Dayan had arrived from the Northern Command, where the situation was difficult and dangerous. The Syrians had breached our front line during the night, and since morning we had been trying to stabilize things. The Israeli Air Force had been operating, and the small reserve armored units had been rushed there to reinforce beleaguered regular troops.

The previous night, 6 October, Dayan had taken part in a cabinet session at which the chief of staff reviewed the situation on both fronts. At that meeting Dayan had disputed the chief of staff's assessment about the southern front. It was already clear that in the north our small forces were deployed to meet the enemy in accordance with the plan, whereas in the south a serious mistake had been made in that the forces had not been moved into a forward deployment condition (*Shovach Yonim*). During the night the picture was that the enemy was crossing the entire length of the front uninterruptedly. Dayan thought that after the failure of the regular forces to prevent the Egyptian crossing, it would be best to withdraw to a new and deeper defense line. At this line we would await the massing of all the reserve forces and only then move to an armored counterattack.

After hearing discouraging reports during his visit of 7 October to Southern Command, Dayan became even more convinced that our forces should fall back to a new defense line. Moreover he could not understand why the canal strongpoints had not been evacuated during the previous night, since they were never meant to prevent a crossing. Unlike Gonen, Dayan did not believe we would be able to link up with them soon. Weighing these problems, Dayan said that we should evacuate the strongpoints and withdraw to a second line in the rear. He left the exact location of the new line to Gonen.

I don't know whether this was an order or a piece of "ministerial advice" (this was the phrase used by Dayan himself to emphasize that his comments were not actually an order) to Gonen. But the moment the defense minister left the Southern Command war room, at 1206 hours, we division commanders received orders from Southern Command to form a new defensive line along the Lateral Road, 30 km east of the canal. We also were to maintain small mobile forces on the Artillery Road, 10 km from the canal to report on and delay the enemy advance. In addition, Gonen ordered the evacuation of the strongpoints wherever conditions permitted. At 1310 hours Gonen informed Dado Elazar that he was deploying our forces along the Lateral Road, which henceforth would be the main defensive line. At Gonen's request, the chief of staff ordered the entire air effort concentrated on the southern front.

Upon his return to Tel Aviv that afternoon, Dayan hurried to brief Prime Minister Meir on what he had learned. In her office he met Ministers Yigal Allon and Israel Galili. Dayan explained the situation to them, expressing his view that since the first phase of hostilities had resulted in relatively few enemy casualties, while we had suffered heavy losses, implications for the continuation of the fighting were grave. Although on the previous night he had believed we could counterattack when the reserve divisions arrived, he now thought we had to deploy the reserve formations for a long and stubborn defensive battle deep in our territory. Dayan said we would not be able to drive the Egyptians back across the canal until we received more planes and tanks from the United States and Europe.

Golda was appalled. From what she had learned previously, she knew that Israel was in a difficult situation, but she thought that as soon as the reserves entered the fray, we would be able to launch an early counterattack and drive the enemy back across the canal. But now Dayan was proposing a deployment in depth for a protracted defensive war.

At 1600 hours Dado was called into Golda's office and asked for his assessment. The chief of staff thought we should counterattack the narrow bridgeheads on the eastern bank the next morning, 8 October. He said that Sharon and I favored an immediate counterattack and then a crossing to the west bank of the Suez, but this he considered too great a risk. Dado did not accept Dayan's notion of resigning ourselves to the defensive. He suggested, however, that he personally go to the Sinai and decide after a closer look at the situation. Dayan did not object. Today I know that Sharon called Elazar to tell him he favored an immediate crossing. I do not know where he got the impression that I was also for this, since I had had no chance to speak with him since the previous day. But his arrival at Southern Command would enable him to learn that I actually held a different view.

Prior to leaving for Sinai, Dado met with his staff and summed up his ideas. He told them that two counterattacks should be planned for the next morning, 8 October, a massive full scale action on the northern (Syrian) front and a limited offensive in the south. This was the background to the meeting that was to be held at Southern Command Headquarters with Dado, Gonen, and the division commanders — Magen, Sharon, and myself. Early in the evening of 7 October Magen and I took off from Baluza in a light plane.

I do not know how many times I had flown between Baluza and Refidim (near where the meeting was to take place), but I always loved to fly over the sparkling white sand dunes and see the green patches of palm groves along their edges. From time to time, I would spot tiny shepherds with their small scattered flocks. As the plane continued farther across the dunes, the atmosphere changed completely. I always felt a fusion of wildness and purity in those white dunes, a feeling of something still unspoiled by the touch of human hands. Whenever I flew over the desert, the sight of it would conjure up memories of my first days at Dangur, a place in the Negev Desert where my friends and I had settled to build a new kibbutz exactly twenty-seven years earlier, on the night following Yom Kippur in 1946. Today that kibbutz is called Nirim, and many of my friends still live there. At that time we were a small group — just twelve young men and three young women — and we aimed to carry out agricultural experiments and strike roots in the Negev. I remembered how we liked to lie on the clean white sand that filled the yard, as if it were our lawn. Since then, the Negev has been transformed, much of it now covered by green fields. But this time everything seemed different — absolutely quiet, as if everything were at a standstill, in stark contradiction to the scene just a few miles away where our soldiers were fighting for their lives. The scene looked unreal; the quiet was utterly deceptive.

I reflected on the situation in my sector. We had received warning of an Egyptian thrust deep into our territory. "Thank goodness it hasn't commenced yet," I thought. I had managed to prepare against such a move by deploying Natke's brigade to contain the enemy, while Rami's armored infantry brigade dug in around Baluza. I assigned Gabi the tank battalion from Rami's brigade, hoping that together with the remainder of his brigade and the new tanks he was now recovering from the dunes he would be able to resume operations. Those were all the forces I had.

The trouble was that traffic on the main communications road between El Arish and Qantara was barely moving, and Aryeh's brigade was still far off. Although Aryeh was approaching Katia, 40 km from the canal, his last units were 70 km from the front, near Nahal-Yam. Fedale's mechanized brigade of armored infantry battalions and Sherman tanks had been transferred from Central Command only that morning, 7 October, and was not expected to arrive before about noon on the eighth. My division's artillery battalions were ordered to proceed southward on their own tracks, without waiting for transporters. That order had been given at noon on the seventh, so when we learned about the situation on the El Arish-Qantara Road, we could not expect them to arrive at the front before the evening of the eighth. At present, I could count on only ten guns available to my division, those which were in the sector before my arrival.

My greatest concern was for the men in the strongpoints, besieged and fighting for their lives. All attempts to link up with them had failed completely, and they had taken heavy casualties. Natke's experience fighting against the stubborn Egyptian commandos who tried to cut off the road around Romani showed again that this was no longer the same Egyptian army we had crushed in four days in 1967. We were now dealing with a well-trained enemy, fighting with skill and dedication.

Our plane finally landed on an emergency runway at Umm-Hashiba, and we were taken to Southern Command Headquarters in a jeep. Upon arriving there, I had to force my way through scores of male and female soldiers crowded in the bunker's corridors. Some were wrapped in blankets, taking naps, while others sat on stairs, talking. I saw the familiar faces of friends and colleagues but also noticed many outsiders and reporters. The war room was jammed with staff officers and visitors. The place was a mess; you could barely find your own feet. Looking at maps and listening to transceivers, I tried to follow reports from our forces along the front, but in vain. So deafening was the noise in the room and so distorted the sound from the radio that it was impossible to understand anything. It was a frustrating and depressing situation. I could not help thinking that it had to be impossible to work out any coherent plan amidst such disorder.

At 1845 hours Dado arrived, and I was taken to General Gonen's private room. This small office was approximately 3 x 3 meters, simply furnished with two sofas, a few chairs, a coffee table, and a larger table against the wall with a big plastic-covered map on it. Dado welcomed me warmly as we shook hands and took each other in. From his calm, serene face one could never guess that this was a chief of staff whose army was facing a critical situation. I glanced at the other men in the room. I saw Yitzhak Rabin, the former chief of staff who would later become prime minister; his features were expressionless, and he took no part in the discussion. On his left sat General Gonen and his deputy, Gen. Uri Ben-Ari, both of whom looked tired, almost exhausted. On the right was Mandler, who had borne the burden of the first twenty-four hours of fighting all along the Suez front. This showed on his face. The atmosphere was oppressive; we all knew that the IDF had undergone a difficult twenty-four hour period, the like of which we had never expected. I shook hands with everybody and took my seat.

Dado asked, "What's happening in your area, Bren?"

I described the situation in my sector, the progress of my forces, and our struggle against the Egyptian commandos who had ambushed us near Romani. I also related what I had learned from Alush, Kalman, and Gabi about the events that had taken place before my arrival. Most of the questions from the chief of staff, Gonen, and his deputy seemed to seek an answer to the mystery that concerned us all. Why were the Egyptians doing so well, and we so poorly? Were they fighting better than they had in the past? Were they really different from the enemy we had met in 1967, 1956, and 1948?

To answer these questions, I gave several examples: how Egyptian commandos, blocking the road to Strongpoint Budapest, had twice held their fire until Lapidot's troops came into close range; how, even though pinned down by our tank and mortar fire, they allowed our sector reconnaissance unit to advance, holding their fire again, and then inflicting heavy casualties on them. I told how Egyptian soldiers had reblocked the road between El Arish and Qantara with effective fire although we had counterattacked and killed many of them. Then I recounted how they had fought against Natke's tanks, continuing to fire in the face of a head-on assault, and how the captured Egyptian commando unit commander had expressed so much bitterness about his failure to complete his mission for lack of reinforcements. Unpleasant as those facts were, no one suggested I was exaggerating.

Dado turned to Gonen, "What's happening with Arik Sharon? Why hasn't he arrived yet? When can we actually start the discussion?" Gonen explained that he had ordered Sharon to come to headquarters, but there had been some misunderstanding and Sharon would arrive late. Dado decided to wait no longer and opened the discussion.

He began by briefing those present on events on the northern and southern fronts, emphasizing that in both places we had failed to prevent the enemy from breaking through our lines and had suffered considerable losses in men, tanks, and aircraft. Now that the reserves were nearing the front lines, he wanted our opinion about what steps should be taken.

The intelligence information we had about the enemy dispositions was that they had twelve bridges spanning the Suez Canal; five infantry divisions with perhaps hundreds of tanks were crossing along the length of the canal, seeking to move east. The main tank concentrations had been observed in three places: near Qantara, in the northern sector, and Firdan, in the central sector, and on the road to the Mitla Pass, in the south. We did not yet know where they would make their main effort.

One grave problem of concern to all of us was the situation of the men still in the strongpoints, all of which were under siege. Most had many wounded and dead, and all were crying for help.

Gonen was the first to speak. He reviewed the situation from the beginning, praised the support provided by the air force, and recommended that the IDF cross the canal on Egyptian bridges, with my division near Qantara and Sharon's near Suez City. General Mandler recommended waiting until around noon the following day, and then, with the greater forces available, launching a concentrated two-division attack in a narrow sector in the southern section of the canal and crossing to the west bank.

Now came my turn. I did not believe in our capacity to cross or even approach the proximity of the canal at this time. It was a moment of truth, a very difficult moment.

I was about to recommend not to attempt a link-up with the strongpoints because it would cost too much and probably end in failure. But this was a terrible course to recommend. It went against my grain, against the tradition of IDF, and against the ideals which we had always upheld. We often had paid dearly to rescue our people. That was exactly how we had been able to establish and keep the confidence our soldiers held in their commanders, why our soldiers in the strongpoints would not imagine that they might be left behind, and why they continued to fight so bravely and stubbornly. I knew, however, that my responsibility as a senior officer obligated me to make my decisions logically. What good would it do to try to rescue those in the strongpoints, if we were doomed to failure, thus increasing enemy success by adding more casualties to our forces?

I began describing the disposition of my forces and gave my assessment that by dawn I would have about two hundred tanks available, with the rest arriving by that evening, 8 October. But I pointed out that I only had ten guns in my sector and that my artillery battalions could not arrive until the following evening or the day after, on 9 October. Moreover, Fedale's brigade was still on the move and it would not arrive until noon on the eighth. Until then, we would be short of infantry units.

Our experience of the past twenty-four hours indicated, I noted, that the Egyptians were dug in along the canal with many antitank missiles, using the area's unique topography to good advantage. The artificial ramparts and barriers on both sides of the canal were helping them control the canal zone and impeding our ability to maneuver. Therefore, any attempt to break through to the strongpoints would be costly and, in my opinion, could not succeed. I recommended a limited counterattack instead, aimed only at taking the initiative from the Egyptians and halting their advance eastward, while destroying that part of the Egyptian armored force which had thrust deeply into our territory, no longer protected by the ramparts near the canal.

I was not confident that my approach would be accepted, since it did not include a rescue of the besieged strongpoints. I suggested that each strongpoint that could be evacuated, should be and right away, but I knew that many would not make it. I added that if we decided to try a rescue, it would first be necessary to use both divisions (mine and Sharon's) with all our tanks and all our artillery battalions as well as massive air support. Such an attack could not be prepared before noon the following day, which meant that we would be leaving the initiative with the enemy for the time being. I concluded by asserting that I favored taking the initiative in order to halt the momentum of the enemy's advance as soon as possible. With the forces that would arrive by morning we would be able to mop up and seize the area not dominated from the ramparts and barriers. For the rest, we would await the arrival of all our reserves. Ben-Ari expressed a similar view.

Dado summed up: As the situation looked now, we would proceed the next day with a limited gradual counterattack from Qantara southward, unless we received information during the night that would force us to attack from Qantara to the north. In that case, my division was to contain the northern sector, while Sharon's division would attack from south to north. If no such reports were received, my division would attack from Qantara southward to Bitter Lake, while Sharon's division would serve as a containing force and act as the reserve for my division; and Mandler's division would defend its sector. It was Dado's estimate that the attack would begin in the morning, after most of our forces had arrived, and would be over before noon.

In the afternoon Sharon's division would attack from the central sector southward to the southern extremity of the canal. At that stage Albert's division would be a containing and reserve force, while my division would stabilize in its sector (from the lagoons to Bitter Lake). These graduated divisional attacks would be executed with extensive artillery and air support.

The chief of staff added: "I would like to emphasize that in these attacks we will stay away from the canal zone, from that area swarming with infantry equipped with RPGs, and from the area where the enemy is employing tanks and antitank weapons from his ramparts. Obviously we will *not* link up to the strongpoints and we will *not* initiate a crossing operation." Therefore, the chief of staff concluded, every effort should be made to evacuate all that could be evacuated from the strongpoints during the night. This was only an outline of the plan, Dado said, adding that he would now return to GHQ and await the arrival of the detailed plan in the course of the night.

It was now 2200 hours. To save time, I told General Magen to call my deputy, Dovik, immediately and have him plan a diversionary attack towards Qantara to cover the attempted evacuation of the men from Strongpoint Milano and their link-up with our forces.

I accompanied the chief of staff as he left the headquarters. As we were emerging from the bunker, General Sharon showed up. He shook hands with the two of us and impatiently announced that he had just arrived from the field, had spoken by phone with our men in the strongpoints, and they were relying on us to rescue them. The Israeli army had never abandoned its soldiers, he asserted, adding that he had already planned a link-up operation. Actually, he concluded, he regretted that he had been called to this meeting, since hours of darkness were being wasted, and he wanted to rescue them that night.

Dado listened, then told Sharon that we had just completed a situation assessment, and we had agreed upon a different plan. He said he had to leave but suggested that Sharon talk to Gonen, who would give him all the details.

Sharon's outlook, I saw, differed from mine. How to explain this, I wondered: It was my impression that had he seen the reality in the field as I had seen it all that day, he would be talking differently about approaching the strongpoints and the canal. I had the impression that in addition to his concern that the IDF should not abandon its soldiers (which we all shared), he was overly influenced by the fact that he had been talking with the men in the strongpoints and had promised to extricate them.

In my opinion, Sharon's suggestion was a dangerous one. I decided to join him, and we both went to see Gonen. When Sharon expressed his ideas, I found it necessary to repeat my own view. It was a sort of second round that ended with our original conclusion. Gonen did not give approval for a link-up to the strongpoints. At the same time, though — perhaps because he felt uncomfortable refusing Sharon, who was more experienced than he was — Gonen did not turn him down flat. He said only that at this stage we were not going to approach the strongpoints, though developments during the night might lead to a change of plan. Gonen agreed that Sharon should prepare for a link-up with the strongpoints in his sector. Southern Command, Gonen said, would examine the situation towards dawn and would then make its decision.

CHAPTER NINE

GONEN MAKES CHANGES

Sharon, Kalman, and I left by helicopter. The noise of the helicopter made conversation impossible. Tomorrow morning we were going to attack, I thought to myself. I wondered what was happening on the front under cover of darkness. The Egyptians were no doubt continuing to move armor to our side of the canal and advance eastward. In fact, we had received no reports in the past few hours of any further advance by them. Maybe they had bypassed our thin forward forces, or perhaps they were concentrating on transferring additional forces and preparing for an offensive with first light. I hoped our troops were overcoming the traffic jams on the road here and that most of the tanks would have arrived by morning. If I found that over half the tanks had already arrived and that they were complete and ready for action, I would have them move west in the coming hours. The night was short; the work immense — I still had to plan the attack, issue the appropriate orders. This was not how I had imagined the division moving into battle, hastily and not in full complement. But there was no alternative: we had to take the initiative from the Egyptians. It was good the chief of staff had decided on a limited offensive. Despite the difficulties, I felt we would achieve our goal.

We dropped Sharon off at Tassa and continued to Baluza. From there I went on towards Reactia, the main concentration area on the Lateral Road for my division forces coming from the north. It was approximately midnight. I was driven in a jeep among the many tanks on the road. I called the brigade commanders by radio to come for orders at my tactical forward command post on Pushkin Hill, on the Lateral Road. At the same time, my deputy, Dovik, and some of my staff officers were busy moving the division forces toward the front.

The Qantara-El Arish Road continued to be jammed, and Aryeh's brigade was still making its way along the road between Nahal-Yam and Romani, 20–70 km away. Taking part in that planning meeting, then, were the intelligence officer, the operations officer, and the communications officer from my tactical command post. Together we worked out the plan of operations according to the chief of staff's outline. The plan was to attack with two brigades — Natke's and Gabi's — from north to south and to hold Aryeh's brigade in reserve. I did not determine specific terrain objectives; the emphasis was on a coordinated advance to search out the enemy and destroy him, but without entering the 3-km zone adjacent to the canal.

I gave the order and my detailed instructions to Gabi, Natke, and Kalman, who were close by (Aryeh was still far off). In those instructions, I spoke of our heavy losses during the past two days and summed up our intention of taking a limited initiative while avoiding the area near the canal. I told them to proceed cautiously, watching out for dunes and dangerous swamps.

It was because I wanted to be ready to move out as soon as we got the okay that I decided Aryeh's brigade, still en route, would become our division reserve concentrating in the rear at the center of our sector opposite the two main roads, Ma'adim and Spontani, leading to the canal. For the same reason I decided to move Natke's and Gabi's brigades from the Lateral Road westward in a "creeping deployment," ready to operate southward when ordered. "Creeping deployment" is not a military phrase but describes a technique I developed during the 1948 Independence War. It means that instead of organizing a military formation that is to be moved to another sector in a certain way and at a specific place when so required, you organize on the move, deploying stage by stage into the desired disposition, thus saving considerable time.

At 0400 hours Natke's and Gabi's brigades began moving cautiously west. I had delayed my own advance for a time, waiting for Aryeh. Even though tanks from his brigade were already passing nearby, Aryeh himself had not shown up and was not replying to my radio calls. I was impatient: my two brigades were already advancing towards the front, and I was stuck in the rear. I told Dovik to give Aryeh the order and sped forward to take my place in the center, between the two brigades, en route to a good observation point on Beroslav Hill.

Aryeh was an old-timer in the Armored Corps. I had known him for many years — from the time the Corps was so small that every officer knew all the others. He was in his forties, of medium height, heavy looking. But he was the opposite of ponderous in his work as an officer. Having worked closely with him, I knew that he was energetic, had initiative and organizational ability, and knew how to imbue his men with motivation. In 1956 as a platoon leader, he took part in the conquest of Gaza. In the 1967 war he commanded a tank battalion in Mandler's brigade and took part in the conquest of the Golan Heights, including the town of Quneitra. In the period when I was commander of the Armored Corps, he was commander of a reserve armored brigade and was also in charge of the main training center for the reserve armored units. I considered him a very talented officer, a thorough professional with leadership ability. The fact that he had not arrived in time to get the order worried me. I would have expected my brigade commanders to push forward and leave traffic problems to their deputies. I had no idea what was delaying him, but it would later emerge that the roads were so jammed and chaotic that Aryeh had preferred to stay behind and ensure that his brigade continued to advance.

While the various echelons of the Southern Command were busy working on plans and orders in the wake of the conference with the chief of staff, Dado himself arrived at GHQ in Tel Aviv. He assembled his augmented staff at about midnight and briefed them on what would happen the next day, 8 October, in line with what had been concluded in the meeting at Southern Command.

Dado began by making the overall intention clear: "Tomorrow

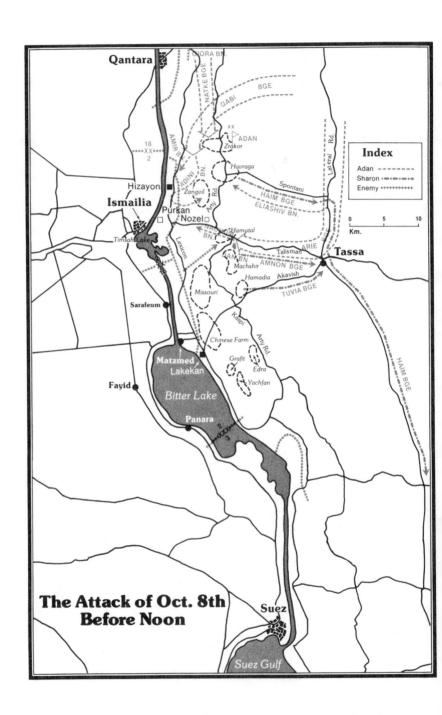

Qantara

GIORA BN.

NATKE BGE

GABI BGE

18
XX
2

ADAN
Zrakor

Havraga

AMIR BGE

ADINI BN.

Hizayon

Zangvil

Spontani

Ismailia

Purkan
Nozel

Arty Rd

HAIM BGE
ELIASHIV BN.

Lateral Rd.

Index
Adan
Sharon
Enemy

0   5   10
Km.

Lexicon

NACHSHON BN.

Hamutal

Timsah Lake

Lexicon

SAMIR BN.
AMNON BGE

Talisman

ARIE

Tassa

Sarafeum

Machshir

Hamadia

Akavish

Missouri

TUVIA BGE

Kaspi

Chinese Farm

Arty Rd

HAIM BGE

Matzmed
Lakekan

Grafit

Edra

Fayid

Bitter Lake

Yachfan

Panara

2
XXX
3

**The Attack of Oct. 8th
Before Noon**

Suez

Suez Gulf

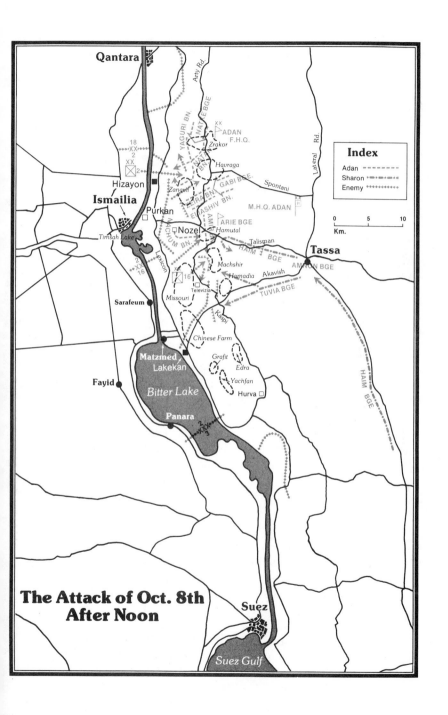

The Attack of Oct. 8th After Noon

we move to a counterattack.'' But at once he qualified this: ''The offensive will not include an initiated crossing but attacks on the Egyptian forces which have crossed the canal. The idea is not to move close to the canal but to attack and destroy the forces inward from the canal.'' The chief of staff went on to explain that there was no intention of dealing with the infantry occupying the barriers and the area around them: ''The Egyptians are using masses of infantry equipped with plenty of antitank missiles deployed on the barriers. And they've placed a lot of missile-firing troops along the roads as well. So tomorrow will not see a total 'clean-up' of the canal; rather, we shall attempt to destroy the forces in the area.''

The chief of staff added that the attack would be accompanied by extensive artillery shelling and a concentrated effort by the air force, including the use of cluster-bomb units, against the infantry — ''so they [the divisions] will be able to move along and rip apart tanks.'' When he described the IDF's consolidation following the attack, he explained: ''Again, we will not again be on the canal unless there is a *general collapse* of the Egyptian forces. The intention is not to mop up the barriers.''

General Elazar then went on to outline the plan that had been decided upon in the meeting at Southern Command. Before noon, my division would attack from Qantara southward, towards Deversoir, with Sharon's division containing the enemy in the sector under attack and standing by in reserve to support my attack. Then in the afternoon, Sharon's division would attack from Deversoir southwards, towards Suez, with Mandler's division containing the enemy and standing by in reserve to support Sharon's attack. The chief of staff asserted that H-hour would be determined only after the detailed plans were received from Southern Command.

From the standpoint of correct staff procedure, there is no doubt that the chief of staff's summation was meant to serve as a guideline for his staff so that they could allocate, coordinate, and direct the air force to the various territorial commands and also so that Elazar's staff could integrate and supervise the plans of both Northern Command and Southern Command.

At about the same time that Dado Elazar was updating his staff and I was doing the same in my headquarters, some unexpected changes in the Southern Command's plan took place. I would hear about them only after the war.

At about 0100 General Gonen went to his quarters to take a nap, ordering his aide to awaken him in two hours. But his deputy, General Ben-Ari, woke him thirty minutes later, because a written order had to be issued. I don't know what caused Gonen to deviate from the chief of staff's summation, but the fact is that Gonen issued a written order substantially different from the plan that Dado had summed up. Nor did the division commanders ever receive that written order. The finalizing of the new plan apparently took thirty-five minutes, because (according to the logbook) Gonen went back to sleep at 0205. Meanwhile, the operations department at GHQ was asking for a copy of the order. At 0245 Gonen's headquarters reported that the order was being flown to General Staff Headquarters.

A written order usually specifies exact objectives for each subordinate commander. It sets out precisely the main axis of attack, objectives, and intermediate objectives. In addition to setting out the tasks and missions for each subordinate force, such as the divisions, the successive stages of the operation are generally outlined along with the arrangements for coordination of forces, either by a fixed timetable or by intermediate objectives and phase lines.

Gonen's written order, however, was what is known as an "overlay order," commonly used in armored forces. Usually issued under the pressure of time, a brief text explains and complements the overlay sketch, and the two parts together constitute the complete order. The written text must state precisely the mission of each force and include also time schedule coordination and the code words for executing each phase of the operation.

When I had the opportunity to see Gonen's order after the war, I found the text to be unclear, particularly with regard to method and to coordination of the operation's phases. Nor was there any hint of the two principles decided upon earlier in our meeting with the chief of staff: a limited attack and staying away from the canal. Instead Gonen's order called for action that had been considered and expressly rejected: "Mopping up the zone between the Artillery Road and the canal water line; destruction of the enemy forces in that area while extricating forces from the strongpoints and pulling out stuck tanks; and readiness for a crossing to the other side of the canal."

The log shows that Gonen discussed with his staff two alternative attacks, depending on the number of tanks available by dawn. One alternative was code-named *Aryeh,* and the other code-named *Dov.* But a reading of the overlay order gives the impression that these two alternatives became two stages of one plan. In phase *Aryeh,* my division would attack from Qantara southward to Bitter Lake. This was to be followed by phase *Dov,* in which Sharon's division would attack from the northern section of Bitter Lake south to the Suez Gulf. For phase *Aryeh,* Gonen's order stated our respective missions this way: "Sharon's division: containment in the west and reserve. Bren's division: containment in the west and north, attack southward and reserve. Mandler's division: containment."

Phrasing such as "containment in the west" or "containment in the west and north," and "reserve" is vague. We usually expect to find "X will contain in his sector." When drawn on the overlay, a sector is a very specific area, but in this case no specific sectors were drawn on the overlay nor was there even an arrow to show where Sharon was to cross. In my division's sector, arrows did indicate crossings at Hizayon and Matzmed, and two lines pointed to where I was to form up for defense on the west bank.

The order contained a very important qualifying note, a leftover from our discussions with the chief of staff. This stated: "Beginning of the operation: not before accumulation of enough forces, at 0800 and only by order." This meant that the 0800 time was only tentative. The actual start of the operation would depend on the number of tanks we had ready in the morning. But the order did not suggest how many tanks would be enough for the operation to go ahead.

At his staff meeting around midnight, the chief of staff had noted: "It is not clear yet how many tanks we will have by tomorrow, but if we take into consideration the forces on their way right now, we can count on something between 650–700 tanks." Gonen's order set out the assessment that by the start of the operation I would have 200 tanks, Sharon 180 tanks, and Mandler 150 tanks. That made a total of 530 tanks.

Actually, I only had 170 tanks available by 0800 on 8 October. At about 0530 I reported that 44 tanks I was expecting had not yet arrived. Magen reported that 50 Sherman tanks from Fedale's brigade were encountering delays too. Sharon told Gonen that he had only 170 tanks. These updates seemed to have had no effect on the starting time of the attack, even though that time had been made contingent on the accumulation of strength.

Even after having made a thorough study of the background, it is difficult for me to explain what really happened or what caused Gonen's plan to deviate so much from that of the chief of staff. It may be that in order to understand the causes for the change, we have to go back to midday of 7 October. That was a time of grave danger on the front. General Mandler reported that the enemy was breaking through his lines, and Gonen ordered me to deploy forces along the Lateral Road, 30 km from the canal. At the same time, Dayan arrived at Gonen's headquarters, and their discussion resulted in steps being taken to retreat to the Lateral Road and in guidelines being issued for evacuation of the strongpoints. When Dayan left, at 1256 hours, Gonen ordered deployment for defense on the Lateral Road.

Ten minutes later, however, when Gonen heard from Sharon that in three hours he would have eighty more tanks, Gonen changed his line of thought. Sharon was told to rush all his forces to Tassa to establish a defensive line on the Lateral Road, leaving only outposts along the Artillery Road. That made sense. Then in the same breath Gonen told Sharon to prepare for counterattacks southward and/or to the northwest and, surprisingly, to be ready to cross the canal north of Bitter Lake at Strongpoint Matzmed.

Four minutes later, Gonen told Dado by phone of his orders to Sharon. Dado cautioned him: "Shmulik, you have to view the situation as it develops in stages. Right now we are at the stage where we have to stabilize a defensive line. So it's important that Sharon deploy his forces on your second line. I also want you to hold the Mitla [Pass] firmly."

At 1500 Gonen called to ask how many tanks had arrived and learned that I had only eighty-nine. Staff officers around Gonen heard him reflect aloud: "How long before the situation on the front changes substantially?" And he answered his own question: "If the air force is successful and the Egyptian flow is frozen, then we can proceed with a counterattack on the Ma'adim Road and another on the Listim axis." Therefore, he added, "It is very important that we know where there are prepared [i.e., Egyptian] bridges across the canal."

Four minutes later he spoke with Mandler, who reported seeing three concentrations of fifty Egyptian tanks each; some were advancing toward Stronghold Nozel (on the Central Road, near the Artillery Road). Gonen's reply indicated his line of thought: "If the situation freezes, we will move to the offensive!"

At 1539 hours Gonen called Dado, asking how things looked on the Syrian front and then sharing his reflections. He said that as soon as our forces arrived at the front that evening, he would move Mandler's division eastward and attack southward with Sharon's division, destroying all the Egyptian forces that had crossed the canal. Then, he went on, when Sharon reached the southern end of the canal, he would seize an Egyptian bridge and cross to the other side, capture Suez City, and establish a defensive line 20 km deep in Egyptian territory on the Marze'ach-Odeda-Metzila line. Gonen went on to tell Dado that my division would attack along the Aleket and Listim axes [in the northern sector] and would execute "Great Zfania," code name for a crossing operation to seize the western, Egyptian bank of the Suez Canal from Qantara to the Mediterranean.

At 1544 hours Gonen received a call from Sharon about the arrival of his units at the front. Gonen spelled out his ideas again: "I see two possibilities. Number one, Mandler will go on containing. You [Sharon] will attack toward strongpoints Hizayon and Purkan [i.e., the Firdan Bridge and Ismailia]. At night you will cross the canal and capture the area north of the Suez-Ismailia Sweet Water Canal." Gonen continued: "At the same time, Bren, whose forces are located at the junction of Kartisan and Spontani [on the Lateral Road], will move along the Ma'adim and Listim roads. He, too, will cross on the Egyptian bridges and will capture the entire area north of his crossing point, including 'Politura' [code name for Port Said]." Gonen went on to explain to Sharon what he regarded as "possibility number two," by which "Bren will execute his part as in possibility number one and you [Sharon] will attack southwards, mop up, cross on an Egyptian bridge, and then capture Suez and proceed 20 km westward to establish a defense line." (This latter alternative was consistent with what he had just told Dado.)

It will be recalled that at the conference that evening (7 October) with the chief of staff, at Umm-Hashiba, Gonen recommended a canal crossing with two divisions in two separate sectors. His recommendation had *not* been accepted, but Gonen had not opposed General Elazar's summation.

It emerges then that from midday on 7 October, Gonen, although in real trouble, never stopped having optimistic hopes that were clearly unrealistic and irrelevant. He burned with a desire to bring about a change in his difficult situation — and fast! Evidently he did not perceive our grave situation that afternoon as being one with deep ramifications for the present and future course of the war but as a minor hitch easily overcome, an idea coming, apparently, from the profound contempt he felt for the Egyptians. He never stopped thinking about a crossing operation and counterattacks. Every shred of positive information — such as the possibility that Sharon would soon have eighty tanks — fed his optimism. Gonen expressed his ideas to me, Sharon, Mandler, Dado, and to his own staff officers. Each of us heard it once or twice, and all assumed that it was simply wishful thinking, or perhaps aimed at raising morale. But no one imagined that Gonen's thinking was fixed in this direction.

Some will say that there was nothing wrong with Gonen's optimistic ideas, especially considering the fact that he expressed them as suggestions or intentions. Surely this shows that he never lost his spirit even during the bleakest moments, never abandoned hope of a counterattack or of taking the initiative. In my view, however, Gonen, while nursing these ideas, neglected realistic approaches, failing to take measures really needed to deal with the actual situation. Eventually, this led him to issue additional orders, irrelevant to the situation on the battlefield.

Once the plan was drawn up, Gonen faced two problems: first, to get it approved by the chief of staff; and then to issue the order, either in writing or orally, to his division commanders. His attempts to call me via the radio failed because of noise interference. (It is possible that the enemy was jamming our transmissions.) Since the attack was to begin just five hours later, at 0800 hours Gonen should have flown by helicopter to the various division headquarters to give the order orally, especially since the plan had been altered so drastically. Moreover, he could have used that opportunity to get a closer view of the real situation in each of his divisions. But Gonen preferred to issue the order by radio.

At 0354 hours when Gonen was unable to contact me, he called General Kalman Magen in Baluza, where a larger antenna made reception possible. He asked about the number of tanks in my division. Magen told him that I had 180 tanks and added that when my division began the attack, only one tank company would be left at Baluza until the tank battalion from Fedale's brigade arrived. Magen, who had attended my briefing to our commanders and staff, then informed Gonen of my plan. Gonen said that it would be impossible to launch the operation without communications, but then, after some thinking, decided to issue the order through Magen. He told Magen that my division was to link up with strongpoints Milano and Mifreket, near Qantara, and with strongpoints Hizayon and Purkan, near Ismailia and the Firdan Bridge respectively.

Magen remarked that the men from Strongpoint Milano were on their way to join Natke's brigade and that the Mifreket Strongpoint had been taken by the enemy. Gonen simply continued: "All right, when Bren arrives opposite Ismailia [Strongpoint Purkan], if he finds an Egyptian bridge he is to have one of his brigades cross the canal and deploy for defense along the Michal/Tirda axes" (i.e., a 20-km-wide deployment 15–20 km deep into Egyptian territory). Gonen added: "If Bren doesn't find an Egyptian bridge or if we don't get the go-ahead to cross, he is to continue to attack southward to Bitter Lake and cross there at Strongpoint Matzmed on an Egyptian bridge. In this case, too, the crossing is to be made with one brigade, which will establish a defensive line west of the Havit road [5 km west of the canal] or on the Vada'ut Road [20 km west of the canal]."

Magen replied that I had given a totally different order to my brigade commanders and had already dismissed them one hour before. The brigades were already on the move, Magen said, and he didn't see how I could call them in time to issue new instructions.

Following this discussion, Gonen tried to call me again. When he failed to establish communication, he called Magen again at 0413 hours and gave him a "correction" to be relayed to me: "Cancel the crossing operation in the Firdan area. Cross only in the Bitter Lake area [Matzmed] and establish the defensive line, with one brigade, along the 'Havit' axis [5 km west of the canal in Egyptian territory]." Gonen then gave Magen another instruction: "Since Bren has already dismissed the brigade commanders and they are already moving, he should call just the brigade commander who will cross the canal and brief him."

Magen replied that in his opinion, even the link-up operation presented many problems, since it called for special preparations of small units and briefing many forces, so that to call just one commander would not solve the problem.

Gonen reconsidered his instructions and informed Magen: "Okay. Bren should get organized in his present location. I'll assign the link-up operation to Arik [General Sharon]. He'll link up to the strongpoints and return, and only then will Bren proceed southward and cross the canal at Matzmed."

At 0420 hours Gonen tried to call me again to give the order he had just given to Magen, but again disturbances made comprehension very difficult. I told him that I would try to climb a high hill in the area and use special equipment to enhance reception. Finally, at 0430 hours we established contact.

Gonen: "I have a question to ask you. Could you move to the Hizayon, Purkan and Matzmed strongpoints and link up with them while proceeding with your mission?" He asked if I had anyone familiar with the area and continued: "Your mission is: One possibility — attack south to destroy enemy forces down to Matzmed. At Matzmed, move west until 'Havit' [i.e., to cross the canal]. Do you see any problems in your mission?"

I replied: "I'll be able to tell you only after first light."

Gonen: "Another possibility is that Arik [Sharon] will first link up with the strongpoints and return. Does that look simpler to you?" I replied: "I'll be able to answer you only in the morning, after I see how the situation develops."

Gonen: "Be prepared for both things!"

This conversation deserves further explanation. One must remember that I didn't have the slightest idea about Gonen's *new substantially altered plan*. I did notice certain deviations from the original plan, such as the notions of linking up with the strongpoints and crossing the canal, but these were formulated as suggestions, as questions: "Could I move to the strongpoints?" "Did I think Sharon should move to the strongpoints?'' My impression was that we were still speaking of moves included within the framework of the original plan. That is, I was being asked whether, as part of the plan to attack south to Matzmed while avoiding an approach along the entire water line, I could, nevertheless, move to the canal at certain points. My reply was perfectly simple: How could I know *now*? If the situation in the morning develops in a way that would permit that action, *then* I will answer your question. Moreover, at 0442 hours and at 0445 hours, Gonen called me again and insisted on an answer regarding a link-up with the strongpoints. I reminded him that the conditions for such an operation, as discussed the previous evening (i.e., in the conference with the chief of staff), did not yet exist. I said that I did not have any artillery or air support and that I could only answer as the situation developed. Gonen replied, as if there was no problem at all: ''You will receive both kinds of support. Right now we're coordinating the support you asked for earlier.''

And what was Gonen telling Sharon at that time? At 0432 hours, ten minutes before he spoke with me, Gonen had contacted Sharon. In that conversation before the fighting had begun, he told Sharon that he ''must have him in the south'' so that he could cross the canal at Strongpoint Nissan, capture Suez City, and advance to 20 km west of the canal. Gonen then told Sharon: ''Plan the move to link up with the strongpoints in your sector. In the morning you will liberate them and then return.'' Then, Gonen explained, ''Bren will attack south to Matzmed and you will proceed further south.''

It will be recalled that at Umm-Hashiba, Sharon had asked to link up with the strongpoints, had received permission to make preparations for such an action, and had made his plan and forwarded orders to his brigades; now the moment had arrived when Gonen was ready to approve the operation. Sharon answered Gonen that the strongpoints were in desperate straits and that there were good people in them. He added that he wanted to update his information about the enemy in the area and expected to be ready for the rescue mission in forty-five minutes. But forty-five minutes passed, ninety minutes, two hours. Sharon, who had planned the operation and had issued an order to his subordinates, was in no hurry to implement it. When he heard, after the two hours had passed, that he was not going to the strongpoints after all, he made no protest. But he did take the trouble to call me in order to remind me that the Hizayon, Purkan and Matzmed strongpoints were still held by our soldiers and to emphasize that we had to rescue them.

So much for what Gonen had told us, the division commanders. What was the picture at headquarters? Coordination and supervision of operations in the territorial commands fell under the responsibility of the chief of the operations department at GHQ. In the General Staff itself, supervision and coordination of the work of the branch chiefs and of the chief of the operations department were in the hands of the deputy chief of staff and head of the General Staff Branch, Maj. Gen. Israel Tal.

At about 0400 hours 8 October the chief of the operations department called his aides together in order to examine the orders arriving from the territorial commands. They noticed that Southern Command's overlay order failed to coincide with the directives of the chief of staff. They discussed the matter, but no steps were taken.

At about 0530 hours the chief of staff entered the operations room for an update on the situation. Officers were monitoring the major radio nets and marking maps in line with the new information coming in. Each wall was given over to a territorial command theater and had its own situation maps, a large table for written work, and a battery of telephones. Dado was updated on the situation with regard to the plan of Southern Command. Apparently no attention was paid to the deviations in the command's plan. He was told, however, that if Egyptian bridges were seized intact, the intention was to cross the canal with one brigade.

At 0605 hours, while he was still being updated, the chief of staff was called to his room; Gonen was on the line. There is no written record of what Gonen said, but a record does exist of Dado's end of the conversation. He replied that the plan had been approved but cautioned Gonen not to approach the water line. He said he was pessimistic about the prospects of crossing on an Egyptian bridge, adding that they would discuss this again later that day. When Dado replaced the receiver, he remarked: "By the way, it came out just about the way I summed it up with them, with Bren."

I don't know what he was referring to when he said "just about," but I tend to think that the chief of staff thought he had approved the plan he had summed up the previous night, along the lines I had suggested, and that the "just about" referred to the canal-crossing issue. Following this conversation, he ordered the chief of operations to issue a corrective cable that there was to be no canal crossing without his, Dado's, personal approval.

The chief of staff, then, seems to have believed — especially after issuing his corrective cable — that he had approved the plan he had summed up the night before. Gonen, however, thought he had received approval for the plan he had submitted to GHQ — in the form of the overlay order — earlier that night (0300 hours). Encouraged, Gonen went ahead with his ideas. At 0617 hours he contacted the chief of staff of Sharon's division, Colonel Gideon, and told him: "Arik is not to attack towards the strongpoints before noon, [instead] he should attack around noon in the south, destroy the enemy forces and 'get a lift' on a bridge [Egyptian], cross westward, take Suez City, and consolidate a line between Mafzeah and Atakah [20 km west of the canal]. No more than one brigade, or a brigade and a battalion, is to be moved in [on the west side]."

At 0649 hours Gonen took a nap, asking to be awakened at 0730 hours, shortly before the start of the attack. Gonen's perception was, apparently, that he had closed the circle of orders and coordination: that he had received the chief of staff's approval for his plan and had given me an order to link up to the strongpoints and cross the canal — all this in line with his *Aryeh* Plan. He had even given Sharon advance notice to be ready to operate in the far south around noon when he would cross the canal in the Suez City sector.

In fact, however, the actual situation was totally different. I assume that Sharon, too, knew nothing of the *Aryeh* and *Dov* Plans. Certainly I knew nothing of the *Aryeh* Plan.

Thus, as the Israeli attack of 8 October was about to get under way, there existed misunderstandings within the IDF hierarchy. There was no common language between GHQ and Southern Command, and certainly none between Southern Command and the divisions in the field.

CHAPTER TEN

FIGHTING BEGINS

The general notion that prevailed in Southern Command Head-quarters about Egyptian intentions for 7 October was that the enemy would attack eastward deep into our territory. With this in mind, orders were given to deploy our main forces along the Lateral Road 30 km east of the canal, while leaving small forces on the Artillery Road, 10 km from the canal, and to evacuate the strong-points where this was feasible. Today we know that the Egyptians planned to advance no further than 10–12 km at that stage of the war — as far as the Artillery Road — although they did not achieve even that objective and remained for the most part east of Lexicon Road.* But our lack of reconnaissance units for maintaining contact with the enemy precluded information that could have altered our erroneous impression.

The Egyptian Army's 135th Independent Infantry Brigade was active across the northern lagoon road (Asher), ambushing our forces and attempting to attack the strongpoints in the sector north of Qantara. During the night, after getting orders to evacuate their posts, nineteen soldiers from Strongpoint Ktuba and fifteen soldiers

---

*According to other sources, they planned to reach the Artillery Road position by the evening of 8 October.

117

from Drora managed to escape on armored half-tracks without a fight. Forty soldiers from Strongpoint Orkal tried to make their way out on two tanks and an armored half-track. They managed to overcome several ambushes, but their vehicle was hit near Lahtzanit. After heroic fighting, during which many of them were killed or wounded, the survivors were taken captive. The men of Strongpoint Lahtzanit were also taken prisoner.

The Egyptian 18th Infantry Division and 15th Independent Tank Brigade were active opposite Qantara near Strongpoint Milano. By the morning of 8 October, the Egyptians had 130 T-62 tanks across the canal, along with thousands of infantrymen who filled Qantara and its outskirts. It was no easy task for forty of our soldiers to try to break out of Strongpoint Milano and link up with our forces. They kept running into Egyptian forces throughout the night. Finally they split into two groups; some were ambushed and either killed or taken prisoner, but twenty-four soldiers managed to get to our lines and reached Natke's brigade. The very few fighters still alive in Strongpoint Mifreket were captured. The Egyptian 2nd Infantry Division, reinforced by the 24th Tank Brigade from the 23rd Mechanized Division, was active in Sharon's sector, across from Balah Island down to Ismailia. The Egyptians managed to get 120 tanks across the canal there by dawn of 8 October. For some reason, the strongpoints in that sector had not received the evacuation order.

In the morning of 8 October, the Egyptians had 600 tanks on the Israeli side of the canal to our 500. Since their original missions had not been fully achieved, the task of the Egyptian forces for 8 October was to complete their bridgeheads up to 10–12 km deeper into the Sinai until they seized the Artillery Road. Then they were to fan out until continuous contact was established with all adjacent divisions. But our thin forces along the Artillery Road did not come under any pressure on the night of 7–8 October, so both Sharon and I began to move our units from the Lateral Road forward to the Artillery Road.

By about 0600 forces from my two attacking tank brigades were already deploying to their line of attack, after having advanced from the Lateral Road. Both brigades were badly understrength. Natke's brigade, with seventy-one tanks, was in the north of the sector. Gabi's brigade advanced south of him, with two battalions of twenty-five tanks each. Aryeh's brigade, still awaiting its forces, was serving as the divisional reserve. General Magen was left in charge of the sector from Qantara north. He had Rami's understrength mechanized brigade (just two armored infantry battalions), a tank company from Aryeh's brigade and Lapidot's tanks — all told, about twenty tanks. Fedale's mechanized brigade was moving towards our sector on the Rafiah-Baluza Road.

As dawn broke, our airplanes started attacking the enemy in my sector. From time to time, unfortunately, they also attacked Natke's brigade. Natke reported seeing enemy tanks 2 km west of him. I was trying to coordinate and establish physical contact between my two brigades on the common boundary line that defined their sectors. I also tried to learn what was happening in Sharon's sector and was begging Southern Command to let my own forward air controllers coordinate the air strikes in my sector, since they were with the attacking forces and could handle it the best; but headquarters did not accede to this request.

About 0700 I decided to move up my reserve force, Aryeh's brigade, whose third battalion had arrived by then, giving it sixty-two tanks. On my way west I had seen that some of our tanks had lost their tracks in the dunes; I decided to have Aryeh move towards the Artillery Road on two roads that ran through Sharon's sector. I asked headquarters for permission to do so and received an okay. The two attacking brigades advanced farther west, toward the Hazizit and Lexicon roads. We began to come under enemy artillery fire, and Egyptian MIG fighters attacked Natke's force.

At 0753 hours I gave the order to attack from north to south. Since Natke was engaged and I couldn't take him from the Qantara area, I made a change in the plan and ordered Gabi and Aryeh to attack southward toward Bitter Lake (Strongpoint Matzmed). Gabi was to advance in the western sector on the hills between the Artillery Road and Lexicon Road, and Aryeh was to move east of Gabi. I told Natke to stay where he was, opposite Qantara, and be ready to proceed south, upon order, behind the two attacking brigades as the division reserve. Because of my conversations with Gonen in the early morning hours, I also told Gabi that he should plan to link up with the Hizayon and Purkan strongpoints, but to do so only upon a specific order.

At 0806 hours, six minutes after Gonen gave the order to attack, I reported that we were taking artillery fire as well as fighting "tank-hunter units" from Egyptian commando forces, so I asked for artillery and air support. In reply, Gonen reminded me of something I remembered very well — not to get too close to the canal. (Subsequently, Gonen would cite that one and only statement to claim that he warned me against moving to the canal, and that the attack on the canal had been my own initiative.)

Since 0800 the entire division began advancing under artillery fire, with Gabi's and Natke's two forward brigades deployed in a breadth and depth format. Sharon's forces, watching the attack, reported that it was an impressive sight. Contrary to our estimates, we encountered virtually no enemy forces. Around 0900 Gabi reached Zangwill, the plain between the prefortified stronghold of Havraga, on the Artillery Road, and the Firdan Bridge. In the hours to follow, that area would become the main battlefield of the 8 October counterattack. My tactical command group was constantly on the move between Natke's brigade and Gabi's on three armored personnel carriers and two half-tracks and was now about to ascend Zrakor Hill, the central and highest dune in that area.

In the meantime, Natke reported that he had advanced westward as far as was possible, had destroyed seven enemy tanks on his way, and had encountered several Sagger missile teams; he was now ready to attack southward. Gabi reported that he had made contact with some tanks belonging to Sharon's division at Havraga. He also informed me that he had killed a few enemy soldiers and had taken several prisoners. He was now deployed with one battalion near the Arov Road and a second battalion near the Haviva Road. I told Gabi to update his information via Sharon's units on the enemy to his immediate front around Strongpoint Hizayon. At about 0900 I instructed Natke to plan his brigade routes all the way down to Strongpoint Matzmed (on the north shore of Bitter Lake) but to move there only on my order, after I was certain that there would be no further enemy activity in his sector.

Gonen now radioed to ask what my plans were. I felt a certain discomfort because the time had come to develop the situation in line with the guidelines he had given me. I told him that I was ready to move to Hizayon, but only if I could get plenty of close air support to silence enemy artillery, and directed by my own air controllers.

In a long radio discussion, I tried to grasp his intentions. Should I first destroy as many of the Egyptian forces as I could or give priority to linking up with the strongpoints? Or should I reorient my attack to cross the canal? The answer I got was to do all of these and more: to annihilate all the enemy forces that had crossed between Qantara and Matzmed, then cross the canal in the Matzmed area. It was very important, therefore, that we move south "like a current." Moreover, he said, if en route when we linked up to Hizayon we should find a bridge in the area, it was very improtant that we cross with a small unit there too.

I replied that my forces were too small to send some of them to the other side of the canal, as this would weaken me even more.

Gonen answered: "All the same, it's worth it. A foothold on the other side is a whole new situation." I replied: "All right, I'll be listening to the signals and decide as the battle develops. Over."

Gonen summed up: "So two things are very important: one, to establish a foothold or two on the other bank; and second, to advance southward very fast, cross the canal at Matzmed, then to continue further westward and establish a defensive line on the Havit Road. Out."

As soon as I finished my radio conversation with Gonen, I learned that Natke was engaged with enemy T-62 tanks of the 15th Brigade and was also contending with infantry equipped with Sagger missiles. These battles were taking place around Qantara and south of it. I cautioned Natke not to get involved in built-up areas or marshy terrain. Gabi was also engaged with enemy tanks and antitank missiles fired from a palm grove in a swampy area, 3 km east of the canal on the Arov Road. Gabi asked for artillery and air support.

At 0938 hours Gonen radioed again about our progress toward the Firdan Bridge (Hizayon). I explained that we were now engaged in battle and that the link-up to Hizayon would therefore have to be postponed. I added that I needed air support very badly. I was astonished when he told me that I was *getting* air support. I said I was unaware of this and pointed out that my air support liaison officer had just been told by his (Gonen's) own staff that my requests could not be complied with. Gonen went to clarify the situation and answered that due to the difficult circumstances, the Israeli Air Force was operating by means of a special technique and therefore would not be able to let my own forward controllers direct the strikes supporting my units. I then asked him to break off, since I was busy trying to command and control my forces in a difficult situation. Meanwhile, I told him, it would be helpful if he could arrange for close air support for our attack towards Hizayon.

Fifteen minutes later, at 0955 hours, Gonen contacted me again as if we had never spoken before, asking me to speed south much faster to an area near Bitter Lake to establish contact with the Missouri and Chinese Farm (Amir) areas, about 20-25 km south of Hizayon.

I said: "I understand that you want me to get to Missouri and to Amir. I am not interested in overextending my forces, but if it's very important I can try and make it."

Gonen: "It's very important. Moreover, when you link up with Hizayon, seize the other bank with a small force. That will be a substantial change."

In view of the repeated pressure to move south, I considered sending Aryeh into action southward. At that time, his battalions were continuing to advance toward the canal. Aryeh, along with Dan's and Nahum's battalion, was moving on the Talisman Road, while Eliashiv's battalion was on Spontani Road. Bearing in mind our mission concerning Hizayon, Gilad — my operations officer — suggested that when Eliashiv reached the Havraga area he be told to halt and be held in reserve. I wasn't enthusiastic about this idea, because it would leave Aryeh with just two battalions, but it did make sense to hold at least one battalion as the divisional reserve. Also should we not need it for Hizayon, the battalion could be returned to Aryeh's brigade. I accepted Gilad's suggestion and sent the appropriate order to Aryeh.

Meantime Natke was enjoying a lull in the Qantara sector, but Gabi, in the Firdan sector, was still heavily engaged. I told Gabi that I would soon be in his vicinity at Zrakor Hill where I intended to deploy my forward command post and install effective communications.

My deputy, Dovik, was then in a helicopter. Since before dawn he had been engaged in breaking up traffic jams and pushing units from Katia toward the front. But from the time our advance to establish contact with the enemy got under way, he had been helping with control by assisting slow-moving tanks and units en route in the heavy dunes. Dovik now called to tell me that Gonen was trying to raise me by radio to give me an urgent and important message. I told Dovik that I was en route to Zrakor, where communications might be better. I added that if he received the message, he should come to Zrakor and deliver it to me there.

By 1005 hours I was settled in at Zrakor and at once made contact with Southern Command. Gonen's deputy, Uri Ben-Ari, came over the air and gave me a very surprising and certainly "important" message: "I hear you well. There are some slight indications that the enemy has begun to collapse, so it's very important, very important, to rush at maximum speed with all your forces along your entire axis from the north, from Qantara, to down below to make contact and destroy. Otherwise they're liable to get away!.."

Ben-Ari had been my commander at the end of the War of Independence and in the Sinai Campaign. I esteemed him as a serious officer. So, of course, I took what he told me seriously. I also knew that Southern Command had means to collect intelligence from sources unavailable to me.

To execute this new thrust, I would have to move Natke's brigade southward from Qantara. The Egyptian tanks of their 15th Brigade, which had already engaged Natke twice, had pulled back and disappeared in the concealed area of Qantara. I wondered if these were part of the retreat indicators Ben-Ari had spoken of? I knew I could not simply abandon the sector, lest the enemy exploit the situation and penetrate our rear zone. In reply, then, I raised the question whether, according to their information, Natke could evacuate the Qantara sector since he had just been engaged there twice with the Egyptians' 15th Brigade. It's quiet there now, I added, but I was not sure what would happen if we were to leave.

Ben-Ari: "I suggest leaving a small force to secure the sector, but the major part of Natke's unit should advance along the Lexicon Road and destroy anything west [of the road]. Otherwise the enemy may flee. It is also very important that you cross at Hizayon and ensure yourself a way across because it [the passage] is liable to be closed off."

Ten minutes later, Ben-Ari contacted me again and told me what I already knew and had told him earlier, that there were still enemy forces in Qantara, and I was to destroy them. I answered that I wasn't ready to move into the built-up and swampy areas there. Ben-Ari then pressed me again concerning a push southward to Missouri and Amir (that is, an advance to Bitter Lake). My response was that I wanted Gabi to be reinforced by one of Sharon's battalions deployed at Havraga and doing nothing. Ben-Ari's answer surprised me: "Negative! Sharon is about to move southward."

I had had no conception of what was being cooked up at Southern Command or of their assessment of the situation. I did not know that they had already decided to move Sharon southward. However, I did not acquiesce to Ben-Ari's negative reply. It was Gabi who suggested getting a battalion from Sharon, and I still thought it a good idea. On the one hand we were dispersed over a broad zone, while on the other I was getting orders to speed things up because "the route across is liable to be closed." And adjacent to Gabi was a battalion doing nothing. I made my request to Gonen, who promised to attach the battalion to my division.

Meanwhile, in order to enable Natke to move from Qantara southward, I contacted General Magen about replacing Natke at Qantara. But as Magen did not have sufficient forces to deploy there either, I had no choice but to detach one battalion from Natke's brigade and attach it to Magen. Natke, then, would have to move south with just two reduced battalions.

At 1037 hours I told Natke to be prepared to move toward Gabi and instructed him: "There you will have to update yourself. My intention is that you move on the Lexicon axis from north to south, carefully, with plenty of artillery and air support (which had been promised me by Gonen). There are three crossing sites there. Your task will be to cross them and get a foothold on the other bank. But before you go ahead enthusiastically, study the site well. We'll discuss it further. And wait for my final approval."

I now turned to Gabi, to see whether there were in fact signs of an enemy collapse. I asked him: "There is an intention of taking Hizayon as soon as possible and crossing to the other bank. Do you have a plan? Do you feel that you can implement this with the forces you have on hand?"

Gabi replied: "No! I have just come under heavy artillery fire and am engaged with enemy tanks and missiles. I have already suggested getting Sharon's battalion which is deployed behind me doing nothing. And I need more artillery and strong close air support."

The pressure on me from above continued unabated; communication with Southern Command was like a dialogue with the deaf. At 1020 hours Gonen: "I intend to give you the mission [establishing] many small outposts on the west bank."

I told him: "What I really need, if you can, is to provide me with air support."

Gonen: "We'll get you some, but it's urgent that you take the other side near Hizayon."

At 1025 hours, Ben-Ari: "South of Amir (the Chinese Farm) the terrain is crisscrossed with dry irrigation canals. You have to be very careful there."

I replied: "Roger. Understood. It will be some time before we reach there."

Then at 1040 hours, Ben-Ari: "After finishing with Missouri, we want you to cross in three places" (and he indicated the names).

I replied: "These three places are clearly marked on my map, but I wonder what reports you've been getting. Here in the field it looks completely different. I also can't understand why I am not getting Sharon's battalion."

Ben-Ari, reconsidering, said, "Take the battalion!"

I told him, "Okay. I will take it. I am also calling Natke's brigade to move down — but I still need lots of air support because there are plenty of enemy tanks and missiles up on the hills there!"

Ben-Ari: "What is the situation concerning Missouri and the rest of the sector?"

I answered, "We'll be getting to Missouri much later, so let's talk about it later. Meanwhile, I have to deal with Hizayon."

As to the internal coordination at Southern Command, the call to me from Gonen at 1054 hours is instructive. Now, after I had radioed Gonen's headquarters about Natke's engagements with Egypt's 15th Brigade tanks near Qantara and after I had worked to move Natke's reduced brigade to Gabi's sector, Gonen suddenly came on the radio and "revealed" to me that, according to a "new report" he had just received, a T-62 tank brigade was located in Qantara. In the wake of this, Gonen said: "Since you have not met up with the brigade, it is still there. Can you secure Natke's rear? Secondly, I want Natke to engage that brigade with one battalion which would enter into Qantara.''

I told Gonen: "It doesn't make sense, I have just ordered Natke to carry out another mission. Why disrupt it?''

To Gonen's query concerning Natke's mission, I explained that Natke was moving south to join Gabi's sector and that the Qantara sector had been placed under General Magen's command. I took the opportunity to complain again that the battalion from Sharon's division had not yet been ordered to join Gabi.

Gonen: "Fire the battalion commander and appoint his deputy [in his place]!''

This remark was typical of Gonen's leadership style. Was the battalion commander to blame because he hadn't received approval to join Gabi? I continued to press to get the battalion but in vain. Gonen promised to solve the problem but nothing materialized. Today I know that Gonen had not even talked with Sharon directly but made do with directing his order to Sharon's chief of staff, Lieutenant Colonel Gideon. Nor does this mean that Sharon did not know of Gonen's order; he simply chose to ignore it. Gabi made repeated efforts to get the battalion. When he contacted its commander directly, he was told that the brigade commander was withholding approval. Gabi then got hold of two of Sharon's brigade commanders, who told him that they had no approval from Sharon. At one point, Sharon's operations officer, Lieutenant Colonel Aharon, approached him and said: "I am listening on Bren's radio net; they are having trouble around Hizayon and are requesting one of our battalions, which is situated there, to help them.''

Aharon later related that Sharon seemed to reflect on this before replying: "We are about to move south, and we will need this battalion.''

The situation was nerve-wracking: Gabi's brigade, thrashing about under heavy artillery fire, was awaiting reinforcement. Southern Command had given its approval; the battalion was deployed on Havraga; and the battalion commander was ready to join up with Gabi, but Sharon would not approve.

When Gabi received the reply of the battalion commander, Lieutenant Colonel Ami, he burst out over the radio net: "You are arguing among you, and meanwhile my men are being killed.'' This unpleasant affair left its mark on Ami's own tank crews. When his battalion moved out, he saw Sharon standing by the side of the road near Tassa. He stopped his tank, went up to Sharon, and said that his conscience was troubling him because he was precluded from coming to Gabi's assistance by Sharon's objections. Sharon replied that Ami should leave it to the division commander's (i.e., Sharon's) conscience. Moreover, Sharon added, there was a disaster in the Mitla Pass, and they had to rush there. Ami returned to his tank, but his company commanders kept coming over the radio, to ask: ''Why didn't we help Gabi? Why didn't we help Gabi?''*

*An examination of the time schedules involved shows that handling of the matter of trying to attach the battalion to Gabi's brigade began at 1000 hours and that Sharon objected to this from the beginning, before he got orders to move south. Sharon would later argue that he hadn't understood why I had asked for his battalion because as he left the sector he happened to see one of my battalions, that of Eliashiv, idle near Havraga. The truth is that Eliashiv's battalion arrived there only at 1100 hours, while we had been trying since 1000 hours to get Sharon's battalion transferred to Gabi. Moreover, it would not be long before it became clear that Aryeh's understrength brigade was in a critical situation, being left with only two small battalions after I had had to transfer Eliashiv's battalion to Gabi's brigade.

CHAPTER ELEVEN

OPERATIONAL MISTAKES

B efore continuing with the story of the fighting of my division, I think it worthwhile to elucidate how and why Sharon moved southward. This move, along with various others, was the result of deliberations going on at the levels above me.

All during the time Gonen and Ben-Ari were pressing me to cross the canal and expand deep into the south, Gonen was also busy trying to obtain approval of the chief of staff for these two fateful steps — and for changing Sharon's mission. The chief of staff was unfortunately compelled to base his decisions on inaccurate and even misleading information that Gonen sent him.

It will be recalled that according to Gonen's plan, Sharon's division was to be in reserve during the attack carried out by my division. But at 0430 — that is, three and a half hours before he gave the order to attack — Gonen had for the first time expressed his new idea that deviated from the plan he had sent the chief of staff. Gonen had explained to Sharon his plan of having him move south, cross the canal at its southern extremity, and capture Suez City. At 0617 Gonen spelled out his notion to Sharon's chief of staff, Colonel Gideon.

Then, at about 0925, in a long conversation with me, Gonen "clarified" his intentions, and I agreed to try to get close to the canal. Gonen's behavior seems to indicate that his having clarified his intentions to me meant that they had already been carried out. Otherwise it is difficult to explain the conclusions he reached ten minutes later in what his aide records as a "situation-reassessment" conference with his staff, focusing on the question of whether Sharon should be ordered to move southward. It was just then, at 0938, that I informed Gonen that both the link-up to Strongpoint Hizayon and the canal crossing would have to be postponed because I was engaged in a difficult battle: Gabi's brigade was fighting against tanks and missiles originating in the Hizayon sector. However, this information did not prevent Gonen from reaching the conclusion that Sharon's division should be disengaged and moved far to the south. Nor did it prevent him from reporting, at 0955 hours, to Maj. Gen. Rechavam (Gandi) Ze'evi, the chief of staff's assistant, that the forward elements of my division were already close to Hizayon, that the area was relatively free of enemy forces, that there was a bridge there, and that I was preparing to cross the canal.

It is difficult, then, to see any connection between the true situation and the "situation assessment" that Gonen had made or between the reports I was transmitting to Gonen and those he was, in turn, passing on to the chief of staff. Dado heard the optimistic report but still withheld approval. But this did not prevent Gonen from ordering me, at 0957 hours, to seize a foothold on the other side of the canal opposite Hizayon.

From 1000 hours until 1125 hours, the chief of staff was busy attending a cabinet session. I assume that Dado felt that this was an unfortunate time to be tied down in such a meeting, as all the indications were that events were moving quickly on the battlefield. Contact with Gonen was maintained via General Ze'evi, who, after speaking with Gonen by phone, would pass notes containing both information and requests for approval of various steps to Dado in the cabinet room.

At 1015 hours Gonen asked Ze'evi for air support, without which, he said, he would not be able to approach the canal. He also requested approval to move troops across the canal to take footholds to a depth of 200–300 meters, so as to ensure that the Egyptians did not destroy their own bridges. Ze'evi delivered the message in the form of a note to Dado. The chief of staff replied in a note, asking how many footholds would be involved, expressing apprehension that small forces were liable to be cut off, and instructing Ze'evi to ascertain that the areas in question were free of enemy forces and that the Israeli troops involved were not too small in number.

Encouraged by this reply, Gonen went on to explain that he had already given an order to cross at one point — at Hizayon — and was now requesting approval for an option to cross at four or five additional points. He added that he would operate in line with the chief of staff's directives, crossing at sites free of enemy troops and with forces that were not too small. He noted, however, that the crossing force would also not be too large, to prevent a situation in which we would be committed.

When Dado received yet another note from Ze'evi, with Gonen's reply, he apparently assumed that if Gonen had already given the order to cross at Hizayon, all the conditions he, Dado, had laid down must exist there. At 1035 hours Ze'evi informed Gonen that the chief of staff had given his approval for seizing the footholds on the other side of the canal.

Unfortunately, Dado was compelled to base his decisions on imprecise information from Gonen. The chief of staff did not even imagine that Gonen was requesting approval after approval unless things were changing in the zone of operations. When I learned of all this, after the war, it was my impression that Gonen behaved in this matter as if we were conducting some kind of war game, an exercise involving no troops — neither ours nor the enemy's — and in which there was no battlefield reality. It would seem that for him the battle, which one would expect to be long and complex, ended the moment he had had his say. The moment he made a decision, he could move ahead to the next stage. Now that he had obtained approval for my division to cross, he moved energetically to deal with the matter of altering Sharon's mission.

Reflecting on the "time and space" factors concerning Sharon's move south, Gonen reached the conclusion that it would take Sharon about four hours to get to the southern end of the canal — so that if he were to attack at 1600 hours, he must be moved out as quickly as possible. Losing no time, Gonen told his chief of staff: "Give Sharon an order to concentrate for a southerly crossing on the Gidi Road." At the same time, Gonen contacted Ze'evi, explaining that in order to save time he was requesting the chief of staff's approval to have

Sharon move south, at this stage, only as far as the Gidi Pass route. At 1040 hours, Ze'evi informed Gonen that the chief of staff had approved his request. Twenty-five minutes later, Gonen requested approval to move Sharon farther south, to have him proceed on the Lateral Road as far as the Mitla Pass route. Gonen detailed his intention of having Sharon attack from south to north. Should he find a bridge intact at Strongpoint Nisan, opposite Suez City, he would cross the canal and capture Suez City.

As soon as he emerged from the cabinet session, at 1125 hours, Dado contacted Gonen to discuss Sharon's mission with him. After considering the plan, the chief of staff expressed doubt concerning its logic: it would take four to five hours for Sharon to arrive at his new zone of operations, by which time it would be close to dusk and no time would be left to destroy enemy forces. Dado favored the original plan whereby Sharon was to attack west of the Artillery Road from north to south, from Bitter Lake to the Gulf of Suez (from Strongpoint Lituf towards Strongpoint Nisan). That would leave Sharon enough time to destroy more enemy forces. Gonen replied that fighting from north to south would enable the enemy to do away with the bridge at Nisan (opposite Suez), whereas his plan — which called for disengagement, a quick move south on the Lateral Road, and fighting from south to north — would catch the Egyptians by surprise so that we could take the bridge intact.

Dado suggested to Gonen that Sharon dispatch a small force that would operate from the south, but it was desirable that the major part of the division fight from north to south. However, when Gonen said that he preferred to have the entire division operate from south to north, Dado yielded the point. The chief of staff then saw to it that the chief of the operations department was informed of his approval and of the reasons for the change. This move would achieve surprise at a place where the Egyptians were not so well prepared, as against an attack from north to south, which would allow them to fold up their bridges while retreating slowly.

However, the chief of staff was still not entirely content with his decision. He again called Gonen to express his apprehension that four to five hours of daylight would be wasted without any fighting and without any enemy troops being destroyed. But this round, too, ended with the change in plans being approved. Those who were around Dado at that moment heard him say: "It's a borderline thing, but since it is, let him do what he prefers."

When, at 1045 hours, Sharon's division received approval to move south, it had to disengage in the Ismailia-Bitter Lake sector, pull back 20 km to the Lateral Road, and speed south. And there was one more serious difficulty: if Sharon disengaged from the enemy without my forces replacing him in an orderly manner, and at once, the enemy was liable to advance into the evacuated area and threaten my division from the flank. When Gonen ordered Sharon to disengage from his sector, the hope still existed that the commanders in the field would not make the mistake of disengagement and abandonment of territory before the arrival of replacements. Most of the commanders, in fact, responded correctly.

When Gideon, Sharon's chief of staff, heard the order to disengage, he was aware of the pressure on me to extend my deployment southward and knew that Aryeh's brigade was proceeding on the Tassa-Ismailia Road (Talisman) but had not yet reached the Hamutal, Ziona, and Nozel hills that were held by Sharon's units. He therefore asked Gonen: "How can we move when we are in contact with the enemy at Missouri? And who will replace the forces at Hamadia and Kishuf?" He was, in fact, raising the question: What will happen if Sharon disengages and the enemy takes advantage of the situation, moves forward, captures the abandoned area, and threatens my flank? Gonen replied that Sharon's division should start to disengage from the northern area first, so that forces from Hamadia and Kishuf could disengage last, but he didn't explicitly condition those moves on my forces getting to the area first.

This, it will be recalled, was the third day of the war, when Egyptian forces were to push their bridgeheads to 10–12 km, up to the hill line along the Artillery Road. Forces of the Egyptian 2nd Infantry Division were attacking through Nozel along the Ismailia-Tassa Road. To that division's south, their 16th Infantry Division, reinforced by their 23rd Tank Brigade, was successfully penetrating deep into our territory. They reached the Chinese Farm (Amir), 4–6 km from the canal and were soon deploying heavy concentrations in the entire area between the Chinese Farm and the Tassa-Ismailia Road.

They took Stronghold Televizia and advanced as far as Machshir, 12 km east of the canal and only three km south of the Tassa-Ismailia Road.

Amram, a tank battalion commander who fought at Nozel, later described what happened: "I had been under prolonged heavy shelling; and just when the Egyptian pressure slackened, I was suddenly ordered to withdraw. I said to the brigade commander, why leave now when they're pressing and there's no one to replace me. In the end I got an order: Move! I said to myself that if I'm now getting an order to evacuate a hill which is a key point in the sector, then it must have been decided 'up there' to evacuate the hill before any Egyptian assault." The brigade commanders Amnon and Haim also asked whether they were really to evacuate their position before being replaced, but the order remained: Move out! Colonel Jackie, Sharon's deputy commander, was with a part of Tuvia's brigade at Hamadia when Sharon urged him to cease operations there and move southward. Jackie couldn't believe that Sharon intended to expose the hill, so he called Lieutenant Colonel Aharon, Sharon's operations officer, and asked him how much of his force he should leave behind to secure the sector. Aharon knew that Sharon's order was to evacuate but nevertheless replied that he would check again with Gonen.

At this point Sharon intervened on the radio: "You don't have to check it, I have already checked!" Gideon also clashed with Sharon; he, too, asked who was going to replace them if they pulled out before my units arrived and suggested that they wait. But Sharon told him that Bren was "having trouble" and that there was no need to delay the movement to the south.

So it was that between 1000 and 1130 hours, Gonen obtained the chief of staff's approval and began energetically carrying out his moves that were riddled with these serious operational mistakes. Sharon, who was to have been in reserve for a westward attack, instead of *assisting* me, actually *exposed* my southern flank. Gonen then stepped up his pressure on me to push south and disperse my forces. Sharon's division disengaged and was rushed so far south as to be neutralized — wasted — that entire day.

Having described the contacts among Dado, Gonen, and Sharon, I must remind the reader that when I planned my division's fighting for that day, I did not even know that the original plan had been altered to include an approach to the strongpoints and a canal crossing. Even when it was decided to change Sharon's mission, Gonen did not see fit to update me.

At first I was requested, and then pressured, to seize footholds on the west bank of the canal. Of course I noticed Sharon's forces moving away from the front eastward, but I did not imagine that all his forces were pulling out — and, what is more, doing so just at a time when the enemy was bringing pressure to bear. Nor did I conceive of the demand that I deviate from my plan by moving to the canal and crossing independent of any factual or intelligence data that could justify it. Certainly it never even crossed my mind that I would be called on to do all this without being given assistance, or that steps would be taken which would actually make the situation worse.

I was, in fact, busy making a cautious attempt to carry out what was being required of me.

CHAPTER TWELVE

TACTICAL MISTAKES

Between 1100 and twelve noon on 8 October, Natke's forces were moving to reinforce Gabi's sector. Aryeh's tanks, moving towards the front, met up with Sharon's tanks moving in the opposite direction. The roads were occupied; the tanks could move unobstructed along the sides of the road, but the half-tracks and other vehicles were having difficulties. Aryeh's brigade was moving on two roads. Eliashiv's battalion, which I had taken from Aryeh to be the divisional reserve, was on the Spontani Road and halted at Havraga. Aryeh's two remaining battalions were on the Tassa-Ismailia Road (Talisman): Nahum's battalion, with twenty-two tanks, was leading and was followed by Dan's battalion, which had fifteen tanks (one of Dan's companies had been left with Magen, at Baluza). Aryeh's tank strength was, then, small in the extreme. At this stage, his mission was to move towards Stronghold Purkan to attempt to link up with the strongpoints and seize footholds on the other side of the canal.

For two hours now, Gabi's brigade had been shuffling about in the Zangwill area, being shelled while waiting for reinforcements and air support. To his right, on the Arov axis, Amir's battalion — which consisted of the twenty tanks that had survived the brigade's battles near Qantara on the night of the sixth — was also being hit by artillery and was engaged in a battle with enemy tanks and antitank missiles. The battalion hit some tanks but also suffered casualties of their own. But by about 1100 Amir was already short of fuel and ammunition, so asked permission to withdraw several tanks and resupply them; permission was granted. To Gabi's left was his second force, Adini's reserve battalion, consisting of twenty-five tanks. Deployed south of the Haviva Road, some 3.5 km from the canal, Adini's companies were under artillery fire, constantly moving back and forth, right and left. He asked permission to leapfrog to the rear but was refused. When his radio net to brigade headquarters malfunctioned, he monitored the division net, where he had heard something about Southern Command orders to cross the canal and seize footholds on the other side. The area between his position and the canal looked unoccupied, so he began moving forward. Ten minutes earlier, he and his artillery officer had seen bombs dropped by our planes landing in front of him near the canal, as well as explosions of artillery shells. Certain that the air support would continue, he launched his assault.

Once on the move, he realized that he wasn't getting air or artillery support, but he thought that to stop or to retreat would be worse than continuing to charge forward. When he reached a point 800 meters from the canal he found himself under tank fire from ramparts and barriers on both banks of the canal. To his right, he noticed one of his tank commanders signaling him, pointing toward Egyptian infantry who were fleeing, but in front of him he saw salvos of Sagger and RPG-7 antitank missiles being fired. Within minutes his tanks were being hit, one after another. Then Adini himself was wounded, his hand broken by a small-arms round. After evaluating the situation, he ordered a retreat. One of his company commanders, Captain Ze'ira, assumed command. Six tanks were burning, totally destroyed, with crewmen running about. Ze'ira evacuated the casualties and helped tow some of the other disabled tanks. All told, only seven of the battalion's twenty-five tanks remained operable. The battalion suffered twenty killed, including two platoon commanders. Among the dozens of wounded were the battalion commander, two company commanders, and two platoon leaders. It was a severe blow, but the battalion would continue to fight until the end of the war under Ze'ira's command.

I did not know until later of the assault by Adini's battalion and of the drama played out next to the canal, since I was located on Zrakor, a high dune hill about 8 km from the canal. It was a good observation point. I could see most of the area between the canal and the Artillery Road ridge line on which Zrakor was located. I saw the two roads, Arov and Haviva, along which our main attack was to be launched, but there were still many parts of the area concealed from my view. From the dust cloud his tanks raised, Natke's approach from Qantara was visible. Our radio nets were jammed, partially due to interference by the enemy and atmospheric noises, but also because Gonen and Ben-Ari would burst into my net, since the Southern Command net was hardly functioning.

Between 1120 and 1140 hours, I managed to hear some fragmentary radio reports indicating that Gabi's brigade was in grave trouble. First there were frantic demands for urgent and heavy air support, then messages about burning tanks and crewmen being cut down. I immediately asked for urgent air support, but Southern Command replied: "Impossible now, the planes are engaged in air-to-air combat." Then added, "What's happening with your advance southward?"

It is hard to describe how I felt, especially since the timing of Gabi's attack was off, coming while we were still massing additional forces. While I didn't know just how severe a blow had been inflicted on Adini's battalion, the fragmented messages I could hear seared my heart. But this was not the time for despair or to divert my attention from the mission. I began to work for Gabi's reinforcement and to hurry Natke to the area so that we could launch a two-brigade attack.

At 1215 Aryeh reported that Nahum had seized Nozel, destroying eight enemy tanks there. Aryeh told Dan to deploy at Hamutal because of a threat that Aryeh saw developing to his south from the direction of Missouri: he could see thousands of infantrymen advancing, reinforced by tanks, and was worried that they might cut his forces off at Hamutal or Ziona. I now attached Aryeh's third battalion, under Eliashiv — which had been held as the divisional reserve — to Gabi who was reorganizing his forces. Gabi also received a reconnaissance company of two tanks and five M-113 armored personnel carriers. Gabi then told Amir's battalion to pull back and replenish their tanks with fuel and ammunition.

With Natke's brigade on its way to reinforce Gabi's sector, I told

Natke to rush ahead personally to meet with Gabi for updating on the terrain and the enemy. On his way, Natke tried to verify whether the picture he had formed, from fragmentary radio messages he had heard while still in the northern sector, was correct. First he contacted Gabi and then he asked me: "What I don't understand is whether we have forces on the other side."*

My reply: "Absolutely not!" Then I explained to him his brigade's mission to capture two out of the three Egyptian bridges in the sector and transfer small forces across the canal. I made it clear to him that he would have to wait for close air support and that he should use the time until it arrived to improve his positions.

Gabi and Natke met at 1230 hours. By 1245 Natke was back with his brigade. Just then, Gabi, who was south of the Havivah Road, reported that "many enemy tanks" and other vehicles were crossing the Firdan Bridge to our bank and then moving southward towards the Purkan sector. This unceasing flow southward made both Aryeh and me apprehensive that the enemy was building up a force to attack Aryeh. Colonel Gideon, Sharon's chief of staff, burst over our radio net to repeat over and over that Sharon's troops were in the process of evacuating their sector near Missouri, but that they saw many Egyptian tanks coming in. He suggested that Aryeh rush to take over the sector. He was told, however, that Aryeh was busy in the Purkan (Ismailia) area. I assumed that under those circumstances, Sharon's troops would hold their positions until we could get there. Once again I asked for air support. Meanwhile at 1315 hours, Natke moved his brigade into the area, and I fixed the Haviva Road as the boundary between his brigade and Gabi's.

I now faced a dilemma. Usually a divisional attack is launched only after precise coordination. Such an attack will normally be supported by at least fifteen artillery batteries and massive air support, particularly if the enemy is well organized for defense. Under cover of the artillery, the tanks advance, with their attached armored infantry. The tanks inflict damage by direct fire, the artillery support the attack with covering fire, and then the tanks assault with the mounted armored infantry.

But in this case I had only two understrength brigades, each with

---

*The General Staff bunker was monitoring several radio nets. Apparently one of the monitors picked up part of this exchange and formed the impression that I had crossed to the other side of the canal. Thus, the report circulated there was that we crossed the canal.

just two reduced battalions of about twenty tanks each. I was also very short of armored infantry and had only three understrength artillery batteries. I had been promised further artillery support and massive air support — indeed, massive air support was the only available element that could now compensate me for my lack of firepower. But I was not able to get that air support. I had no choice but to adjust our plan of attack to advance very slowly, improving positions by closing in on the enemy and deploying for the major assault when the air support arrived. Southern Command assured me that we would have air support within thirty minutes.

Observing the field through binoculars from my position on Zrakor, I could see some of my forces moving forward, improving positions. The radio net was "clogged up" with noises, fragmented messages, and outbursts from Southern Command's intermediate stations.

At 1330 hours I noticed that Natke's right battalion (Natan) had halted, while the battalion on the left (Assaf) was still moving forward. I pointed this out to Natke, who said he was aware of it and told me that Natan was engaged with enemy tanks and Sagger missiles fired from the palm grove (the same forces that had previously engaged Amir's battalion, from Gabi's brigade). He added that two of our tanks and a half-track had been hit and that there were casualties, among them Natan's deputy battalion commander. He also said that Natan was about to renew his movement, so I called Aryeh, ordering him to support Natke's and Gabi's forward thrust by advancing his forces and also putting pressure on the enemy in the direction of Purkan.

At 1415 hours, indications of failure began coming in. Natke reported that his tanks were being hit and set afire one after another and asked for more forces to be pushed forward. My heart skipped a beat. Again our tanks were being set afire! I bit my lip and, making an effort to speak calmly and quietly, replied that he should be careful, that he should not push too energetically forward, that it would be better to wait for air support. But it was too late. Natke was paying a heavy price, and I ordered him to move to the rear. Before I could find out exactly what was going on there, Aryeh came on the radio net to say that his forces were too small for the area in which he was operating. He told me that two of his tanks had been hit on Nozel, but what was really worrying him was a buildup of enemy forces threatening him from the south. He asked urgently for air support.

At 1430 hours Natke informed me that he had lost radio contact with his forward battalion commander, Lt. Col. Assaf Yaguri. Some time would pass before the situation was clarified, but I had a hunch that something was wrong. I had no time for reflection, however, because Aryeh called again to report that scores of enemy tanks — apparently those that had crossed the Firdan Bridge and had moved southward — were now attacking him from north to south, and he was also taking very heavy artillery fire.

What really went wrong in the second attack toward the Firdan was that the final assault was executed by only one battalion. Natke had approved the delay of Natan's battalion, which was on his right, because of the hits it had sustained. On his left was Gabi's very small brigade, made up of Eliashiv's battalion and the reconnaissance company, but they halted at the edge of the hills so as not to advance into the flat terrain until air support could suppress the enemy. Natke himself was with Yaguri's battalion, and they continued to advance into the flat terrain under very heavy enemy artillery fire. About 1,500 meters from the canal, they suddenly found themselves almost on top of enemy trenches from which infantry opened fire on them with machine guns and antitank RPGs. At the same time, scores of enemy tanks opened fire from the ramparts and barriers on both sides of the canal, and Sagger missiles were also directed at them. Tanks were hit one after another and crewmen could be seen jumping out of the burning vehicles.

Natke ordered a retreat, but within minutes fourteen tanks were hit. Only four tanks, including those of the brigade commander and of company commander Brik, managed to make it back. On the way back they picked up five more tanks which had been delayed due to technical faults. Of Yaguri's twenty-five tanks, only nine made it through that day. The fate of the battalion commander, his deputy, two of his company commanders and many platoon leaders, tank commanders and crewmen was unknown. Many were killed or wounded; others were taken prisoner. That evening Natke's brigade would report fifty-four men missing in action.

It was a terrible blow but unfortunately not the last one to be inflicted on my division on that long day of fighting.

Company commander Brik received permission to try to rescue

any surviving crewmen who might still be wandering around in the field. But as he approached the area he saw through his binoculars that the Egyptians were assembling prisoners and evacuating them on an armored personnel carrier. It also looked to him that an Egyptian attack in his direction was about to be mounted. So he withdrew and joined up with the few tanks left from Assaf's battalion.

It is difficult to describe what I felt and what I went through in the course of those long hours. War-tested, I had been in pressure situations before. But this time I was commanding a large formation which, on orders from above, I was compelled to disperse over a broad expanse so that it was difficult to maintain control. Despite my excellent observation point, I could see only two of my brigades. Aryeh's brigade was operating beyond the hills, and my only contact with it was via the radio. Communications were terrible. The Egyptians were apparently jamming our nets. I could have overcome this because of my proximity to the brigade commanders, but Southern Command kept bursting into my net. Because we were far from Southern Command HQ, the jamming of that net was more effective. The Command's intermediate stations would override my division command net, trying to relay messages. The intermediate communication procedure was time consuming, and meanwhile the net was occupied.

Critical battlefield situations compel bursting into communication nets. Commanders are trained in and sensitive to the need to free the net for this purpose, but this is not so with the operators in the intermediate stations. Of course, I tried to break into the brigade nets for updating and to issue instructions; but the pace of events taking place simultaneously in each of the three brigade sectors made it exceedingly difficult to keep abreast of the situation, the more so as the brigade commanders were engaged in intensive communciations efforts. And all this was under heavy enemy fire. I realized that I was receiving the reports too late and too slowly.

But the report that something had gone wrong in Natke's brigade reached me precisely as it was happening. How could this be, I wondered, since the assualt order had not yet been given?

While I was still waiting impatiently and under terrible tension for supplementary reports on the exact situation, Aryeh radioed that he was facing a serious threat from the direction of Hamutal. Thousands of Egyptian infantry, supported by many tanks, were approaching from the south. He was worried that they were about to cut off the road (Talisman) between him and Tassa. He therefore asked permission to evacuate Nozel immediately in order to move Nahum's battalion from there to Hamutal to support Dan's battalion.

At that moment, the Egyptians let loose with a terrific shelling on Zrakor. Shells exploded near my forward command post vehicles; smoke and sand flew into our faces. Afraid, as we all were, I crouched in the armored command vehicle. I had been under heavy fire many times in the past and knew exactly what our chances were. We needed plenty of luck. My personal fear was mixed with anxiety for my division if I were killed or wounded. "All vehicles of the forward command post, move out after me! Driver, move out!" I heard myself order. When the smoke cleared, we discovered that our communications half-track had been hit; my forward command group's communications officer, Captain Yosef Desheh, was killed, and several men were wounded. My communications officer and my deputy took charge of evacuating the casualties while I ordered the forward command group to move to Havraga.

I now decided to let Aryeh withdraw from Nozel quickly, without hesitation. I felt that under the circumstances, without proper communication with or observation of the area in which Aryeh was fighting, no time could be wasted in any examination of the situation. On the contrary, I felt that I had already "missed the boat."

And, in fact, after only a few minutes, Aryeh radioed me that the enemy had taken Hamutal. This created a wedge between our forward forces and the Tassa junction, thus posing a serious threat to the division's flank. I decided that Hamutal must be retaken by a counterattack. Aryeh again asked for reinforcements and suggested that I give him back Eliashiv's battalion, but that battalion was engaged with the enemy, along with Gabi's brigade. Gabi suggested that he send Amir's battalion instead, since Amir had just completed replenishing his ammunition and fuel. The trouble was that Amir's battalion had only twelve tanks. But it was the only unit I could dispatch immediately. So I told Aryeh to be prepared to receive Amir's battalion, which would arrive from the north and once it arrived, to counterattack and retake Hamutal. Immediately thereafter, communication with Aryeh was lost again.

CHAPTER THIRTEEN

HOURS OF CRISIS

O ur situation was grave, and as this long day wore on, things grew worse. From 1415 hours, when fragmentary information first began to arrive that something very wrong was taking place with Natke's brigade, until 1500 hours, while I was awaiting clarification, reports kept coming in about a continuous flow of enemy tanks crossing the canal over the bridges in the Firdan area.

From my observation point I could see that my forces were unorganized. Tanks could be seen moving to the rear, while others were grouped in small clusters but not in firing positions. I tried to radio my brigade commanders of the situation but to no avail. Each one averred that the tanks in question were not his. So I sent my operations officer to find out whose they were and orient them toward their units. Because of the communications difficulties, I felt I was not getting a true picture of the situation. I could see that there was considerable disorder in the units, and I knew I had to tighten my control, but I felt there was no way to do it by radio.

I had the possibility of withdrawing to the rear to reorganize, but I feared that the enemy would take advantage of such a disengagement to intensify the pressure. I decided to move to the Hazizit-Haviva junction and have Gabi and Natke meet me there to assess the situation and receive my orders. On my way I could hear fragments of messages from Aryeh asking for air support and for helicopters so he could evacuate his wounded.

It was close to 1630 hours when I met with Gabi and Natke. I took off my headset and jumped down from the armored command vehicle, map in hand. The three of us bent over the map on the soft sand. I was astonished to find that the crash of exploding shells was more pleasant to my ears than the noise of the radio set that had been drumming into my ears for so many hours. I looked at Gabi and Natke and wondered how we would look to an outside observer. Three commanders, all short with broad shoulders — and what a heavy burden had been laid on them.

For three days and nights we hadn't slept a wink. I thought of all that Gabi had been through that first night, at Qantara, and during the past few hours near the Firdan Bridge; and of Natke, who only two hours before had barely made it to the rear. Each of them had lost a battalion within the last several hours. We were now badly disorganized. What to do to get things straightened out? My thoughts were abruptly interrupted as Natke and Gabi simultaneously got calls from the radio operators on their vehicles: their deputies were calling them urgently. An enemy attack had just been launched from the west! Just what we needed, I thought: the enemy attacks and both brigade commanders are with me. "Get back to your brigades fast!" I shouted, but they were already on their way.

At about 1700 my division was in real trouble, and I was undergoing the worst crisis I had experienced in four wars.

Natke reported by radio: "They are coming on the Haviva Road. They are coming towards us. This is a really serious attack, one hundred tanks at least . . ."

And Gabi: "I don't know what's with Eliashiv, I don't see him here."

I told Gabi: "We have communication with Eliashiv. I am sending Natke to help you. Meanwhile, hold the enemy." Gabi replied: "They are coming on a very broad front at him [Natke] and at us, in huge numbers. They are moving straight ahead, across the whole front. Give us air support, because we don't have enough forces."

Then Natke broke in: "They are coming in masses, they are coming in masses. We have to have planes right away, because we don't have enough strength.''

It was a very difficult moment. I had no communication with Aryeh, but I knew that the enemy was attacking him also, that he was withdrawing and had asked for helicopters to evacuate casualties. Gabi and Natke, under heavy attack, were crying out for air support, reporting that they didn't have enough forces to stop the enemy advance. The entire division was now under attack from two directions: from the west by forces of the 2nd Egyptian Infantry Division and from the south by forces of the 16th Egyptian Infantry Division. From each direction came thousands of enemy infantry accompanied by scores of tanks, while we were few, worn down, disorganized.

In the command vehicle with me were my operations officer, Gilad, and my deputy, Dovik. I looked at them; they were looking at me. Silence. I thought to myself: Should I give the order to retreat? "There is no choice," I burst out. "We must retreat."

Sometime between 1700 and 1710 hours, I ordered Natke and Gabi to withdraw.

At 1710 hours, Sharon's operation's officer radioed my operations officer to find out what was happening: Where was the enemy and where were my forces? Gilad updated him on our situation and then, hearing from him that Sharon's division was about to attack west toward Missouri, asked whether they could attack northward instead, so that we could repel the enemy by a joint effort of both divisions. He said he would ask Sharon.

I still felt very uncomfortable about the retreat order I had issued. A thought crossed my mind that situations of near collapse frequently come up on the battlefield simultaneously for both sides, and the force that finds the inner strength to hold out just a little longer can sometimes alter the course of the campaign. I didn't know if Sharon would come to my assistance, or, if he did, how long it would take, but I clung, like a drowning man clutching a straw, to the hope that he would come.

"Gilad!" I said: "Ask Natke and Gabi if they can hold their present positions until Sharon arrives." Gilad radioed: "A large force of ours is coming from the south. Can you hold your positions and repel the enemy together?''

Natke and Gabi replied: "Affirmative! Meanwhile, we are setting them afire!"

Gilad, simply: "I love you!" I was pleased that he had handled the transmission because I could not have expressed myself so freely.

One of Natke's messages conveyed the "fog of battle" which prevailed then: "The attack seems to be contained. We have hit many tanks. It looks like there were many enemy forces here. Some of them are burning, and some of them have halted. But what's happening is that our boys are falling back too far to the rear. It's enough that one does it, and then others do it too."

I replied: "Some of those who fell back have begun to return. We will send back the others too."

The Egyptian attack was halted by small groups of tanks. Shilo, Gabi's deputy, was deployed on the Haviva Road with six tanks that he had assembled. On his left was Eliashiv, with a relatively large battalion of twenty-two tanks. To the right of Haviva Road, Captain Brik commanded the nine tanks remaining from Yaguri's battalion, and to his right was Natan's battalion, with about twenty tanks. Natke's operations officer was moving into position between Brik and Natan with six tanks he had collected in the rear. As the enemy attacks began we had the sun in our eyes, but soon dusk fell and then darkness. Our tank crews fired like devils out of hell as the Egyptians closed range, and we could see flames from the disabled tanks and pillars of smoke all across the front. The defenders thought they had stopped the attack, and their confidence increased.

But after the sun set, scores of enemy armored personnel carriers passed among the Egyptian tanks and advanced toward us. Emotions intensified again. Artillery bonfires, smoke, and dust compounded the confusion. More fires appeared on the battlefield, most of them on the enemy side, but our tanks were also hit. As the darkness grew, reports came in of enemy infantry attacking on foot. Requests for illumination shells were radioed, and the battlefield was soon brightly lit.

Actually, dismounted infantry never attacked. What my front line troops saw were enemy troops jumping from their personnel carriers when they began to take hits. They were rushing about among the vehicles but bent on panicky retreat, not attack.

Meanwhile, another fierce fight was under way in Aryeh's sector. It will be recalled that Amir's battalion had set out southward from

Havraga at about 1530 hours; after moving some twelve km on Hazizit Road and after some mutual identification difficulties, he linked up with Aryeh. The latter deployed Amir between Nahum's and Dan Sapir's battalions and finished issuing his orders for a counterattack. According to Aryeh's plan, Nahum's battalion had taken up positions for covering fire on Hamutal. The two remaining reduced battalions, Amir's with twelve tanks and Dan's with fifteen tanks, launched their assault in a southeasterly direction.

As the charge began, Egyptian tanks began taking hits, but at a point 1,000 meters from the peak of Hamutal, two of our tanks were hit. One of the battalion commanders, Lt. Col. Dan Sapir, was killed, and his battalion's assault was disrupted and then halted. Amir's battalion continued the charge on its own. The battalion moved on Talisman Road, which bisects the long, flat dune atop Hamutal. Amir closed range very quickly, then turned south across the dunes. In a short time his tanks began taking hits from missiles fired in front of them and from tanks which were sited close to their rear. The fighting was bitter. Three of our assaulting tanks took up positions and began firing at the enemy tanks in the rear. The others continued to charge, but they became fewer and fewer in number. Amir's own tank was hit three times, and its gun barrel exploded, but he continued to charge, using his machine gun only and trying to crush the enemy infantry with the tank tracks.

Five hundred meters in front of them they saw two Egyptian tanks and some missile launchers. By now, four of the Egyptian tanks in their rear had been destroyed, and the others were abandoned by their men. The two tanks in front of them had also been abandoned after the stubborn Israeli charge. At the same time, however, more of Amir's tanks were hit. It was getting to be twilight. Amir, realizing that his battalion was in a critical situation, ordered the evacuation of the wounded and a general pullback to Talisman. Of the twelve tanks that had begun the charge, only five were capable of returning to the road under their own power. Some of the casualties were evacuated by the crews of the five able tanks, while others made their way on foot to Talisman.

As Amir now turned to withdraw from Hamutal, he was astonished to see concentrations of tanks east of him — most of them near Ziona, others moving and firing toward Machshir and Hamutal. He sensed that these were Israeli tanks, so asked Aryeh, who told him they were in fact part of Haim's brigade attached to Sharon's division. Aryeh added that he was trying to get them to stop firing. My communication with Aryeh was renewed just then. With no little irritation we tried to coordinate a cease-fire both with Sharon's HQ and directly with Haim's brigade.

Haim's brigade had left the sector before noon in order to move to the southern part of the canal and was now returning to its sector, which had become part of my division's sector. The fog of battle that attended their activity was best described by brigade commander Haim himself, after the war: "As we approached with the aim of capturing Hamutal, we had no idea that a fierce fight was already under way. Aryeh's brigade had not been informed of our movement either. He also thought we were joining in the assault." Haim goes on to relate how he deployed two battalions as a base of fire near Ziona to cover him from the east, and how he dispatched Shimon's battalion along Talisman Road in order to charge Hamutal.

Shimon described what happened: "Then I arrived at Ziona and I saw a terrible fight. I saw tanks burning, tanks moving, one on top of another . . . Centurion tanks [Israeli tanks] were burning and moving. Suddenly I noticed two Centurions coming from the direction of Machshir toward Hamutal. It was already dark. The sky was lit up by flares. Then I saw that my tanks were beginning to take hits from missiles fired at us from Machshir and from south of us. Three of my tanks were hit and three of my men were killed at once."

As these descriptions make all too clear, the confusion on and around Hamutal was tremendous. Aryeh, of my division, and Haim, of Sharon's division, had had no prior information about each other. During the fighting they managed to avoid firing at each other, and as Aryeh called Amir to descend from Hamutal, forces of Haim's brigade were already ascending it. Miki, Shimon's deputy battalion commander, recalls: "We advanced, and we replaced one of Aryeh's units. When we ascended the objective, they left it." Later, Haim ordered Shimon to evacuate Hamutal.*

---

*After the war, Sharon claimed that Aryeh had never been on Hamutal and that he (Sharon) had in fact left the sector with Nozel, Hamutal, Machshir, and Ziona in his hands, but upon his return they were all in enemy hands. Sharon said that he could not understand why Aryeh had not seized, or why he had lost, those sites, in whose attempted recapture precious blood

How did it happen that Aryeh and Haim met on Hamutal without one knowing about the other? To answer this question, we must go back to about noon that day.

Sharon's division had disengaged from the enemy at about 1100 hours, moved to the Lateral Road, and then began moving southward. Between 1130 and 1200 hours, Gonen received reports of our difficulties and heavy losses and our urgent appeals for air support — this having to do with our attack towards Hizayon (the Firdan Bridge). At this time most of Sharon's division was on the Lateral Road (near Tassa). Gonen did not change his plans, and Sharon continued southward. At 1430 hours the second attack towards the Firdan Bridge failed. This time Gonen decided to halt Sharon and at 1445 hours Sharon stopped. Although compelled to deviate from his previous plan, Gonen still wanted very much to cross the canal. He changed Sharon's mission, instructing him to attack directly westward and to capture Missouri and the Chinese Farm (Amir); following this, Sharon would return to his previous mission, to continue southward and cross the canal there.

Sharon answered that the planning and preparations would take time. He thought he would be able to start the attack at 1700 hours and began to move his forces back to deploy for the new mission. His intention was to attack with the entire division through the Akavish and Puton roads. Haim's brigade returned to the Talisman sector, which by this time was part of my sector. At about 1715, a spate of radio communications began between my operations officer and Sharon's, between Gonen and me, and between Gonen and Sharon. At issue was our request for Sharon to attack from south to north in order to ease the terrible pressure being exerted on my division by two simultaneous Egyptian attacks: one from the direction of the canal against Gabi and Natke, the other from the south against Aryeh, the attacks that almost forced me to withdraw.*

---

was later shed. An examination of the facts shows that the Egyptians had seized Machshir on the morning of 8 October, when the sector was under Sharon's responsibility. The only site first captured and later evacuated by Aryeh was Nozel, which was done to preclude the risk of our being cut off at Hamutal.

*We subsequently learned that we had been attacked by two mechanized brigades.

From the conversation between Sharon and Gonen it emerged that both were listening to my radio net and were discussing the line I was holding, ostensibly after a minor withdrawal, and where Sharon's forces were deployed. Sharon now explained that his forces were holding Machshir and that Haim's brigade was at a point on Talisman which was 6 km east of Hamutal (where my forces were fighting desperately).

Sharon told Gonen: "I hear Bren's requests that I should attack in his sector, but that doesn't look right to me, because the moment we do so our flank will be exposed. Instead, I suggest we reconsider an attack on Missouri and Amir."

Gonen rejected Sharon's proposal to attack toward Missouri, because, he said, if Sharon became engaged there, there would be no uncommitted forces left in the sector. Gonen told him: "You'd better stay where you are now; that is good for me. If Bren has to go down [i.e., move east], then you will be the second line, the depth. We'll conduct this game until we overcome in another way." What the other way was he didn't say.

Sharon: "I definitely understand it, and I think what you are saying is a very serious consideration."

Apparently, my continuing pressure to get support caused Gonen to reconsider, and a few minutes later he contacted Sharon again. Gonen: "Arik, is the brigade near Talisman 39 okay?" (This was Haim's brigade, 6 km east of Hamutal.)

Sharon told him: "The brigade is okay."

Gonen asked: "Can you send the brigade to Machshir? Or maybe it can launch a counterattack from south to north?" (An attack from south to north would of course have helped my division.)

Sharon: "I don't suggest that now, at night. I think that might wear them [the brigade] down. We are sitting now and thinking about the situation. I'll call you back in fifteen minutes."

Thirty minutes later, Sharon replied to Gonen: "Regarding your previous question, about assisting Bren, I can't see it. I also have the problem that Machshir isn't in our hands." Sharon then explained that in order to establish a good defensive line it was vital to capture Machshir.

Gonen asked him: "What do you intend to do?"

Sharon: "I don't intend to allow Haim to move from south to north to the place where Bren was today."

Gonen: "I'm not interested in your taking Machshir."

Sharon: "I *must* take Machshir; it isn't complicated, it's a little thing."

Gonen: "It isn't a complicated matter. But I assume that Bren will soon pull back again, and then you're left with your back exposed. As long as you are here, we have a second line."

Sharon: "You think that Bren is going to move back?"

Gonen: "He is engaged now with enemy infantry equipped with RPGs and other antitank weapons."

Sharon: "Okay, fine, but in any case I am not committing Haim's brigade now to assist him because we did not talk with the brigade."

The lay reader may form the impression that this was a very serious conversation replete with military considerations. Actually, I find it incredible even today. As I fought there, I did not imagine that my request for support would be discussed in such a manner. It was clear to both generals that I had decided to withdraw under enemy pressure and that I might have to withdraw again. Gonen, the front commander, was wavering: to save forces and so do nothing or to attack nonetheless — and if to attack, whether toward Machshir or from south to north. But an attack toward Machshir and an attack from south to north were, after all, hardly the same thing.

As for Sharon, he had no qualms: at 1445 hours he was given an order to attack toward Missouri and Amir and would be ready to do so by 1700 hours. That hour had already passed, and before he was ready Gonen rescinded the order. When Gonen suggested he attack in order to support me, Sharon objected to exposing his flank, to wearing down his forces. On the other hand, he had some "wearing-down" suggestions of his own: he was ready to press toward Missouri and Amir, he "must" capture Machshir. Astonishingly, in the end, despite Sharon's opposition, Haim's brigade went into action on Hamutal — but without any coordination with us.*

---

*Haim's move to Hamutal was undertaken within the framework of getting to Machshir, but his brigade never got there.

An hour after dark there was a lull on the front line. The illumination flares faded out, and we realized we were no longer under attack. The main problem I now faced was how to enable my division, which had been cut to pieces, to lick its wounds and reorganize for further fighting. My intuition told me that the enemy would also need a period of reorganization and would probably not renew his attack overnight. But even so, I couldn't afford to leave my forces or the sector unsecured, especially when the division would be busy rearming, refueling, and repairing damaged tanks. My reconnaissance unit had already entered battle and was halted in Magen's sector. When Dovik informed me that Mandler's reserve reconnaissance unit, which had not taken part in the fighting, was moving toward us, I assigned tanks to it and gave it the mission of establishing a security and patrol screen on the Hazizit Road.

I moved the brigades about 5 km to the rear: Natke on the Ma'adim Road, Gabi on Spontani, and Aryeh on Talisman. To the credit of the officers at the main HQ and to that of the Divisional trains* it must be said that despite the jams and disruptions on the coastal road, they managed to get convoys of fuel and ammunition and repair crews through. These at once positioned themselves at the points selected for the night bivouacs and awaited the arrival of the brigades.

As I stood with the command group watching the flow of tanks to the rear, I found it a little difficult to believe my eyes. There had been moments when I was no longer sure I had a division, but now I saw organized columns of tanks moving by, the fighters' silhouettes visible in the turrets. I felt my heart spilling over with pride and affection for the soldiers. We had undergone a day of terrible fighting, but despite the heavy blows inflicted upon us, despite the disruptions due to commanders who had been hit, the division was functioning.

My commanders had a host of problems: many tanks had been hit; many others broke down; some had been repaired by their crews, but others had to be towed out of the battle zone. We had to be on the alert in case Egyptian infantry or commando units had set ambushes for the tanks. The area had to be combed to ensure that no

---

*An important support element of the division which provides logistical services for all organic and attached divisional troop units. It encompasses the functions of supply, repair, ancillary transportation, medical services, and evacuation of personnel and equipment.

abandoned tanks or wounded soldiers had been left behind. Aryeh's jeep company reconnoitered the Hamutal area and directed tanks and crewmen who had lost their way to our bivouacs. The doctors and medics had plenty of work; some of the casualties were evacuated by helicopter, others in vehicles.

Manpower had to be reassigned, new commanders appointed. Three battalions, one in each brigade, were in severe shape, virtually wiped out: Adini's battalion in Gabi's brigade; Yaguri's battalion in Natke's brigade; and Amir's battalion, which was now in Aryeh's brigade. Of the battalion commanders, Dan Sapir had been killed, Adini had been wounded, and one battalion commander, Assef Yaguri, had been taken prisoner. Many company commanders, officers, tank commanders, and crewmen had been killed.

We had started the fighting on the morning of 8 October with 170 tanks and finished with 100. About 40 tanks were severely damaged, of which 25 had to be left behind in enemy-controlled territory. Of the remainder, many had less severe damage and had to be towed to the rear, while other tanks had been assigned in the morning to Magen.

Dead tired, hurting for our friends who had fallen, downcast over the blows taken but determined to prepare for the resumption of the fighting, the men girded themselves for the task and threw themselves into the work. Despite our losses on 8 October, the division had about 120 tanks ready for action by the following morning. The forces had been reorganized under commanders, many of whom were new to the post. Some had reached the battlefield as reinforcements, and some had taken command during the fighting and had been approved to continue in their new task.

A small division but ready for battle.

CHAPTER FOURTEEN

REASSESSMENT OF 8 OCTOBER

Victory has many fathers, but failure is an orphan, goes the proverb. The unfortunate truth of that saying is reflected in much of what has been written and said concerning the eighth of October. Gonen spared no effort to cast the blame for the failure mainly on me, but the Agranat Commission, which investigated the events of that day, did not agree with him, writing:

"[Gonen] did not prepare a detailed operational plan, and he did not see to it that an operational order was issued and reached the commanders of his troops. He did not ascertain whether his forces had in fact arrived in full and were deployed in the manner required for the operation . . . When the battle began, he conducted it without any effective control system or staff work; he refrained from taking personal command of his troops, and consequently did not know firsthand what was happening on the battlefield. He took crucial decisions on moving an Ugda [division] from one sector to another hastily and without ascertaining by every possible means that the objectives, as defined to him by the chief of staff as a condition for moving the division, had in fact been attained. He frequently changed the objectives of divisions and gave them new ones without providing his forces with information concerning our own or the enemy's forces. He caused a gradual erosion of the objective and of

154

the method with which he was charged by the chief of staff, being impatient for a quick canal crossing before the essential conditions for such a decisive step had been created.''

Gonen was not the only one who made mistakes that day; those above him and those under his command, myself included, also made mistakes. But what set Gonen apart was not only the fact that his mistakes were many and severe, but also the fact that he created the circumstances for many of the mistakes made by others. Gonen did get the approval of the chief of staff for his moves, but this came in the wake of Gonen's reports, which created for Dado a picture of the situation that differed markedly from reality. After the war I asked Dado how it came about that he had approved a canal crossing that day in order to establish footholds on the other side and how it was that he had approved Sharon's move southward. Showing some discomfort, he replied: "What could I do? I tried to be cautious, but Gonen time and again created the impression that things were going better than we expected." Dado was one of those commanders who gave subordinate officers freedom of initiative, and he was open to the suggestions of those under him. Outstanding among his qualities were his ability to analyze complex issues and his capacity for persuasiveness. I liked his leadership style, but I was sorry that he erred in appointing Gonen and in the unreserved trust he placed in him.

I knew Shmulik Gonen well. Several times he had been under my direct command. In 1956 he commanded a company in my battalion. When I assumed command of the 7th Brigade, he was there as a battalion commander. When I was given command of the Armored Corps, he was commander of the 7th Brigade, which was under my responsibility. I knew he had good points. He was awarded a citation for distinguished performance in the Sinai Campaign of 1956. He gained wide fame in the Six Day War, when he fought as commander of the 7th Brigade. He was brave and master of his profession, armor.

Gonen created for himself a showy image and had the reputation of being a very strict disciplinarian, and it was over this point that I had reservations about him. Gonen enforced discipline by intimidation, both in style and content. More than once I had seen him throw things, tear maps, shout at those around him, and rashly confine soldiers to jail, often acting on impulse.

Amazingly, though, for one who was so impulsive vis-à-vis those under him, he could get along well with his superiors with whom he was soft-spoken and self-disciplined, showing extraordinary self-control. He was what is known in the army as a "bicycle rider" — one who presses hard downward but is always looking upwards. Gonen's method seemed to aim at breaking the personality of his staff officers.

When Gonen was promoted to major general, we were equal in rank and both of us were members of the General Staff. In that capacity, we restrained our mutual hostility and worked harmonious-ly. But now, with the outbreak of war, an embarrassing situation arose. Gonen, the young and inexperienced commanding general, was commander of the front, while under him were two veteran generals: Arik Sharon and myself. I was not disturbed by this because I preferred to command a battlefield division and be with the troops at the front rather than at a command post in the rear. I could not help doubting Gonen's ability to command the southern front. But there and then I made my decision: we already were at war — a war which had begun very badly for us. It was clear to me that in war we had to act in the IDF spirit of "let's do and *then* talk." I did not realize then how crucial a decision this was. At all events, I abided by it until the end of the war. Gonen himself bore this out just after the war, when he said: "Bren behaved correctly toward me throughout the war."

Nor, in my opinion, can or should the division commanders shirk responsibility for what happened on the grounds that they were following orders. There is always a place to ask what they knew, what they thought about the orders they received, and what they did to rectify mistakes they noticed.

At first glance, Sharon's division saw virtually no action on 8 Oc-tober. Its move toward the strongpoints was canceled in the morning, it disengaged from the sector in the forenoon, and returned in the afternoon. Nonetheless, mistakes occurred in the way the division was run and operated. While Sharon did get an order from Gonen to move out of the sector, his behavior as a military commander must be termed surprising. After all, his subordinates also received a like order (from him), but they saw at once that its implementation would involve abandoning an area that the Egyptians were then liable to seize. They put forward questions: Who would replace them in the sector? How many troops should be left behind until the replacements arrived?

Sharon cut them short: You don't understand, you're not in the picture — disengage at once! This eagerness to pull out at once was subsequently explained as stemming from the need to rush south because of a "catastrophe" there — though no such catastrophe occurred in the south. (Even if the report, radioed at 1210 hours, concerning an Egyptian armored division threatening us in the southern area of the canal is taken as the source of the notion of a catastrophe in the south, the fact is that Sharon evacuated his sector at 1045 hours — almost ninety minutes before that report.) The sector was abandoned on Gonen's order to mass on the Gidi Road, preparatory to a canal crossing in the south. Sharon, who was in possession of information on the enemy's activity in his sector, erred in not clarifying the picture to Gonen and erred again in not leaving behind small forces to engage the enemy until the arrival of my replacing forces.

Another of Sharon's mistakes was the way he held the sector prior to his disengagement. When I attacked from north to south, Sharon was to contain the enemy in his sector and press westward. His forces were at Havraga, around Nozel, and on the Talisman Road near Hamutal, but they did not seize the peak of Hamutal, south of the road, or Machshir. Moreover, from the morning hours Sharon's men had seen that Machshir was being taken by the Egyptians, who were starting to dig in there, but he seems to have been unaware of this. (As noted earlier, Sharon would subsequently say that he could not understand why important hills that his men held when he left the sector were in enemy hands when he returned — and among these hills were, he said, Hamutal and Machshir.) Sharon erred, then, in not holding his sector properly and in not updating HQ concerning enemy activity.

In addition, an important component of overall battlefield strength is readiness and sensitivity, at all levels, to hurry support to friendly forces that are in trouble. I must, then, strongly criticize Sharon for not attaching a battalion to Gabi for the attack on Hizayon and for his refusal to support me, towards evening, by launching an attack from south to north.

It must also be borne in mind that this was the first day of fighting for the reserve divisions, which were not yet organized. The absence of coordination and control was apparent at all levels in Southern Command and found its most extreme expression in the return of Sharon's division to the very sector it had left. We did not even know of Sharon's return. At first Aryeh thought that the enemy had taken Ziona, then it emerged that these were Sharon's forces.

Sharon for his part thought that Machshir was in his hands and that the enemy was holding Hamutal, though his deputy, Jackie, did know that "Machshir is not in their hands." Haim fired on Hamutal, where, at the time, Aryeh's brigade was engaging the enemy. Sharon kept on trying to clarify the situation: for some reason he found it difficult to believe that he was not holding Machshir. Meanwhile, Aryeh and Haim had discovered each other's location. The picture formed at Southern Command was that Ziona and Hamutal had been recaptured from the enemy. Haim attacked Hamutal, but his assault suffered from lack of coordination and control, just like Aryeh's attack at the same site. Finally, Haim's force ascended Hamutal, and Aryeh descended; and finally Haim also evacuated Hamutal.

And what were my mistakes? My biggest mistake was my attack toward the canal. I have since reflected on this a great deal, and I feel that it is related to my personal background. I had always set myself certain criteria. I expressed my views and differences of opinion in the planning stage; when it came to implementation, I always acted in line with "We'll do and we'll listen." One listens, one understands, one implements. After all my past experience, it simply did not occur to me that orders could be issued without the balanced consideration I believed there must be.

In all the wars I fought, I was alert to the possibility of initiating things and of taking advantage of opportune situations. In the 1948 war, for instance, when two columns made their way to Eilat, one, mechanized, along the level plain of the Arava and the other — my infantry company on foot — through mountainous terrain from the central Negev, I was quick enough to get there first and raise our improvised "flag of ink." In the Sinai Campaign (1956) when I was commander of a tank battalion, my brigade commander, Uri Ben-Ari, ordered me to penetrate deep into the enemy's rear via Wadi Daika and to attack Abu Agheila. I soon advanced out of effective radio communication range and by the time the brigade was able to reach me in order to stop me and change the order, my battalion had already captured Abu Agheila. As a result, the battalion was left on its own, and the brigade moved south. For twelve hours we fought, cut off and under attack from all directions, because we were as a bone in the enemy's throat, disrupting its continuity between Nitzana and El Arish. At dusk I received an order to take the Revpah Dam, which we did, after a bitter fight.

In 1967 I was deputy division commander under Major General Yoffe. We were advancing quickly from Bir-Hassna toward the Mitla Pass when suddenly our forces halted; in front of them they saw a seemingly endless level stretch on which hundreds and thousands of enemy vehicles were moving. At once our commanders began to deploy for contact. My observation led me to conclude that what we were seeing was a disorganized force beating a hasty retreat toward the Mitla Pass. I had one of our tank battalions rush to seize and block the Mitla Pass — a daring move, but it enabled us to close off the route of retreat of Shazli's forces and to capture them along with many weapons.

In earlier wars, then, my commanders never had to push me, but on 8 October 1973, I felt I was being pushed. I did not know that the plan had been changed, and I mentioned "last night's summations." As the pressure continued, while I was still hesitating, I was aware of Ben-Ari's remarks about the collapsing enemy. This led me to attempt an attack toward the canal. I made this attack conditional upon my receiving massive air support, reinforcement by a tank battalion from Sharon's division, and artillery support.

In spite of the pressure on me, I did not press or push my brigade commanders. Nor do I think that it was a mistake on my part, with the data and information I then had (a disintegrating enemy and the promise of support) to try to carry out what I was being called on to do. But I definitely regard it as a mistake that, at a certain stage, after I saw that we were shuffling about without HQ sending us the promised support and reinforcement, I did not make it unequivocally clear to Gonen that I had no intention of attacking westward.

I do not shirk responsibility for what happened in my division. The running of the battle was faulty; my coordination and control were insufficient. In the second attack I was unable to prevent a situation in which Natke's brigade made an assault on its own. The brigade commanders were also at fault in coordination and control. Gabi, Natke, and Aryeh did not succeed in preventing an assault by just one battalion from their brigades.

Nonetheless, our failure must be viewed within the general context of all the circumstances. There was no justification for dispatching us to attack toward the canal while at the same time bringing pressure on us to extend ourselves southward. He who dispatched us also created the conditions for our failure. We constituted the major effort of Southern Command. Of the three divisions, only mine was to attack: without infantry, without artillery, and — what is less understandable — without air support. Gonen promised such support, but it subsequently emerged that the available air support was dispersed every which way. Of the many dozens of sorties carried out in support of ground forces, seventy were carried out in the sector of the Egyptian Third Army. Most of the sorties were carried out in the Second Army sector but only twenty-four of them around the Firdan Bridge — of which ten took place early in the morning, before we arrived in the sector, two around noon, and the other twelve in the later afternoon when we threw back the Egyptian attacks.

Much has been said about what happened on 8 October and about what should have happened. In his attempts to blame me, Gonen claimed that his orders made sense and could have been implemented. Had I but attacked from north to south and en masse — instead of frontally from east to west — I would have rolled back the enemy's flank.

In fact, the general direction of our attack was from north to south. And, indeed, such an attack made sense as long as one kept away from the area of the sand barriers and the ramparts. But the moment Gonen pressed for a link-up with the strongpoints, for a canal crossing, and for the seizing of footholds on the west bank, of course I attacked from east to west. An attack from north to south near the canal would have meant exposing my flank to the enemy, who was holding sand barriers and ramparts and operating tanks and firing both short-range and long-range antitank missiles from them. Moreover, the topographical and artificial structure of the terrain near the canal allowed the enemy to operate against me while the marshy area and the obstacle of the canal itself protected him against possible assault by me.

As to the claim that I did not attack with a concentrated force, it was Gonen himself who played a major role in that. When on the evening of the seventh the various options for the eighth were discussed, General Mandler suggested a concentrated attack in a narrow sector with two divisions and a canal crossing. The chief of staff decided against approaching the canal and against a crossing. If despite this, Gonen decided to attack the canal and to cross it, why not in full massed strength? And if Gonen already decided to attack with one division, why not Sharon's division? His division was deployed in the sector; he was demanding to move to the strongpoints, had planned it, and was preparing for it. Why bring my division from far off to carry out an operation it had not prepared for? Or was this done in order to increase the force concentration, with me attacking from the north and Sharon pressing from the east? If so, why did Gonen pull Sharon out even before my attack west began, thus exposing his sector, and consequently press me to move south fast at the same time?

Of all the possibilities, Gonen brought about the one that he had "locked on" already on the evening of 7 October: a simultaneous crossing by two divisions at two widely separated points. He thus caused the maximum dispersion of forces.

Sharon later argued, against Gonen and the chief of staff, that we had enough forces on the eighth and had they been sent into action in concentration to attack and cross the canal, the Egyptians would already have been vanquished. I believe that had we tried to do this, we would have suffered even greater losses and achieved nothing. On the eighth we had only three reduced disorganized divisions. We later learned that the Egyptians' bridges were incapable of carrying our heavier tanks. We could not have crossed. Lacking the capacity to destroy the enemy on the far side of the canal and with the enemy's antiaircraft missile batteries preventing our air force from providing effective support to the ground forces, an approach to the canal by two divisions under those circumstances would have ended in disastrous failure.

In retrospect, it may be asked whether the IDF would not have done better to refrain from attacking altogether on 8 October? Had we known then about the "operational hold" phase of the Egyptian attack plan, it would certainly have been preferable to wait and concentrate stronger, better organized and better balanced forces — but the fact is we did not know.

On 7 October Dayan proposed that no attack be launched. At first, on 6 October, Dayan seems to have felt that the regular army with a partial reinforcement from the reserves could contain the enemy; thus, on 6 October he opposed general mobilization and a preemptive air strike. When he realized, after a few hours, that we had failed to prevent the canal crossing, he apparently began to wonder whether this was due to mistakes we had made or to mistaken basic assumptions. At all events, in the cabinet session at 2200 hours on 6 October, Dayan put forward a realistic assessment when he argued that we must recognize that the first defensive line was lost and that until the reserves could arrive we should withdraw to a second defensive line. He reasoned that after the arrival of the reserves, on the eighth or the ninth, armored counterattacks could be launched.

On the afternoon of 7 October, after he returned north from Southern Command HQ, Dayan reported to the prime minister. This time he was very pessimistic. He still favored a retreat to a second line, but he no longer believed in our ability to launch counterattacks with the armored formations. Dayan's apprehension was that such an attack might sustain heavy losses and fail; then our situation would be critical. This time he said he believed we were facing a protracted war, and we had to adopt a defensive strategy in Sinai and await arms shipments from the United States and perhaps from Europe. Only after we had built up more power would we be able to move to a counterattack. The chief of staff's view was different, and Dayan gave him a mandate to meet with the commanders in the south and decide on the spot. Dado decided on a limited attack.

Who was right — the chief of staff or the minister of defense? There is no doubt in my mind that the stance of the minister of defense was too pessimistic that day and expressed a lack of faith in the ability of the IDF "to throw the Egyptians back across the canal" before we received more weapons from abroad. Taking Dayan's notion of "throwing back the Egyptians" in its military sense — vanquishing the Egyptian army and destroying major parts of its forces — that is just what the IDF ultimately did, until it was stopped by the intervention of the superpowers. And the IDF did this before reinforcements of tanks and aircraft from the United States reached the fronts.

Should the IDF have attacked quickly on 8 October, even though the reserves were still far from being in full force or organized? In my view — yes. Under the circumstances as we understood them and in line with our basic assumptions, there was not one of the southern front commanders who recommended waiting until we could build up strength and organize fully. Everyone believed that we had to take the initiative from the Egyptians as soon as possible. The operation was intended to gain the initiative, to slow the Egyptian momentum, and to retake a substantial part of the territory we had evacuated. This would have given us time to concentrate and organize the reserves and prepare the way for a major counterattack that would include crossing the canal and crushing the enemy. Such an attack would have been based on our crossing gear, which would be readied in the area retaken; the attack would then have been launched from a distance of 3-5 km from the canal.

If we continue this line of thought, we may ask what should we have done in line with that plan once it became clear that the enemy did not penetrate any further than he did in reality? Even then, we should have stuck to the original plan and dealt only with Hamutal, Machshir, Missouri, and the Chinese Farm — which had been taken by the enemy and lay beyond the bounds of the 3 km adjacent to the canal. Only after our mission had been completed in full would there have been room to place Sharon's sector under my responsibility and to have Sharon operate from north to south in Mandler's sector against those enemy forces that had advanced past the area of 3 km from the canal.

The defeat of 8 October had a considerable effect on the subsequent course of the fighting on the southern front, though not necessarily as a result of that day's failure in itself but as a result of the accumulated effect of the blows we sustained on the sixth and seventh. On the evening of 8 October, Southern Command had only one division left intact: Sharon's. The other two, Mandler's and mine, were both reduced and worn down due to the loss of tanks, crews, and many commanders of all ranks.

My division bore the main burden of the fighting that day. Terrible blows were inflicted on us. For some of the officers and men it was their baptism by fire. For the regulars, it was a relentless continuation of the blows they had sustained on the sixth and the seventh. Many of them could not grasp just what was happening, but their fighting spirit never broke.

As night fell on the eighth, every battalion of my division had withstood a difficult Egyptian attack. Thousands of enemy soldiers and scores of tanks had assaulted us. We were few in number, dead tired, beaten, badly organized — and we had almost retreated. (Actually, we did withdraw at Hamutal but quickly counterattacked.) But thanks to the courage, the bold spirit, the camaraderie, and the readiness for sacrifice of the division's men and officers, we hung on and repelled the attacks. In spite of our losses that day, our determined fighting — especially the containment of two Egyptian mechanized brigades that afternoon — certainly left its mark on the Egyptians.

The Agranat Commission later wrote of that day: "One reserve division did not succeed in fulfilling its mission of destroying the enemy bridgeheads. But this division's fierce fighting that day contributed much to the containment and blocking of the enemy's advance, and thus prepared the ground for the IDF's major counterattack, at the end of which it crossed the canal."

Brigade forward command post in defensive battle.

Repairing a tank in the dunes.

Major General Gonen, Commander Southern Front, on the right; division commander Major General Adan in the center with his deputy, Brigadier General Dovik, on the left.

A tank towing a unifloat raft. Ramp can be adjusted by hydraulic pressure.

Evacuation of the wounded, usually by helicopter.

Lieutenant General Bar-Lev, now in command of Southern Front. Near Havraga, on 11 October.

Half tracks on Spontani Road with tanks moving beside them.

Three Gilowa rafts joined together can support a tank.

Unifloat rafts made of iron cubes. The two armored compartments that protect the engines from fragments are concealed by camouflage nets. The raft weighs sixty tons.

President Ephraim Kazir at division headquarters with Lieutenant General Elazar on the left; author on the right.

Replacing power plant of a tank in the field.

The roller bridge (400 tons; hauled by sixteen tanks). In front, a unifloat raft can be seen.

Dangerous congestion on the roads.

Moshe Dayan and author conferring.

Senior division commanders, from left to right: Aryeh, Amir, Bren, Gabi, Natke, Dovik.

PART III

BUILDING UP STRENGTH

CHAPTER FIFTEEN

AFTERMATH OF 8 OCTOBER

On 8 October, the general staff had hoped to begin repulsing the enemy from our territory by means of counterattacks on both fronts. On the northern front this hope materialized, and we began throwing the Syrians back. On the southern front the counterattack failed, and we suffered heavy casualties. This failure led to more considered thought and greater weight given to preparations and the accumulation of strength as preconditions for a renewed offensive. At the same time, we did strive to launch that renewed attack as soon as possible, for fear of a cease-fire being imposed while the situation in the field was not in our favor.

In a conference held at 1800 on 8 October at the GHQ bunker, the director of Military Intelligence still assumed that the Egyptians were operating according to Soviet military doctrine, which meant that they would seek to complete the extension of their bridgehead to a depth of 12 km that evening and would follow with an attack eastward the following day. In his view, the crossing of the canal by the Egyptian 4th and 21st Armored Divisions, along with the landing of commandos in our rear, would be indicators of an imminent armored attack deep into Israeli territory.

At 2100 the chief of staff updated the cabinet on the events of 8 October, and some three hours later, around midnight, he and the minister of defense left for Southern Command HQ for a meeting with Gonen and the division commanders.

I too was about to convene my staff officers for a situation assessment. After I ascertained that my three brigades were on the move toward their night bivouacs, I moved my tactical command post to my main command post which, camouflaged, was deployed at the junction of the Spontani and Kartisan roads. There, at a point called Kurkar, in the deep sand, the war room was set up in a large tent stretched between two trucks. Around it were the vehicles and posts of the staff officers, with the division's communication vehicle stationed close by. When I entered the war room, for the first time since we had left for the front, I encountered staff officers who were not part of my forward command post. They looked active but tired, their eyes bloodshot and their voices hoarse — just like the rest of us.

The war room was designed to be the planning, coordination, and control center for my main command post. It had been equipped with telephones, radios, maps, and various data tables that were constantly updated. But the dimensions of the war room had been determined by the fact that it was also intended to serve as a conference site for dozens of officers. As I entered the tent, it looked large and empty. On one side a few officers and NCOs were working on the maps and communications sets while on the other side several of the division's liaison officers were grouped. I knew most of them personally. They were veteran Armored Corps men, reservists generally around my own age, who had held active staff and command posts in the past but had now been replaced by younger, more *au courant* officers. They held ranks of captain, major, or lieutenant colonel. Two of them were very old friends indeed, having served with me as company commanders in the Negev Brigade during the 1948 War of Independence. I was very happy to see them.

At 2050 hours I assembled my staff officers. I had not yet met with the brigade commanders so did not know the reasons for their premature assault or for the failures, but I was well aware of the effect Southern Command had had on our activity. I said we had undergone a terrible day of fighting in which we had been committed on an over-risky basis, that we had been hard hit and gravely weakened. At this stage, I added, I did not know why Sharon's division had been disengaged from the front line. Our situation obliged us to weigh our steps with caution. The questions facing us were what the enemy was likely to do and how we should respond?

The first speaker was my intelligence officer, Yoram, who noted that the Egyptian armored divisions had not yet begun a canal crossing. Therefore, he expected that they would now continue to consolidate their narrow bridgehead, though the likelihood was that the divisions would soon cross. Dovik, Gilad, and others also spoke. All of them discussed the option of destroying the Egyptian forces on the east bank as against the possibility of crossing the canal. All agreed that the correct solution was to cross the canal, and so attack the enemy from the rear. At the same time, they pointed out that we would be incapable of carrying out such a move without precise advance planning and without the accumulation of more strength. Gilad estimated that we would need a week to prepare. Dovik recommended that we wait for the Egyptians on the ridge line and move against them only when they tried to advance toward us.

Summing up, I said we had been worn down and were additionally facing the fact that the air force was having to contend with antiaircraft missiles, while the Armored Corps was coping with antitank missiles. From the experience of the fighting that afternoon, when despite our weariness and reduced ranks we had repulsed the enemy and caused him losses, it was my conclusion that at this stage we should enter a defensive posture in order to cause the enemy further losses and improve the balance of forces. We could prepare for a crossing, but it would have to be a concentrated and coordinated attack by two divisions, with air and artillery support. The emphasis, then, would be on defense, on economizing force, and on accumulating strength. This would be my recommendation to Southern Command.

Meanwhile a helicopter had arrived to pick me up for a conference at Southern Command HQ at Umm-Hashiba. I said I would be convening the brigade commanders later that night, and I would inform them about the meeting before I returned.

I arrived at Umm-Hashiba at 2330 hours, and I noticed one difference since I had been there the previous night. Around the command bunker there were more vehicles parked and more antennae reaching into the sky. There were more reserve soldiers wandering about inside, along with various "guests" and media people. The disorder was even more glaring than it had been.

When I entered Gonen's room, the division commanders were already seated. This was the third straight night I hadn't slept a wink. Although I was aware of only a few of the many mistakes that had been made during the day, I did perceive that I had been placed in intolerable and unjustified situations. I was furious over the deviation from the agreed-upon plan and over the hours of helplessness when we could do no more than shuffle about statically under heavy artillery shelling, waiting for reinforcements and air support that never arrived. I knew nothing of the fact that the plans had been changed, nor did I know what the considerations had been for disengaging Sharon from the front. I was too involved all that day in intensive fighting and too weary to ask questions that night.

Even though we had borne most of the burden of that day's fighting on the southern front, and I was more than aware that even the little help I had requested had not been forthcoming, I refrained from expressing what I felt and thought. I just told Gonen that I would wait until after the war for an examination of why I had been put under pressure to attack toward the canal and to seize small footholds on its western bank, while being given false information that the Egyptians were fleeing.

At twenty-five minutes past midnight Dayan, Dado, and Maj. Gen. Aharon Yariv entered the room. Their expressions, like ours, indicated the seriousness of the situation, but their manner was quiet and restrained. After Gonen had asked for and received permission to open the conference, he related how, since things had been going well for me, he had given Sharon an order to disengage and move south; but because Sharon's advance was too slow he had been compelled to stop him and divert him for an attack on Missouri and the Chinese Farm. Gonen went on to say that I had had communications difficulties and, it had emerged, I was facing a too-large enemy force. Because the situation was unclear, he had decided to stop Sharon and have him return to his original sector. Gonen continued by indicating what he thought should now be done. His remarks constituted an admission that the attack towards the canal should be called off. Nor, in his view, was it possible to link up with the strong-points or to cross the canal. Instead, he recommended raids on the other side of the Gulf of Suez.

The three division commanders gave their views. Mandler again recommended a concentrated attack with all available forces in a narrow sector as soon as possible, with the aim of getting to the canal and crossing it. Sharon was against basing the assault plan on the seizing of an Egyptian bridge because it was uncertain that it would indeed be seized. At this stage, he went on, we were pretty well deployed; the Egyptians were on open terrain, and we should make plans to cross based on our own bridging gear.

I said that we must not act as we had done that day. The "gung-ho" approach would just not work. I pointed out that a crossing involved a difficult and serious breakthrough to the canal. We must, I repeated, wait, accumulate strength, and carry out a combined operation with artillery, infantry, and air support — with greater caution and better judgment. I dwelled on the difficulties of operating our bridging gear, which was heavy and intended for use from a near to a far bank, whereas now it would have to be dragged in from a considerable distance. I noted that this equipment had never yet undergone any test where it was dragged in from a distance. It would be prudent first to test the gear and train some units in its use. At this stage, I concluded, we were holding our ground firmly, and we should maintain the defensive while gaining strength to prepare for a crossing.

The chief of staff summed up: He had been given an overly optimistic picture in the course of the day. The truth was that since the beginning of the war we had sustained heavy losses, nor was the air force enjoying the freedom of action that we had grown used to. The immediate consequence of this state of affairs was that we could not attack on two fronts simultaneously. Therefore, the attack would continue in the north while the southern front would move to defense. The main problem in the south was to avoid attrition, prevent enemy successes, and at the same time build up strength for returning to the offensive. The divisions were understrength and the men were dead tired, so we would not search for contact with the enemy or initiate combat. If the enemy tried to break through eastward, we would try to contain him without being worn down, as long as we prevented him from breaking through east of the Lateral Road.

Meanwhile, we would try to rest as much as possible, reorganize, repair as many tanks as possible and move in reinforcements, all with the aim of gaining strength for an offensive. Dado concluded by issuing some immediate instructions: Mandler's and Bren's divisions were understrength; Sharon's division was the only one to have sustained virtually no losses, so it was being charged with preparing for a canal-crossing within a day or two in the Port Said-Port Fuad zone. Concluding, Dado reminded those present that the strongpoints should be evacuated, if that was still feasible.

The defense minister wrapped up the discussion by expressing his profound concern that the heavy losses we had suffered would seriously affect the rest of the war. Moreover, he added, the small force in the south — the estimate was about 400 tanks — was the only one between the Egyptian Army and Tel Aviv. We could not expect reinforcement, so it was essential to economize strength.

At the end of the conference, each of us returned to his headquarters knowing that a new phase was beginning, a defensive posture based on avoiding attrition with the hope of gathering force for a canal crossing in the very near future.

Dayan and Dado returned to Tel Aviv, where they took measures to implement the conclusions reached at the conference. Meeting at 0430 hours on 9 October, they decided to give priority to a strategic move aimed at vanquishing Syria. They decided to resume the ground attack and employ most of the air force in the Syrian sector, including strikes deep into that country against its war infrastructure. The defense minister ruled out a crossing in the Port Said-Port Fuad area. Only after Syria's defeat, after we could transfer forces to the south, would we move to a crossing there and a counterattack. These decisions were later brought for cabinet approval and for further deliberation at General Headquarters.

The other issues with which Dayan dealt that day indicate that he had reached a crossroads. So far the war had developed contrary to what we had imagined; but why, and what were the practical implications of this? Dayan had long enjoyed a special standing within the IDF and within the nation. He was the victorious chief of staff in the

1956 Sinai Campaign and the defense minister during the Six Day War eleven years later. While a defense minister is generally expected to have political acumen and strategic insight, Dayan also had the advantage of being an ex-army man who had attained the top position of chief of staff. But even before this appointment and certainly after he became defense minister, Dayan always showed more of an interest in political and strategic issues than in the purely military sphere. As the years passed, he became less and less familiar with the actual running of the armed forces in the field on technical, tactical, and operational levels. He rarely intervened in these matters. When he had to, he relied on intuition. Dayan's lack of confidence regarding operational and tactical matters found expression in his not imposing his own view but couching it as "ministerial counsel," meaning, this is my opinion — take it or leave it, as you wish.

Dayan was known to be very discerning and sober minded, but the events since the outbreak of the war had overturned many of the concepts and assumptions previously presented to him by the IDF's senior command level. He began to have reservations about the General Staff's assessments. Contrary to expectations, the air force was not overcoming the enemy's antiaircraft system, and, likewise, Israeli armor had been unable to thwart the Egyptians' canal crossing. His perception that it was too early to launch a counterattack toward the canal had proved right, and the expectations of the senior commanders concerning the attack of 8 October had proved unrealistic. As a result, Dayan began taking a more pessimistic stance than the chief of staff. He saw the war as difficult and protracted; the IDF must now organize itself for that kind of conflict.

With his tendency to look one step ahead and his desire to draw immediate lessons from what had happened so far, Dayan went on to analyze the events on the southern front: the regular forces had not been deployed in time; the strongpoints had not been evacuated while this was still feasible; on the eighth only one of Southern Command's three divisions had been put into action, and that unsuccessfully. Along with this, GHQ had been fed overly optimistic and misleading data. The conclusion: Gonen was incapable of holding his post; he must be replaced at once.

The chief of staff was not eager to replace Gonen, but under Dayan's pressure it was agreed that he would be replaced by the former chief of staff and the present minister of commerce and industry, Lt. Gen. (Res.) Chaim Bar-Lev. Bar-Lev, who on the evening of 7 October had already been dispatched to the northern front, would now take over command of the southern front. Dado got Dayan's consent that if Gonen so wished, he could stay on as Bar-Lev's deputy.

Dayan brought his second conclusion — a highly pessimistic one — before the prime minister: he suggested that seventeen-year-olds be mobilized and trained and that Israel take urgent steps to procure arms from abroad. Dayan envisaged the possibility that we would have to withdraw well to the rear, to a line more defensible, such as the Sharm el-Sheikh – Santa Katerina – El Arish line. There we would hold on until we had improved the balance of forces, and then "throw the Egyptians back across the canal."

Dayan's picture was indeed gloomy. The prime minister must have been stunned, and many criticized him for having lost his head. In my view, Dayan's line of thought was correct. It was his duty to see that the resources for fighting a war were available, and all indications were that this could well be a long and difficult campaign. But there were more aspects to Dayan's pessimistic outlook. These have to do with his third conclusion: that the nation must be told the truth, or, as he put it, we must "play straight with the people."

Dayan met with the chief editors of the Israeli press and updated them on the fall of the Bar-Lev Line and on the IDF's inability to throw the Egyptians back across the canal in the near future. He was scheduled to go on TV to tell the nation the facts, but the editors, badly jolted by what they had heard, appealed to Prime Minister Meir to prevent Dayan's TV appearance. Recalling Dayan's electric effect on the nation when he was appointed defense minister on the eve of the Six Day War, it is no wonder that the prime minister had him call off his TV appearance. Instead, General Yariv appeared. I believe that, in the long run, hiding the whole truth from the public caused greater harm to national morale and confidence in the leadership than the short-term advantage gained by not revealing the true picture.

Thus it was that as 9 October approached, the fourth day of the war, all the official levels were beginning to understand that we were facing a very difficult and probably protracted war.

CHAPTER SIXTEEN

CONTAINMENT: 9 OCTOBER

I t was 0300 when I returned to my main command post. Since the brigade commanders were situated an hour away from my post, I decided not to call them in but to give my orders and guidelines by radio. My staff updated me. The brigades were still hard at work, reloading ammunition and refueling. This was arduous and drawn out because the supply vehicles were unable to move off the road into the deep sand. The tanks did move close to the road, but jerrycans of fuel and ammunition still had to be carried across the soft sand between the road and the tanks.

I briefed my staff on the decisions that had been reached at Southern Command. The mission was to deploy for defense along the Lateral Road while sending a patrol screen forward to the Artillery Road. Our sector was about 30 km wide, from the Ma'adim Road in the north to the Talisman Road in the south. Since the policy was to refrain from contact with the enemy as far as possible, I decided that we would send a reconnaissance unit forward. We would thus increase the area in which we could carry out a mobile defense by means of shifts backward for the main body until we reached the ridge line just before the Lateral Road; there we would halt for a stubborn defense.

A small part of the 18th Infantry Division, reinforced by the 15th Tank Brigade, and the bulk of the 2nd Infantry Division, reinforced by the 24th Tank Brigade were deployed opposite my sector. My three brigades were deployed in bivouacs on three axes: Natke on the Ma'adim Road with about forty-six tanks, Gabi on the Spontani Road with about twenty-five tanks, Aryeh on the Talisman Road with about forty-eight tanks. The division of the subsectors among them was schematic, i.e., equal in width. I had attached brigades to the reconnaissance units that had been deployed along the Artillery Road since the previous day.

Beginning at 0300 hours we radioed instructions to the brigades, and at 0530 hours we began a slow, cautious advance. I informed the brigade commanders that I wanted to meet with them at 0630 hours at a certain point on the Spontani Road. Until that time Gabi's and Natke's brigades advanced to west of the Artillery Road, but Aryeh, who found the Talisman Road occupied by forces of Sharon's division, encountered rough going in deep dunes.

As vision became better, around 0700, a surprising sight revealed itself to the troops in the center of our sector. About 4-5 km in front of them they saw thousands of Egyptian soldiers feverishly digging ditches, preparing entrenched positions, putting up fences, and laying mines. Trucks were crossing the area to unload mines. There was no such activity on the flanks, i.e., opposite Natke's and Aryeh's brigades.

At first, our sector was quiet. Activity was focused on both our flanks. Giora, the battalion commander who had been left near Qantara the previous day under Magen, reported from there that he had destroyed twenty enemy tanks. There was combat to the south as well. At about 0830 hours contact was made between Sharon's operation officer, Aharon, and his counterpart in my division, Gilad. Aharon radioed that Haim's brigade was attacking Hamutal and that a force from Amnon's brigade was about to break through, via Haim's brigade, and link up with about thirty men from the Purkan Strongpoint who had evacuated that point during the night and had made their way eastward toward our lines.

Aharon, explaining that Sharon's division was encountering difficulties and was apprehensive over its northern flank, requested that we expedite the capture of Halutz. Aryeh's brigade was in fact on its way to Halutz, but they were advancing slowly, with jeeps looking for routes of passage through the deep dunes north of the Talisman Road. Aryeh pointed out that if he were able to use the road it would speed up his advance. Talisman formed the boundary between Sharon's and my own divisional sectors. Both Haim's brigade, from Sharon's division, and Aryeh's brigade, from my division, had bivouacked by the road overnight; and both had made use of the road. Generally when a road is determined as a sector boundary, it is assigned to one of the forces. Following Aryeh's request, I suggested to Gonen that the road be included within my sector. At first Gonen acceded to my request, but at 0900 hours, after he had spoken with Sharon, Gonen changed his mind and stated that the entire road would be in Sharon's sector. I then pointed out to Gonen that whoever has the road should also have the area dominating the road: I therefore suggested that the sector boundary be moved to the dominating ridge line 3–4 km north of Talisman. In the end, Gonen amended the sector boundary in line with my suggestion.

It was now 1000 hours. Gabi and Natke were deployed on the hills near the Artillery Road with no contact between them and the enemy. I decided to move them westward with caution, while preparing to employ the divisional artillery against the Egyptians who were working in front of us. Just as we got under way we came under enemy artillery fire. Since we were to refrain from situations of attrition and from seeking active contact with the enemy, in line with the plan, I ordered Natke to move back close to the Artillery Road; but I did commit Gabi and Aryeh to assist Sharon's division on its northern flank. Gabi reported that he was shelling Halutz and Nozel — the two hills dominating the Tassa-Ismailia axis — and was sending a reconnaissance unit to collect information. Aryeh continued to complain about the difficult terrain of deep and hilly dunes and at 1230 hours I received permission for him to advance along the Tassa-Ismailia Road (Talisman). Natke reported that he was busy extricating and towing away tanks that had been hit the previous day.

Around 1300 hours the relative quiet in my sector ended. Gabi reported that tanks, accompanied by mounted infantry, were moving from the west toward Zrakor and Havraga and that he could overcome them on his own. I was apprehensive, however, since Gabi had just twenty-five tanks dispersed over a broad area — most of them on or south of Havraga and the rest, reinforced by a small reconnaissance unit, on Zrakor. I decided to have Natke move southward close to Gabi's sector, so I issued an order to that effect. Within forty minutes a critical situation had developed. Gabi reported that Egyptian tanks and infantry had moved into areas near him which because of intervening terrain were out of his sight, and they were continuing to pour in forces and advance. Gabi asked for urgent air and artillery support so I gave him all the divisional artillery. I urged Natke to speed up his advance, but he reported he was still 15 km away to the north.

My forward command post, in four armored personnel carriers, was moving along the ridge line trying to avoid coming under artillery fire. I now noticed that Gabi's tanks were firing at enemy tanks from long distances, causing their fire to be ineffective. I told him to let the enemy come closer and then open fire at short range. Gabi replied that the trouble was that the enemy tanks and infantry were very close in "dead" areas. Since the terrain was hilly, there were many such "dead" areas — compartments, as it were, that shielded their occupants from sight. This, combined with the fact that Gabi's force was greatly understrength and spread out over too broad an area to prevent enemy entry from his flank, caused considerable anxiety and led to nervous activity. We were particularly concerned about the Zrakor area, held by only a company. I was afraid that the enemy was preparing for a final assault in the dead areas, so I ordered Gabi to move infantry and reconnaissance units forward in the few armored personnel carriers he had at his disposal. I continued to urge Natke on. I was worried that he would arrive too late; again and again I looked northward, but there was no sign of him.

Tanks and troops of the reconnaissance units at Zrakor were now being hit. There were some signs of disintegration. The commander, Menashe, was wounded and asked permission to withdraw; his deputy took over and continued to fight and hold on. To the left of this unit was Eliashiv's battalion. In a short time two of his company commanders were wounded. Eliashiv was busy briefing the replacement commanders while engaged in combat. Gabi ordered Eliashiv to reinforce the reconnaissance unit on Zrakor with a tank platoon. To Eliashiv's left, Ze'ira's battalion was embattled. Within one and a half hours nine of Eliashiv's tanks were hit, and the situation grew increasingly grim.

Finally at 1430 hours, the possibility of a shift in the course of the fighting arose. On the hills to our north we saw Natke's tanks, climbing carefully. In front of them was a confusing battlefield picture. Amid all the smoke and dust and with all the tanks moving about and firing, it was hard to tell which were ours and which the enemy's. Procedures for radio link-up began; we were still not as practiced in this as we would be later, so the process was lengthy and irritating. Each of our units was as concerned about being hit by our own tanks as about being hit by the enemy. When the radio link-up was at last completed and, in its wake, identification in the field made, Natke deployed his force on Zrakor and, gradually, also between there and Havraga.

Now our fighting intensified. The enemy broke and retreated. Gonen radioed to warn us not to pursue the enemy toward Lexicon; I did not see the sense of such a warning. I had not intended a pursuit. We could not tell yet how badly we had been hurt. Two things, however, were clear. In front of us, on the slopes of Zrakor hill, there had been fighting at close quarters. We had inflicted heavy losses on the enemy, and he was in retreat. Secondly, Gabi's reports made it clear that our ammunition was rapidly running out.

At 1500 we saw new Egyptian concentrations in front of us, and at 1555, a second assault began. I had reinforced Gabi, on Havraga, with a company from Natke's brigade, but I wanted to create conditions that would enable me to support Gabi with Aryeh's brigade. This was now also my only uncommitted brigade. I had ordered Aryeh to take Halutz and then open up the Hazizit Road, but he explained that in order to get to Hazizit he would have to take Nozel, which dominated the area. I gave my approval, but Gonen intervened and forbade it.

The entire area was now under a heavy artillery barrage that lasted for about an hour. Then Katyusha rockets began exploding all around us, landing in bursts with a terrific impact, forming craters 1 meter wide and 2 meters deep. When the Katyusha attack ended, we found ourselves under renewed artillery shelling that produced a thick pall of phosphorous right across the sector. Apprehensive that the smoke, which was obscuring the entire area, would cause intense anxiety among the troops, I at once radioed the brigade commanders: "Make sure that the men are not upset by the smoke. Get them all into position and have them keep their eyes open. The enemy might launch a charge under the smoke cover or he might be using it to disengage.''

During the barrage I continued to move about on the ridge line with the four armored vehicles of the forward command post, trying to stay clear, but the shells seemed to be pursuing me. I wasn't sure that my dodging about made any sense, but I kept moving.

Two or three times we passed Gabi's forward command group, also in armored vehicles and also moving about trying to avoid being hit. Through the pillars of smoke I could see, though only from time to time, tanks, armored personnel carriers, and half-tracks among my troops. Was it possible? Under such heavy, brutal — murderous, in fact — shelling, we were still moving in the field. Would the men be able to withstand the pressure, or should I order a withdrawal? After all, our mission enabled us to delay the enemy by pulling back. But no, we would not withdraw. If we had already managed to seize the ridge line west of the Artillery Road — a position of vital importance — it would be a mistake to withdraw. Enemy artillery would reach us even in our fall-back position; the enemy charge as yet had not approached us closely.

At about 1600 the shelling ceased and we had a brief lull. When the smoke lifted, we saw no close enemy troops opposite Havraga. But opposite Zrakor, Natke's tanks continued to exchange fire with the enemy at a distance of 2,000 meters. Reports indicated that four enemy tanks had been hit, while a few of our tanks had taken direct hits from the heavy shelling. Gabi and Natke reported that they thought the enemy had quit the area. Meanwhile, I reimposed order among our forces, dividing the sector with Natke concentrating his troops on Zrakor and from Zrakor to Havraga and Gabi concentrating on Havraga and southward. A number of units went back to refuel directly from tankers that had been moved up to the rear slope of the ridge line, near the Artillery Road, about 2 km from the front line.

But we were unaware of a very important development. Under cover of the artillery barrage, the enemy had moved considerable numbers of infantry forward. They were now hastily digging in, in the dead areas very close to Zrakor and in the valley between there and Havraga. They were in fact waiting to launch the final charge of the day, which would begin at 1700.

At 1625 Gabi's observation points reported indications of a concentration of forces as a prelude to a new attack. Then they reported an Egyptian advance eastward. I told Gabi and Natke to hold their fire and let the enemy draw close. I also asked HQ for air support. At 1655 hours our forces came under another massive artillery barrage — though this one was shorter in duration — followed again by a volley of Katyusha rockets. Gabi and Natke reported that the area was swarming with enemy troops. What had happened was that the troops who had been concealed opposite Zrakor and between Zrakor and Havraga approached to head the new assault. The whole area was now covered with charging enemy forces — their third attack that day.

Excited messages began coming over the radio net that there were gaps and disruptions in our deployment. Many of our tanks had moved back to refuel and take on new ammunition, then came the order to break off that activity and rush forward into battle. Again the same phenomenon occurred, tanks moved forward under shelling and in front of them more of our tanks along with Egyptian tanks and armored personnel carriers, all at close range. The battlefield seemed to seethe with activity, and the fog of battle made it difficult to know what was happening. The radio net was alive with nervous exchanges trying to clarify who was on the left, who was on the right, which tanks were ours, which were the enemy's and where were the forces who were on the flank? Interspersed among a stream of calls and appeals asking me to ascertain that our troops did not fire at each other came reports of the enemy being hit, of us being hit by the enemy, and requests for evacuation of wounded men. Aryeh again suggested taking Nozel and joining battle from the south, but again Southern Command said no.

Meanwhile our planes came over and began releasing their bombs. At once came a cry from Natke: "Bren! Stop them! They're bombing too close to my troops!"

And Gabi: "I see tanks moving behind me — whose are they?" And again: "Many tanks moving on the road behind me — whose are they?"

I replied: "Wait. I don't know. We'll find out." I sent Dovik to the road to see what was going on and to send every tank there into the fray. Dovik found that these were tanks that were returning after being fueled. I ordered a halt to all resupply operations and had the brigades send runners to direct all the newly advancing tanks into position.

At 1730 hours the enemy attack hit a crisis point. Silence. Now calmer reports of enemy retreat came over the radio. Suddenly Gabi's voice, weary and complaining, came over the radio: "I don't remember when the war started or how many days we've been fighting already — don't we have a picture of what is going on? What's happening north of us? What's happening with our neighbors to the south? Where are the Egyptians? How far did they get? What is the IDF holding? What's the situation on the northern front? Can we get some information? Can someone tell us where we are and what's with us?"

I don't know why but of all the messages I received during the war, this one made the deepest impression on me. I was profoundly affected. All at once it dawned on me that Gabi and his men had gone into battle one day earlier than the rest of us. This was the fourth day without sleep, the fourth day of desperate fighting in one continuous battle for their lives. They hadn't had a second to think about anything beyond what they were doing in order to survive. Suddenly I thought of the hundreds of tank men who for the past few days had seen nothing but what was visible through their periscopes — a narrow field of vision filled with masses of Egyptian soldiers in tanks and armored vehicles and swarms of enemy infantry, all charging at them while they kept firing and firing, and still the enemy kept coming. Gabi's outburst surely reflected their collective question: What's going on here? When will it all end?

Why had I not thought of this myself, I wondered. I contacted all stations and informed them that I would soon broadcast a kind of news bulletin that was to be passed on via the radio nets until every last soldier had heard it. I then called Southern Command to get updated on what was transpiring on the rest of the southern front and on the northern front. Within a half-hour I broadcast a bulletin to the brigade commanders. This news service became a daily thing. It may not have been too detailed or accurate, but it did give the men some sort of picture of what the situation was beyond their own immediate battle zone.

Towards nightfall we were shelled again, and this time phosphorescent smoke covered the area adjacent to the canal, apparently to hide the Egyptians' activity there, and flares lit up the sky. This same procedure repeated itself in the days to come and became the sign that another day of fighting was ending.

It was now 1745. I decided it was time to disengage the brigades so they could reorganize. We still had a lot to do to prepare for continuation of the fighting: replenishment, repair of tanks, reorganization of units and subunits, assigning new commanders to replace those who had been hit, drawing lessons from this first day of containment, and planning the next day's fighting. To prevent the enemy's monitoring any orders to pull back, I radioed hints to the effect that we would repeat the previous evening's "exercise." Then I made arrangements to have our sector's contact line held by outposts of armored infantry that were to be reinforced by tank squads and deployed at the junctions of the Spontani and Ma'adim roads with the Artillery Road. The brigades would do their reorganizing at the same places they had on the previous night. Gilad, who had helped me throughout the day in controlling and coordinating the forces, now relieved me. Standing beside him, I could rest a bit as he moved the troops back, coordinated their movement, and ascertained that they would secure themselves, both while on the move and around the bivouacs.

Traffic moved slowly in the total darkness; many tanks, armored personnel carriers, and half-tracks were towing disabled vehicles. Convoys carrying fuel, ammunition, food, and water were waiting in the rear. The bivouacs were prepared by about 2230 hours, but there were various signs of lax discipline among the troops. Here and there bonfires had been lit in the bivouacs. I was acquainted with this phenomenon. The unavoidable noise that accompanies refilling, maintenance, and repair of vehicles persuades the men that the lighting of fires in addition to all the noise cannot make a difference. I had to act vigorously via the radio nets to pull the troops back into line and reimpose night discipline. This was a warning symptom of the kind of negligence that manifests itself in the ranks when fighting is difficult and protracted. We will have to be on guard, I thought to myself. I would take the matter up with the brigade commanders later that night.

The logistical nets were now very active, which meant that the work of reorganization was proceeding apace. My forward command post stopped close by the bivouacs so we could get the feel of the pace of activity among the units. The bivouacs hummed with activity. Crewmen were carrying jerrycans of fuel and rounds of ammunition while the sound of hammering attested to the repairing of vehicles. The tanks were parked close to one another, and I could see the guards and the security set up around the bivouacs.

To backtrack at bit — from around noontime, Natke's and Gabi's brigades had been engaged in combat and had come under artillery shelling, while Aryeh's brigade had been separated from the divisional zone of operations. Deep and virtually impassable dunes were cutting him off from the rest of the division. The only way he could move quickly into our zone was directly north via the Artillery Road (Hazizit). As will be recalled, at 1530 hours I had ordered Aryeh to capture Nozel — which dominated the road — but Gonen had intervened, forbidding the attack on either Halutz or Nozel. Consequently, I told Aryeh to advance and put pressure on Nozel, while searching for a bypass into our sector. From 1545, Aryeh began improving his position in front of him and exchanging fire with Nozel.

Meanwhile, at 1625 hours, when there was another Egyptian attack against Natke and Gabi, I pressed Aryeh to join in, and he asked for air support against Nozel. Again Gonen intervened, this time through intermediate radio stations, to forbid the capture of Halutz and Nozel. I replied that I was perplexed by this ban, because Nozel, and even more so Halutz, constituted a "wedge" on the Artillery Road that was preventing the linkage of our forces.

But Gonen said: "I want containment, not attack!" At about 1700 hours there was a third attack in Natke's and Gabi's sector. I pressed Aryeh to find a route to our sector without attacking Nozel or Halutz. I had to reiterate to him that there was no approval for an attack. Finally, as darkness began to fall, I ordered Aryeh to pull back in order to reorganize and bivouac for the night.

In order to understand the series of prohibitions that prevented Aryeh from attacking Nozel and thus joining in the division's fighting, we must see what was happening in the sector of the adjacent division.

I learned of the events of 9 October in the other sectors and at

Southern Command only after the war. Parallel to the Egyptian 2nd Division's attempts to advance in my sector by an attack of a mechanized brigade reinforced by a tank battalion, they also attacked to our south. Before they could get their attack under way, however, Sharon attacked them. Sharon's sector extended from the Talisman Road in the north to Kishuf in the south. He also had a small force at Hurva, further yet to the south, on the ridge line opposite the center of Bitter Lake. Sharon did not content himself with the containment mission he had been given. When he returned to his sector the previous night from Southern Command HQ, he had already planned attacks to be launched in his sector. Haim's brigade was to capture Hamutal, Tuvia was to plan the capture of Machshir, and Amnon was told to prepare to rescue the men of Strongpoint Purkan, who would then make their way toward our lines. The thirty-three men of Purkan had left their strongpoint in coordination with Sharon and were to wait at a point 1 km west of the junction of the Hazizit and Talisman roads; the link-up with them was, by the plan, integrated in the attack on Hamutal.

With morning, Haim's brigade attacked Hamutal — with Shimon's battalion deployed as a base of fire from the east; Giora's battalion assaulting on the road and moving under minor resistance toward Nozel; and Ami's battalion charging at the southwestern section of Hamutal, the same strongly held part of the objective where our forces had run into difficulties on the previous day. About a minute after Ami announced, "I have taken the objective," his troubles began. The fighting against the tanks that operated from the west port of Hamutal and from Machshir was relatively easy, but the fighting against the entrenched infantry and the antitank missile launchers was far more complicated. Ami's armored infantry had been left behind because the terrain was impassable for half-tracks. He got artillery support, but that was not enough. The men fought bravely, charging at the enemy infantry in the trenches, but the Egyptians did not turn and run. After the tanks had passed them, they stood up again and fired at them from behind. Casualties mounted rapidly; all three company commanders as well as platoon leaders, tank commanders, and crewmen were hit. Even the battalion commander's tank was hit. The brigade commander approved a withdrawal which the battalion carried out while evacuating casualties. Of twenty-four tanks, only seven were not hit. Three were abandoned at the objective while the rest were able to withdraw.

While the battle was raging, a small force of two tanks and four armored personnel carriers from Amnon's brigade moved along Talisman Road near Hamutal. They were to evacuate the men of Strongpoint Purkan, so they bypassed Nozel from the west and found the waiting soldiers. Three of the force's armored vehicles were hit on the way, so the battalion commander, Shaul Shalev, continued to advance on his own, loaded all thirty-three men of Purkan onto his tank and made it back with them. Who would have believed that over thirty men could find room on one tank? Indeed, the astonished men who remained near Nozel would experience a few tense minutes until they were able to grasp that the advancing "monster" was a troop-covered tank.

There were now two battalions opposite Nozel: Giora's and Shimon's, the latter having joined Giora after completing its task of supporting Ami from a base of fire. Haim suggested taking Nozel, but Sharon would not approve this. Shimon's battalion pulled out the casualties from the three armored vehicles of Amnon's brigade.

At about 0730, while Ami was fighting on Hamutal, Sharon gave the order to capture Machshir, and Tuvia moved a tank battalion forward to take it from the east. The approach from this direction was very difficult because of deep dunes, and the situation was made still more difficult by enemy artillery fire. The advance was disrupted, with the battalion commander among those hit. The deputy brigade commander was dispatched to replace him, but he, too, was hit. The attack had failed.

Two tank battalions of Haim's brigade were west of Hamutal, a tank battalion from Tuvia's brigade was stopped east of Machshir, and now the Egyptians attacked. At about 0930 hours some sixty tanks from the Egyptian 14th Tank Brigade advanced toward Hamadia, which was being defended by a battalion from Tuvia's brigade. Artillery fire was directed at the Egyptians, and this separated the advancing tanks from the armored personnel carriers that had slowed down. The battalion let the Egyptian force draw closer, took up positions, and within an hour had hit thirty-five enemy tanks with a loss of just two tanks on our side. At 1030 hours the enemy retreated westward.

Following this success, Sharon proposed launching an attack

across a broad zone with two brigades toward Televizia, Missouri, and Amir. Sharon's notion was contrary to the decision on a containment posture adopted the previous evening, and now an argument broke out between Sharon and Gonen. Gonen told him not to launch an attack, but Sharon said he wanted to maintain contact with the retreating enemy. In the end Gonen agreed that Sharon could "tail" the enemy as long as he was on the move but would halt when the enemy stopped to take up firing positions. However, over four hours would elapse before this "pursuit" began, so that it's hard to view it as tailing.

Sharon sent his deputy, Jackie, to supervise Tuvia's attack. At 1500 hours Tuvia ordered an attack from east to west. One of his battalions, which had failed in the attack on Machshir, now wanted to join the brigade by flanking Machshir from the north. The other two battalions began moving, one from Hamadia toward Televizia, the other from Kishuf toward Missouri. The southernmost battalion was the only one to escape almost unscathed. The northernmost battalion, which was seeking to bypass Machshir, came under a vicious Sagger missile attack while it was between Hamutal and Machshir. Thirteen tanks were hit, and seven of them were left behind. Some of the wounded were evacuated, but twelve men were declared missing in action. The battalion that was moving south of Machshir, toward Televizia, also came under a missile attack. Four tanks were hit and the battalion commander was among the casualties. His deputy took over and continued the assault to a point west of Televizia, but by then Sharon had already ordered a pullback. All told, Tuvia's brigade that day sustained twenty-five tanks hit, thirteen of which were left behind on enemy-held territory.

While Tuvia was attacking westward, Sharon deployed Amnon's brigade in Tuvia's sector. When Tuvia's attack was halted, at 1630 hours, Sharon ordered Amnon to attack in a broad zone on both sides of Akavish Road. The attack was launched at twilight. One battalion attacked from Hamadia toward Televizia. The battalion commander, Shaul Shalev, was killed; but the battalion captured Televizia and consolidated itself there. Four tanks of the other battalion that was moving from Kishuf toward Akavish were hit by missiles. The battalion halted and eventually returned to Kishuf.

South of Akavish Road, however, things took a different turn. There in the Grafit area an armored reconnaissance unit, commanded by Lieutenant Colonel Yoav, made its way westward. To their surprise, they encountered no enemy forces. They reached Lexicon Road and soon Bitter Lake; turning north, they advanced to Strongpoint Lakekan and from there to the Lexicon-Nahleh junction, which was quite close to Strongpoint Matzmed. It was already dark when Sharon heard of the reconnaissance unit's course of advance and present location. He contacted Gonen and suggested leaving the unit where it was and making preparations for a canal crossing the following morning. Gonen spoke with the chief of staff, who opposed the idea. Gonen now ordered Sharon to have the unit withdraw to Kishuf, but Sharon did not give up. Once again he tried to convince Gonen that a golden opportunity would be lost. After Gonen had again contacted the chief of staff, he ordered Sharon, at 1920 hours, to withdraw the unit and deploy in line with containment forces on the front line but with the bulk of the troops held in reserve at Tassa. With a heavy heart Sharon ordered his unit back, though it did not in fact return until the following morning.

The Egyptians' intention for 9 October was to complete the consolidation of their bridgehead up to the Artillery Road and to advance along the Gulf of Suez toward Ras-Sudar. The Egyptians' advance was contained in my sector and in Sharon's, but they were more successful in Mandler's sector, south of Sharon's.

Mandler had 145 tanks organized in three brigades: Dan's tank brigade, deployed on the Artillery Road in the Mitla area; Avraham's tank brigade, on the Artillery Road in the Gidi area; and Biro's mechanized brigade, deployed as a second line at the entrances to the Gidi and Mitla passes. The Egyptian attempts to attack toward the Gidi Pass were blocked, but they gained successes in the Mitla sector. Dan's brigade came under heavy pressure from the Egyptian 7th Infantry Division. Despite his destroying some 20 enemy tanks, Dan retreated, enabling the Egyptians to take the highest terrain in the dunes of the southern sector, Qarat Moura (Polygon), and to cut off the Artillery Road by holding it near Notsa.

At about 1410 hours some 20 tanks and 10 armored personnel carriers of the Egyptian 1st Mechanized Brigade moved toward Ras-Sudar. (By then, that sector had already been transferred from the responsibility of Southern Command to that of the Southern Sinai District under the command of the former Commander of Southern

Command, Maj. Gen. (Res.) Yeshaya Gavish. A force of paratroopers was deployed in the Ras-Sudar zone. North of there, about 8 km south of Ayun Mousa, a small task force made up of a reconnaissance unit along with a few tanks, some recoilless guns and a battery of 120mm mortars. This force blocked the Egyptians causing them to withdraw with losses. As the Egyptians advanced, they left the shelter of their antiaircraft missile umbrella. Now, as they retreated, Israeli Air Force planes attacked them, adding to their losses. The Egyptian breakthrough attempt failed.

Gonen and his HQ dealt with three main matters on 9 October: running the containment battle, organizing Southern Command's logistical rear zone, and planning the crossing operation in the Port Said-Port Fuad area. Conducting the containment fighting was no simple matter. As early as the morning Gonen's impression had been that Sharon was deviating from the operational policy which had been decided upon. The reports on the fighting at Hamutal and Machshir indicated that Sharon's division was attacking and being worn down. When Sharon sought to attack again on a broad front, after he had repulsed the Egyptian attack toward Hamadia, Gonen refused to give his approval. At 1315 hours Gonen ordered Sharon not to attack but only to maintain contact with the enemy from a distance. Ben-Ari repeated this order at 1332 hours. At 1345 hours, apparently apprehensive that Sharon did not intend to abide by his guidelines, Gonen flew by helicopter to Sharon's sector. Gonen later explained that at 1520 hours he found Sharon was attacking toward Televizia and Missouri, contrary to what had been concluded between them. By then, Tuvia's brigade had already been hit hard and had lost many men and tanks. Sharon acceded to Gonen's directions and ordered a withdrawal.

About this same time and apparently under the influence of his experience with Sharon's sector, Gonen ordered me not to allow Natke to pursue the enemy westward. Shortly thereafter he refused to permit Aryeh to capture Nozel. Later, at about 1730 hours, he ordered Sharon to halt Amnon's attack toward Missouri and Akavish and at the same time he again forbade Aryeh to attack Nozel. Between 1720 and 1830 hours, Gonen was getting Sharon to withdraw the reconnaissance unit from the Lexicon-Nahleh junction.

Gonen in fact worked hard to carry out the directive to refrain from an initiated attack. Nonetheless, Sharon launched an attack early in the morning and continued to attack from noontime until evening, despite Gonen's consistent opposition. It was on that day that a rift began to develop between the two.* Gonen also prevented me from having Aryeh attack Nozel and Halutz. In my case, I wanted to attack only to create a tactical situation whereby Aryeh's brigade could join the division's defensive battle. Fortunately, we were able to throw back the Egyptian attacks without Aryeh, but I could not know this during the battle and I wanted to develop the option to employ all my available forces flexibly.

The picture on the southern front was not especially encouraging following the first day of defense. In general we had managed to contain the enemy — except for their successes in Mandler's sector — but the rate of attrition was too great, largely due to Sharon's attacks. Eighty tanks were hit that day in containment battles, fifteen of them in my division, but those remained in our territory and would be repaired. Sharon's division lost about fifty tanks, eighteen of which were left behind in enemy-held territory; most of the fifty were hit in the course of attacks.

There is a difference between the attacks carried out by Sharon on 9 October and my attacks the previous day. I had been pushed to attack, unwillingly and under pressure from HQ very soon after my arrival at the front and before my artillery had arrived. Sharon, on the other hand, initiated his attacks contrary to the aims of Southern Command and GHQ, in a sector he had been familiar with since 7 October. But he had more time to organize and had more forces and artillery support. Nevertheless, there are similarities between the attacks of 8 October and 9 October. Both days saw attacks by single battalions, without sufficient concentration of forces or sufficient field intelligence.**

It is difficult to understand either the logic behind Sharon's at-

---

*Gonen submitted a formal complaint against Sharon over this affair. It was decided that the Agranat Commission of Inquiry would investigate the complaint, but under the influence of the Defence Minister at the time Shimon Peres (after the resignation of Golda Meir government in the spring of 1974) Gonen withdrew the complaint.

**It is in fact surprising how much has been said and written about the eighth of October and how little about the ninth, despite the serious results — in terms of losses of both men and equipment — of the ninth. Why the Agranat Commission decided not to look into the events of the ninth, it alone knows.

tacks or his failure to learn from others' experience the previous day. There may have been some point to the attack on the eastern extremity of Hamutal in order to allow the passage of Amnon's force to rescue the men of Strongpoint Purkan, but there is no comprehending the attacks on Machshir, Televizia, and Missouri. I have nothing to say against the reconnaissance unit's penetration all the way to Bitter Lake. On the contrary, this is the classic task of reconnaissance, and, as long as it was carried out in line with the policy of noncombat, it was fine. However, I believe that Sharon was misguided and impractical in his demand that the force be left where it was and that troops and equipment be quickly assembled for a crossing operation the next morning.*

Fortunately the reconnaissance unit moved from Kishuf to Bitter Lake as twilight was approaching, and no columns of dust were raised due to the sand dunes. Thus unnoticed by the enemy, the unit discovered the open "seam" between the Egyptian Second and Third Armies. This was invaluable intelligence for the subsequent crossing operation. It would have been a critical mistake to accept Sharon's demand and leave the unit at the site before conditions were ripe for a crossing.

Even as Southern Command was rejecting any immediate crossing near Matzmed, it was busy planning just such an operation for the Port Said–Port Fuad zone. Magen was charged with this task around noontime, but there really did not seem to be sufficient forces to carry out the mission. In the evening, Magen was flown to Southern Command HQ in order to plan the mission jointly with the staff there, but the deputy chief of staff, who also arrived at Umm-Hashiba, canceled the operation.

At noon on 9 October, Maj. Gen. Menachem Meron arrived at Southern Command HQ in order to organize the defense and the administration of the rear zone in Sinai. Responsibility for the rear had rested with the regular Sinai Division, but when war broke out Southern Command assumed responsibility. Now General Meron, by making this a separate command, would help restore order in the field. Placed at General Meron's disposal were T-54 and T-55 tanks

---

*The reader will be able to grasp the full complexity of the preparations necessary for a crossing operation in Part IV Chapter 27.

captured in 1967. Not many days would pass before the seed that was sown in the rear of the front would sprout a divisionlike military formation that would take its place on the battlefield.

The first day of containment and defense had ended. Some 80 of the 400 tanks that had begun the day had been hit. According to the reports, a similar number of enemy tanks were casualties. Even as the fighting raged along the entire front line, reserve units kept arriving. This night, too, would be devoted to work.

CHAPTER SEVENTEEN

10 October: THE SECOND DAY OF DEFENSE

Thirty minutes past midnight, October 10. Officers were assembling in the war room tent for briefing and orders. The atmosphere was unique: on a bench opposite the large operations map sat the three brigade commanders, meeting after forty-eight hours of bitter fighting and ninety-six hours without sleep. Behind them were the staff, standing behind them were the liaison officers. When I saw the faces of those assembled, I suddenly felt that invisible threads of fate bound me to these men, especially to the brigade commanders. Together we commanded, together we were responsible for a sector — a front only 25 km wide, true, but each of us knew full well whose fate was at stake if the front were breached in that sector. I felt very close to them, and though nothing was said, I knew that they felt the same way. Our emotions were intensified by the seriousness of the situation. We were all very tired and burdened with problems of combat and logistics, and ultimately, with the questions of life and death.

I looked at the brigade commanders: grimy, unshaven, with bloodshot eyes and hoarse voices. The only one to manage a weak smile was Natke. They reported on their day of fighting. They seemed to have changed in the past two days, to be harder. Their reports were serious, their views on what should be done well thought out —

though Natke added a bit of spice, "Today only two of my tanks were hit. If you manage to get me back to Giora's battalion (which had been left in Magen's sector), I know we'll screw them tomorrow until the smoke comes out."

A thought crossed my mind: what was Natke doing here anyhow? I had known him for years, having seen him in many assignments since he joined my battalion as a young officer on the eve of the 1956 Sinai Campaign. He stood out among the officers of the Armored Corps as zestful, full of life, someone who knew how to have a good time. At officers' parties his clear, infectious laughter would gale across the room. In the Six Day War of 1967, he was seriously wounded in both legs while serving as a tank battalion commander. He spent months at Tel-Hashomer Hospital, underwent about twenty operations, but his left leg seemed incurably infected. I helped Natke and his wife, Drora, with the various problems they encountered because of the new reality they had to cope with.

They had put in a request that he be sent to Switzerland for further treatment after he had despaired that his infection could be overcome in Israel. I spoke with the IDF's chief medical officer who at first opposed the idea on the grounds that the medical level in Israel was among the highest in the world and that it was precisely in treating war casualties that Israel had accumulated considerable experience. Finally, however, he agreed with me that "the customer is always right."

Natke was sent to Switzerland and returned walking on both legs, though with the help of a cane. As he came off the plane he said to me, "In three months you'll see me dancing!" This I took as the kind of jest that typified his courage. He had lost the kneecap of his right leg, and the leg was fixed in a permanent stiff position. To move his right leg forward as he walked, he had to raise himself on the toes of his left foot and move his stiff right leg in a wide semicircular motion. His lameness was very pronounced. Nor was his left leg strong, as a metal pin had been inserted in it.

Our problem was an acute one: what next? He was badly crippled, and his future as a commanding officer seemed doubtful at best. I suggested that he become an instructor in the Command and Staff College, having in mind that initially we would reabsorb him in a military environment and then gradually prepare him for rehabilitation and retirement. Three months later Natke could be seen dancing happily — not that his legs had healed, but he just wanted to physically express his outlook on life: "Yes, I was wounded and my legs aren't what they were, but what's done is done, and I won't let my way of life be changed just because of that."

Natke's main strength before he was wounded lay in instruction and in assignments in the field. He was not the staff officer type. After a time, he became a "troublemaker," coming to see me time and again in personal interviews, asking to be made commander of an armored brigade in Sinai. This was in the midst of the War of Attrition, when brigade commanders came under frequent shellings while supervising our strongpoints and had to run into shelters. I admired his will power, but I thought it would be irresponsible on my part to accede to his request. We had long arguments — some of them far from pleasant — but not only could I not conceive giving him a brigade in Sinai, I could not even imagine making him commander of a reserve brigade. It seemed to me that to assign an officer who was restricted in his personal mobility to a command post on the battlefield was to act cruelly toward that officer, even if he wanted the assignment.

Finally he won. I compromised with myself and offered him command of a reserve brigade. To tell the truth, I took this decision thinking that war was nowhere in sight. Chances were, I thought, that within two years Natke would complete his tour of duty and retire. Of course I was mistaken, not only concerning the possibility of a war, but also regarding Natke's ability to command despite everything. Now I glanced at him: he was short, broad-shouldered, had a round open face, piercing green eyes, straight short hair supposedly combed to the side but which kept falling over his brow, and his expression exuded confidence. Even now it seemed to me that his report tended to the optimistic side and that he was with difficulty trying to conceal his natural cheerfulness and seeking to lend his report a serious tone.

Having consulted with my staff officers earlier, I now issued orders to the brigade commanders, completing the plan for the next day's fighting. We had returned to our bivouacs with 120 tanks, and according to the report by the ordnance officer we could expect to start the day with 130 tanks. We had also been assigned an armored infantry battalion, commanded by Lieutenant Colonel Baruchi, that was already deployed in safeguarding the line of contact at night. Our mission had not changed, nor had the division of the subsectors between Gabi and Natke. Natke would hold the area of the Artillery Road on both sides of the Ma'adim Road, and Gabi would be around Havraga and Zrakor. What was new had to do with Aryeh's brigade, which I hoped would increase our strength. This plan was for Aryeh to move back before dawn along the Talisman Road, then move on the Spontani Road, and deploy, as the divisional reserve, at a point north of the Spontani Road 5 km from the front line. In addition, the last of our artillery pieces had arrived the previous day so that now, on 10 October, we would have at our disposal several 155mm howitzer batteries, 160mm heavy mortars and 120mm mortars — all told, forty pieces.

Moving, now, to my briefing and referring to the bonfires I had seen at some of the bivouacs, I dwelt on the danger that lay in forego- ing the standards we had set ourselves during training exercises. Ex- haustion, I noted, was causing a slackening of standards, with the result that not everything was being properly seen to. I warned that we were only at the beginning of the war and that many difficulties still faced us — and woe to us, the commanders, if we were unable to maintain strict operational and professional discipline. I was not sure, I said, whether the hits our tanks had taken today were not to some extent due to the neglect of professional standards. I urged the commanders to speed up the restocking process, so that the tank crewmen would have time to sleep. The meeting broke up with the brigade commanders returning to their sectors. At best, I thought, they would be able to catch an hour's sleep.

At 0330 hours (10 October) I called all my commanders over the command net: "All 'karish' stations: Commanders to microphone for orders! Over!" We were about to begin our fifth day of fighting and our second of defense. In the last two hours reports had come in from our forward screening units concerning various noises and movement in their sector. These forward forces were very small, and we feared that the enemy might advance during the night and seize footholds on our ridge line.

"Natke here, over . . . Gabi here, over . . . Aryeh here, over. . . ."

The division's commanding officers had a "wrist coder." This was a device made of leather and transparent plastic that contained a card listing useful terms of IDF jargon, and alongside them the code words for them. The coder was strapped to the left wrist, like a watch, and allowed officers to refer to it at their convenience during radio communication. I wanted to remind them that they had to look at the appropriate code for the day. But by then I had pretty well lost track of the days and so, probably, had my comrades. So I thought of preceding my order with a reminder of the day and the date. I then radioed, echoing the way in which Israel Radio opened its broadcasts each day: "This is Wednesday, the tenth of October. This is the day on which the Levites in the Temple would chant . . . ". (Here would follow the opening verse of the relevant Psalm.) So far I was quoting from memory, and I then shifted to more immediate matters but retaining a Biblical style: "With care you shall move to positions in your sector, and you shall see to your men, and should the enemy come you shall strike him cunningly. Over . . . ". I can imagine that such a broadcast would cause a few smiles, and perhaps a little astonishment. From that morning on I opened every new day of fighting with a similar broadcast in ancient Biblical style, but the content, of course, was adapted to the particular mission at hand. When the cease-fire finally came into effect, on 25 October, and I no longer opened the daily radio contacts with that kind of message, Natke came over the net to ask: "And what happened to the Levites in the Temple today?"

Natke and Gabi took their positions on the front line — the ridge line — at 0600 hours. By 0700 hours I finished briefing Aryeh, who had just arrived in our sector with his brigade. I informed Gabi and Natke that Aryeh was reconnoitering on their flanks. Now the Egyptians were shelling our ridge line, and we replied with artillery fire directed at a lower ridge line, some 3–5 km in front of us. Here we could see the Egyptians laying mines and digging in. Gabi reported that Sagger-launching infantry troops were moving on his southern flank. Dovik, who was scanning the area from a helicopter, reported that he could see Egyptian infantry troops infiltrating into the empty area between Natke and Gabi. I ordered Natke to expand westward and southward in order to close the gap, but now Gabi said Egyptian infantry was moving toward Zrakor. The sector was in fact too broad for us. I asked Gonen for a battalion of armored infantry that would patrol and block the Artillery Road behind the ridge line we were holding. Gabi now reported that Egyptian tanks were following the infantry by advancing into the dead areas near Zrakor; they were forming for an attack.

At 0950 hours the Egyptian assault began: one infantry battalion accompanied by a tank battalion opposite Zrakor and an attack of the same strength toward Havraga. Natke reported that his sector was quiet. Gabi's brigade had fewer than thirty tanks along with a reconnaissance unit consisting of two platoons of armored infantry. I therefore decided to move two of Aryeh's battalions forward to Gabi's southern flank, between Havraga and Halutz, in order to attack the enemy on his flank. At 1015 hours Gabi was under heavy pressure; he had hit some enemy tanks, but some of his tanks had also been hit. From the helicopter, Dovik said he thought the Zrakor defense was too weak, and he recommended moving Natke closer. Although there were no enemy forces visible in Natke's sector, I hesitated to evacuate it completely, so I told Natke to leave one battalion in his sector and move toward Zrakor with another battalion.

At 1022 Gabi said that the Egyptian attack from the direction of Haviva was at its height, and he was taking hits as the enemy advanced. I ordered Aryeh to dispatch his third battalion into the area between Zrakor and Havraga. At 1040 there was a salvo of Katyusha rockets followed by phosphorous shells, which, as we already knew, was their signal for an assault. Problems arose in the division: Aryeh, who was on Gabi's left, moved too far and encountered orientation difficulties. The hilly terrain with its many dead areas together with the constant firing and smoke, made identification of forces difficult. I had Dovik hover close to Aryeh in the helicopter and direct him. Gabi radioed that the entry of Nahum's battalion had created a crowded situation on Zrakor. When Natke reached the zone he, too, reported that it was overcrowded and that he preferred to wait on the side.

I realized I had made a mistake by moving forces in response to the enemy's threats without first regrouping. I should have attached Nahum's battalion to Gabi's brigade. I tried to bring about a quick regrouping via the communications nets, but it was too late. All the forces were already heavily engaged at short range against tanks and against thousands of infantry troops who were firing Sagger missiles as they charged our tanks. We took some hits, and the radio nets were "hyper-nervous." However, I did manage to bring Nahum into Gabi's net and divide the sector between Gabi and Aryeh, with the Haviva Road marking the boundary between them.

At 1100 Gabi reported that he had repulsed the attack on Havraga; many enemy tanks were burning, with some of ours hit too. But north, in the broad valley between Havraga and Zrakor, a fierce battle was under way. In front of Nahum's crews, at ranges from 80 to 2,000 meters, the entire area was swarming with charging Egyptian infantry. Enemy tanks tried to move in from the flanks, but our scout jeeps situated on high ground and on the flanks reported their movement, and our tanks moved forward to await them, destroying them as they approached. But the infantry pressure continued. Closer and closer they came. Although our tank machine gunners fired as fast as they could, our casualties mounted. Among the wounded were deputy battalion and company commanders, with a company commander killed. Sagger missiles launched from afar and RPGs fired from short range hit our tanks. The situation was critical. Gabi asked for help.

My forward command post was deployed on the Spontani Road, about 2–3 km from the front line. To my right, on Zrakor, I could see a tank company seemingly idle, with its guns aimed in my direction. I called Natke and told him to move his tanks forward into battle, adding angrily that I could not understand why the guns were aimed at me instead of at the enemy. But Natke replied that these were Pattons, and he had no Pattons in his brigade. In fact, it quickly emerged that these were Gabi's tanks, and they were already moving into battle. I was increasingly concerned over the fog of battle and the confusion under which we were operating.

I told Gabi that the entire divisional artillery was at his disposal. A few moments later my divisional artillery commander, Lieutenant Colonel Haim, informed me that Gabi's artillery liaison officer was situated in such a way that he was unable to employ his fire effectively. Haim asked permission to leave the forward command post so that he could move forward and help direct our artillery fire. Permission was granted, and Haim, in his armored personnel carrier, moved up to an observation post; he now concentrated all our artillery fire in a 4 km area. After fifteen minutes of heavy and rapid fire, the enemy attack was broken. The enemy retreated westward on the Arov Road, leaving many casualties behind. That evening Haim reported that the divisional artillery force had that day fired 4,700 shells, weighing 250 tons, all of which had been brought in fifty trucks. Each crew had unloaded and fired some 8 tons of shells, despite the fact that they were being harassed by Egyptian counter-battery fire.

Lieutenant Colonel Haim, forty-two, of just average height, gave the impression of being a heavyweight boxer. His speech was rapid and unclear and at first I took him for a rather coarse, heavy-going type. Actually, I soon found he was a well-educated, battle-experienced artillery officer. The IDF had sent him to the Haifa Technion, and he had graduated cum laude. At the age of eighteen he joined the IDF and began moving up in the ranks of the Artillery Corps. In the Sinai Campaign of 1956 he served as an artillery forward liaison officer with the infantry and took part in the capture of the Rafiah bases. In 1967 he commanded an artillery battalion in Sharon's division. Now, in 1973, he was commander of my division artillery. Haim had three children; news of the birth of his fourth child reached him two weeks later, when he was on the other side of the canal, near Suez City.

I decided to make use of the lull in the fighting to reorganize my forces and simplify control: to pull out tanks that were hit, return Nahum's battalion to Aryeh, and redivide the sector so that Gabi would be concentrated on Zrakor only, Aryeh would defend Havraga, and Natke would be deployed north of Zrakor. Gabi reported that in this last attack several of his tanks had been hit and his deputy brigade commander was among the casualties, with three tank commanders killed. At this rate, I thought, we would soon remain without any unit commanders. I had a feeling that a new enemy attack might be launched before we had completed our reorganization, so I urged the brigade commanders to speed things up. Nahum left to join Aryeh and stopped to reorganize on the Spontani Road.

At 1300 hours a new Egyptian attack was begun, again by thousands of infantrymen supported by tanks, this time from Arov

Road toward Zrakor. Fifteen minutes later Gabi reported that he had
sustained casualties, that he was under heavy enemy pressure, and
that he wanted Nahum's battalion back. The entire area now came
under a terrific artillery barrage, and even as I was watching my
troops, I could hear and make out the closing "note" of the artillery,
the thunderous explosions of the Katyusha rockets and the ensuing
haze of the phosphorous shells.

Gabi: "Things are bad here; tanks were hit on Havraga. They are
charging on the right, the north slope of Havraga; on Zrakor too,
they're using everything — tanks, infantry, Saggers. We have plenty
of artillery, and I would like as much as possible."

I replied: "There is nothing to be done. Fight calmly. I am sending you back Nahum, so direct him." At once I told Natke: "Commence moving forward again."

Natke: "Understood, will improve forward fire positions."

"There is heavy pressure," I told him, "move quickly but
carefully."

Natke now wanted to call up his battalion that had been left in the
Ma'adim Road sector. I weighed the matter: there could be a gap
created which the enemy might exploit; on the other hand, all indications were that the enemy was concentrating his efforts opposite
Haviva and Arov. In the end, I approved Natke's request. Gabi now
expressed concern about his left — his southern — flank, asking if
there were tanks present. I allayed his fears and told him that Aryeh
was operating there. The Egyptian attack continued with Gabi and
Aryeh under heavy pressure; Gabi asked for air support and requested that Natke be committed toward Zrakor. I replied that this
had already been done, and Gabi asked that I urge Natke on. An intermediate radio station intervened on behalf of Gonen. I asked them
not to interfere with the conduct of the battle.

At 1340 Gabi reported that pressure from the direction of Arov
had eased and that the enemy had retreated, though not before their
heavy use of many Saggers had caused us casualties. Gabi also said he
needed more ammunition. Natke reported that he was continuing to
advance along the top of Zrakor but that the peak went on and on,
and no enemy were in sight. Aryeh came over to say he was engaged
against enemy infantry and asked for artillery support. At that moment Gabi radioed that a new wave of Egyptians was surging toward

him. It was now about 1400. The latest attack had caught us in the process of reorganizing. When I had returned Nahum to Gabi's brigade, I also canceled the shifting of sectors. Now Gabi asked that his sector be reduced. Aryeh reported that three of his tanks had been hit by Saggers, and he was under heavy pressure. Natke said he was being pounded by artillery. I alerted them over the radio to prepare for a third Egyptian assault.

But the third assault failed to materialize — perhaps our artillery had disrupted it. The brigades were now busy evacuating casualties and pulling out disabled tanks, all under a heavy artillery barrage. I tried to get reports from the brigade commanders. Aryeh said he had taken a number of POWs but that he was engaged in a firefight against Saggers and was unable to pull back to reorganize.

At 1433 Natke reported that he was engaged against a new assault under way from the dead areas. He complained about our tanks that were moving to the rear and said he was trying to stop them. Many tanks and armored personnel carriers did in fact move to the rear that day — I could see them from my position. Vehicles loaded with fuel and ammunition had been moved forward on the Spontani Road to a point in the center of the sector 2–3 km from the front line of the fighting. When Gabi had asked for more ammunition, I told him to send a few armored vehicles to load up and then distribute it among the tanks. A forward medical station was also deployed in the same area. During the fighting, each time the troops came under the pressure of an enemy assault, tanks could be seen moving to the rear, sometimes one tank alone, at times even three at once. When I found that the brigade commanders were not aware of this movement, I began to worry. I sent Dovik to stop these tanks and as a result of his activity a "checkpoint" was set up at Spontani 32, a supply point for fuel and ammunition, for a forward medical element, and for ordnance men to repair tanks. It was at this point, 2–3 km behind the line of contact on a rear slope, that the tanks moving off the battlefield were stopped.

It emerged that there were many reasons for leaving the field of battle but not desertion. For example, a tank commander was badly hit while standing in the turret, and the frightened crew rushed to get him to the medical station in the hope of saving his life. More complicated situations were also created when a platoon commander was hit, and his tank moved to the rear to get to the medical station. The two tanks subordinate to that of the platoon leader would try to clarify, via radio, what was going on. Failing to get any reply, they acted in line with the rule in small armored units: "Watch the commander and do as he does." Thus the two tanks turned around and followed the lead tank off the battlefield. Such things could happen because of the extreme conditions under which we were operating. Small forces were fighting with considerable gaps between them, the area blanketed by artillery fire, and the atmosphere an inferno. This was also the reason for the great concern in the units not only over what was in front of them but also for what was happening on their flanks. Under such extreme pressure, there are fighters whose effectiveness diminishes. Under less extreme circumstances they could overcome the hitches or improvise a method of action despite the problems. Now they would need counsel and encouragement.

Our procedure was to halt a tank at the checkpoint, and the crew would report their problems. The officers there would see to the evacuation of the wounded, then combine crews from two tanks that had been hit. After giving them a "pep talk," they would send the men back to the front. Malfunctioning tanks would either be repaired on the spot by mechanics or the crew given another tank so they could get back to the battlefield. There was considerable improvisation at the checkpoint, and many tanks and crews were able to be sent back into battle quickly. This checkpoint procedure was a lesson we learned in the course of the fighting; the next day such checkpoints operated in each brigade's sector.

But now another assault had begun. Gabi reported that he had many casualties and that he was under fire from Sagger missiles. He asked for reinforcement by mechanized armored infantry. Our intelligence officer reported that he had information on an impending attack from the south, so I alerted Aryeh to keep his eyes open in that direction.

At 1455 Natke reported that he was heavily engaged with enemy tanks and armored vehicles; then silence. Finally contact with him was reestablished. Up to about 1555 most of the reports came from Natke: he was fighting against thousands of infantry troops — he himself had no infantry — he was in urgent need of infantry — he had taken casualties — "But I broke them . . . they are retreating . . .

we are trampling them with the tank tracks . . . they are abandoning their trenches and fleeing . . .''. And time and again Natke exclaimed, ''I need infantry! I need infantry!''

Where could I get him infantry troops? We did have infantry, but they were mobile, on half-tracks, and I was apprehensive about committing them. This was because at best they could only crawl across the sandy terrain under intense artillery fire in open half-tracks. It was only at night, when the tanks were moved back for reorganization, that we would move the armored infantry forward in order to hold the front line. Although I felt that to commit our infantry in their half-tracks was a bad solution and would, moreover, take time I ordered the brigade commanders to have their armored infantry move forward nonetheless, because the need for infantry was now so acute. In the meantime, as a quick ''first-aid'' measure, I told Gabi to send his few new M-113 armored personnel carriers (Zeldas) to help Natke.

Our planes were in the air now and were asking where to drop their payloads. It was my impression that Natke was not attacking where he was supposed to attack and, fearing that our planes would hit him, I requested that the planes hold off for a bit until I could get Natke to report his precise position. Natke replied that he was charging on the slopes of Zrakor, but this sounded strange, particularly his reports concerning thousands of Egyptian infantry troops deserting their entrenched positions. I told Natke to recheck his position, and he soon came on with a correction: ''I shifted westward and assaulted their low ridge line west of Avnit. I overcame them with my tanks, and I also used the few armored personnel carriers I had. Our tanks took many hits, but they're all moving.''

''Well done, Natke,'' I replied, ''but get back to Zrakor fast.'' By 1600 hours he had returned to Zrakor and reported that he needed ammunition.

Just before that, at 1550, Gonen called with the good news that Lapidot's battalion was en route from Magen's sector to join my command. Gabi and Aryeh said they thought the Egyptians were forming up for yet another assault. We were under a heavy artillery barrage. Lapidot contacted me, and I told him to move west on the Ma'adim Road, turn south on the Artillery Road, and advance until Havraga, where he would join up with Gabi's brigade.

At 1650 hours Aryeh reported suspicious movements on his southern flank; at the same time Lapidot was approaching Zrakor from the north, via the Artillery Road. I was very moved: a column of twenty tanks was coming, our first reinforcement. We were getting stronger. My thoughts were broken off by the boom of explosions, and Lapidot's battalion disappeared from sight behind a cloud of smoke. We had undergone some heavy shellings in the past two days, but this barrage seemed particularly ferocious, far and away more intense than anything we had experienced yet, or did it just seem that way? The Egyptians, I thought, were venting their anger. For two days they had made charge after charge and had been repulsed over and over again. Perhaps they had taken consolation in the fact that they were at least wearing us down when suddenly a new battalion had appeared to reinforce us.

Gabi: "The incoming guests are taking a record pounding."

Gilad: "We can see it. Combat experience is a healthy thing."

It was evident that the men had quickly become seasoned fighters, that they had learned to live with the fears of the battlefield. Near the canal the daily screen of white smoke was rising, and the skies were lit up with illumination flares. Another day of fighting was ending. We seemed to have entered a defensive routine, I thought to myself. It was time to pull back for reorganization and to prepare for the next day of fighting.

It was 1720. I radioed the commanders to carry out "yesterday's exercise" once more. Gabi attached Lapidot — who had arrived unhurt — to his brigade, briefed him on the sector, and then helped him deploy around the junctions of the Artillery Road and Zrakor and Havraga. I attached armored infantry companies and forward observers from the divisional artillery force to Lapidot. The brigades began moving toward the bivouacs, towing damaged tanks and half-tracks. A few tank retrievers could be seen making their way to the front to help out with the towing operations. Traffic control that evening was more complicated because there were now two brigades on the narrow Spontani Road, Gabi's and Aryeh's. Because of the heavy dunes on either side of the road, the tank crews preferred to move on the road only. There were some traffic jams at the junction, but the long columns continued to move slowly in the growing darkness.

Suddenly we heard shooting behind us, and within moments, machine guns were joining in the firing all along the column. The automatic fire of hundreds of tracers blasted the air. Very soon the length of the convoy could be made out, as tanks and armored personnel carriers became visible moving in a line many kilometers long. The machine gunners kept firing into the sky, as the Arabs do in their "fantasias."

What is this madness? I wanted to shout into the radio net, but as I looked up I saw two fireballs moving slowly across the sky from west to east. What in the world is that? I wondered. From afar I could now hear the barking noises of our antiaircraft fire. The two fireballs exploded, and then four more were visible. "Kelt missiles," I heard over the radio net. When the fireballs had passed, our firing ceased. But in the distance the muted sound of other units firing at the fading missiles could still be heard.

We continued moving toward Kurkar, where my main command post was situated. As I reflected on the fighting day just ended I found myself thinking about an issue that was a painful one for me: the armored infantry forces. When I took over command of the Armored Corps this was one of the subjects I had wanted to promote and to improve in all respects — gear and weapons, quality of the personnel, combat doctrine, and training. In fact, I had done so, but the achievements were far from satisfying. The difficulty lay in the IDF's scale of priorities in general and that of the Armored Corps in particular.

There were three types of infantry in the IDF. The highest level and the highest standards were to be found in the paratroopers and reconnaissance units. There, only volunteers were accepted, including *Nahal* (Hebrew acronym for "pioneering fighting youth") soldiers who would later establish new settlements along the borders. One rung below the paratroopers were the men of the Golani Brigade. The quality of the manpower there was lower, but in order to develop the command level the Brigade was given a certain ratio of high-potential manpower. The third type was the armored infantry, which was built on manpower similar to that of Golani with one exception — it received a smaller ratio of command-level manpower.

The armored infantry served in the Armored Corps alongside the tanks. The Armored Corps commanders, however, devoted most of their attention to the tanks and their crews. There were reasons for this, of course. The tank is a more complicated and more expensive weapons system, and its fighting potential is far greater. The tank is the nucleus of the armored formations, and around it are added all the supplementary elements, including armored infantry. When I took over the Armored Corps I got into debates within the corps itself and General Headquarters on this issue. I argued that it made no sense to assign the armored infantry a lower level of priority than that which the other types of infantry had. In war, I pointed out, the IDF's mobile armored elements would constitute the spearhead of the attack, would be well to the fore, and would penetrate into the enemy's depth — in short, they would fight more intensively, would take a more active role in the fighting, and would in fact carry the main burden of the work. It would be a paradox, then, to have this breakthrough element — the tanks — supported by armored infantry that was of a lower level. Meanwhile the best infantry troops — the paratroopers — would remain in the rear or would be called in to take part in a mobile armored battle without having been trained for this.

Of course counterarguments were posited. The Armored Corps, it was said, was ipso facto giving priority to tanks, so that the potential of the infantry could not make itself felt. Moreover, independent infantry activity is more difficult and thus requires a higher standard of manpower.

It seemed to me that the state and status of the infantry was largely the result of the historical development of the IDF in the immediate post-1948 period. At that time, in the fifties, the IDF engaged in a series of reprisal raids across the borders in reaction to Arab raids into Israel. The paratroopers bore the brunt of all these raids, gained distinction and were accorded a high status in the armed forces. And as a result they were given priority of resources and manpower. Thus it was that tradition and conservatism made it difficult to change views and bring about a shift in resource allocations, particularly where manpower was concerned.

I tried to demonstrate that the Armored Corps was capable of training the armored infantry, raising it to a high professional level. I decided to make an extra effort in this direction — in fact, to bring about a veritable revolution. Unprecedentedly I decided to divert incoming recruits of tank-crew level into armored infantry units. We formed armored infantry companies whose members were all of command level, and I was able to convince some tank officers to have themselves assigned to armored infantry units. During the period that I commanded the Armored Corps youth were flocking to it, although we were not recognized as a select volunteer branch. In practice, most of those who entered the Armored Corps did so because they wanted to. Some of these recruits were appalled to find themselves in the armored infantry and not members of tank crews. At first they thought there must be some mistake and tried to use their "connections" to get transferred to tanks but to no avail.

The steps taken to enhance manpower quality were accompanied by a struggle to have the IDF acquire American-made M-113 armored personnel carriers (code-named Zelda). The Zeldas were intended to replace our aging half-tracks of 1941 vintage. They were superior to the half-track in three key spheres: armored protection, mobility, and technical reliability. The half-track was open, hence vulnerable to shelling; the fact that it had two front wheels made it slow or unable to move altogether over rough terrain, especially sand dunes. There was a period when the half-track's slow pace could be coordinated with the IDF's Sherman tanks, which were just as slow and as technically unreliable as the half-tracks. However once the Armored Corps began using Centurions and Pattons (M-60s), there was a total mismatch. The Zeldas had a roof that could be left open or, in case of shelling, closed. Its armor also gave the men better protection. Moreover, it moved entirely on tracks, had a stronger engine, greater mobility and speed, and infinitely better maneuvering ability. In fact they were able to advance even faster than our tanks.

Even though the impossibility of coordination between the new tanks and the obsolescent half-tracks was so obvious and cried out for change, I encountered two major difficulties in my attempts to equip the armored infantry units with M-113s. First, the armored personnel carriers cost several times more than the obsolete half-tracks. The second major difficulty was the active and vigorous opposition to the purchase of M-113s voiced by the man whom I had replaced as commander of the Armored Corps, Gen. Israel Tal. Tal was now working in the Defense Ministry on the development of a new Israeli-made tank. We were at odds on many issues, among them this one of the best approach to armored infantry.

I held that the armored infantry should fight from their vehicles, on the move, and should dismount when that became necessary. Tal's approach was that the armored infantry was mounted only so as to enable it to accompany the tanks and that when it came to fighting they should dismount. Interestingly, the doctrine of the American Army, which developed and manufactured both the half-track and the M-113 armored personnel carrier and which had made extensive use of armored infantry since World War II, was that these armored vehicles were intended only to transport the infantry troops as close as possible to their objective, so that they could then dismount and fight on foot. This was also the doctrine held by European armies, such as those of the British, the French, and others.

It was precisely the Armored Corps of IDF that developed the concept of armored infantry fighting not only on foot but also from their vehicles. To provide for mounted combat, the IDF attached machine guns and other weapons to the half-tracks and later to the Zeldas. It is noteworthy that the Americans, the Russians, the Germans, and others changed their minds and adopted the IDF's approach — and rightly so — for armored infantry is, after all, intended to be a supplementary component for the nucleus of any armored force, the tanks.

Armored warfare is characterized by mobility. It is in the nature of the battlefield that not all of it is fortified. There are in fact fortified compartments that are difficult to breach or capture and that call for fighting on foot. Armor usually seeks to go around these or to break through them in a narrow sector in order to penetrate into the enemy's rear. Those rear areas are mostly unfortified, and it is there that armored forces of both sides are likely to engage in mobile combat. In the course of battle, each side tries to gain additional footholds for defense by seizing key terrain locations with infantry or armored infantry troops, but these hastily established footholds are less fortified and thus can be overcome by mounted troops. Moreover, even when the infantry has to dismount to fight on foot, the half-track or armored personnel carrier does not withdraw — as it used to when it was considered a vehicle for transportation only — but remains in the field, manned by a small crew that supports the infantrymen with its firepower.

The weak point of this kind of mounted warfare lies in the fact that when the vehicle is penetrated by enemy fire, the men on it sustain many casualties because they are such a concentrated target. Tal rejected the notion of mounted warfare and objected to the purchase of Zeldas because, he argued, they did not provide sufficient armored protection for the men. This point brings us to one of the basic questions concerning the fighting power of the tank itself.

From the outset of the historic competition between the production of armored vehicles and the development of armor-penetrating weapons, those working on the latter had the upper hand. Whenever a heavier tank appeared on the battlefield, its advantage was short lived. A new armor-piercing shell or antiarmor missile would soon be developed that could penetrate the new tank. It was not by strengthening the vehicle's passive penetration-withstanding capacity that this problem could be overcome but by increasing survivability by means of improved battlefield tactics. Like the tank, the armored personnel carrier seeks to enhance its survivability by means of high mobility and increased firepower. Its high mobility and agility enable it to move more quickly out of fire-blanketed areas. Its high rate of firepower enables it to suppress sources of fire and prevent them from endangering it. The aim in mounted fighting is to combine rapid movement with intensified firepower, this accompanied by tanks and artillery support. The idea is to bring about a "shock" effect that overwhelms the enemy and paralyzes his will to resist.

As noted, when the objective is fortified and includes many obstacles, it is not possible to make full use of mounted fighting potential. One of the difficulties in employing armored infantry on the battlefield has to do with the question of timing, the decision on whether and when to move from mounted fighting to fighting on foot. This is left to the commander's decision, according to his specific assessment of the situation in view of the strength and effectiveness of enemy resistance.

In opposing acquisition of the Zelda, Tal showed up the truth of the adage that "the enemy of the good is the best." That is that the cost of the Zelda and then the resources needed to maintain and operate it would make it very difficult for the IDF to procure Zeldas at a rapid rate. This was all the more the case with a heavy armored personnel carrier (which is what Tal wanted), whose initial price and even more its maintenance and operation costs made it almost as expensive as a tank. In practice, not one of the world's armies has received the kind of allocations that would enable it to purchase heavy armored personnel carriers in any great numbers. Even the United States and the USSR rely to this day on light armored personnel carriers, such as the M-113. The Americans are developing a heavy armored personnel carrier, but this is intended for only a small part of their infantry. And the Germans have just a few hundred heavy armored personnel carriers, which are not especially successful.

Tal also argued that even the best armored personnel carrier is inferior to the tank. But this is a claim that is not to the point but typical of one who is opposed to mounted warfare. The armored personnel carrier was conceived as a means of compensating for the disadvantages of tanks. Indeed, the Yom Kippur War underscored how vulnerable tanks were to infantry well equipped with antitank weapons. The tank is closed and to a large extent it is "blind." Its gun and coaxial machine gun can fire only in the direction that the turret is facing. On the other hand, the men on the armored personnel carrier can make use of several pairs of eyes to scan the area in all directions, and they can quickly fire many weapons in a flexible manner, either concentrating their fire in one direction or spraying the area. In sum, there is not much point in making comparisons between the tank and the armored personnel carrier, because each is better than the other for its own specific purpose. The important thing is their cooperation in combined and complementary use on the battlefield.

My view was that a relatively small army, such as the IDF, must provide all or most of its few infantry forces with mobile capability, so that its full potential could be realized, especially in combined warfare with tanks. I recommended the acquisition of the Zelda because it provided better protection than the half-track against most of the weapons to be found on the battlefield and because its mobility made it compatible with our new generation of tanks, thus enabling us to employ our armored forces more efficiently. An additional important consideration guiding my recommendation was the fact that the M-113 had potential for improvement in the future in all three of its key aspects: armored protection, mobility, and firepower.

Eventually my recommendation was accepted, and the IDF began purchasing M-113 armored personnel carriers. The first Zeldas arrived in Israel while we were engaged in the War of Attrition. We needed time to get to know them, to adapt them to our needs and our manner of fighting by mounting machine guns on them and installing various instruments. Further we had to develop doctrine and prepare instruction booklets for maintenance crews and for instructors. But the chief of staff, Chaim Bar-Lev, pressed us to get them into action at once in the War of Attrition on the "hot" canal front. So we had to absorb the new weapons system under pressure, but with intensive work we were able to introduce the Zeldas fairly smoothly. The armored infantrymen welcomed them enthusiastically, especially when they saw that even when they hit mines, the men inside remained virtually unscathed.

Further difficulties in upgrading the armored infantry stemmed from concepts concerning the scope of the subject. When Tal was commander of the Armored Corps, consistent with his concept that armored infantry was not intended for mounted fighting, he canceled plans to have armored infantry officers attend a course for Armored Corps officers and instead sent them to the longer course for infantry officers. As a result, confidence — and with it the capacity for mounted fighting — dried up. It took some time until we were once more able to have armored infantry officers attend courses in armored warfare.

From the very notion that armored infantry must fight in two ways — mounted and on foot — stemmed the conclusion that they had to be trained in both kinds of warfare. However, longer training time means less time for operational duties. It is the General Headquarters that decides on the ratio of time given to each of these two activities. The period of time allotted for training armored infantry was identical to that allotted for the training of ordinary infantry, which only fights on foot. All my "battles" were of no avail: the official concept of the IDF was that armored infantry should specialize in armor-oriented activity, while the more difficult infantry tasks — such as capturing a fortified objective or fighting in a built-up area — would be left to the ordinary infantry or the paratroopers.

Despite the mass of difficulties, we succeeded in promoting the cause of the armored infantry. The new priorities, the special efforts made, the influx of better manpower, the new armored personnel carriers, and the improved instruction and training all began to bear fruit, and for the first time the image of the armored infantry began to change. Its *esprit de corps* changed positively. Suddenly the armored infantry could carry out more tasks and do them better. Because of this and because of the compatibility between the Zeldas and our tanks, various operational issues were reexamined and promoted, such as armored reconnaissance, mountain warfare, fighting in built-up areas, and desert warfare.

But all this applied only to our few regular armored infantry units. We had already begun to equip and train the reserve units as well, but no more than preliminary steps in that direction had been taken when the war broke out. There were few Zeldas, and the bulk of the reserve armored infantry units were still using the old half-tracks.

The lack of understanding for the importance of armored infantry found expression a short time before the war erupted when, as part of a proposal to reduce the period of compulsory service in the regular army, then Deputy Chief of Staff Tal suggested eliminating the one armored infantry unit in the regular army altogether. The IDF had already experienced situations in which a certain branch or element did not have a "live" active unit in the regular army; the result was, inevitably, stagnation. In this case, it would have meant killing the whole process of promoting the armored infantry just as it had taken a new lease on life and was absorbing a new weapons system.

There were further grave effects of Tal's other proposals in this sphere, particularly those coming from reducing the size of an already small army such as ours. Many generals were strongly opposed to the idea of cutting down the period of compulsory service. Tal asserted that we were not taking the broad view of the country's security needs, because social and economic factors also affected our capacity to stand firm. Most of those who took part in this debate did not ignore this, but they argued that it was the General Staff who should alert the government to the serious effects cutting the period of service would have.

Now en route to my main command post after this second day of defense and containment (10 October), I was thinking how unfortunate it was that the rate of acquiring Zeldas had been slowed down. Nonetheless, we were fortunate to have even these few, for they were reconnoitering in front of us, protecting our flanks, and even distributing fuel and ammunition in the midst of battle. My thoughts were broken off by a radio message informing me that there would be a conference of commanders that evening at 2000 at Southern Command HQ.

Subsequently, I learned what had transpired in the other divisions and at Southern Command HQ on 10 October. In Magen's sector a link-up to Strongpoint Budapest was carried out after it was found that the Egyptians' commando blockade, which had been preventing access to the strongpoint, had gone during the previous night. In Sharon's sector an attempt was made to comb Hamutal in order to evacuate any wounded who may have been left behind during the previous day's attack. At dawn, under cover of an artillery barrage, five tanks and four armored personnel carriers of Haim's brigade moved toward the area; but three of the tanks were hit by Sagger missiles, and the task force retreated to the Ziona area. On the southern wing of Sharon's sector, Tuvia's brigade replaced Amnon's brigade on the front line (the latter had pulled back to reorganize), but in the course of the switch Televizia was evacuated by Amnon before Tuvia arrived there, with the result that the enemy retook it. Further in the south sector, the Egyptians again tried to advance toward Ras-Sudar, but this time they were thrown back by small forces operating on the Yoreh Road, and again the air force completed the job. Avraham's brigade tried to reopen the Artillery Road near Notsa but failed.

Throughout the day the entire Suez front came under heavy Egyptian shelling. The main pressure was directed at my division; why, I do not know. It may have been because of the personality of the commander of the Egyptian 2nd Infantry Division, Gen. Hassan Abu Saada or perhaps it came from the fact that in my sector the Egyptians had been unable to gain a foothold on the Artillery Road.

CHAPTER EIGHTEEN

BAR-LEV TAKES OVER, 10 October

On the morning of the tenth, an important change had already taken place at Southern Command HQ. At 0730 the chief of staff called Gonen to inform him that Lt. Gen. (Res.) Chaim Bar-Lev was en route to assume command of the southern front. Bar-Lev arrived at about 0900 and he and Gonen closeted themselves for a lengthy conversation. Gonen found himself in a highly unpleasant situation. Some days later he expressed to me his disappointment over the fact that his friends in high places had been unable to withstand the pressure exerted by the defense minister for his replacement. But now what was he to do — resign in the middle of a war? Gonen agreed to stay on and act as number-two man. To his credit it must be said that he continued to function without falling into despondency; in fact, he functioned better alongside Bar-Lev.

When they emerged, Gonen informed his staff that Bar-Lev was now the front commander and that he, Gonen, was under him. In a rather bitter jest, Gonen added that he had received his own private chief of staff to assist him. It was in the same manner that Gonen gave the news to the division commanders when we arrived for the meeting at 2000 hours.

Right off Bar-Lev had an urgent problem to deal with. He joined a staff conference called to consider the fate of our southernmost strongpoint, Masrek, the so-called "Quay" fortification. Now that our forces had linked up with Strongpoint Budapest, Masrek remained the last besieged strongpoint still holding out. Gonen favored replacing the soldiers there with other soldiers on the grounds that evacuation of the strongpoint would mean loss of a source of information on enemy activity along the canal. Specifically, we would not know when the enemy's 4th Armored Division crossed the canal. However, Bar-Lev decided in favor of evacuation without any replacement of the men. The complicated operation to extricate the besieged soldiers, which was carried out on the night of 11–12 October by the navy, failed because the Egyptians spotted the approaching rubber dinghies.

At 1400 on 10 October, the defense minister arrived at Southern Command HQ, and a discussion was held on the plan to capture Port Fuad and Port Said. Bar-Lev and Gonen were in favor of an operation there to be carried out by paratroopers supported by a massive artillery barrage and the navy. Dayan, however, opposed the plan, saying it was unnecessary. It would amount to no more, he said, than seizing a few acres and causing a host of political problems. Dayan then left to visit Sharon's division, and Bar-Lev set about "making order." He issued instructions to organize the war room so that each division would be allotted its own separate follow up and control corner, where there would be maps, a logbook, and an officer responsible for updating information. In addition, Bar-Lev decided to reduce the rather chaotic overcrowding in the war room by moving the main command post to nearby Refidim and having only the tactical headquarters remain at Umm-Hashiba. Following these moves, Bar-Lev had the division commanders called in for an evening meeting and then held a conference with his staff in which he was updated in preparation for the evening session with the division commanders.

At our conference, which began at 2000 hours, I was surprised and pleased to find that Bar-Lev was now commander of the southern front. I had got to know Bar-Lev well in another difficult campaign — the War of Independence. I remembered him from peril-filled days, days of near desperation when he was a battalion commander in the besieged Negev, and I was one of his company commanders. Afterwards I served under him when he was commander of the Armored Corps as his operations officer and again during the War of Attrition when he was chief of staff and I was commander of the Armored Corps. I knew we could rely on his careful judgment and his inner fortitude. This was a timely replacement, I thought, and its effect would soon be felt on our front line.

Bar-Lev opened the meeting by outlining the situation on the Syrian front, from where he had just come. The Syrians had been pushed back across the border. He told us that IDF's main effort would continue to be in the north for the time being. We then reported on the situation in our divisions, followed by a discussion of what strategy we should adopt.

Sharon said that we had taken no initiative since the outbreak of the war. He suggested that we attack, with divisional force, through the empty zone opposite Bitter Lake, mop up the area toward the south, and push the enemy as far back south as we could as fast as we could. To me, this proposal seemed overly risky in our present condition. Sharon's division had only 170 tanks, I had about 160, Mandler around 140, and Magen had just 80 tanks. I said that the area being proposed for penetration seemed the right one, but that we should commit no more than one brigade there. Mandler put forward a more far-reaching idea: to mop up the area south of the lakes and then to continue by crossing the canal.

It was precisely Gonen and Ben-Ari who proposed the most realistic plans. Ben-Ari said we should not carry out an offensive operation at this time; rather, my division should be pulled back to reorganize, even if the Egyptians pushed us back as a result. Only after we had accumulated more strength could we carry out an attack in the sector proposed. Gonen noted that we only had about 600 tanks instead of the 1,000 required for an all-out assault. Therefore a crossing attempt at this time would be dangerous and doomed to failure. His recommendation was that we preserve the tanks we had and build up to 1,000 before launching an offensive; he would agree to Sharon's plan only if a cease-fire was about to be imposed.

Bar-Lev then summed up. It was his evaluation that the Egyptians would continue to attack, which would continue to wear down their forces. The attack ideas that had been proposed could not be implemented without prior planning and preparation. Bar-Lev said he attached importance to the capture of Port Fuad and Port Said. Such a move would have political ramifications because we would then hold a section of the canal, and it could be opened only with our consent. As to the operational plans, he charged Southern Command Intelligence, along with Sharon's intelligence staff — Sharon's division was now situated opposite Bitter Lake — with the task of collecting data toward a future crossing. Bar-Lev stated that we would not launch an attack in the immediate future. He then went on to speak of the tactical lessons we could learn from the war so far and of how we could improve our operational techniques in the defensive battle that would continue.

In retrospect I believe that our situation did not yet enable us to move to the offensive. In fact neither political nor strategic circumstances required us to rush to attack. Today it is easy enough to see that we were prisoners of our own doctrine: the idea that we had to attack as fast as possible and transfer the fighting to enemy territory. Of course there were advantages and disadvantages in either moving to an early attack or delaying to accumulate more strength and so wear down the enemy. A commander must examine the specific situation with which he is faced. Sharon's suggestion that we attack in divisional strength through the seam between the two Egyptian armies made some sense, although the reasoning that we had not yet taken the initiative since the outbreak of the war was neither sufficient nor accurate. We had in fact taken the initiative on 8 October and he had taken it on the ninth. And we had paid dearly. Moreover, if his idea were to be accepted and carried out successfully, it would still not bring about a decisive shift. A part of the Egyptian Third Army would be hit, but we would also sustain casualties, and at that time we did not yet have the forces to exploit any initial success to the point of vanquishing the enemy. A partial victory — one that would not bring with it a rout of the enemy — could, given the condition and strength of our forces, become a Pyrrhic victory. My own suggestion was, if anything, even less logical. If it was already decided to attack to the point proposed, better a full division than just one brigade. Mandler's suggestion to drive southward and then cross the canal was theoretically the solution called for by the circumstances, but practically we had neither the strength nor the means to carry it out at that stage.

Thus it was that Gonen's and Ben-Ari's were the wisest proposals at the time. Bar-Lev in fact concluded that we should continue with our containment operations while gathering strength for a canal crossing. As to Bar-Lev's idea of capturing Port Fuad and Port Said, this was unrealistic, and Bar-Lev himself apparently intended that it should be implemented mainly by forces not under his command at present. However, even if this were his intention, the idea was still not a good one, because we would need all possible strength composed of both the air force and paratroops, when the time came to launch our main counterattack. Bar-Lev may have been deferring, here, to our doctrine of aggressiveness.

The conference ended. I departed for my command post with the feeling that the worst of the crisis was behind us and with the hope that things would begin to get better.

It was midnight by the time I got back to my main command post at Kurkar, and my staff and brigade commanders were waiting for me — a bone-weary group. This was already the fifth straight night of action. I couldn't remember if or when I had slept or dozed — perhaps I had learned to live without sleep. Something was buzzing in my head, a constant irritating noise. It was something I was familiar with from previous wars; even when I did have the opportunity or time to get a little sleep, I was unable to doze off in this condition. Perhaps, I thought, it's possible to get along without sleep after all — but only on condition that things aren't dull. Dull it certainly was not. My mind was unceasingly active: What have I forgotten to do? What to do next? What to say?

All the reports had been collected and analyzed prior to my arrival, and I was now updated. We had had a difficult day of fighting: of the 130 tanks we had at the start of the day, some 20 had been hit. Many of our men — including a considerable number of commanders — had been hit. Nonetheless, it was expected that the division would have 160 tanks for the next day's fighting; Lapidot had joined us earlier in the evening with 20 tanks, and we had been informed by Southern Command that we would be getting back Giora's battalion, which Natke had left on the morning of the eighth in Magen's sector. Giora's battalion, with its 20 tanks, would return to Natke's brigade, I decided.

Another source for our buildup of strength lay in the retrieval and repair of tanks by our ordnance units. The chief ordnance officer of the Armored Corps, Lieutenant Colonel Yoram, was now my divisional ordnance officer. He was a real character: tall, broad shouldered with blond hair and moustache to match, energetic, loud voiced and enthusiastic. He was always ready to fight for "his tanks." In fact, he knew his tanks better than he knew his office furniture. Now he was in control of an ordnance system that was spread out over the desert. Close to the battalions, near the Artillery Road, the ordnance team attached to the battalions were working. About 15 km to their rear, on the Ma'adim and Spontani roads, the forward companies of the divisional ordnance unit were deployed. Still further to the rear, around Romani, the base company was at work. But most important of all, ordnance teams were dispatched to patrol the roads — to extricate tanks, repair them, and push them to the front.

Yoram reported that a team under Lieutenant Colonel Razon had repaired ten tanks along the coastal road, but Magen's division had "confiscated" them as they were on the way to join up with our forces. The lesson was learned; in the future an officer insured that any tanks repaired by our teams got to our division. Yoram went on to say that tanks whose turrets were malfunctioning and for which there were no spare parts were being used to tow out tanks stuck in the heavy dunes. Yesterday only ten tanks had been made serviceable again, but that was because a great many of the still-functioning tanks had returned from the fighting "screwed up" and had to be restored to high operational capacity.

Suddenly we heard the close barking noise of heavy machine guns. It was the antiaircraft battery deployed around the main command post firing like mad. Except for the duty officers, the war tent emptied in seconds flat. We burst out, scanning the night skies, but we saw nothing, not even Kelt missiles. Very bad, I thought; someone was edgy, opened fire, and others joined in. But when the firing stopped and the report came in, it emerged that helicopters had been spotted moving not far from us toward the northeast. It was thought that these were Egyptian helicopters seeking to land commandos to our rear. The radios were alive with activity. The reports coming in made it clear that none of our helicopters were airborne and that other helicopters had been spotted at various places. At once orders were issued, units were sent out to comb the area, and security measures around the bivouacs were increased.

When we returned to the war room, the ensuing discussion on the past two days of fighting was interesting and fruitful. The brigade commanders had mostly recovered from the first shock of the Sagger missile panic. We now knew what to watch out for, from what directions, and at what ranges such attacks could be expected. Moreover, all units now had observers whose job it was to warn of incoming antitank missiles. They would call out, "Missile from the left!" or "Missile from the right!" — and the tanks would succeed in maneuvering so as to avoid the missile. Everyone thought that whenever Zeldas had been sent in ahead of the tanks the results were excellent, as the armored personnel carriers had been able to deal with the Egyptian infantry that had moved into close range. We were used to the artillery barrages by now. We would close the hatches, shift position, and go on operating. As I listened to the reports, it crossed my mind that the division resembled someone initially ill with a high fever over whom everyone had been greatly concerned. Now, even though some fever remained, the crisis point had passed.

After we had analyzed battle techniques and the tactics of cooperation among tanks, armored personnel carriers, and artillery, I decided to redistribute our Zeldas. We would be fighting with small tank battalions the next day, but now each battalion would have armored infantry troops mounted on Zeldas grouped to protect its flanks. I then issued the order for the coming day of fighting. I began by stating that on the basis of the experience of the past two days we would deploy differently the next day. Because the area was hilly, with many dead areas, and because our forces were relatively meager for such a broad sector, there would be no reserve brigade. Rather, we would deploy three brigades abreast on the line, with each brigade maintaining its own reserve and employing it as needed. Since, as we had found, the enemy was attacking mainly in the center of the sector from the direction of the Arov Road toward Zrakor and from Haviva Road toward Havraga, Gabi's brigade would deploy on Havraga, Aryeh's brigade on Zrakor and in the valley between there and Havraga, and Natke's brigade would operate on both sides of Ma'adim. This, I pointed out, did not mean that they would not be called on to attack in an adjacent sector to help out another brigade, but the primary idea was to achieve better disposition of forces for more effective fighting. The overall aim, I repeated, remained to contain the enemy while conserving our strength.

I then checked the personnel situation — crews and commanders. My division G-1, Hanoch, reported the arrival of officers who had returned from the hospital or abroad and had been dispatched from the rear by Armored Corps HQ. Hanoch asked the brigade commanders to take crewmen now assigned to administrative tasks and reassign them to tanks. I dismissed the participants with the feeling that tomorrow would be an easier day.

It was 0300 on 11 October. Because I feared that the brigade commanders might be ambushed by the Egyptian commandos who had landed, I forbade them to return to their command posts and ordered them to sleep until dawn at my HQ. At this directive they just guffawed and went to their command jeeps in order to coordinate from there the thousand and one matters that still remained to be done before the new day of fighting, which would begin soon.

CHAPTER NINETEEN

11, 12, 13 October: STALEMATE

The third day of defense, 11 October, began as usual. Natke's reconnaissance unit was observing the enemy from the ridge line. Far to the west, near the canal, they could see suspicious-looking dust clouds. Early in the morning Gabi sent his reconnaissance company to join Lapidot. The dozens of burned-out Egyptian tanks scattered across the area were pointed out to Lapidot's men so that they would not waste ammunition by hitting them again. Then the reconnaissance commander took up position on Zrakor. Aryeh dispatched a reconnaissance unit to the hills south of Havraga.

Natke was waiting at Kurkar for a helicopter to take him to his brigade which was on the Ma'adim Road when he found that Giora's battalion had not yet arrived from Magen's sector. He therefore ordered Mulla's battalion to deploy on the ridge line west of the junction of the Ma'adim and Artillery roads. While in the helicopter en route to his sector, he heard his reconnaissance unit reporting that the approaching dust clouds were being raised by T-62 tanks of the 15th Brigade of the Egyptian 18th Infantry Division. They were trying to penetrate along the boundary between Magen's sector and mine. Natke immediately advanced Natan's battalion northward to Voroslav hill. Meanwhile, Giora's battalion was approaching on the

Ma'adim Road, and Natke had him make a flanking movement toward the Maror Stronghold. Natke was behaving coolly. When I told him that the entire division artillery was at his disposal, he replied that he preferred not to have the guns open up just yet but to let the enemy come closer. At 0730 hours a pitched battle was raging; within minutes fifteen T-62 tanks were burning, and the rest were in retreat. In Natke's brigade one tank and one armored personnel carrier were hit. The entire tank crew was killed, including the company commander, Avi Ostrovitz. In the armored personnel carrier the battalion commander, Mulla, was killed. He was the battalion's third commander lost in six days. Natke at once sent his operations officer to take temporary charge of the battalion. That evening, he was replaced by the battalion's fourth commander, Lieutenant Colonel Ze'evik, who was sent from the division.

At Zrakor and Havraga, Aryeh and Gabi followed the enemy's activity with concern. When Egyptian concentrations were observed west of Havraga, Gabi moved up his reserve battalions. When reports came in that enemy tanks were on the move from Missouri toward Nozel, this was seen as a potential threat to our southern flank, and Aryeh reinforced his deployment south of Havraga.

In practice it was enough to land a concentrated barrage on the enemy with our divisional artillery to make them think twice about attacking. Various events, which actually constituted relatively minor threats but were added to other reports concerning Egyptian intentions, occupied us too much and caused us to react with too much force. While we were still worrying about our southern flank, three enemy armored personnel carriers and two tanks suddenly appeared from one of the dead areas just 500 meters in front of Eliashiv's battalion. They were destroyed within minutes.

Then a column of five Egyptian tanks was observed along the seam between my sector and Sharon's, in the sea of nearly impassable dunes on our southern flank and deep within our territory. Perhaps they were lost; perhaps they were the vanguard of a larger force that sought to attack us from the rear. In any event, we dispatched tanks to close in on them from the north while tanks from Haim's brigade (of Sharon's division) pursued them from the south. Dovik, who was coordinating the operation from a helicopter, directed the two forces. Finally Haim engaged them, and all five enemy tanks were destroyed.

At 1110 hours I radioed a news bulletin about the northern front. The news was encouraging. Our forces had launched a counterattack and were moving toward Damascus, while the air force had bombed the Syrian Ministry of Defense, which was on the outskirts of Damascus, as well as other infrastructure targets deep in Syria.

A painful event occurred that day in my sector. In a show of daring, the Egyptians dispatched planes that carried out short, low-altitude sorties over our lines. Two of these planes hit a point on the Ma'adim Road where four tanks from one of Natke's battalions were reloading with ammunition; two platoon leaders were killed and crewmen were wounded. At 1400 hours two other enemy aircraft bombed a point that was some 15 km east of the front line, on the Ma'adim Road. This was a working site for one of our forward ordnance companies, repairing tanks. Fuel tanks were there also, as well as vehicles loaded with ammunition and nearly two hundred men. The dunes made it difficult to disperse vehicles, so that the company was crowded in an area close to the road. The men overconfidently thought that our air force was in control of the skies and that the Egyptians would not dare send their planes into our territory. This was a serious miscalculation, and we paid dearly for it: fuel trucks caught fire, ammunition began exploding all around, and eighty of our men were wounded. At 1415 helicopters were called in to evacuate the wounded, but it was rough going. My chief of staff, Ami, took charge of the evacuation process. Bulldozers had to be called in to clear the road, and it took about two hours to extricate all the burning vehicles and reopen the road. The wounded behaved in exemplary fashion, as did their comrades who had not been hurt and who now assisted in the evacuation. But the scene was an appalling one and the damage heavy. The ordnance company was seriously hurt, but they were reinforced and continued to work wonders in repairing tanks under immense pressure, particularly in the bridgehead area after we had crossed the canal.

In the afternoon Natke reported that he had captured a commando squad that had been hiding deep in our territory in his sector. With the squad, which was equipped with observation and communication equipment, was an artillery forward observer. This fact, along with the earlier penetration behind our lines of Egyptian tanks, was warning enough for me. I decided to set up ongoing surveillance during the daylight hours in our rear and behind the front line area, to be carried out both from the air, by helicopters, and on the ground, by jeep-borne units. I made a note of this for the nightly briefing of the brigade commanders. In the meantime, I attached a jeep company to take up observation points in order to safeguard the area around my forward command post, which was situated in an isolated position on a hill amid dunes 3 km from my fighting forces.

This was the first day on which I was not under relentless enemy pressure. I took the time to contact General Headquarters and speak with Brig. Gen. Mordechai Zippori, my former deputy, who was now chief Armor officer. This was the first opportunity I had had to learn of his activity. Heading a small staff, Zippori was working on sending reinforcements of officers and tanks to the front.

Zippori was engaged in building up forces, organizing all reserve Armored Corps personnel arriving from abroad, mating them with the repaired tanks and sending them off to the fronts. He had also reopened the Armored Corps school, using wounded commanders who could not return to the battlefield as instructors. From Zippori I learned that General Staff was drawing up lists of equipment and weapons that, it was hoped, the Americans would send via an airlift.

"Zippori," I said to him, "I want you to know that even though many of our tanks have been hit, our most urgent need is for armored personnel carriers. We cannot make use of even the few infantry troops we have in our half-tracks. Also, it's very important that you ask for plenty of antiinfantry ammunition for the tanks. These assaulting infantry forces are our main problem."

Zippori told me not to worry, because they were asking for everything. Then I reminded him that dozens of new Zeldas, which had arrived a short time before the war began, were now in various workshops being fitted out according to our specifications. I urged him to get them forward as fast as possible.

At 1535 Bar-Lev arrived for a visit to my forward command post. He was my first visitor. I was the only divisional commander whose HQ was "out there in the dunes"; the others commanded from bunkers: Sharon at Tassa, Mandler at the Mitla, and Magen at Baluza. So far I had been cut off from the external world. Gonen had not paid a visit since the war began; Dayan had made do with a visit to Sharon. Even the newspapermen who had been assigned to cover our part in the fighting "dropped out" on the way and found shelter and hospitality with Sharon.

Bar-Lev joined me in my armored command vehicle, and I briefed him on the situation. Egyptian artillery shells exploded around us, and Bar-Lev remarked that in his view I was situated too close to the front. I replied that we had already got used to the Egyptian shelling and that it was not very effective. In fact, I told him, we hadn't yet had to switch our own artillery to alternative positions even once, because the Egyptians lacked effective counterbattery fire. He informed me that a battalion of paratroopers was en route to my division, and a similar unit was to be attached to Sharon's division, the intention being to have them operate by night behind enemy lines. In addition, Bar-Lev said, GHQ had approved the planning of a crossing operation to take place near Deversoir, north of Bitter Lake. This would be the subject discussed that evening at 2000 hours with the division commanders, and Bar-Lev suggested I prepare for this conference.

After he left, Gonen informed me that things were going very well on the northern front and that Yanosh (Col. Avigdor Ben-Gal, commander of the 7th Armored Brigade) was approaching Damascus. This, I decided, called for a special edition of my news bulletin. After raising my brigade commanders on the radio net, I began: "All 'Karish' stations, this is 'Karish' speaking. The Syrians are getting royally screwed. Our forces on the northern front are advancing relentlessly. Things are going well for them and Yanosh is already at the gates of Damascus." Then — I don't know what happened to me, but suddenly I began broadcasting to the Egyptians. I suppose it crossed my mind that they must surely be monitoring our nets. "Oh Egyptians! If you are listening to us, then listen carefully, you sons of bitches: your turn is coming!" Then Natke came on the air and launched in with some zestful cursing. No matter that Yanosh had not yet, in fact, reached the gates of Damascus — morale, which had been very high since the previous evening, was now higher than ever.

Darkness was about to fall. The Egyptians' daily "farewell artillery shelling" was leveled at us; a white smokescreen went up adjacent to the canal, and flares lit up the sky. Yes, this series was now repeated for the third day running, as though speaking to us in a language both sides understood: "That's all for today — see you tomorrow."

Activity had already entered a set routine. As night fell, I radioed: "Repeat yesterday's exercise," and the tanks pulled back into their night bivouacs to prepare for the next day's fighting; the armored infantry and reconnaissance units moved up to hold the front line. At night there was another meeting of brigade commanders so orders could be issued, and then, in the morning: "Today is the twelfth of October, Friday, the day on which the Levites in the Temple would chant: 'Why should you run about the hills to seek out the enemy? Surely it is better that you should post lookouts and do as in days past, as it is said: Each with one hand shall labor in the work [reorganizing] and with the other shall hold his weapon' [ready to join battle]."

For the fourth day of the defense (12 October), my orders were to deploy only one battalion in each brigade sector and that even if Egyptian forces should appear in front of us, the activity of the nondeployed battalions — organizing, tending tanks, preparing for future operations — was not to be disturbed except on my order. That morning I was informed that Yoel's brigade would be taking over our sector and replacing us in the defensive battle, so that my division could move out and prepare for the crossing operation. Yoel arrived around noon; his brigade was made up of Soviet-made T-54 and T-55 tanks captured in the 1967 war and afterward incorporated into the IDF.

Colonel Yoel had been on my staff in the Armored Corps for some years. I was quite fond of him. He was a very professional officer, energetic, efficient and courageous. He told me what he had been doing since the war broke out. In the main, he had been engaged in blocking Egyptian breakthrough attempts, particularly assisting Mandler in the southern canal zone around Ras-Sudar and at the Jundhi Pass. I then briefed Yoel on the enemy in our sector, the terrain, the manner of fighting of our own forces and of the enemy. To my own surprise, I found that my briefing took quite a long time. Without being aware of it, we had in fact accumulated a considerable amount of information and experience. Yoel now issued his orders to his subordinates as his brigade, led by his deputies, approached. It arrived in a fine, broad deployment, which is a pleasure for every armor man to see. I decided that his brigade would replace us on the line only the following morning, after his commanders had accompanied my commanders on the front line that afternoon.

On 12 October additional tanks were repaired, and we were even able to begin reorganizing. In addition, a new battalion was on its way to join and reinforce my division. It was headed by Ehud, who had returned from the United States when war broke out. In fact, all his subordinate commanders and crewmen had also returned home from their studies in the United States. Ehud had thirty-eight tanks, of which ten were Centurions and the rest Pattons; he also had ten armored personnel carriers. Ehud and his force would join us on the thirteenth.

The work of reorganization was complex and delicate: first, because we had to be ready to enter battle at any moment. (As things transpired, I helped Yoel not only with the division artillery and Zeldas, but also by dispatching battalions to assist him when the going got rough.) Secondly, we had to try to balance the brigades as regards the number of tanks each had and to create homogeneity where the types of tanks were concerned. Moreover, this had to be worked out in light of several factors. On the one hand, battalions wanted to return to the brigades with which they had undergone training; but on the other hand, they also wanted to stay with the brigade in whose framework they had just fought life-and-death battles. Furthermore, many tanks had been "snatched," among both divisions and brigades, mostly from repair points or workshops. The Israeli mentality regarded such "grabs" as an expression of initiative, fellowship, and the ability to "make out." All in all, the good spirit that prevailed in the division helped overcome problems.

For the first time since the war broke out, most of the division was not engaged in contact with the enemy that day. The work of repair and treatment of tanks was at its height. The brigade and battalion commanders assembled their men to discuss with them the lessons of the past few days and what the future held. We now had 272 tanks, of which 15 were still undergoing repair. That meant, if Yoel's tanks — which would stay behind to hold the sector — were deducted, we would carry out the canal-crossing with some 200 tanks, a large, battle-tested division now functioning like a well-oiled machine.

In the morning hours of 13 October I was called to attend a meeting with the chief of staff that was to take place in Sharon's HQ at Tassa. Arriving early, I had two experiences that reminded me "civilization" was still in existence. First I met Colonel Amnon, of Sharon's division, who had served as my operations officer in the Armored Corps for about two years and with whom I had become fast friends. Amnon recounted the terrible hours he had undergone at the beginning of the war when his tank brigade was deployed on its own along the entire 160 km of the Suez Canal, with him in the central sector. By the time the other brigades arrived from the rear, most of his brigade had been decimated; some of the remnants of his battalions had been absorbed by reserve brigades in other sectors. During the containment phase, he had gradually built up his strength and now had almost a full brigade again. Amnon wouldn't let me go until I had showered in his now empty brigade HQ at Tassa. I had become used to the dirt and to being unshaven, and I had forgotten that there were such things as showers. It was refreshing, but it felt a bit strange, out of place.

My second experience came as I awaited the arrival of the chief of staff. I was wandering about the many corridors and small rooms in which officers, equipped with telephones and maps, controlled Sharon's field forces. The place looked well organized. There was little communications activity. Sharon's chief of staff, Gideon, and the communications officer, Hillel, seemed to be engaged in routine activity. Suddenly I heard one of the officers tell Sharon that it was time to partake of some of "the fine cheeses." So partake we did, and there was a wealth of cheese to choose from. I have to admit that life here was much more pleasant than it was at my own HQ: showers, cheeses, bunkers — and as long as I was a guest here, I enjoyed it. For myself, however, I preferred being in the dunes. In all the wars I had been through, from the time I was a company commander to this day, when I was commanding a division I had always kept away from built-up areas or from buildings of any kind. These, I felt, were liable to make you remote from your men and to divert you and your staff from concentrating solely on the task at hand.

Meanwhile the chief of staff arrived, accompanied by Maj. Gen. (Res.) Ezer Weizman (former commander of the air force), along with Bar-Lev and Gonen. As we were all entering one of the rooms a shocking piece of news arrived. General Mandler had been critically wounded and was being evacuated to Refidim. He had been visiting one of his brigades, which was deployed on the front line in the Gidi sector, when the area came under heavy shelling. The brigade commander implored him to wait for the barrage to abate, but Mandler said he could not. There was much to do, and he had moved to a road junction that the Egyptians had already shelled. Just as he got there the enemy shelled the place again. Mandler's armored command vehicle took a direct hit. Within minutes we learned he was dead. There was silence in the room. Images of Avraham "Albert" Mandler passed through everyone's mind. He was to have transferred command of the Sinai Division to General Magen the day after the war erupted; but he had smelled the tension in the air and had refused to leave. Then, when the war did break out, he had gone through that terrible first night when his regular division alone against the masses of the enemy was crushed before his eyes. During the days of the containment battle the division had begun to recover and to be rebuilt. Now, when we were on the verge of moving to a counterattack, he had fallen. He would not be able to see the shift the war would take.

The silence was soon broken. It was proposed that Brigadier General Magen, who was to have assumed command of the Sinai Division in early October, be flown from Baluza to take command. Magen's place at Baluza would be taken by Southern Command's chief of staff, Brigadier General Sasson. Forty-five minutes later, Magen entered the shelter and in our presence was given command of the Sinai Division. There were no badges of rank around, so Ezer Weizman removed his own insignia, and he and the chief of staff pinned them on Magen.

Our conference opened in an oppressive atmosphere. The question of the date for the canal crossing and for launching our major counterattack was on the agenda. The dilemma confronting us was whether we should wait for a possible enemy attack, which might after all never take place. The conclusion was that come what may, our crossing operation would begin in the evening of the fifteenth of October. If the Egyptians attacked before then, we would first defend and contain them and then move directly into our counterattack. If they delayed their attack, we would wait no longer but would launch the crossing operation as planned.

As I returned to my command post to prepare for the crossing, I wondered who would break the deadlock that had descended on the front. Our forces, or the Egyptians?

CHAPTER TWENTY

STALEMATE BROKEN: EGYPTIANS ATTACK ON 14 October

T he front-line situation had remained unchanged since the evening of 9 October; this, despite the shelling that took place all along the front and the small-scale attacks, mainly in my sector. The Egyptian offensive activity went on through 10 and 11 October, and on the following two days they tried to press forward by what we termed "creeping defense." In both camps, the Israeli and the Egyptian, there were deliberations and debates, plans and preparations.

The Egyptians were in their "operational hold" stage. Their consolidation along the east bank of the canal afforded them considerable satisfaction and pride. Our last isolated and besieged strongpoint, the Maoz of the quay point, received permission to surrender on 12 October, and its men were taken into captivity. Egyptian television was able to show the masses that their army was continuing its fine work. But among the Egyptian high command, there were major differences of outlook.

War Minister Ahmed Ismail and Chief of Staff Shazli were polar opposites in character, and their differences were already present at the beginning of the war. Ismail, fifty-six, a rather bland type and intellectually limited, nonetheless had some compensating virtues that were appreciated by the Egyptian hierarchy; his very serious approach to the military profession and his complete devotion to the army gave him the reputation of being "every inch a soldier." In 1970 when I initiated the armored raid on the western side of the Gulf of Suez, Ismail was commander of that sector, and Nasser had dismissed him. Sadat brought him back, first as chief of the Intelligence Branch, and then, following Sadat's quarrel with War Minister Sidki, Ismail was appointed minister of war. Sadat viewed Ahmed Ismail as a man after his own heart, as the right man in the right place, because Ismail wholeheartedly agreed with Sadat that it was best to go to war with what was available — even if only partial attainments resulted — in order to break the political deadlock. Another major factor in Ismail's favor, as far as Sadat was concerned, was that he had no political ambitions.

In contrast, General Shazli, fifty-one, a paratrooper, was a colorful figure, a real character. Arrogant, given to theatrical behavior, his comrades often described him as a prima donna. In 1967 his reputation preceded him, and even before the war began he was being talked about on our side. This was the first time in our conflict with the Arabs that the myth of an Arab commander developed. During the period of tense expectation — about a week before the Six Day War broke out — Shazli, at the head of a task force, arrived by train at El Arish. Following some of the deceptive maneuvers we carried out, however, his force was rushed southward and was deployed opposite Wadi Kuraiya. When the fighting began, most of his force fled and was captured while trying to get through the Mitla Pass. I took part in the quick blockade of the Mitla, and I really wanted to capture Shazli, but he ruined his reputation by being one of the first to flee. The legend was shattered, to be replaced by contempt. Following the Yom Kippur War, I had the opportunity to peruse some of the wealth of intelligence material we captured from the Egyptian Third Army. Shazli's operational orders, which appeared among this material, showed that he was a very capable officer indeed.

The dispute between Shazli and Ahmed Ismail, then, began very early in the war. When Shazli saw how successful the Egyptian crossing operation had been, he wanted to take advantage of the surprise move and burst through into our rear area. Ahmed Ismail was dead set against such a move, his chief aim being to preserve the integrity of the Egyptian force and not endanger it in any way. His inclination was to keep extending the phase of the "operational hold." However, as the days afer 8 October passed, it became apparent to the Egyptians that this stage of their plan was not achieving its purpose, because there were no further Israeli armor attacks after the ninth. On the eleventh and twelfth it became clear that the situation on the Syrian front was extremely grave for the Arabs. The Egyptians now began to fear that the IDF would rout the Syrians and then transfer more forces to be concentrated against the Egyptians. It may have been this consideration that was decisive when Ismail finally gave his consent for his forces to begin their third operational phase, that of the breakthrough from the bridgehead eastward.

The internal debate in the Egyptian high command was intertwined with an acrimonious dispute between the Egyptians and the Syrians. The Syrians initially broke through our lines on the southern Golan Heights and took advantage of this to move in more armor and to penetrate deep into our territory toward the Jordan River and the Sea of Galilee. Their prospects were in fact quite good, had they kept up the momentum of their initial thrust. Once they had penetrated into our depth, however, they began showing hesitation, and their momentum was broken. When our reserve formations arrived, we launched a counterattack. Our professional superiority in tank gunnery and in mobile warfare and the boldness of our men led to the destruction of most of the penetrating tanks. As a result, the invading Syrian forces were pushed back across the border. On 11 October we launched a second counterattack; our forces broke through the Syrian lines and were approaching Damascus.

In the light of this situation, the Syrians demanded that the Egyptians cease their "operational hold" and resume their offensive in order to step up the pressure on the IDF and prevent it from concentrating its main efforts (especially the air force) on the Syrian front. It soon became apparent that there was a misunderstanding between Syrian President Assad and the Syrian high command on the one hand and Sadat and the Egyptian high command on the other hand. The Syrians claimed that the agreed-upon plan called for the Egyptians to continue with their first operational phase until they reached a line about 100 km east of the canal; only then would the "operational hold" phase begin. With that completed, the Egyptians and the Syrians would move to the "liberation of the territories occupied in 1967."

The Egyptians, however, said their implementation was in line with the plan. But the Egyptians were slow in preparing for the breakthrough attack into our depth. On 12 and 13 October, we noted many indications that an Egyptian attack was imminent. (Their attack was in fact set for 14 October, but we did not know this.) We thought that the Egyptians would once again land commando forces behind our lines and try to break through with the 21st and the 4th Armored Divisions, followed by the 23rd and the 6th Mechanized Divisions.

On the Israeli side, too, conferences, debates, plans, and preparations were under way. The stalemate on the front line, our increasingly professional adaptation to a defensive containment battle, the Egyptians' fatigue, and our success in economizing forces and building up strength had improved conditions for a counterattack on the southern front. On 11 October General Headquarters gave Southern Command HQ the green light to prepare a canal-crossing operation. The following day General Bar-Lev presented the plan, which was proposed for the night of 13–14 October. The conference in Tel Aviv was attended by the chief of staff, his deputy, the director of Military Intelligence, the commander of the air force and Generals Yariv and Ze'evi. The air force commander, Major General Peled, favored the operation, pointing out that because of the ongoing attrition being experienced by the air force, delay was impossible. Peled also pointed out that if the crossing were successful, the ground forces would be able to destroy the antiaircraft missile batteries on the west bank, thus helping the air force gain freedom of operation.

The director of Military Intelligence, Major General Ze'ira, also supported a crossing operation, but the deputy chief of staff, General Tal, opposed the idea strongly. He argued that such an operation depended on a breakthrough to the canal which would be difficult and cost many lives. It was, therefore, preferable to him to engage in armored combat on the east bank of the canal. The chief of staff tended to support the proposed crossing operation, but he thought that the defense minister should also take part in the discussion and decision-making process. Dayan, who was then on the northern front, was requested to come to GHQ upon his return. He decided to have the prime minister make the final decision. Thus the same forum moved, that afternoon, to the prime minister's office where Deputy Prime Minister Yigal Allon and Minister without Portfolio Israel Galili also joined the discussion.

The two contradictory positions were put forward, with Tal against the crossing, and Bar-Lev rejecting an unlimited wait for an Egyptian attack. In the midst of the discussion, however, reports that an Egyptian attack was imminent arrived. Under these conditions, all agreed that it would be better to wait, contain the Egyptian attack, and carry out the crossing operation later. Bar-Lev at once directed Southern Command to plan the containment of the Egyptian attack but without neglecting the preparations for the canal-crossing operation. This was also the intention of the chief of staff.

The plan at Southern Command HQ was to block the enemy armor while letting them move deep into our territory away from their infantry support and antiaircraft missile umbrella. It was decided that Magen's, Sharon's, and Sasson's divisions would deploy for containment in their sectors, with Sharon also holding one brigade in reserve to deal with any possible local Egyptian thrusts in his and Magen's sectors. Since Yoel's brigade had already been sent to replace me, my division would take up a position in the rear, to prepare for the crossing opportunity, while at the same time serve as the major reserve striking force to repulse any Egyptian penetration. Accordingly, on the night of 12 October I held a planning session with my staff and then issued pertinent orders to my four brigade commanders.

On 12 October the Egyptian forces on the east bank of the canal had already begun to prepare the terrain to absorb the forces that would be crossing the canal for the breakthrough. Their transfer of forces commenced on the night of 12–13 October and continued on the thirteenth. By the morning of 14 October the Egyptians had already sited fourteen antiaircraft missile batteries, including six mobile SAM-6 batteries. Many artillery and mortar battalions had also been moved up.

We expected two main efforts. In the Second Army's sector, the 21st Armored Division would lead the attack, while in the Third Army, the 4th Armored Division would be the spearhead. In their wake would come mechanized divisions along with independent tank brigades and infantry divisions. We feared a night landing of many commandos in our rear, along with a 750-tank thrust by the Third Army toward the Gidi and Mitla passes, and another 750 Second Army tanks toward Tassa and from there to Refidim. We were even apprehensive that these two forces would link up north of the Gidi Pass, moving this massive concentration of 1,500 tanks into the Refidim Valley. Against this immense force, we had only 750 tanks deployed along the entire front.

What actually happened was not what we expected. The Egyptians transferred only a part of their second-echelon forces to the east bank. The Third Army moved just one tank brigade across from the 4th Division, while the other tank brigade, the mechanized brigade, and the divisional HQ all remained on the west bank. The Second Army moved the 21st Armored Division across along with one tank brigade and a mechanized brigade, while its second tank brigade — which had been operating on the east bank under the command of the 16th Infantry Division — now returned to its parent division, putting the 21st Division at full strength. The 23rd Mechanized Division, except for its 24th Tank Brigade, remained on the west bank. As a result of this deployment, the Egyptians had just 1,000 tanks on the east bank on the morning of 14 October. Moreover, instead of the extensive commando landings we had expected, only about one hundred of these troops were landed before dawn on the fourteenth near Tassa. They were attacked and wiped out even before the Egyptian attack got under way. Apparently after their failures in massive commando landings at the beginning of the war and the many casualties they had sustained, the Egyptians were in no mood to repeat this exercise.

The attack began at 0620 hours with a heavy artillery barrage along the entire length of the front. Egyptian aircraft carried out a few sorties here and there, but these were brief and shallow and left no mark on the battlefield. At about 0700 hours tanks and infantry of the first operational echelon advanced in support of the breakthrough effort by armor of the second-echelon forces. But instead of concentrated attacks, they tried to break through in brigade strength at nine separate points along the front line.

Most of the Egyptian tanks were stopped short before our contact line, suffering heavy losses. The only division sector where fighting occurred in the depth of our territory was that under Magen. Two columns of tanks from the 3rd Tank Brigade, reinforced by one tank battalion, began advancing at 0700 along the broad Wadi Mab'ouk. In their vanguard mechanized infantry equipped with antitank weapons moved, and bringing up the rear were artillery and antiaircraft batteries. Magen's long-range observers spotted the advancing force and alerted our troops, but by the time our tanks engaged them the Egyptians had almost reached the Lateral Road. Suddenly the enemy columns came under heavy artillery fire, and their way was blocked by an armored infantry battalion. Two reduced tank battalions attacked them on both flanks, and after brief engagements most of the forward sections of the columns were annihilated. Air force planes, which were able to operate undisturbed because the Egyptians had moved away from their missile umbrella, finished off the job. About fifty Egyptian tanks were left burning in the wadi.

Another column, which was making its way south on the Yoreh Road, was made up of tanks of the 22nd Tank Brigade and remnants of the 1st Mechanized Brigade. The story here was similar. Israeli paratroopers, supported by 81mm and 120mm mortars and a few tanks, halted the column, causing heavy losses; the air force completed the work. The third force of the Egyptian Third Army that made its way into Magen's sector was composed in the main of the 25th Tank Brigade, which sought to advance into the Gidi Pass. Avraham's brigade stopped them twice: first at 0800 hours at long range with five enemy tanks hit, and then at 1200 hours, when the Egyptians tried a flanking movement south of the Gidi and lost fifteen tanks.

Second Army armor attacked in Sharon's sector, in Sasson's, and in mine. In Sharon's sector the 21st Armored Division operated; its 14th Tank Brigade advanced on the Puton Road toward Ziona. There Haim's brigade was waiting for it with one of his battalions blocking the Egyptians in front and another hitting from the north. By 1500 hours the Egyptian 14th Tank Brigade retreated, leaving behind around forty smashed tanks. Just two of Haim's tanks were hit. South of this column, the 1st Tank Brigade made its way toward Hamadia. There they encountered Amnon's brigade. Two battalions blocked the Egyptians in front while the third struck them from the south. Another forty Egyptian tanks were left behind, destroyed.

In Sasson's sector about sixty tanks of the Egyptian 15th Tank Brigade tried to advance along the Qantara-Baluza Road. In addition, two smaller forces began to make their way parallel to the road, but farther from it on each side. Fedale's brigade let them approach and in the ensuing battle destroyed some thirty enemy tanks.

Things got a bit more complicated in my sector. On 12 October I had already planned and issued orders for the forthcoming battle. When the Egyptian attack failed to materialize on 13 October, we continued defense operations in our sector while at the same time preparing for the canal crossing. On the night of 13-14 October we were engaged in studying the various possibilities for crossing. Early in the morning of 14 October, Yoel's brigade deployed on the ridge line, and I sent Dovik to set up a small, improvised forward command post on the Spontani Road. I remained in the rear along with the brigades commanded by Natke, Gabi, and Aryeh.

At about 0700 hours Egyptian planes attacked our forces on Havraga, the ridge line came under an artillery barrage, and enemy tanks began advancing simultaneously toward Ma'adim, Zrakor, and Havraga. At the same time Gonen called, informing me that the Egyptians were attacking all along the front line and ordering me to move a brigade at once to a point south of Tassa and prepare to launch a counterattack. I was faced with a dilemma. The Egyptians were attacking in my sector, but my division had been assigned the task of being the reserve division for Southern Command. Now in the sector that we knew so well, where we had fought so intensively for five days, and had had no more than 120 tanks for some periods, Yoel was deployed with only 75 tanks. He was under heavy pressure across the entire sector. Was I to leave him to his fate?

I decided to split the division and to attach Aryeh's brigade to Dovik as well and have him take command of both brigades. At about 0900 the fighting in our sector was at its height. Gonen called again to have me rush a second brigade — Gabi's brigade — to the Tassa sector. This meant that I must move out and leave Dovik to improvise hastily a command set up. He had three reduced brigades under him, two of them engaged in combat on the front line (under

Yoel and Amir), and one (Aryeh) in reserve. Thus my force was now deployed as two small divisions, one defending force and one moving toward Tassa. We had two forward command posts, with the main command post supporting the operation of both forces.

The first wave of the attack in my sector was taken by Yoel's brigade alone. It was quite a baptism of fire for most of the men. They fought bravely and made the best use they could of their T-55 tanks (captured in the 1967 war), but their lack of experience in the sector was apparent. They suffered many losses and about fifteen of their tanks were hit. Two battalion commanders were among the wounded. The turret of Yoel's tank was also hit, and he was thrown from the tank, but he returned and continued to command his force.

The second wave of the Egyptian attack began about 0930, shortly after Dovik had sent Amir's and Eliashiv's battalions along with some armored infantry troops in Zeldas to the front line for reinforcement. This was a timely move. After some bitter fighting, the Egyptian attack was broken at about noon, and they retreated leaving about forty burning tanks behind. Dovik's command was exemplary. Unruffled, he was in complete control of the situation and made full use of the knowledge and experience he had gained over the past six days of fighting. Yoel, too, did very well, even though he found himself under heavy pressure in a new sector.

In the evening Yoel's brigade pulled back for reorganization, and Aryeh's brigade deployed on the contact line. The next morning (15 October), when Yoel moved up to deploy in the sector, he found that Egyptian infantry had infiltrated Havraga, so he had to retake it while mopping up the area. Since only about twelve hours remained before the canal-crossing operation was to begin, Aryeh's brigade and Amir's battalion were pulled out of the sector so they could take part in the final preparations for the crossing. We thus left the sector where for six days we had been on the defensive. At 1600 Sasson arrived to take over responsibility for the sector from Dovik. Yoel's brigade was now on its own.

As my division moved southward toward Tassa, I flew there by helicopter, met with Gonen, and received from him directives and explanations on how Southern Command expected the battle to develop. On the way back, just as the helicopter was about to land at my forward command post some 10 km south of Tassa, the helicopter abruptly lifted and began flying due east.

"What happened?" I asked, dumbfounded.

"An order from central control," was the pilot's reply.

We flew about twenty minutes, as far as Refidim, and the pilot said: "We can return now, but I suggest we refuel here first."

"That makes sense," I replied.

On the way back, just as we neared Tassa, the helicopter again suddenly turned around and moved eastward. This time I was furious. I shouted at the pilot. Nothing helped. The order was from air force central control. At my demand, he explained to central control that his passenger was a division commander who was arbitrarily being separated from his division — but the sergeants at central control were not impressed. I told him to try to raise the commander of the air force. The reply was that the commander of the air force confirms that orders issued by central control must be carried out. (I would subsequently learn that the matter never reached the air force commander himself.)

I began to "go wild" and to threaten the poor pilot, who was frightened and made the "concession" of stopping his flight eastward and of circling around instead while he communicated with the anonymous men at central control. Finally, he was "persuaded" to drop me off at my forward command post. This "exercise" consumed about two hours. The commander of the reserve force was for that length of time a "prisoner" of the air force. There could be no illustration more striking of the state of cooperation between the air and ground forces at that time.

Fortunately, the Egyptian attack failed without the need for the reserve division to go into action. The attack was easily repulsed, with some two hundred enemy tanks destroyed. Twenty-five of our tanks were hit. In line with Soviet doctrine, the Egyptians tried to break through on many axes, the intention apparently being to concentrate forces at those places where success was thought to be attainable. But our superiority in tank gunnery and mobile warfare dashed their hopes. They were thrown back, generally on the forward line of contact, with heavy losses of men and equipment. The results of the battle favorably affected our strengths in relation to the enemy, just as we were about to launch the major counterattack. Yet I thought, a crossing is a complicated operation, and the main work still lies ahead.

The six days of defense and containment — from the ninth to the fourteenth — were at an end. At the beginning we were fighting for our very survival, but toward the end of this period we were simultaneously defending and planning and preparing for the next stage, that of crossing the canal. When the Egyptian attack on 14 October failed, we thought that they would not resume their offensive in the next few days. Therefore, if we wanted to end the stalemate and overcome the enemy, the only way was to attack. And that was the decision: to attack and to cross on the following day, the fifteenth of October.

Egyptian aircraft overflys Israeli forward command post facilities. (p. 350)

"War Council" in the dunes near Kishuf; Dayan, Bar-Lev, author. Sharon not yet arrived.

Sweet Water Canal in the green belt. Note passage prepared by Egyptians to ease crossing. Usually the water obscures the stones.

Landscape of the green belt.

Tanks operating in the green belt south of the stone bridge.

A missile launcher. Note the sophisticated gear in the rear for fire control.

Israelis taking over captured Egyptian missile site.

Only the dogs were left. (p. 357)

Charging an Egyptian command post.

Israeli paratroopers assaulting near the Chinese Farm.

Charging with all battalions in wide formation, 22 & 23 October.

Soviet mobile assault bridging equipment.

Typical Egyptian quarters for military families, near Suez City.

Our tanks in central street of Suez City.

Crossing the Suez Canal on assault bridge.

Combat on Geneifa Hills.

Carrying rations to Egyptian Third Army after the cease-fire.

PART IV

THE CANAL CROSSING

CHAPTER TWENTY-ONE

OPERATIONAL BACKGROUND

U ntil 1967 the IDF had no means for water-crossing operations, nor had we any special interest in the subject. But Israel's new boundaries, the Jordan River and the Suez Canal — two water obstacles — created a new situation. Our strategic doctrine always held that the best defense is offense and that the war must be transferred to enemy territory. Thus the new defense lines obligated us to develop a water-crossing capacity as quickly as possible.

We ran into difficulties in trying to purchase modern and efficient bridging gear abroad. The equipment that we bought confronted us with many problems. What we purchased were floatable iron cubes — uni-floats — each of which was 5 × 2.5 × 1.2 meters and weighed 3 tons. These cubes could be linked together in order to form platforms of various size, which could then be used as rafts capable of carrying tanks or even to form an entire bridge.

In the immediate post-1967 period, things moved slowly; it was only in early 1969 that the subject was given its first major thrust. The initiative came from Col. Moshe Peled, who was then chief of doctrine in IDF's Training Branch. He organized a bridging demonstration as part of an advanced course for the IDF's high command.

The demonstration was effective and showed just how complex a water-crossing operation was, particularly in the face of enemy resistance. There were tactical, technical, and organizational problems to be solved.

Naturally the means available to the Engineering Corps and the methods they employed influenced the solution considerably. First, infantry troops crossed in light rubber dinghies in order to take the far bank and safeguard the bridging work on the near side of the obstacle. This was followed by the arrival of a convoy of trucks at working points along the water barrier. A huge crane began unloading the uni-floats, which the engineers then began assembling in the water. When a square made up of nine of these floats (3 × 3) had been formed, two triangular approach ramps were attached to it. These two ramps could be elevated or lowered by hydraulic power, adjusting them to various bank contours. In addition, two small floats were attached to the flanks of the raft, enabling two engines to be installed. It took about an hour to assemble such a motorized raft. The engineers could then begin moving tanks from one bank to the other. Only then, after they had several such rafts in operation, could they begin to construct one linked bridge across the entire obstacle.

The method demonstrated was reasonable and acceptable for heavy, awkward bridging gear such as we had. Other armies made similar use of this kind of equipment. Many armies, however, also had light, mobile equipment that enabled them to bridge a gap relatively quickly. Many troops and much equipment could then be transferred on rafts and on the light bridges to expand the bridgehead. Only then would heavy equipment be brought in to construct massive bridges.

I saw that the first method would make the assaulting infantry troops fight alone for a relatively long period, without tank — or even armored personnel carrier — support. Moreover, these troops would be able to seize only a narrow bridgehead, and the enemy would remain close to the assembly site of the bridge, employing small arms and flat trajectory fire to disrupt the construction work and damage the equipment. What we really needed, I thought, was some sort of assault gear; tank-towed bridging equipment would enable us to cross quickly even in the face of strong artillery fire, and within a few minutes we would have tanks to support the infantry on the far bank. If we had armored infantry and tanks on the other side, we would soon be able to expand the bridgehead.

Immediately following this demonstration, I had Armored Corps HQ undertake an energetic research and development program with the aim of finding our own water-crossing means and methods. Our underlying concept was that the basic element would be the raft, rather than the single uni-float cube. A fully assembled tank-raft, consisting of nine cubes, two approach ramps and two engines, was 22 meters long, 11 meters wide, and weighed about 60 tons. The idea was to have such preassembled rafts towed to the shore by tanks. The rafts would then be pushed into the water so that tanks could at once begin to be ferried across. Once eleven rafts were afloat, they would be joined together and form a bridge across the 180-meter-wide Suez Canal.

A series of experiments shows us that a pair of tanks could tow a preeassembled raft across typical Sinai terrain without damage to either the raft or the tanks. At the same time, we developed a simple sledge, in order to reduce the friction as the raft was towed along. We also came up with a way to attach gigantic wheels to the raft so that even one tank could tow it.

The entire matter was given a major thrust forward by Exercise Oz, held in the winter of 1971–72 and the largest such exercise held until then by the IDF. The exercise was designed to test many subjects. The primary one was the new structure of the regular armored division, this against the background of a crossing operation, penetration deep into enemy territory, mobile combat against enemy armor, and capture of key terrain features. My division would perform the exercise. Southern Command at that time was commanded by General Sharon, who ran the exercise; his deputy was General Gonen. We were three ambitious generals. Sharon and Gonen set elaborate objectives, while I aspired, with my regular HQ staff and trained troops, to prove that the problems that confronted us could be solved smoothly and professionally.

Sharon had a great idea. Through relatively minor engineering work, he was able to enlarge the small Ruafa'a Dam, located in the middle of the desert in northern Sinai, which absorbs the flood waters that flow through the El Arish wadi during the winter rains. Thus a small water obstacle was created that would enable us — despite the limitations of its location and its size — to conduct a "wet" crossing operation combined with a fire exercise.

We wanted to cross using our new "assault" method but at that time our crossing means were in the experimental stage. With an intensive effort, we succeeded in quickly constructing additional models of the type of raft then undergoing experiments. On the day of the exercise the division advanced while towing the bridging gear. Artillery softened the opposite bank, tanks took up positions to support the infantry, and the infantry crossed in rubber dinghies. Armored personnel carriers, which had been provided with floating capability, crossed to the other side. Being mounted, the men in the APCs were able to conduct mobile combat and so mop up a greater area. Now the bridging equipment was lowered into the water. Hastily constructed, the crossing means were far from sophisticated so that the actual bridging took a considerable time but still far less than previous tests. Tanks were quickly transferred to the far bank on rafts and joined battle. After about an hour we had a bridge. We then continued our deep-penetration assault by night with two tank brigades along a line several kilometers wide.

A few days before the exercise I visited the engineering units in the field with General Tal, who had just been appointed deputy chief of staff. I showed him the water-crossing means that were being developed. Tal had just returned to the IDF after a period of working in the Ministry of Defense, and the entire subject was new to him. I briefed him on our new solutions which would provide us with flexibility to select the crossing sector we wanted and then move the bridging gear there with relative ease.

Tal promised to help give things a push, and he was as good as his word. He met with Col. David Laskov of the Engineering Corps. Laskov is a unique character. The oldest officer in the IDF, he was then pushing seventy. He was known for his innovative mind and his abundance of ideas on how to solve various battlefield problems by engineering or technical concepts.

Laskov suggested, and Tal helped implement, the development of a roller bridge. Such a bridge consisted of more than one hundred iron rollers, two meters in diameter, which were attached together to make one rolling bridge 180 meters long. The main advantage of a roller bridge was that it could be pushed into the Canal. It could float and hit the far bank. This process was truly an assault process. However, the bridge had many disadvantages: it took three days to assemble, weighed four hundred tons, and had to be towed by sixteen tanks. It could only be towed straight forward on a wide, previously cleared road. Because of its weight and inability to change direction, there was no flexibility to maneuver from sector to sector. In unforeseen battle circumstances, this could be disastrous. Furthermore, this monster had not been tested adequately.

Besides the uni-float rafts, the Engineering Corps purchased — as salvage, in Europe — mobile bridging equipment. Named Gilowas, these were very large vehicles with correspondingly large wheels that were capable of moving to the water, floating, and — by means of hydraulic power — opening up two treadways suitable for tank tracks. The linking together of three such vehicles formed a raft unit capable of traveling across the water from bank to bank while carrying one tank. Six of them joined together would create a raft that could carry two tanks. The coupling together of a considerable number of them resulted in the construction of one continuous bridge. The Gilowa had two main disadvantages; the first was logistical maintenance problems of these well-worn vehicles. The second drawback was operational; we were worried by its vulnerability. The vehicle was floated with the help of inflatable rubber sleeves that were fitted around the Gilowa, but these sleeves could be punctured by enemy fire, thus sinking the vehicle. This problem could be overcome by filling the floats with a light foamy material. Although the vehicles were purchased relatively cheaply, it was a fairly costly process to overhaul them. But their high mobility on the ground gave us a much needed means of assault.

During the state of alert declared in April–May 1973, when we thought war was liable to break out, Tal allocated funds for enhancing the mobility of the uni-float rafts. However, this was limited to about twenty rafts only, and overhaul of the Gilowa vehicles was halted in midwork, leaving us with only eighteen of them.

Every IDF commander was deeply imbued with the idea that we would have to cross at some point; this was an organic part of the IDF's doctrine of transferring the war to enemy territory and terminating it there quickly. We had spent years preparing for this. Now, since the beginning of the war, the Egyptians had succeeded in consolidating a narrow bridgehead that was supported by weapons sited on the west bank, including protection afforded by an antiaircraft missile umbrella. There were two courses open to us in order to end the war on the east bank: either to wait for the Egyptians to launch an offensive that would carry them beyond the strong defensive disposition they had occupied since the "operational halt" phase or to launch a frontal attack of our own, without our being able to maneuver into their rear.

Virtually no one on the Israeli side doubted that the war would be decided only after we had crossed to the west bank and destroyed the main enemy force. The crossing idea was like some siren song, beckoning the commanders on, teasing them to dare and reach for the prize. As I saw it, the clever thing was to withstand the temptation but to watch out for just the *right* moment to cross. On 10 October, Bar-Lev arrived at Southern Command HQ. Gonen had suggested a crossing in the Port Fuad–Port Said area, but Bar-Lev said we were not yet ready. (Incidentally, our chief engineering officer made it clear that the bridging equipment would not be ready before 13 October.) That night, in a conference of the division commanders with Bar-Lev, Mandler was the only one to suggest a crossing. In his summation, Bar-Lev said we were not yet prepared to implement this, but preparations for a crossing should continue. The following day, 11 October, saw a shift on the battlefield, as Egyptian pressure slackened. Following discussions held that day at GHQ, the chief of staff decided that the crossing would take place in the Matzmed area. In the wake of this decision, Bar-Lev assembled his staff that evening at 2130; they decided on 13 October as "D day." Gonen proposed a second crossing, on 14 October, north of Qantara. At about 0200 hours on 13 October, reports came in to the effect that Great Britain was about to submit a cease-fire proposal to the United Nations. We were apprehensive that this was liable to be adopted while the military balance in the field was not in our favor. At once the suggestion came to execute a quick crossing at the canal's northern extremity toward Port Said. Suggestions for a crossing in this area had already been put forward as early as 9 October.

In fact, the terrain in the northern corner of the canal is unique. Port Said and Port Fuad are isolated, being bordered on the north by the Mediterranean and on the south by large lagoons. Hence, it was relatively easy to cut the area off and block the few avenues of approach on which reinforcements might arrive. Moreover, the area's isolation would facilitate an attack on the antiaircraft missile batteries, thus affording the air force freedom of action without any covering support fire from adjacent sectors. In the light of all these conditions, a crossing and an offensive with relatively small forces but with massive air support seemed feasible. Because the area was so tempting, the proposal to cross came up over and over, even when we lacked both sufficient forces and enough time. The disadvantage of a crossing there was that even a successful operation would not contribute to a decisive destruction of the Egyptian forces. On the other hand, the value of such an attack was that if a cease-fire were to be declared, the Egyptians would not hold the entire canal; the keys to its opening would be in our hands, to be used as a political bargaining card.

As it turned out, we learned on the morning of 13 October that Sadat was refusing to accept a cease-fire, so we returned to our original plan of a crossing around Strongpoint Matzmed.

As will be recalled, on 12 October Bar-Lev flew north to GHQ and put forward his suggestion for a crossing on the night of 13–14 October. The discussion was a prolonged one. General Tal opposed the plan. Dado and Dayan decided to put the matter to the prime minister for her decision. While the conference was still in progress, reports were received concerning enemy intentions of transferring armor to the east bank with the aim of launching an offensive. Everyone agreed that in view of these reports the crossing should be postponed until the Egyptian attack was halted. At all events, this postponement gave us time to commence preparations without which we would be unable to execute a crossing operation.

It was only on 13 October that crossing equipment began to be moved from various places and to be concentrated in Sharon's sector. The roller-bridge was assembled that day, and a tank company began to train in towing it. In addition, eight mobile uni-float rafts and sixteen self-propelled Gilowa-type vehicles were moved forward from Refidim to the Lateral Road. With regard to the other twelve mobile rafts that were at Baluza, Southern Command was unable to make up its mind who should detach tanks to tow them — Sharon or Sasson. It was only on the morning of 15 October that it was decided that Sasson would tow them to Sharon's sector. But postponing the decision so long caused a delay in their arrival on D day.

On the night of 13–14 October Southern Command HQ issued a written order under the code-name Operation *Abirei-Lev* (literally, Operation Valiant). There was still some hesitation on the fourteenth, because we weren't sure whether the major Egyptian offensive had been launched already or was still to come. Finally, it was decided that whether this was or was not the big Egyptian attack, we could wait no longer. At 2240 hours on 14 October, following the total failure of the Egyptian attack, an oral order was issued to supplement the written order. It directed that the crossing attack commence at 1700 hours on 15 October.

The crossing was not an end in itself but a means to support a general IDF counteroffensive designed to knock out the Egyptian army. Following the failure of the Egyptian armored attack on the fourteenth, most of its greatly reduced army remained on the west bank. There were five infantry divisions on the east bank and another seven tank brigades, numbering about 650–750 tanks. On the west bank two reduced divisions were deployed, one armored and one mechanized, as well as two tank brigades and paratroopers; all told, some 650 tanks.* While the forces on the east bank were deployed in high density in a narrow bridgehead with the Suez Canal protecting them from an attack from the rear, the forces on the west bank were positioned over an immense zone, from the outskirts of Cairo to the canal. This disposition of the Egyptian army afforded us a good chance of overcoming the reduced forces on the west bank, encircling part of the Egyptian Army and moving to annihilate the bridgeheads from the west while threatening their rear.

We had just 700 tanks at that time, organized in four divisions. Two of them were stronger than the others and were intended to cross

---

*In the sector of the Second Army on the east bank the 18th, 2nd, and 16th Infantry Divisions, the 21st Armored Division and the 15th and 24th Tank Brigades were all deployed. In the Second Army sector on the west bank only two mechanized brigades from the 23rd Mechanized Division were deployed. In the Third Army sector on the east bank were the 7th and 19th Infantry Divisions, the 130th Amphibious Brigade, and the 3rd, 22nd, and 25th Tank Brigades; while on the west bank were the 4th Armored Division (minus the 3rd Tank Brigade) and the 113th Mechanized Brigade from the 6th Mechanized Division.

Along Bitter Lake on the west bank was a Palestinian brigade reinforced by a battalion from Kuwait. Farther in the rear, in the Cairo area, were reserve forces of the Egyptian GHQ that included two tank brigades and four brigades of commandos and paratroopers; the tank brigade of the Guard of the Republic, along with two or three tank battalions from the School of Armor; the 35th Tank Brigade; and three paratroopers brigades and one commando brigade at Inshas (near Cairo). The location of the 3rd Mechanized Division was unknown.

the canal and attack on the west bank: Sharon's division with 240 tanks and my division with about 200 tanks. The other two divisions — Sasson's with 125 tanks and Magen's with 140 tanks — were to defend the east bank. Southern Command's objective was to take control over the area between the canal carrying sweet water from the Nile toward Ismailia and Mount Ubaid, Mount Ataka, and Suez City. This was an area some 100 km long and 30 km wide in its northern zone and 50 km wide in its southern part. The aim was to destroy forces on the west bank within this designated area and to encircle the Third Army and annihilate it from the rear.

Between Cairo and the Suez Canal lies the Sweet Water Canal, which is also called the Ismailia Canal. Near Ismailia, this canal branches into a northern and a southern section. Both branches run parallel to the Suez Canal, at a distance of from 1-3 km. Egyptian farmers cultivated both banks of all three canals; it was a mixed area, orchards alternating with cornfields and vegetable gardens. This greenbelt was a muddy place with considerable undergrowth that hampered tanks but was favorable to infantry. It was in the greenbelt area that the Egyptians had constructed much of what they needed for their crossing operation: high ramps for firing as well as roads and bridges across the Sweet Water Canal.

For us there were many advantages in the Matzmed area as the crossing site. It was adjacent to Bitter Lake and was located in the unheld seam between the two Egyptian Armies. The fact that no enemy troops were on the east bank provided us with a secure southern flank from the outset. Beyond Deversoir (opposite Matzmed on the west bank) lay an open desert expanse — the Plains of Aida — so that the moment we broke through to it from the greenbelt we would have excellent maneuverability in all directions. At a distance of about 15 km on either side of Deversoir were two key objectives that were very important to capture as quickly as possible. On the northwest were four to five bridges across the Ismailia Canal; capturing these would enable us to cut off the enemy forces to the north. To the southwest were the Geneifa Hills, which dominated their surroundings in all four directions. These cleft hills extended some 30 km to the southeast, while their width varied from about 15-20 km. Their eastern face was characterized by steep cliffs, but movement was possible along the hilly terrain from north to south and from east to west through the wadis or across the peaks. Many of the Egyptian surface-to-air missile batteries were dug in on the Geneifa Hills. To the north the hills dominated the Plains of Aida; to the west they overlooked the plain extending to Cairo; to the south they dominated the wadi-broken plain that extended for 25 km to Mount Ataka and Suez City; and to the east they overlooked the coastal strip along the Bitter Lakes. To the east of that strip was the Havit Road, on both sides of which were many large military camps. Slightly to the east of the camps were two more north-south roads: Test, which ran along the Suez Canal itself, and Masecha, which ran along the Sweet Water Canal. This, then, was to be our zone of operations. It was here that the battles which would decide the outcome of the war would be fought.

We were ready now to implement the *Abirei-Lev* plan that called for Sharon's division to cross at Matzmed, seize a bridgehead, construct bridges across the Suez Canal, and secure the bridgehead on both banks. As soon as the bridges were in place, forces would cross and rush to seize the bridges over the Ismailia Canal in order to isolate our zone of operations. The second division to cross (at the briefing it was decided that this would be my division) would move quickly to take the Geneifa Hills, and then continue south to Mount Ataka and be prepared to capture Suez City. At the same time, Sharon's forces would continue toward the southwest — on our right — until Mount Ubaid and secure the zone of operations to the west. Magen's division was to defend on the east bank in the first stage, along with Sasson's division, and then replace Sharon on the bridgehead so Sharon could speed south.

The planners expected that the taking of the bridgehead and the construction of the bridges across the Suez Canal would be completed during the first night of fighting, that the advances to the north and to the south would take up the day following, and that within twenty-four hours after that Suez City would have been taken and both banks of the canal mopped up.

As early as 12 October, when we realized that a crossing operation was likely in the near future, I began to study the crossing options available in my sector. On the night of 12–13 October I sent out a detachment from the paratroop battalion attached to my division to reconnoiter a broad zone and find avenues of approach to the canal. They brought back information on an open approach north of the Firdan Bridge.

In Sharon's sector there were two parallel east-west roads, about 3 km apart, leading to the crossing site: Akavish, a narrow asphalt road, and to its north, Tirtur, a dirt road. The entire zone north of these roads to Ismailia was vigorously defended by the Egyptian 16th Infantry Division and the 21st Armored Division, which had 110–140 tanks. They were also holding Missouri and the Chinese Farm. The farm was an extended area marked by a series of dry irrigation canals; generally, it ran from the Tirtur Road northward, but some of the ditches continued south of the Akavish Road as well. In the Amir area of the Chinese Farm were structures housing large water pumps, as well as buildings for settlers who had not yet arrived.

Sharon's division was reinforced by a paratroop brigade, two engineering battalions, and three reduced infantry battalions. Sharon's order said that he was to capture the Amir-Missouri area and consolidate a bridgehead on both sides of the canal that would extend at least 4 km northward. This objective was in fact insufficient. The accepted rule among armies everywhere is that a bridgehead must be continuously expanded to the point where its bridges are no longer in reach of enemy artillery. In our case, however, the 4 km would be enough only to prevent the enemy from employing flat trajectory fire or light mortars.

When the plan was presented, I agreed with the overall intention but expressed criticism of the method. I proposed a simultaneous crossing by two divisions, each in its own sector. The plan called for two divisions to cross — but following each other in one divisional sector only. Two reasons were advanced for this decision: the shortage of crossing equipment and the desire to keep one division fresh so it could maintain the momentum of the initial attack by penetrating deep into enemy territory. I could understand the advantage of leaving my division out of action in the first stage in order to throw it into the fray in the second phase while it was still fresh, but the price of not pushing the enemy far enough away from the bridgehead seemed to me not worth paying. I suggested that even if we lacked sufficient crossing equipment to establish two crossing zones, it was still worthwhile for my division to attack northeast to southwest, along the Puton and Sipur routes simultaneously with Sharon's south-north attack. Such an attack, using the four hundred tanks of the two divisions, would enable us to apply the "concentration of force" principle and would increase our chances of totally wiping out the 16th and the 21st Divisions. This might cause some losses in the two divisions, but we would emerge with an extended enemy-free area, from Deversoir all the way to Ismailia.

Sharon supported my view, though not with his usual forcefulness, and it was his crossing plan that was accepted. This plan called for Tuvia's tank brigade (minus one battalion) to advance from the east toward Televizia and Missouri under cover of artillery fire by the artillery units of both Sharon's and my division. This, however, would be a diversionary attack, to begin as darkness fell. Under cover of darkness and of Tuvia's advance, Amnon's brigade — consisting of four tank battalions (one of them having been detached from Tuvia) and three reduced infantry/reconnaissance battalions on half-tracks — would set out. Amnon's brigade would penetrate the open, empty area of the seam from the ridge line near Kishuf toward the shore of Bitter Lake near Lakekan, and from there they would surprise the enemy by bursting onto the Lexicon Road in the Egyptians' rear. The brigade would push about 12 km northward up to the Usha Route and occupy the area astride the Lexicon Road, to its west along the canal bank from Deversoir up to Mifras, and to its east, the Chinese Farm and Missouri.

Amnon's brigade was also to open the Akavish and Tirtur roads from west to east. It was for this that the battalion from Tuvia's brigade had been attached to Amnon. After the two roads were open, the battalion was to return to Tuvia's brigade. As soon as these two roads were open, two crossing brigades would advance to the canal, carrying with them the crossing gear. Colonel Danny's paratroop brigade would move along the Akavish Road, carrying its rubber assault boats on half-tracks; while Haim's brigade would advance on the Tirtur axis, towing the roller-bridge, and also on the Akavish Road, towing the uni-float rafts and the Gilowas. Forces from the Engineering Corps were attached to these brigades to manage the crossing equipment and assist the brigades in making a smooth crossing to the west bank. The plan had a good chance of surprising the enemy.

My division was engaged in studying and planning its mission on the west bank. I foresaw difficulties in our advance to the bridges. Southern Command had not specified avenues of approach for us. Intuitively and contrary to the suggestions of some of my staff officers, I decided not to move along the Akavish Road but rather to advance across the dunes. I expected that the Akavish axis would be jammed, and since I had to ensure that we crossed the canal fully fueled, I set up special ad hoc refueling units that would advance in M-113 Zeldas along with the tank columns.

Most of our plans were general in nature and focused on our advance to the west bank in a formation that would afford us operational flexibility. I stressed the importance of taking the Geneifa Hills quickly and avoiding the big army camps and the greenbelt area. I also noted the intention of leaving the Egyptians a way to flee westward from Suez City, to prevent even stronger resistance than was to be expected when we moved to take the city. At the second orders conference in Tassa, I was informed that Aryeh's brigade was to be left on the east bank as the Southern Command reserve force. This decision would again leave me with a reduced division of two brigades, with about seventy tanks each. Naturally I tried to get this decision changed but had only partial success: I was promised that the brigade would be returned to the division after we had crossed the canal.

The brigades had begun to pull out of the defensive zone the day before, 14 October. However, this movement had been disrupted because we had had to assist Yoel's brigade, which came under attack. Improvising, I had left behind my deputy, along with Aryeh's brigade and Amir's battalion from Gabi's brigade, to help defend the sector. Now on the morning of 15 October, these troops were on the way to the massing area south of Tassa.

We all felt that we were at a crossroads. Ten long, hard days of fighting were behind us, but we could not know how many days of battle — and what kind of battle — still lay ahead. Preparations for the crossing and the counteroffensive were made energetically at all levels. The entire division was busy around its tanks. The second orders conference ended as darkness began to fall. Since, according to the plan, we were not to move out until midnight, I was happy to have the chance to speak to the men. I ordered the brigade commanders to assemble the troops so I could address them.

The scene repeated itself in each of the three brigades. In the darkness, about two thousand men sat on the sands in one shadowy mass. "Attention!" The men rose as the brigade commander and I

arrived. The two of us climbed onto a tank. He would introduce me
and I would speak. Lighting provided by the headlights of a jeep, and
a loudspeaker were the only aids.

As I stood on the tank and looked at the mass of fighters, I felt a
profound identification with them. I well knew the course of battles
they had been through, the agonizing path of the first days and the
increasing strength of the days that followed. I was bothered by the
fact that I could not distinguish individual faces. I saw only a solid
bloc in the darkness. But I knew that mass was made up of individuals, each with his own thoughts and problems, his own fresh
battle experience, and his own store of the sights he had seen in the
past few days.

I had assembled them because I wanted to explain to them how
important it was for each man to surpass himself and fully exhaust
his potential in the offensive we were about to launch. No less was
my desire to meet with the thousands of soldiers I had commanded
over the past ten days in the difficult and bloody, but heroic, course
of battle — a continuous series of fierce engagements such as I had
not known in all my previous wars — not even in 1948.

I had no written notes, but I knew what I wanted to say. I wanted
to share with them my information concerning the course of the war
so far as well as my assessment of what the future was likely to hold. I
had always told my men the truth, without rhetoric and embellish-
ment, and I did so this time too. I opened by telling them that we had
been surprised and that the way the war began had serious consequences and ramifications for our fighting. Certainly there were
those who bore responsibility for the fact that we had been caught by
surprise, but all that should be left for after the war. I went on to
review the hard days experienced by the IDF on both fronts, but
despite the critical situations we had faced, the enemy had been
repulsed on both fronts. Pointing out that in the north the enemy had
already been pushed back to the gates of Damascus, while suffering
heavy losses, the time had now arrived for a counterattack on the
southern front as well.

I continued by evaluating our own fighting so far. In a personal
tone, I said that since 1948 we had experienced only "deluxe wars"
— in 1956 and in 1967 — as a result of which I had more than once
found myself wondering whether youth that had been raised on such

wars could hold out in difficult campaigns in which they might have to retreat at times. I told them that I had always admired the British people who had known many defeats and retreats in the Second World War, but whose spirit had never faltered. Now after ten days of bitter fighting, not only was my mind at ease on this score, I said, but I was full of admiration for our soldiers too. The most difficult stage was behind us, I told them.

I described the savage fighting we had experienced, how we had been reduced in number by our losses, and went on to recount how we had been strengthened and forged anew as the fighting went on. Noting the blow we had inflicted on the Egyptian armor as they sought to advance into our territory — resulting in the good conditions that now existed for our counteroffensive — I pointed out that the original high morale of the Egyptians had by now worn away. Turning to the political aspect of the situation, I related that the Russians had cooperated in the Arab aggression, not only by sending arms to the Egyptians and the Syrians, but also by frustrating American attempts to arrange a cease-fire. Since yesterday, however, an American airlift had been flying arms and military supplies to Lod Airport.

As regards our counteroffensive — which was already now in progress as Sharon's division moved to cross the canal — I said that our forces were few and the mission a gigantic one. We had already suffered many losses, so it was vital that we should fight intelligently as well as boldly and resolutely to break the Egyptians' spirit and achieve our objective — the final defeat of the enemy. We would be crossing fresh — only after the termination of the crossing battle. When our turn to go into combat came, we would have to burst across to the west bank and continue the momentum of the attack deep into the rear of the enemy. No doubt we would encounter some hard moments in the course of our attack, I concluded, but the division has been forged in battle and is now working like a well-oiled machine.

Now a surprise awaited them. That afternoon, one of Israel's best known singers, Yaffa Yarkoni, had joined the division. Yaffa, who was of my generation, was known as the "singer of the four wars." She served in the Givati Brigade in 1948 and had ever since maintained close ties with the soldiers of the IDF, appearing before them in all four wars before 1973 and, of course, between wars as well. In this war, too, Yaffa — along with other performers — had been entertaining the troops since the fighting broke out. But, because my division had been fighting deep in the dunes for the past ten days and because all the troops were committed to battle — we did not even have a military camp in the rear of our sector — we had not enjoyed any entertainment so far.

I had run into Yaffa around noontime. She was traveling along the road in a car and had asked to join us and appear before the troops. I introduced her to the men. Tall and thin, she stood on the tank, and within moments she was in close rapport with her audience. To our west Sharon's division was already moving into battle. In a few hours my men would also be in the fray, but just now they were listening to Yaffa sing, joining her in the songs they knew.

While I was standing alongside Yaffa on a tank in Natke's brigade, I felt someone pulling lightly on my leg. I bent down to see who wanted to talk to me, trying to make out a face in the darkness. I saw a young man with a smiling face. Within a few seconds I recognized him — Ilan, Ilan Gidron. I jumped off the tank, we shook hands, I embraced him. Ilan — or Ilanon, as I fondly called him — was the youngest son of our next-door neighbors, Tamar and Musik Gidron. I had known him since he was six. After graduating from high school, Ilan, like many young men from our town, had joined the Armored Corps.

Smiling and in a good spirit, Ilan told me briefly what he had undergone so far in the war. A young officer in the regular army, the outbreak of the war had found him in Gabi's brigade. While breaking through to Qantara his tank was hit. Together with his crew he managed to get to Strongpoint Milano, where he had fought until the night of 7–8 October. Then, along with the rest of the men of the strongpoint, he evacuated it and set out to try to get through the Egyptian troops who were already surrounding Qantara. As will be recalled, they had to link up with Natke's brigade, which was then engaged in a diversionary attack designed to facilitate the link-up operation. While making their way they encountered Egyptian soldiers, and the group split into two. One group took up positions in Qantara, and the men were subsequently taken prisoner. The second group, including Ilan, continued on its way, encountering Egyptians time and again and sustaining casualties.

On the morning of 8 October, after suffering many hardships, contact was made between a force from Natke's brigade and the group from Milano. Initially it was fire contact, as Natke's troops opened fire on the men who were kneeling behind the bushes in the dunes. It was a foolish situation, but no less dangerous for that. Boldly, Ilan held up a *talith* (Jewish prayer shawl) and waved it like a white flag. In short order, the group was picked up and evacuated to Baluza. Showing initiative, Ilan assembled crewmen and took them to the regional workshop. There, after no little difficulty, he managed to obtain three newly repaired tanks and to round up equipment and ammunition. Eventually he succeeded in organizing a tank platoon and joining the Lapidot "task force" attached to Magen's division, which he fought with for two days in the Baluza area. When Lapidot's unit joined up with my troops on 10 October, Ilan came along. During the days of our defensive fighting, Ilan had ended up in Natke's brigade, though not without first undergoing some more adventures.

I was very happy indeed to meet him. I looked at him in disbelief — the kid had gone through some terrible ordeals but seemed not to have changed in the least. Still the same smiling Ilanon. It was a brief meeting — and a final one. Four days later, Ilan fell in battle. But as I talked with him alongside the tank there in the dark, waiting to go into battle, it was like meeting someone almost from my own family.

Suddenly I started thinking: where is my son Omer now? He was serving as an officer — somewhere. And what of my daughter, Netta? She, too, was in the army, stationed in the Gaza Strip. At home were my wife, Miriam, and my youngest daughter, Talila, sixteen. What are they doing now, I wondered. But at once my repression mechanism did its work: I repressed and expelled these thoughts, said goodbye to Ilanon, and left to speak to the men of another brigade.

A few hours earlier, in the afternoon, and then even more as evening approached, I had been seriously worried. From my command post as I traveled from one brigade to the next, I saw that all the roads around Tassa were jammed with huge convoys making their way laboriously. From time to time I spotted the massive crossing equipment moving ahead with considerable difficulty. I saw the Gilowa vehicles and the heavy rafts coming from Refidim, but the rafts from Baluza were still nowhere in sight. The apprehensions that had led me to decide to have the division advance in the dunes instead of on the Akavish Road now were materializing.

While I had all along pictured the chaos that would develop on the roads, I had no detailed information on the situation and location of the crossing equipment. Sharon, however, seems to have had such information. At about 1500 hours he considered requesting a postponement of the operation because he would not have enough rafts to construct a bridge. But in the end he felt that any postponement could be dangerous, and that the approval given for the crossing operation should be used before the higher echelons changed their minds. Nonetheless he put the problem to Bar-Lev, suggesting that he cross using the Gilowas, the roller-bridge, and some of the rafts, with the remaining rafts to arrive later. Bar-Lev gave his okay and things kept rolling.

There were more indications that the operation had not been properly prepared. The roads were blocked; the crossing equipment was barely moving. The air strike began, as planned, in the afternoon hours. Initially, the planes attacked across a broad zone so the enemy would not realize that a crossing operation was about to be launched in one specific area. It was only toward evening that they were to strike at both banks of the crossing area with cluster bomb units. However, the artillery shelling, which was also to get under way in the early afternoon, was delayed.

Danny's paratroop brigade, which was to cross first in rubber dinghies, was still deployed in the Mitla Pass on the night of 14-15 October. It was only on the morning of the fifteenth that it was relieved there and set out for Refidim and went on to the staging area, 30 km east of Tassa, waiting in vain for the rubber boats. At 1400 hours Danny dispatched officers to locate the boats and to get them moved forward to the Akavish Road. At 1600 the brigade continued on its way in sixty half-tracks and buses. But the roads were blocked, and Danny reached the boat area behind schedule. The boats were loaded on the half-tracks and he was ready to move out at 2230. He now had a tank company from Haim's brigade attached to his command. Meanwhile, battles were already raging to the west.

CHAPTER TWENTY-TWO

15-16 October: FIGHTING FOR THE BRIDGEHEAD

At about 1700 the operation went into high gear. Tuvia's reduced brigade launched a diversionary attack with two battalions that moved from the Puton Road toward Missouri. Tuvia left behind one tank company on the Hamadia Road to secure the convoy-laden Akavish Road against the possible threat of Egyptian forces from the direction of Televizia and Machshir.

Amnon's brigade was deployed on the Caspi Road, south of Kishuf. A reconnaissance unit was to lead, then three tank battalions followed by three infantry units. With darkness the brigade began to move from Caspi-56 into the area of the seam, still empty of Egyptian troops, toward Bitter Lake. When they reached the Lexicon axis they turned north, bypassing Lakekan. The column was headed by Yoav Brom's scout unit, to which about twenty tanks and twenty APCs had been attached. In line with the plan, the force turned west on three axes — the Nahala, Tirtur, and Shick roads — and reached the canal without any hitches on a front 3 km wide. They were followed by Amram's battalion of twenty-two tanks, accompanied by Amnon's forward command group. This force continued without any problems until near the Shick Road, where they were to turn northwest, take control of the Egyptian bridging zone at Mifras, and secure the bridgehead zone vis-a-vis the north. Then came Almog's battalion of twenty-one tanks. Its task was to turn east on the Shick Road, north of the Chinese Farm, to deploy northeast, and then proceed toward Missouri. The last tank battalion was that detached from Tuvia's brigade. Two of its companies were to open the Akavish and Tirtur roads from west to east. The third company was split into two parts and attached to two infantry forces advancing behind the battalion — four tanks were attached to Shmulik's task force and five to another reduced (Shaked's) reconnaissance force. Shmulik's force was to follow Almog's battalion and mop up Amir and Missouri, while the Shaked force was to mop up west of the Lexicon Road. Finally, came a paratrooper force commanded by Major Shuneri; this unit, reinforced with antitank weapons, was to remain near Lakekan to secure the zone of operations toward the south and constitute a general reserve.

Until after 2100 everything went according to plan. Tuvia's brigade drew attention toward the east, while Amnon's brigade penetrated deep into enemy territory on the Lexicon Road, with the head of the column nearing the Usha Road and its tail somewhere in the area of Lakekan. Yoav's scout unit reached the canal. Amnon's successful penetration, without enemy resistance, occurred because his forces moved deep in the enemy's rear. Rather than a stealthy penetration, this was a surprise move by large forces on a major road. The various enemy units deployed in most of the area must certainly have noticed the tanks moving close by them, but they needed time to clarify just what troops were involved.

In a split second the entire situation changed. Enemy troops near the Tirtur-Lexicon junction opened fire with tanks and Saggers. Now, at about 2120 hours, the enemy's bewilderment dissipated to be replaced by concentrated fire. At once, the entire area was alive with activity and commotion. Under the full moon Egyptian soldiers and tanks moved aimlessly in all directions east to west and west to east, and north to south and south to north. Even in areas where our forces had passed without encountering the enemy, the Egyptians went into action with fire contact between our tanks and theirs. Israeli tanks that sought to move off the Lexicon axis hit mines. Trucks and tanks of both sides were hit and began to burn. It was next to impossible to know who was who. Tank units often could not decide whether to hold their fire or to open up on an advancing

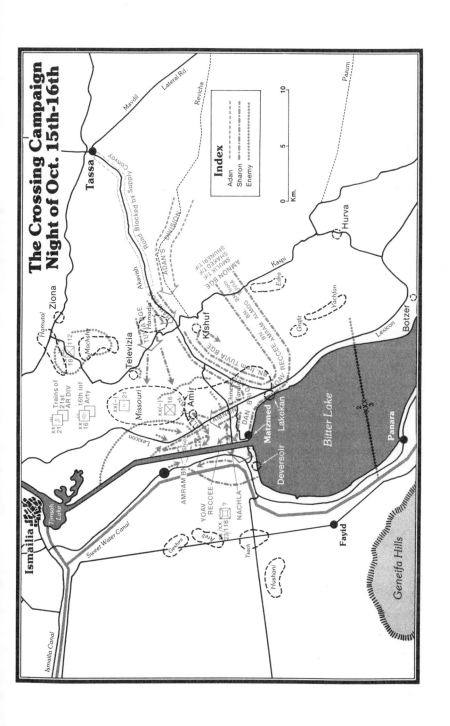

The Crossing Campaign
Night of Oct. 15th-16th

Index
Adan
Sharon
Enemy

Km.
0   5   10

group of tanks. The chaos was compounded by the problems of evacuating the wounded and retrieving tanks.

The initial burst of fire cut Amnon's column in two. Yoav's force had reached the canal, and Amram's battalion, along with ten tanks of Almog's battalion, had reached the Lexicon-Shick junction. But Almog's ten remaining tanks were caught at the Tirtur-Lexicon junction and virtually wiped out. While half of Almog's battalion, aided by Shmulik's task force, was engaged in pulling back and evacuating casualties from the junction, Amram's forward forces continued to advance from Shick northward, penetrating a logistical zone in which tanks were also deployed. Although Amram was causing the Egyptians heavy losses, his tanks, too, began taking hits, mainly from short-range antitank weapons. In view of this, Amnon ordered Amram to withdraw southward and to stabilize a line along the Shick Road. In the course of the pullback, Amram was wounded, and his deputy assumed command. As a result of battles with the Egyptian infantry troops and hitting mines, Amram arrived at the Shick-Lexicon junction with just six of his original twenty tanks. Meanwhile, the first ten tanks of Almog's battalion also arrived. Amnon now established a line, held by sixteen tanks, along Shick on both sides of Lexicon — thus setting the northern boundary of the bridgehead, west of the buildings of the Chinese Farm, which had not been mopped up. Amnon himself decided to move southward in order to overcome the enemy's blocking of the Tirtur-Lexicon junction.

Meanwhile, the battalion from Tuvia's brigade opened the Akavish Road without encountering the enemy. Encouraged by the fact that this road was now open and by the fact that his reconnaissance troops were holding 3 km of the canal bank, Sharon decided to push ahead and move his units according to the plan. Danny's brigade was ordered to advance at 2330 and cross the canal. The brigade set out led by the tank company from Haim's brigade that was to secure the route. When Danny's brigade reached the Nahala-Lexicon junction, it turned west on Nahala, toward Matzmed. Hearing the battle noise under way about 1 km to his north, Danny decided to secure his movement by dispatching his tank company to north of Nahala. From that moment, Danny lost control over the tank company which very soon found itself involved in battles with the Egyptian forces operating at the Lexicon-Tirtur junction.

Danny's brigade itself passed close to Egyptian tanks and troops. However, it took only minor hits to its half-tracks and arrived with its two reduced battalions intact at Matzmed's "yard."

This "yard" was an area of 200 × 500 meters, surrounded by artificial earth barriers and prepared as an embarkation point for the canal-crossing infantry and armor. The crossing itself began at 0125 hours on 16 October, following an artillery shelling of the opposite bank. A few minutes after he set out Danny reported: "Acapulco!" — meaning: We have a hold on the west bank. Danny encountered no enemy resistance. Egyptian artillery did shell the area in general, but they were just groping in the dark. So by 0300 16 October, Danny had completed — without resistance and without losses — the transfer of his two battalions and his forward command post to the west bank. The brigade completed its deployment on the bridgehead on the west bank by dawn: 3 km northward as far as York A and 2 km westward up to the southern Sweet Water Canal. Danny's force numbered about 750 men equipped with an abundance of short-range antitank weapons.

Meanwhile, the brigade commander, Amnon, had reached the Tirtur-Lexicon junction, where he found things to be in a state of great confusion. The remnants of Almog's tank battalion along with Shmulik's force were still evacuating casualties. The Shaked scout force had found a way to bypass the junction and proceed northwest to the Nahala axis, in order to continue with its mission of mopping up the area west of the Lexicon Road. But the force was engaged by Egyptian tanks and infantry and also was concerned with evacuating the wounded. Moreover, the tank company from Haim's brigade that Danny had left behind near the Nahala junction in order to secure the area toward the north was battling with the Egyptian forces there, and most of its tanks had been destroyed.

The tank company from Tuvia's battalion that opened up the Akavish Road from west to east returned and was now south of the Tirtur-Lexicon junction. Another company from this battalion was awaiting an order to open up the Tirtur axis. The Shuneri reconnaissance force was to their south, securing the zone of operations south of Lakekan.

Amnon regarded it as essential to attack the junction and open up the Tirtur Road so the roller-bridge could be moved up. He decided to assign this mission to Shuneri and to attach to him the tank company slated to open up the Tirtur Road. Shuneri left one of his companies, equipped with recoilless guns, to secure the area toward the south and launched an attack with two companies — infantry mounted on half-tracks and a tank company. This attack was hastily launched, with poor coordination between tanks and mounted infantry. The tanks led the attack. While they succeeded in hitting most of the enemy tanks at the junction, most of them were also hit. Finally, two tanks broke through the junction and advanced on the Tirtur Road, but the mounted infantry did not follow. After these tanks had moved 4 km eastward along the road, they were hit.

It was absolutely essential to open the Tirtur axis so that the crossing operation could proceed. At 0300 hours Amnon ordered Yoav Brom to leave the canal bank and attack the junction from west to east with part of his force. As he approached the junction, a few of his tanks were hit. Among those killed was Lt. Col. Yoav Brom. This attack, too, was beaten back, and the force withdrew westward.

As a result of the repeated attacks, Amnon believed that most of the enemy tanks at the junction had been destroyed and that the rest had fled northward. At the junction itself and along the ditches to the east were enemy infantry equipped with RPGs. Amnon decided to commit Shuneri's force once more. Shuneri deployed his troops and tried to break through, basing his assault on infantry mounted on half-tracks covered somewhat by the few remaining tanks but mainly by their own fire. They made it through the junction, but both there and on the Tirtur Road — and particularly at Tirtur-43, where there was a wide ditch — his half-tracks were hit one after another. Only two of them managed to emerge on the east, and the road was closed behind them. Another attempt was made by Tuvia's deputy at 0515 hours. He assembled the tanks from Tuvia's brigade that had returned from opening the Akavish Road, but this attempt also failed. Three tanks were hit, and the deputy brigade commander was wounded.

For some reason, Sharon concentrated on organizing the crossing to the west bank, leaving the combat problems on the east bank to Amnon. It will be recalled that early that night Sharon ordered Tuvia to carry out a diversionary move by bringing pressure to bear from east to west. However, instead of concentrating the pressure on the southeastern sections of Akavish and Tirtur, he oriented it toward Missouri. Tuvia left one of his two battalions to secure the zone of operations around Hamadia, while the second battalion penetrated northward, toward Missouri. At about 2200, when this battalion was deep in the area between Televizia and Missouri, it hit a minefield. The evacuation of the wounded and retrieval of tanks took until close to midnight. In the end, disabled tanks had to be left, and the reduced battalion turned back to Hamadia. Sharon now ordered Tuvia to step up his pressure from east to west, but Tuvia's small force was unable to do so and thus remained distant, east of the Egyptian disposition, making no substantial contribution to the pressure on the Egyptians.

In the course of the night Amnon lost about sixty tanks and was left with forty. His losses of personnel were heavy, over 120 men dead or missing in action. At morning, the remnants of Amram's and Almog's battalions were stationed on the Shick Road, constituting the northern boundary of the bridgehead. For any additional attempt to open the Tirtur Road, he had only the remnants of Yoav's scout unit, encamped near Matzmed, and the remaining tanks of Tuvia's brigade, stationed near Lakekan.

By now Sharon had put a tank battalion from Haim's brigade under Amnon's command and, later, another battalion from Tuvia's brigade. These two battalions were some 10 km east of Amnon, on the other side of Missouri and the Chinese Farm. Sharon ordered Amnon to make another effort to open the Tirtur axis, this time with a coordinated attack from the east and the west. But after all Amnon personally and the remnants of his battalions had been through that night, the task was beyond their strength. Assaults were mounted, but once more they were piecemeal and uncoordinated. First into action was the tank battalion from Haim's brigade. Beginning at 0700 hours they tried to open the Tirtur Road from the northeast, but did not get far. At Tirtur-40 they were hit by a salvo of missiles from the Chinese Farm and were forced to pull back.

Amnon ordered him to mount another attack, this time with the cover of the battalion from Tuvia's brigade. The battalion commander assembled six tanks, each commanded by an officer, to make the attempt with him. This time they reached Tirtur-43 before two tanks were hit, and the entire force had to retreat. As they were withdrawing, they picked up some twenty wounded men from Shuneri's force, who had been there since the breakthrough attempt during the night. An hour later, Amnon ordered Tuvia's battalion to try again, this time from the east and north of the Tirtur Road. The battalion's twenty-two tanks began to advance; three were hit, and the attempt failed in the face of superior enemy armor. Meanwhile, Amnon assembled the thirteen remaining tanks from Yoav's scout unit and from Tuvia's battalion as well as reconnaissance and infantry forces — all the forces west of the junction — and launched still another attack on the junction. Finally, at 0840 hours, Amnon captured the Tirtur-Lexicon junction, with charred tanks and many antitank weapons abandoned by the Egyptians.

From the outset of the operation, while General Sharon was moving his troops up and following the battles for the taking of the bridgehead, his deputy, Jackie, was engaged in controlling the traffic on the Akavish Road and moving the convoys and the supporting forces — especially the crossing gear — along. This was extraordinarily hard work. The Akavish axis was the only paved road leading from Tassa to the crossing zone. It was narrow — no more than 3.5 to 4 meters wide — and flanked on both sides by heavy dunes. Hundreds of vehicles loaded with fuel, ammunition, and engineering equipment were stuck bumper to bumper on this road for 20 km, totally jamming the axis. At various points along the road, vehicles that had tried to pass the traffic jam were stuck in the sand.

Haim's tank brigade, plus three engineering forces, were moving up the crossing gear. One task force, consisting of tanks, engineers, and an antiaircraft unit, was towing the roller-bridge. A second task force was dealing with the heavy, massive mobile rafts. The third engineering force was moving up with the Gilowa vehicles, while one reduced tank battalion was left to secure the zone of operations north of the Akavish Road. Some of the heavy mobile rafts were late in arriving from Baluza, and now they could barely move on the jammed road. Jackie seemed to despair of moving the rafts forward. The task seemed a Sisyphean one, progress was inch by inch and the effort invested was immense. The prospects of getting the gear to the canal that night were negligible. To add to the difficulties, problems in towing the roller-bridge had arisen by midnight; the towing, therefore, would take more time than had been planned for. Failure of the bridging gear to arrive would not only delay the crossing operation, but would mean that Haim's brigade would be stuck in the rear, away from the fighting.

Anxiety was growing at Southern Command HQ; after midnight a conference was held with the chief of staff and the minister of defense both participating. Morning was rapidly approaching, and there seemed no chance that we would have even one bridge in place. At that time no one was aware of the battering Sharon's division had taken. At one point, Dayan suggested that my division be committed in battle on the east bank in order to develop an attack northward together with Sharon's division. But at the same time both Southern Command and Sharon's HQ were trying to decide whether to keep Haim's tanks attached to the slow-moving crossing gear or if it would not be better to release them so they could take part in the fighting — and if so, whether to use them on the east bank or the west bank, because as a result of the delays, Danny's paratroopers were going to be left alone on the west bank without tank support.

At midnight, following consultations between Sharon and Bar-Lev, it was decided to "push" the Gilowas at once to Matzmed and use them in transferring tanks to the other bank to support Danny. After midnight, the eighteen Gilowas, accompanied by a company of tanks from Haim's brigade, set out for the canal. The Gilowas' high mobility enabled them to make their way along the Akavish Road and across the dunes to the canal with relative ease. They arrived at the canal at 0400 hours. Following ground preparations, which included breaching the earth barrier on the east bank, they were set afloat at 0630 hours. They were assembled into two long ferries capable of carrying two tanks in each cycle, with a third raft that could carry one tank.

Meanwhile, the eighteen tanks forwarding the roller-bridge continued to tow it westward. From Yukon until Akavish-55 the bridge was towed on the paved road, but from there the planned route to the canal called for the bridge to be pulled a oss the southern slopes of Hamadia, in the direction of Tirtur. Oi of the slopes, the tanks were unable to work up enough power to brake the bridge, all four hundred tons of which was rolling downhill, and the bridge broke away. When the force had organized to begin towing it again, at 0500 hours, one of the roller connections had broken. The bridge was stuck. Hours would be needed to repair it.

Southern Command and Sharon's divisional HQ were wavering about whether to release Haim's brigade and commit it to battle.

When the roller-bridge broke, the wavering stopped. Sharon decided to leave a battalion under Amnon to fight on the east bank and to break through the Tirtur axis from the east. He ordered Haim himself to rush to Matzmed with the second battalion in order to cross to the west bank. As the morning of 16 October broke, Southern Command was as yet uninformed of the condition of Amnon's brigade. Sharon's desire to transfer tanks to the west bank seems to have been taken to mean that the situation on the east bank was not critical. True, the roller-bridge and the mobile rafts had not yet arrived at the canal, there had been some difficult battles during the night, and there were problems in opening the Tirtur axis. The Akavish road was open, however, the Gilowas had reached the canal, Danny's brigade was deployed on the west bank and had encountered no difficulties. The chief of staff expressed his intentions: Sharon "will commit his three brigades to battle . . . and will mop up the area northward" in order to secure the operation of the rafts and construction of a bridge. Dado also suggested that Danny's paratroopers advance northward on the west bank "in order to seize an Egyptian bridge, or at least to prevent the Egyptians from using the bridge." The commander of the front, Bar-Lev, gave Sharon approval to reinforce the ten tanks he had already transferred to the west bank and to raid missile batteries there. Thus, as morning approached, the expectation was that Sharon was committing all his forces on both banks of the canal.

At about 0900 hours Haim, heading a tank battalion followed by a paratroop battalion mounted on half-tracks from Danny's brigade, was moving on the Akavish Road when suddenly they came under small-arms fire accompanied by a salvo of missiles. Four tanks were hit and began burning. Haim ordered the paratroopers to turn back, while he — with seventeen tanks and some Zeldas — turned south, left the road, and continued toward the canal in a flanking movement across the dunes. As they passed along the Nahala Road they could hear the battle still raging at the Tirtur-Lexicon junction.

Meanwhile, activity at Matzmed was continuing. By 0630 hours the tank company that had accompanied the Gilowas began transferring to the west bank. Danny was given seven tanks; he stationed most of them at the Deversoir airfield, while dispatching one platoon to block the Test Road over the Sweet Water Canal. When Haim arrived at the Matzmed yard, he met Sharon. Sharon told him to cross the canal, then move westward, and strike at surface-to-air missile battery sites. Danny's paratroopers, now advancing northward, began hitting small Egyptian forces and their vehicles. The Egyptians were not yet aware that Israeli forces were on the west bank. The crossing zone was quiet and came under no artillery shelling. By 1000 hours Haim's force had crossed and begun to move west with twenty-one tanks and seven armored personnel carriers. He got as far as Maktzera, some 20 km from the canal. On his way, he destroyed four surface-to-air missile bases, hit vehicles, and surprised an enemy battalion, destroying ten tanks and twenty-five armored personnel carriers. At about 1600 hours he returned to the bridgehead, east of the Sweet Water Canal, his tanks just about out of fuel.

Amnon's attempts to open the Tirtur Road from the northeast and to attack the Tirtur-Lexicon junction from the southwest on the morning of 16 October, and Haim's raid west of the canal during the day marked the end of those operations initiated by Sharon. The division was exhausted, part of it on the west bank, part of it wedged in the enemy's rear between the canal and the Lexicon Road, and a third part — mainly Tuvia's brigade — in the Hamadia area east of Amir and Missouri. The deputy division commander, Jackie, along with the logistical elements and the crossing equipment, waited far to the east on the Akavish Road. Both the Tirtur and Akavish roads were blocked, and the only route linking the forces in the western "wedge" with the forces east of the enemy was the bypass from Lakekan over the dunes south of the Akavish-Caspi Road. After the war, it was Sharon himself who provided the best description of the extent to which his troops had used up all their strength that night: "A supreme effort was made. . . . If we were not successful . . . it was not because we did not want it or didn't try. . . . We just couldn't . . . even with all the forces we employed."

According to the plan, we expected to have a bridgehead on both sides of the canal, continuous and secure, with two roads leading to two completed bridges before dawn on the sixteenth. We even hoped that by then parts of both Sharon's and my divisions would be on the other side. But what we in fact had on the morning of the sixteenth was only a narrow wedgelike bridgehead on both sides of the canal. Moreover, Sharon's division lacked the strength to continue the momentum of assault. A danger also existed that the enemy would launch a counterattack to annihilate our narrow bridgehead. As compared with the original plan, the actual situation showed we had failed in two aspects. We lacked a continuous bridgehead and an unbroken approach route to it, and we had no bridges across the canal. The question was what effect these failures would have on the continuation of the operation. It soon became clear that opinion on this was divided.

Since Bar-Lev's arrival, personal relations at Southern Command had seemed less tense, but from the morning of 16 October a rift became apparent between Sharon on one hand and Gonen and Bar-Lev on the other. Even before the war, the trust between Sharon and each of the other two had not been very high, but now — in the wake of battlefield developments — things became worse. The perception at Southern Command HQ was that Sharon's division had despaired of being able to move up the mobile rafts. HQ came to the conclusion that without at least one bridge and without the bridgehead and the access roads being properly secured, there could be no major transfer of forces to the west bank. Sharon did not agree with this evaluation. On the contrary, he tried to convince HQ that he had created sufficient conditions for continuation of the crossing and that forces from his and from my division should be transferred to the other side. The chief of staff, too, was against basing the transfer of hundreds of tanks, armored personnel carriers, and half-tracks, dozens of artillery pieces and hundreds of vehicles on just three Gilowa rafts. This was because the Gilowas were floated by means of inflated rubber sleeves around them, and shelling could puncture these sleeves and sink the Gilowas. (This did, in fact, happen later.) When Southern Command learned that Akavish and Tirtur were blocked, it ordered a stop to the transference of tanks to the west bank. Efforts were to be concentrated on the east bank.

Sharon was ordered to capture the Chinese Farm, and I was ordered to try to open the Akavish and Tirtur axes and to push the rafts on to Matzmed. Following this, Sharon would secure the bridgehead, and I would cross and then break through westward toward Maktzera. On the strength of this order my division went into action.

CHAPTER TWENTY-THREE

OPENING THE AKAVISH ROAD

All during that long night when Sharon's division was engaged in heavy fighting, my division worked to prepare for a crossing at dawn. We set out at 0145 hours. Gabi's and Natke's brigades moved on the Revicha Road, followed by a fuel convoy towed by Zeldas. Before dawn the two brigades reached the area of the Caspi Road near Kishuf and waited. I went with the forward command vehicles on the dunes alongside the Akavish Road in order to observe firsthand the progress of Sharon's forces. As anticipated, Akavish was jammed with vehicles. Here and there I spotted rafts that could not move any further. I feared that if the situation on the road remained as it was after dawn broke, the enemy might attack from the north — or even from the air — and the death and destruction would be terrible.

Stopping near the broken roller-bridge, I was informed that its repair would take many hours. Even though the transfer of the roller-bridge was not my responsibility, I decided to locate Haim Razon, one of the Armored Corps' top ordnance men, and have him come with a team and special equipment to help repair it. I then turned onto the Caspi Road and positioned myself at the head of my division, near Kishuf, to await orders. I did not know the exact situation, but I did know that the main missions had been carried out, as I had heard that Danny was on the other side and that we had a bridgehead. At 0452 hours I received advance notice from Southern Command to be ready to cross early in the morning, but only on order.

As daylight broke I was standing on a hill south of Kishuf. The mist covering the area was thickened by the fog of battle. As Egyptian artillery shells landed at various points in the area, I prayed that they would not hit the road and the vehicles lined bumper to bumper for kilometers. At about 0700 hours the mist lifted. Natke, Gabi and I, observing from the hills south of Kishuf, could see a broad area below us that included the expanses around the Chinese Farm and areas in the direction of Lakekan and Matzmed. But what was going on down there was far from clear. Tanks could be seen moving about, but it was impossible to tell if they were ours or theirs.

From time to time we heard reports that wounded soldiers from Sharon's division were lying in the ditches of the Chinese Farm in areas close to Tirtur. Amnon's forces were moving between Lakekan and the Tirtur-Lexicon junction. Haim's and Tuvia's forces had tried to attack from the northeast on the Tirtur axis and then withdrew — but we knew nothing of this. On the Akavish Road I noticed a column of vehicles moving westward with tanks in the lead, followed by Zeldas and half-tracks. Haim had been ordered by Sharon to get to Matzmed with a battalion of tanks and cross the canal. It was Haim that we now saw heading the battalion and followed by a battalion of paratroopers from Danny's brigade mounted on half-tracks. As the column reached a point 2–3 km northwest of our observation site, I suddenly saw four tanks begin burning within seconds. But we heard no tanks firing; Haim's tanks had apparently been hit by Sagger missiles fired from the north, from the Tirtur Road. The column was caught by surprise. Many things then happened at once. We saw crews jumping out of tanks starting to run in our direction, half-tracks halted as the troops abandoned them to lay down on the ground and other half-tracks turning around and moving back. The tank column turned south into the dunes followed by the Zeldas.

I told Gabi to dispatch tanks and Zeldas to the road to pick up the "refugees" from the tanks and half-tracks. It was now clear that the Akavish Road was totally blocked.

Now Gonen's deputy, Uri Ben-Ari, arrived by helicopter from Southern Command HQ. He requested that I take charge of "pushing" the rafts to the canal and that I release my deputy, Dovik, and some of my staff officers for this task. In addition, Ben-Ari added, if necessary some tanks would be allocated for this mission from Aryeh's brigade, which was serving as the Southern Command reserve force. I was not anxious to send my deputy or staff officers to carry out tasks that had not been assigned to my division, and I asked Ben-Ari why the change had been made. "Bren, for heaven's sake, it's a delicate thing; we'll talk about it after the war," he replied. I asked no more questions but ordered Dovik to take the job on himself.

Then a second helicopter arrived, from which Gonen emerged. He backed up Ben-Ari's remark but more explicitly. Sharon had been a disappointment. He did not know what had happened to Sharon in this war. I thought this exaggerated but made no response. I discussed with Gonen the fact that my division had now been inactive for hours. We decided that I should go ahead according to the original plan, and that for the time being I should send one battalion forward. Gonen and Dovik then set out by jeep for the Akavish Road. At 0915 I ordered Gabi to send one battalion south of Akavish toward Lakekan and from there to Matzmed, to cross the canal. Gabi passed the order on to Amir, who set out with his battalion. I told the rest of the division to be ready to cross by stages, according to order.

At about 1000 another helicopter arrived, this one carrying Defense Minister Dayan. He found the front in a state of enervation and stalemate. Except for the battalion we had dispatched to Matzmed, we continued to wait for orders. Dayan observed the area for about an hour. Some movement could be seen around the Chinese Farm, but nothing was happening. The lack of activity bored him. He took off his shoes and fell into a deep sleep on the dunes; at about noon he awoke and left.

At 1037 we noticed four tanks moving on the Akavish Road, this time from the west. Even as we were trying to identify them, two of them were suddenly hit and began to burn. We saw the crewmen jumping out. Just then we also saw movement and dust to our north, from around the Chinese Farm. Division intelligence reported on enemy units that were crying for help and on enemy armor moving from the north toward the Chinese Farm.

Amir Yoffe, the battalion commander I had dispatched to cross the canal, arrived at Matzmed at about 1130. There he met Sharon, who told him of Southern Command's ban on the transfer of any more tanks to the west bank. At 1145 Sharon contacted me, and after informing me of the ban, he went on: "Amnon fought like hell all night. He had very heavy losses. What's left of his tanks are still in contact with the enemy, but they're short of fuel and ammunition. I'd like you to leave me Amir's battalion, so Amnon can replenish and reorganize." I quickly told him: "You've got it!" A moment later I updated Gabi and then Southern Command. Amir was dispatched to replace the remnants of Amram's battalion near the Shick Road, and from then until about noon the following day he defended the bridgehead's northern boundary. Amnon had already sent Amram's battalion to Lakekan; now he pulled out Almog's battalion, too, and dispatched them to the Caspi Road in order to reorganize.

The lull came to an end about 1200 hours. I was ordered to open the Akavish and Tirtur roads, and Sharon was to capture the Chinese Farm. At this time one of Natke's battalions was deployed south of Kishuf, near Akavish; Lapidot's battalion from Gabi's brigade was deployed north of Kishuf; and Amir's battalion was deployed along the Shick Road in Sharon's sector. I decided to leave Gabi where he was, in reserve to provide covering fire if needed. I told Natke to move to the hills north of the Akavish-Tirtur junction and to advance from there to open the roads. The division intelligence officer relayed a series of updates concerning the disposition of the enemy in the sector where Natke was about to attack. Natke placed one battalion in attack position with another on the alert behind it. His attempts to move from the hills southward to the ditch-veined plain of the Chinese Farm were met with a salvo of Sagger missiles fired from long range. At the same time, we could see dust clouds raised by enemy armor, moving from north of the Chinese Farm in a southeasterly direction. Concluding that the enemy was developing an attack toward Natke and preferring to meet him from good positions, I told Natke to pull back to the hills behind him, to hold his fire until the enemy entered the killing area, and only then to open up. I ordered Gabi to be ready to join battle from the Kishuf area toward the northwest, and I instructed our artillery to hold its fire as well.

It was 1330. The next half-hour passed in tense expectation, since it was hard to determine whether the enemy armor was continuing to advance in our direction or had turned westward. Finally we saw that they had turned north and were moving away. Natke then tried to renew his attack, but two of his tanks were hit by Saggers. After spotting Egyptian infantry and Sagger crews in the ditches of the Chinese Farm, Natke slowed his advance and proceeded with caution.

Air battles were in progress in the skies above us, with several Egyptian MIGs shot down. Our planes bombed the buildings of the Chinese Farm, but Amir Yoffe, who was deployed near the buildings on the Shick Road, reported that the sorties were largely ineffective. He also informed Gabi of enemy movements toward us in the rear of the farm.

At 1410 hours enemy armor was again seen moving toward Natke. For twenty minutes Natke held his fire, and then, at 1430, he had his artillery face the advancing Egyptians under fire and began moving forward, trying to improve his position. He next reported that he had hit two enemy tanks, but three of his had been hit, apparently by missiles. Natke noticed Tuvia's tanks to his rear at Hamadia. They were far off and were not taking part in the battle, but Natke feared that they would fire on him by mistake.

Coordination between Sharon and me was not good. It was through Natke that I received the reports concerning Tuvia's brigade and learned of the wounded soldiers from Sharon's division lying in the ditches of the Chinese Farm. Zeldas from Weiner's paratroop company (which had been attached to Natke during the period of containment) were sent out, under tank and artillery cover, to evacuate the wounded. In the meantime, I cautioned Natke not to be swept northward, reminding him that the objective was to open the Akavish and Tirtur roads. His reply: "When I try to come down from the hills, I get Saggers fired at me." At 1455 I called Natke in for consultation.

Ten minutes later, at 1505, yet another armor attack seemed to be developing, this time from south of Missouri. We decided to hold fire, hoping that the enemy would enter a killing area. Our attempts to move forward and our maneuverings back and forth went on until 1600. The problem was that the battlefield situation was fluid and variable. Time and again the enemy made threatening armor moves (that we wanted to deal with from good positions), but these always ended in their pulling back. And every time our tanks tried to move forward into the open zone at the foot of the hills, they were hit by Saggers fired from many directions by infantry concealed in the ditches of the Chinese Farm, which crisscrossed an extensive area in front of us. Finally, I concluded that 21st Armored Division tanks were trying to lure us into a trap so that the 16th Infantry Division could finish us off. I reported the situation to Southern Command and suggested that the problem could be solved by having the area mopped up at night by our infantry. My idea was accepted, and I was informed that airborne infantry, commanded by Col. Uzzi Ya'iri, would arrive to carry out the night attack. During this entire period when I was engaged in trying to open the Tirtur and Akavish roads, Sharon did not make a renewed attempt to capture the Chinese Farm.

Also at this time, my deputy, Dovik, was busy trying to concentrate the rafts and push them forward. Dovik had taken two jeep platoons with him. He came on the radio to report that he was making progress and to ask whether the two roads were now open. The rafts were stuck at various places in the bumper-to-bumper convoy on the Akavish Road stretching to Tassa. With the help of bulldozers and with a lot of maneuvering, vehicles had been pushed off the road, opening a route for the rafts. The task required resourcefulness and resoluteness. After many hours of exhausting toil, they were able to move forward with twelve rafts.

It was getting late on the fighting day of 16 October. The uncertainty about the fate of the crossing operation was reflected in the war room of Southern Command, at Umm-Hashiba. After trying unsuccessfully for many hours to make contact with Sharon, Gonen contacted Sharon's brigade commanders directly to find out what orders they had received from their division commander. Gonen himself gave them some instructions, which indicates the mistrust that had developed between him and Sharon. At 1405 hours Gonen spoke with brigade commander Tuvia, who told him that he had left the Missouri area in order to refuel and take on ammunition and that he had left behind eight tanks, most of which had been blown up by mines. Gonen asked Tuvia what orders he had received from Sharon and was told that he had been instructed to leave one battalion to tow the roller-bridge and to prepare another battalion for crossing the canal, but only by order. In his reply, Gonen sought to go over

Sharon's head: "Report to me when Sharon orders you to cross. Without reporting to me, you don't cross!"

At 1500 hours a conference was held at Southern Command HQ. Gonen's view was that the existence of a bridge was a precondition for the transfer of any more forces to the west bank. Unless we had a bridge and uni-float rafts, the forces should be returned, Gonen said, since we could not rely on just the Gilowas. Gonen also expressed the general uncertainty when he briefed General Ze'evi (Dado's assistant) at 1555 hours: "Bren hasn't succeeded in opening Akavish and Tirtur. . . . Another attempt will be made with Bren and Uzzi [Ya'iri]. . . . Uzzi is on his way to the front in buses from Refidim and will get to Bren only in another five hours. If we don't succeed in opening the roads, we'll consider today whether to stay [on the other side] or not."

At 1630 hours Dayan arrived at Southern Command HQ for a brief conference. Gonen stressed that Sharon had not carried out his task of establishing a bridgehead, but the intention now was to open the two roads that night. If that failed, consideration should be given to evacuating the men now on the west bank. Bar-Lev explained that air support could not be effectively utilized, since Sharon had said that his forces and the Egyptians were too closely interlocked. In contrast to Gonen, Bar-Lev said there was no plan to remove the Israeli forces now on the west bank and added that he had information that the situation of the Egyptians at the Chinese Farm wasn't easy either. Dayan stated that in order to take advantage of the air force clear sectors should be demarcated between our forces and the enemy. The defense minister also warned that en route from the front to Southern Command HQ he had seen that the Akavish Road was jammed with vehicles, and that was dangerous.

So 16 October was about to end in a draw and in uncertainty concerning what was to happen next. All the commanders could do was wait, with an oppressive feeling, to see what the coming night would bring. However, developments also depended on what the other side would do. The momentum of our attack had been halted; the enemy now had an opportunity to react. Would he use it?

At GHQ, too, there was an atmosphere of uncertainty mingled with hope — though it was my impression that the hopes overrode the uncertainty. There, in a conference that opened at 1900, they discussed the plans for the next day, 17 October. The participants were briefed on the Soviet airlift to Egypt and on the American airlift to Israel. The director of Military Intelligence noted that the Egyptians were not yet aware of our crossing operations. They had employed neither their air force nor reserves against the crossing forces. The chief of staff said that the operation had been only partially successful, due to the failure to complete preparations prior to its launching. He pointed out that the attack had lost its momentum, but he expressed the hope that during the night we would be able to move the crossing gear up and transfer additional forces to the west bank.

The Egyptians, however, were in fact slow to spot our canal crossing. It is probable that most of the reports came, on the night of 15–16 October, from the 16th Infantry and 21st Armored Divisions, since they were engaged in furious combat with Sharon's forces on the east bank. Danny's brigade had crossed without encountering the enemy, so there was no one to report on it. No operations were carried out by the Egyptians that night to locate our forces. This being so, Danny's soldiers could consolidate their hold and dig in uninterruptedly, and the Gilowas were able to transfer a tank battalion from Haim's brigade in full daylight without artillery intervention.

At first, the Egyptian high command thought we were carrying out a local attack on the 16th and the 21st Divisions. The first reports they received concerning the presence of Israeli forces on the west bank came in only in the wake of Haim's armored raid on four surface-to-air missile batteries. However, at Second Army HQ, that raid was perceived as having been carried out by a small amphibious force — no more than four or five tanks — for psychological reasons, to raise morale in the Israeli camp and perhaps also to impress and frighten the Egyptians. The Egyptians were convinced that the IDF had taken a fearful pounding and was incapable of mounting a crossing operation. An expression of their self-confidence was heard on 16 October, when Sadat addressed the Egyptian Parliament, declaring that the war would continue and proclaiming his decision to begin preparing the Suez Canal for navigation. His remarks show that he did not yet know that the canal was no longer wholly in Egyptian hands. That very same afternoon, Israeli Prime Minister Golda Meir addressed the Knesset (parliament) and declared

that an Israeli task force was operating on Egyptian soil. In his book
The Road to Ramadan, the Egyptian journalist Mohamed Hassanein
Heikal relates that as soon as he had reports of Mrs. Meir's remarks,
he phoned President Sadat, who said "he had no information that
would bear out her claim." Sadat decided to dispatch his chief of
staff, Shazli, to Second Army HQ to find out firsthand what the actual situation was on the front — particularly since Soviet Premier
Kosygin was about to come to Egypt, and Sadat could assume that
his aim would be to convince the Egyptians to accept an early cease-
fire. In addition — as we learned after the war — the commander of
the Second Army suffered a heart attack on 13 October and was
evacuated to the rear. Under these circumstances, it was extremely
important to send Shazli to the front, where he could take all
necessary steps.

On the afternoon of the sixteenth, at the very time that Southern
Command was deliberating whether to continue with the crossing
operation, Egyptian GHQ decided an energetic major counterattack
should be launched on the east bank to annihilate the Israeli wedge.
The Egyptians decided to launch a pincer-movement attack. The 21st
Armored Division of the Second Army would attack from north to
south, and the Third Army's 25th Independent Tank Brigade was to
move north along Bitter Lake and attack from south to north. Until
that attack could materialize — apparently on the morning of the
seventeenth — the 16th Infantry Division was ordered to counterattack in its sector that night. Egyptian War Minister Ahmed Ismail
discussed the matter personally with the commander of the 16th Division. Orders were then issued to rush forces to the crossing zone on
the west bank. Commando forces and a force of fifty tanks (apparently from the 2nd Tank Brigade of the 4th Armored Division)
were dispatched along the shore of Bitter Lake, northward to Deversoir. The Palestinian force stationed at the Faid camps was ordered
to deploy antitank weapons along the routes parallel to Bitter Lake.

Meanwhile, my division was deploying for night security, and I
was awaiting the arrival of Uzzi's paratroopers. I positioned Gabi's
brigade on both sides of the Akavish Road in order to protect the
many concentrated convoys as well as the twelve rafts that Dovik had
managed to bring forward along with the bridging personnel who
had been attached to Sharon's division. I sent Natke's brigade south

to Caspi-57-58 in order to secure the zone of operations against possible attacks from the south. I set up my forward command post by Akavish-55. I had a small tent that was soon unfolded between two Zeldas; my working table opened out from the side of my command Zelda. When the tent flaps were down, I could put on a light and begin poring over maps and aerial photos, planning how best to employ the paratroop brigade that was en route.

Col. Uzzi Ya'iri was stationed at Abu-Rodeis, and his paratroop brigade was deployed and operating against Egyptian commando forces at various points along the Gulf of Suez. Around noon on 16 October he was told to take the battalion commanded by Lieutenant Colonel Itzik — which was operating in the A-Tur area — and fly to Tassa to take part in the crossing campaign. Taking a small command group with him, Uzzi helicoptered to A-Tur, where he explained to Itzik that he himself was flying to Tassa, where they would be assigned a new mission. In the meantime, Itzik was to concentrate his battalion at the A-Tur airfield and wait for planes to take them to Tassa. Upon arriving at Tassa, Uzzi contacted Southern Command HQ and spoke to Bar-Lev. When the latter was chief of staff, Uzzi had served as his aide, and relations between them were close. Bar-Lev briefed Uzzi on the situation in the crossing zone. In summary, we were unable to get the bridging gear to the canal, and the entire operation was at a very critical stage.

Bar-Lev told him: "Your mission, and this is our hope, is for your paratroopers to mop up the antitank units in the ditches during a night battle so that we can open the roads and the operation can continue. You will fly to Akavish-55, where you will be under Bren's command, and he will inform you of your specific mission." Uzzi had already released the helicopter. Glancing at a map, he saw that the distance was not great, and he decided to set out at once in jeeps. But he quickly found that the road was completely jammed and impassable, so he returned to Tassa, where he had to wait a long time for a helicopter. He finally arrived at my forward command post at about 2200 hours.

Itzik's battalion was flown in transport planes to Refidim. From there Itzik contacted Southern Command HQ, which told him to wait because the brigade commander was just then receiving his orders. Itzik called back every thirty minutes. At about 1700 hours an officer from Southern Command HQ arrived with buses and told Itzik that he and his men must get to Tassa fast. As they approached Tassa they could already see what a blocked axis meant. At Tassa they were given a general briefing on the situation at the front and on their mission to open the roads to the bridgehead. Between 2100 and 2300 hours, they were flown by rotation in giant helicopters to Akavish-55. They used the time to adapt their equipment and ammunition to the nature of their mission.

I awaited them impatiently. According to what Southern Command had told me, I had expected their arrival before dusk so that they could observe the arena of battle. The hours passed, and my repeated phone calls to HQ drew the same reply: the force is on its way to you. But 2000 hours, 2100 hours, and still no paratroopers. We had only a few night hours to mop up an extensive area, including two roads 10 km long. Time was wasting! I was very apprehensive that we would not manage to get the roads open during the coming night, and on the morrow we would face the same problems we had today. There was no point or logic in employing the paratroopers in open areas during daylight. We would have to wait until the following night and who could say how things would develop by then?

It was about 2200, then, when a helicopter landed by my forward command post. Uzzi and his operations officer entered my tent. I had known Uzzi a long time. He was a straightforward, devoted, sensitive, and alert officer who always said what he thought. Tall and thin, dark-skinned with brown eyes and close-cut brown hair, Uzzi entered the tent energetically. He unfolded his map at once and laid it against the side of the tent. Only then did we shake hands, and he apologized over the tardy arrival of his force. He knew, he added, how important and crucial his mission was. Within fifteen to thirty minutes Itzik's men would begin landing, and he hoped he would soon go into action.

For the past two hours, as I was considering and planning the paratroopers' operation, my thoughts kept reverting to the most difficult combat situation I had ever faced. It was twenty-five years earlier, when I was a twenty-two-year-old infantry company commander in the Negev Brigade of the Palmach toward the end of the War of Independence, in Operation Horev. My company happened to be in the rear of the Israeli force that broke through into Sinai. Soon, however, we were committed to action like Uzzi's force, had a rather desperate firefight against heavy odds, and gained our objective.

And now here before me was Uzzi Ya'iri, his men being brought from afar because they were the elite of the IDF's infantry. Uzzi had been told how vital their mission was for the continuation and success of the crossing operation. The men were coming to an area they had not seen by daylight. It was unclear exactly where the enemy was deployed and in what strength. This one battalion came from afar even though there were two divisions operating in the area, with hundreds of tanks, plenty of artillery, and considerable armored infantry forces. I remembered how bitter I had felt under similar circumstances and wondered what Uzzi's troops were feeling.

I briefed Uzzi with the aid of a photo map and a 1:50,000 map, updating him about the day's events in the field. Just south of the Chinese Farm, I told him, were low hills that dominated the Tirtur Road where the enemy had set up an antitank system, including 85mm dual-purpose guns. The main problem lay in the broad irrigation ditches that extended southward from the farm to the area between the Tirtur and Akavish roads, and also south of Akavish toward Lakekan. The soldiers of the Egyptian 16th Division were making good use of these ditches, which provided cover for crews equipped with Sagger missiles. It was extremely difficult to pinpoint the locations of these units because the ditches crisscrossed such a broad area. All our attempts to attack the area during the previous night and day using tanks and mounted infantry had failed, with heavy casualties. Even when Tuvia's tanks or Shuneri's armored infantry had succeeded in overcoming resistance at a certain point and breaking through, they were eventually met by infantry firing antitank weapons and forced to withdraw after taking hits. Similarly, I continued, all of Natke's attempts to operate in the area north of the Akavish-Tirtur junction had also failed because of the armored threat of the 21st Division or the antitank missiles employed by infantry of the 16th Division. I told Uzzi that I did not know exactly where the enemy was positioned. What was clear was that they had the flexibility to move about freely in the ditches with the result that the Akavish and Tirtur axes were blocked.

The main aim was to open those two roads so we could move the rafts to the canal and have access routes to the bridgehead. There were not many hours of darkness left, and time was pressing. Since the precise location of the enemy was undefined, my plan was to decide on an area that we would mop up and then defend, freeing traffic on Akavish and Tirtur. I went on to suggest that Uzzi begin by cleaning up the area from the Akavish-Tirtur junction toward Lexicon as well as a few hundred meters north of Tirtur, where we would position forces to isolate the Tirtur axis from Amir.

Since Uzzi had a battalion of four companies at his disposal, I suggested a broad deployment in three companies — one between the two roads, one south of Akavish, the third north of Tirtur — with Uzzi to follow along with the fourth company and a weapons support company that would serve as his reserve. Uzzi would have to leave platoons to hold the ground north of Tirtur and to prevent the enemy penetrating the area dominating Tirtur from the north. Once the enemy was discovered, all the dispersed forces could be massed for an attack. Because of the full moon and enemy's abundance of antitank weapons and in view of the combat experience we had accumulated here, I was not suggesting that any tanks or armored personnel carriers go along — but of course we would have tanks at the ready to come to his aid should the need arise.

Uzzi accepted the plan and sat down with his operations officer to work out the details. Further coordinating discussions between his staff officers and mine revealed that Uzzi had not brought along an artillery liaison officer. It would take about 50 minutes to bring an officer from one of the artillery batteries dispersed in the area. But Uzzi felt that time was running out. He suggested we forego this, and that if needed he would ask for artillery support over my command net. Since he was the only force operating in my division that night and the radio net would be free, I agreed.

Uzzi left to organize his men, issue orders, and brief the force. It was already midnight, and they had still not set out. I began to worry, as the hours of darkness were slipping through our fingers. All the briefings were being given under pressure of time, even though the mission was a complicated one. Such dilemmas are frequent in war: to go into battle underprepared or not to go at all. In this case, at least, there was no need to spur the men on. Uzzi and his soldiers were fully aware that the fate of the crossing operation depended to a large extent on them.

The paratroopers began to move out at 2403 hours, marking the start of the fighting on 17 October. They passed the rafts waiting by Akavish-52 and made their way toward the Tirtur-Akavish junction. A tense combat atmosphere pervaded the entire area. The advancing troops were suspicious of the shadowy figures they saw along the way, and the men guarding the rafts tensed as they spotted the advancing silhouettes. The paratroopers continued on their way. Time passed. All was quiet. How far had they got? Uzzi reported over the radio that they had covered about a third of the way. It was already 0130. I realized that the timetable we had set made it doubtful that the mopping-up operation could be completed in time. I decided to narrow the sector to be cleaned up, and ordered Uzzi to call in the southernmost company and make do with mopping up the Tirtur axis only. It was 0200 hours; the paratroopers were combing the area carefully, with only about three hours of darkness left. The night was going to pass. The bridging equipment was ready to be put into action, true, but the roads weren't open. When dawn broke, we would face yet another day of shuffling about, a very grave prospect. We must do something — but what?

I turned the matter over and over in my mind and came up with an idea. I ordered Gabi to dispatch his scout company in Zeldas along the Akavish Road to the junction with Lexicon to determine if the road was still blocked. This was risky, but there was no choice: it was a calculated risk that I had to take. I told Dovik to be prepared to move out with the rafts, if and when the order came.

Gabi's company set out at 0230 hours. Fifteen minutes later fire contact was made between Uzzi's force and enemy troops at Tirtur-42. At first Yacki, commander of the company that had encountered the enemy, thought he would be able to overcome the Egyptians on his own; the Egyptians' fire was largely ineffectual so Yacki tried to outflank them from the left. In the meantime, Itzik, the battalion commander, moved in his more remote companies and began positioning a base of fire, at which he concentrated machine gunners from all the companies. The brigade commander, Uzzi, who had also come under fire — including Sagger-missile fire — entered one of the ditches along with his reserve company. As had been

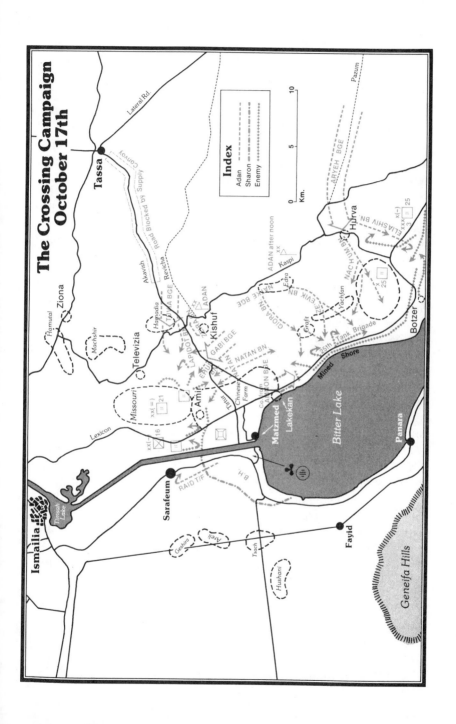

The Crossing Campaign
October 17th

Index

Adan
Sharon
Enemy

Km.
0   5   10

Ismailia

Timsah Lake

Hamutal

Ziona

Machshir

Televizia

Missouri

xx(=) 21

Lexicon

Amir

Thint

Chinese Farm

Sarafeum

B.H.

RAID T/F

Geshra

Areli

Tsach

Hushani

Fayid

Geneifa Hills

Matzmed

Lakekan

Mined Shore

Bitter Lake

Panara

Botzer

Hurva

ELIASHIV BN

MACHUMBI

x 25

3 25

xx(=) 25

25th Tank Brigade

Grafit

Yachfan

GIORA BN

EREK BN

Kaspi

Edra

ADAN afternoon

LAKE BGE

NATAN BN

GABI BGE

Kishuf

ADAN

ZORA

LAPIDOT T/F

TUVIA BGE

Hagadia

Machshir

Coltrah AMNON BGE

xx 16

xx(=) 16

Tassa

Lateral Rd

Convoy

Road Blocked by Supply Convoy

Akavish

Revicha

Reshef

agreed, the division artillery began shelling enemy targets deeper in their territory, far from our forces. Uzzi was afraid to adjust the artillery fire closer to the zone of operations because his men were close to the Egyptians with whom fire contact had been made.

The situation began to deteriorate. Yacki's company, which had attempted the flanking movement, suffered heavy losses. Yacki reported that he could not overcome the enemy on his own and needed reinforcements. Another flanking movement, this time to the right and aimed at easing the pressure and allowing casualties to be evacuated, also failed, resulting in even more casualties. My contacts with Uzzi made it clear that no quick resolution could be expected. Moreover, among the casualties were many officers, including company commanders.

Then, at 0315 hours, the company from Gabi's brigade reported that it had reached the Akavish-Lexicon junction and that the road was open. Should I order Dovik to move out or was it too risky? The equipment was heavy, massive, slow-moving. What if it attracted the enemy's attention? If it were hit we could forget about the crossing operation. The fate of the operation hung in the balance.

Perhaps, I thought, perhaps the situation of the Egyptians at the Chinese Farm is no less difficult than that of Uzzi. Perhaps they, too, have suffered losses and are close to the breaking point. Their attention must certainly be concentrated on the area of fire contact, so this might be a good time to get the bridging gear to the canal. I had to make a decision. I ordered Dovik to wait until Gabi's company returned. Half the company would be attached to him, to patrol in front of the raft column. I ordered Gabi to dispatch the other half of the company to help evacuate Uzzi's wounded men. I then told Natke to forward a tank battalion to north of the Akavish Road, to protect the raft convoy as it proceeded along the road.

Contacting Amnon, of Sharon's division, I requested that he bring bulldozers to clear the charred tanks that were blocking Akavish. In addition, Amnon was to bring bulldozers to the Akavish-Lexicon junction, which according to the map seemed to require too sharp a turn for the rafts to be able to get by. I wanted them to help the rafts at this point, so they would not have to go off the road.

At 0345 the scout company returned, and I ordered Dovik to set out. The convoy included Zeldas from Gabi's company, two D-9 bulldozers, and personnel from the bridging unit attached to Sharon's division. By now, Natan's battalion, from Natke's brigade, was already deployed between Akavish and Tirtur-42-43. A fierce battle continued to rage between Uzzi's paratroopers and the Egyptians; it was under cover of that engagement that the raft convoy moved along the Akavish Road. No other engineering equipment arrived from Sharon's division, but the D-9s were able to clear the road, and the convoy made its way slowly but surely.

Dovik arrived at the Matzmed yard at 0630. At long last we had enough rafts by the canal to build one massive bridge, a bridge whose construction was a precondition for a major crossing operation and for the launching of a counterattack on the west bank. However, we still had the problem of opening the roads so we could maintain a safe corridor to the bridgehead. To that end, we would have to continue to fight and push the Egyptians away from the roads.

At about 0400 hours I ordered Gabi to send a tank battalion to link up with Uzzi's men, and at 0500 hours I told Gabi to dispatch half the scout company to help evacuate Uzzi's wounded soldiers. Gabi also sent Ehud's battalion, which was made up mainly of Israeli students who had returned home from their studies in the United States as soon as they heard that war had broken out. They were about to undergo their first serious baptism of fire in this war. Lieutenant Colonel Ehud contacted Uzzi and then Itzik and was told of their difficult situation and cautioned about the Sagger-missile units operating in the area. Ehud and Uzzi decided that Ehud would wait for daylight before attempting a link-up. In the meantime he would maneuver about in order to deter enemy armor from advancing. When dawn broke, Ehud had identification difficulties, because Itzik's forces were so close to the enemy forces. With the help of colored smoke, Ehud linked up with Itzik. After the two commanders discussed the situation, it was decided that Ehud would try to capture the nearby objectives with a flanking movement to the left.

Ehud commenced a charge with his tanks and Zeldas, managing to cover about 80 meters while running over Egyptian infantry in their trenches and exchanging fire with enemy tanks positioned about 1,000 meters away. But within four minutes, five of his tanks were hit, mainly by Saggers fired from his flank. Ehud withdrew to his starting position, near Itzik, and now the two had to deal with evacuating even more casualties from Ehud's force. As the evacuation operation was under way, another tank and another Zelda were hit, and the number of casualties rose. Ehud pulled back 800 meters and began to count his men. He found that ten had been killed, four were missing and fifteen were wounded. An artillery liaison officer from Ehud's battalion remained with Itzik to help adjust artillery fire on the enemy. Itzik continued to round up the wounded and to evacuate them.

At 0600 Natan's battalion, which had completed its task of safeguarding the passage of the rafts, began moving forward toward the Tirtur Road, southwest of Ehud's battalion. Gabi also moved in, with Lapidot's battalion, so that his brigade was deployed from Akavish-52 to Tirtur-39. Natke was ordered to leave two battalions at Caspi-57-58 in order to secure the zone of operations toward the south, and he personally joined Natan's battalion. I contacted Southern Command to ask for Tuvia's brigade, which had been stationed at Hamadia since the previous day and had taken almost no part in the fighting. Tuvia's brigade was attached to my division at 0745 hours, and I deployed him to the north from Puton-37 to Televizia. Now we were pressing ahead with four armored battalions in a wide arc toward Missouri and the Chinese Farm.

West of Uzzi's paratroopers, we had some immediate successes. Natan's battalion went into action south of the Chinese Farm, while at the same time helping to evacuate wounded paratroopers. When Natke joined him he stepped up his pressure, and his tanks reached Tirtur on the western edge of the arc. In Gabi's and Tuvia's sectors we encountered greater difficulties, but the pressure continued. Gabi was also in radio contact with Amir Yoffe's battalion, which — though operating on the Shick Road under Sharon's command — was keeping in touch with its own brigade. Amir asked for more fuel and ammunition and reported enemy tank concentrations among the buildings of the Chinese Farm and enemy tank movements toward us from deep in their territory. Gabi directed his artillery fire in that direction. At 0730 hours we were already able to allow combat vehicles to move on the Akavish Road, and at 1100 hours we declared the road open to all traffic. The supply convoys began streaming in. The 16th Division, I thought, was starting to break.

After Dovik had brought the rafts to Matzmed, he proceeded northward to visit Amir's battalion. Dovik described Amir's activities as highly effective. While sustaining hardly any casualties among his own men, his battalion had hit a good number of enemy tanks that had tried to attack from the north. The columns of black smoke rising from the vehicles and tanks disabled both during the night and morning battles caused many who saw the scene to compare it to a vale of death. Dovik recommended that supplies be dispatched to Amir in small groups of vehicles. Things were looking better in Sharon's division too. Amnon told me by radio that he was leaving a small force at Lakekan and concentrating forces to send to Amir at the northern end of the bridgehead. Somewhat later that morning, however, Amnon — acting on Sharon's orders — transferred ten tanks to reinforce the troops on the west bank. This conflicted with the orders issued by Southern Command, and Sharon was told to stop transferring tanks across the canal.

Between 0800 and 0830 hours we could see many indications in the field that the Egyptians were about to carry out the orders given to their Second and Third Armies on the evening of 16 October (of which we, of course, knew nothing at the time). From the north, elements of the 1st and 14th Tank Brigades of the 21st Division were attacking toward Tuvia and Gabi, while the 18th Mechanized Brigade of the 16th Division attacked toward Amir. It looked as though large-scale armored battles were about to take place around the Chinese Farm. At the same time, Tuvia informed me that one of his tank platoons — which since the start of the crossing operation had been positioned at Hurva in order to secure the zone of operations toward the south — had spotted enemy tank columns moving from the direction of the Third Army far to the south and west. The lead elements were already advancing on Lexicon along Bitter Lake a few kilometers north of Botzer. Two of Natke's battalions had been left on the hills overlooking Bitter Lake, at Caspi-57-58. I now ordered Natke to leave Natan's battalion and return southward to set up an ambush against the expected enemy armored attack. I instructed Natke to conceal his men among the Edra Hills and to annihilate the enemy when he reached the plain at the foot of Grafit, which had been chosen as a killing ground. Natke asked to concentrate on this one task only and to transfer Natan's battalion, operating at Tirtur, to Gabi's command. But since the enemy was still far off and there was no certainty that they would continue to advance and since Gabi was engaged on a broad sector, I decided to leave Natan under Natke's command.

The advance of the Egyptians' 25th Independent Tank Brigade along the Lexicon axis was incredibly slow; they seemed to be doing more halting than moving. Natke was ready to "welcome its arrival," but it was not arriving. At the same time, armored battles were in progress, and again Saggers were fired from long range at Tuvia, Gabi, and Natan.

From my observation post on a hill near Kishuf, I could see the entire battle area, but the level terrain made it difficult to distinguish between our forces and the enemy's, especially when they engaged in close combat. More and more palls of smoke could be seen in the field, most of them from burning enemy tanks but some from our tanks as well. The armored battles that were taking place over an extensive area on the margins of the Chinese Farm were very difficult to conduct. As on the previous day, the Egyptians moved forward and back, seeking to lure us into the broad irrigation ditches where they could employ combined forces of armor and infantry equipped with Saggers. Our tanks advanced slowly, in the main maintaining fire contacts over large distances. We were gradually pushing the enemy back, but it was mainly the Saggers that impeded our penetration into his depth. The missiles endangered our tanks, the more so because it was difficult to spot them from afar. More than once reports came in to the effect that the enemy was on the verge of collapse, but then our attempts to advance were halted by salvos of Saggers. Again we felt the lack of infantry forces, but the truth is that even if I had had an infantry formation, I would have hesitated to send it into a concentrated attack by the light of day in the flat, open terrain that was our current zone of operations.

By 0930 hours, Uzzi had succeeded in assembling most of his wounded men in one of the ditches. We concluded together that there was no point in holding the paratroopers in the line of contact. Forty of his men had been killed, among them two company commanders, a deputy company commander, and many other officers; and about eighty had been wounded, not all of whom had been evacuated. Their bold fighting during the night allowed us to get the rafts to the canal, but now there was no tactical advantage to their presence.

I reported to Gonen that I was about to pull Uzzi's brigade from the line of contact. To my surprise, Gonen expressed vigorous opposition to such a move on the ground that Uzzi's soldiers were preventing Egyptian infantry from infiltrating into the ditches and thus endangering the open Akavish Road. I argued with him at length, pointing out that while this might be the way things looked on the maps in the rear, the facts in the field were otherwise. I explained that in the battle for the Akavish and Tirtur roads, in which four tank battalions were now involved, the paratroop battalion that had taken such a pounding overnight could not play a major role. There was no justification in prolonging its suffering. However, my efforts to convince Gonen were in vain. His order remained in force. Uzzi's paratroop brigade was not to be pulled back. Meanwhile, I was informed that a helicopter was on its way to me, and at 1030 hours Defense Minister Dayan and the front commander, Bar-Lev, arrived. I put the problem of the paratroopers to Bar-Lev, who approved their disengagement from battle. Shortly thereafter they were taken out, some on foot and others on Zeldas dispatched for that purpose. The area was combed to ensure that no wounded men had been left behind.

From Natke I kept getting reports concerning the threat posed by the 25th Brigade, advancing from the south. At 1045 hours I contacted Gonen and asked for Aryeh's brigade (which was concentrated as Southern Command's reserve), in order to bring it into the battle against this latest enemy threat. Approval was granted, and at 1055 hours Aryeh was ordered to move southward quickly along the Mavdil Road and then to turn west on the Pazum axis. Fortunately the 25th Brigade continued to tarry around Botzer, while its forward screening troops could be seen advancing up to about Lexicon-279. Aryeh had to leave one battalion to secure the Ziona area and set out with only two battalions. Dovik updated Aryeh on the disposition and strength of the enemy and about Natke's location and the route earmarked for him. Natke was likewise informed of Aryeh's anticipated arrival.

At about noon reports were coming in attesting to a positive situation. Aryeh had already covered the 20 km of the Mavdil Road, had turned west on to the Pazum axis, and had to plow through another 30 km or so among the dunes to reach positions from which he would be able to dominate the killing ground. Natke was still lying in ambush among the dunes around Edra and Grafit. Taking time whenever I could, I briefed Dayan on the course of the fighting. He observed the scene for a time and then said he wanted to move up to Sharon, who was in the yard at Matzmed. The yard had been taking a heavy shelling since the morning hours. Knowing that this would not prevent Dayan from going there, I told him that at this time it was impossible to get there. Dayan didn't give up, and Bar-Lev suggested that we ask Sharon to come to us. Dayan did so, and Sharon set out.

Since the early morning the bridging personnel had been working in the yard and in the canal itself on assembling the rafts into one bridge. However, the Egyptians had in the meantime pinpointed the crossing site and were bombarding it fiercely. The shelling continued for hours. Many were killed or wounded, but others took their place. Despite the heavy casualties, the engineers carried on with the bridging work heroically and steadfastly. But the work was hard going and would take many hours more. That morning Sharon had ordered Haim to advance out westward once again and strike at missile and artillery batteries. By now the Egyptians had already taken up positions on the fringes of the greenbelt, west of the Sweet Water Canal, preventing Haim's exit. To break out of this area was no longer a relatively simple surprise move.

Around the crossing area and the corridor leading to it, the Egyptians had concentrated 21 light field-artillery batteries, 5 medium batteries, and 3 heavy batteries — all told, 144 pieces. Because of the massive shelling, Sharon wanted to mop up the nearby greenbelt zone in order to remove the enemy's forward observers and then raid the artillery batteries themselves. He ordered Colonel Danny to send a paratroop force from the greenbelt northward. At about 0900 a company mounted on half-tracks, accompanied by two tanks, set out along the Sweet Water Canal to carry out the mission. But the battalion commander who was leading the task force went too far north; near the village of Serafeum they came under fire at close range, including direct fire from artillery pieces at the Orcha position. The force was split in two. One part, headed by the battalion commander, found itself cut off in some of the village's buildings and at the Serafeum Railway Station. For four hours they fought desperately, until 1700 hours when they were rescued by a relieving force that included a few tanks and paratroopers in half-tracks. Twelve paratroopers were killed and twenty-two wounded. The bodies of the dead Egyptian soldiers were scattered about in the area around them, just meters from the Israeli positions.

This action marked the end of Sharon's attempts, that day, to expand the bridgehead northward. While the Egyptians had not yet managed to mass armored forces on the west bank, paratroopers, infantry, and a few tanks and armored personnel carriers were already containing the bridgehead. There was no choice but to continue the bridging operation despite the massive shelling. Indeed, construction of the bridge cost many lives and proceeded very slowly, but we could already sense that in another few hours we would have a bridge. That bridge and the taking and opening of the Akavish Road provided the necessary conditions for continuation of the operation. Danger still lurked from the 25th Brigade, advancing from the south, and the attacks from the north were still continuing, but the time had now come to decide on renewal of our momentum.

CHAPTER TWENTY-FOUR

17 October: TURN OF THE TIDE: 25TH BRIGADE AMBUSHED

No one had decided that a commanders' conference would be held by my forward command post. It was as though an unseen hand had assembled, at the right time and the right place, the minister of defense, the chief of staff, the commander of the front, and the two division commanders. And so it was that what later gained fame as the "war council in the dunes" was held.

At about noon, Sharon's command vehicle drew up to my command post. I was surprised at how many people were in the vehicle. When it approached closer, I recognized at least one reporter, as well as senior officers, not divisional staff officers but personal friends of Sharon. I left the microphone to Dovik and Gilad, took my 1:50,000 map, jumped off my Zelda, moved about 15 meters away from it and spread the map on the sand. Dayan, Bar-Lev, Arik, and I knelt around the map.

To my surprise, Sharon's friends and the journalist also stood around us in a circle. This was not the custom at my HQ, and I had no qualms about asking them to move away. Just then the chief of staff, accompanied by his assistant, General Ze'evi, also arrived. The fact that a council of war was being held just as a shift became evident in the battlefield stalemate lent it supreme importance. The

Akavish Road was already open to traffic. Repeated attempts by the 21st Division to attack from the north had been checked while causing the enemy losses, and construction of the bridge was proceeding apace. The question now was will we cross on strength and continue the assault momentum with a breakthrough into "Africa"? And if so, who would cross and who would secure the bridge zone? Sharon reported that despite the heavy shelling of the yard at Matzmed, the bridging work was continuing unabated and the raft-bridge would be completed within a few hours. He suggested that his forces cross to the west bank while my division took charge of defending the bridgehead. I suggested that we stick to the plan whereby I was to break through via the bridgehead and attack westward and southward. Bar-Lev came up with a compromise plan: part of my division and part of Sharon's division would be regrouped, under Dovik's command, to defend the bridgehead, while the two understrength divisions would then launch the assault. The chief of staff, who had listened to this debate, concluded it in clear, concise, decisive language: "I do not favor the compromise idea. I have decided: Sharon will continue with the task of consolidating the bridgehead, and Bren will cross westward according to the plan."

It is difficult to describe the relief I felt. When the discussion opened I had no idea it would go the way it did. Ever since the operation began, I was waiting impatiently for the moment when I would be able to cross. I was glad we had been able to widen the corridor to the bridgehead and free Akavish from enemy pressure. I saw the moment of the crossing approaching — and now suddenly the crossing itself was being called into question. Bar-Lev's compromise proposal took me by surprise, and I worried about how the chief of staff would decide the matter. His statement was decisive, not to be questioned.

"Arik," Dado told Sharon, "complete the task assigned to you and then you can cross too!" Sharon made no reply. It seemed to me that he saw the sense of the chief's decision. I said that in order to be able to cross soon, I would have to deal with two problems. First, to destroy the Egyptian armored brigade that was advancing toward us from the south, and second, to hand over to Sharon the combat sector opposite the Chinese Farm and Missouri, where Tuvia and Gabi were engaged in battle. I suggested that Tuvia be returned at once to Sharon's command and requested Sharon to dispatch forces to replace Gabi along the Tirtur Road so he could refuel and prepare for an early crossing. Natke and Aryeh were about to go into battle against the 25th Brigade and would have to replenish themselves later, after the battle. I said I was glad Sharon had sent Amnon's forces to replace Amir Yoffe's battalion around noontime. I pointed out that I had already sent Amir fuel and ammunition and that it was important he get back to us quickly.

Hastily taking my leave of those at the conference, I mounted my command vehicle was told the driver to speed to Caspi-59. My spirits were high. I felt full of energy and self-confident, eager for the fight. On the face of it, I should have been feeling the pressure: I must cross soon, but before that I had to deal with the advancing 25th Brigade. How could I know whether they would keep up their advance and at what pace? How long would we have to put off our own move? What if they should spot Natke or Aryeh? What if we got tied up in a prolonged battle? Moreover, Gabi was still fighting opposite the Tirtur axis, and who could know how long it would take to transfer the contact line to Sharon's division? And what about more fuel and ammunition? After all, the roads were blocked and to replenish stocks in the heavy dunes was a time-consuming process.

I had doubts, but refused to get worked up over them. I felt certain, for whatever reasons, that the engagement with the 25th Brigade would be short and successful. This perception may have stemmed from the awareness that I was getting Aryeh's brigade in time and that Aryeh was now moving to enter battle opposite the rear section of the enemy column. In short, I felt that even though we were facing some complex activity, we would certainly overcome it easily.

As we sped along the empty Caspi Road, I radioed Dovik and Ami, telling them to push supplies to Caspi. Just a few minutes after I left the council, Sharon called to ask why Tuvia's brigade was not yet being transferred to him. I at once gave the necessary order, happily taking this as a sign that things were beginning to go according to plan and that Sharon was already beginning to assume responsibility for the Tirtur sector.

At 1440 hours everything seemed to be going smoothly. Aryeh was nearing the hills close to Hurva and opposite the Tzihzuah area. Natke was deployed in an ambush with one battalion well forward in the Grafit Hills west of Edra, while the second battalion was 2 km east of Yachfan position. I had reached Caspi-59 and could observe the entire area. Even the Egyptians were playing their appointed part in the plan and were now deployed along about 15 km between Lexicon-269 and Botzer. I released Natke from responsibility for Natan's battalion, which was fighting in the western section of the Tirtur axis, placing Natan under Gabi's command. Natke could now devote all his attention to executing the ambush against the advancing 25th Brigade.

The battle began at 1445 hours, but not before some excited calls from Amnon's brigade (in Sharon's division) which had a four-tank company positioned south of Lakekan. At 1230 hours they had opened fire on a few tanks that were moving ahead of the main column, apparently the 25th Brigade's scout company, while Natke's tanks had held their fire. We also blocked attempts to have the Egyptians shelled by our artillery. The enemy halted, but we hoped they would soon renew their advance. Amnon's company now began reporting nervously that a huge armored column was moving toward them along Bitter Lake. His company could not see Natke's concealed troops, but we calmed Amnon, and Natke radioed: "God bless them, let them come in — we're waiting for them!"

When a long-range firefight began between the head of the Egyptian column and the company by Lakekan, Natke's brigade went into action. They dashed forward on the Egyptians' flank and opened fire. Within minutes many Egyptian tanks were ablaze and Natke's tanks began rushing forward to narrow the range. In the midst of the confusion that rapidly developed among the Egyptians who began moving about every which way, a few tanks launched a hopeless attack toward Natke. Even though Natke's brigade was deployed in dominating positions on Grafit, and the Egyptians were exposed on lower flat terrain, there was some excitement among the men in Natke's tanks, who radioed: "They are charging us!" From my observation point I could see the battle. Natke's second battalion, commanded by Ze'evik, was charging down the sand hills toward Yachfan. Some of the amphibious tanks in the Egyptian column tried to flee to the lake, but they hit a minefield. I was worried by the fact that Aryeh was still far off and out of the firefight. Noticing that the entire Egyptian column — even those tanks that were not taking part in the battle — had halted and fearing that they would any moment retreat toward Botzer, I urged Aryeh to dispatch one battalion straight ahead to take up positions south of Yachfan and another battalion to make a flanking movement southward in order to block the rear section of the Egyptian column, where its artillery and many supply vehicles were concentrated. I approved Natke's request to recall Natan's battalion, which was operating opposite the Tirtur axis under Gabi's command. I determined the small swamp in front of Yachfan as the sector boundary between Aryeh and Natke. Near me was Natke's jeep company and I employed them to steer tanks into position and act as a physical liaison on the sector boundary.

More and more fires appeared in the plain before us. The Egyptians, moving in an unsecured column, were caught on the killing ground in the worst possible situation. On one flank Israeli armor was operating against them from good positions while on their other flank was the lake, and adjacent to it was a huge minefield that we had laid back during the War of Attrition. In front of them were Israeli tanks, and more tanks were moving to close off any possible escape route to their rear. By 1600 hours the Egyptians' 25th Brigade had been largely annihilated.

Natke: "I think we can cross off this brigade."

"Don't cross off anything," I told him, "keep cleaning up the road."

Natke: "Okay, I'm continuing to set them alight." And he went on: "Bren, did you see that MIG that just fell among us? He bombed us with napalm and was shot down by a tank."

At 1640 hours Natke reported: "Some enemy tanks fleeing to the south."

Aryeh: "I'm dealing with them, but I don't understand how they're coming through the swamp." But the rear section of the 25th Brigade had managed to retreat toward Botzer before Aryeh could head them off. Eliashiv's battalion gave chase to about ten tanks and other vehicles that were trying to flee to Botzer. Now my chief of staff, Ami, came over the radio to say that he had coordinated things with Magen's division, to the south, which was ready to support us with artillery fire. Aryeh's artillery liaison officer began to adjust their fire as required.

Aware of the need to disengage in order to prepare for the crossing, I ordered Natke, at 1700 hours, to break off and move back to the Caspi Road in order to replenish, while Aryeh was to continue in hot pursuit. Close to dusk, Eliashiv's tanks hit an old minefield of ours near Botzer, and two tanks were disabled; a third tank was hit by a Sagger missile. Those were our only losses in the battle in which we destroyed some fifty to sixty T-62 tanks, as well as armored personnel carriers, guns, and many supply vehicles, all of which were left ablaze in the field.

At this point I ordered Aryeh to return to Caspi, stock up with fuel and ammunition, and organize for a crossing. However, Southern Command intervened and asserted that Aryeh had to return to his earlier role as Southern Command reserve and secure the zone of operations against possible enemy incursions from the south.

The battle itself was an example of a successful divisional "jump-out ambush" which was coordinated for many hours across a broad front. Adjacent small forces — Amnon's small company south of Lakekan, a platoon of Tuvia's at Hurva — helped channel the enemy onto the killing ground. At 1515 hours Natke's and Aryeh's "jump-out" from their ambush quickly sealed the fate of the 25th Brigade. When the remnants of the enemy force made for Botzer, Magen's artillery volunteered to batter them.

While I was busy conducting the battle against the 25th Brigade, Gabi called to report that Sharon's forces had not yet begun to assume responsibility for the battle zone opposite Tirtur; therefore Gabi was still involved in the fighting and could not pull out Ehud's and Lapidot's battalions for refueling and restocking. Gabi also complained that even though Amir Yoffe's battalion had been replaced on the Shick line and had even refueled and taken on new ammunition (I had sent him both), Sharon was still not releasing him so he could rejoin us. At about 1600 hours Gabi called again to say that he could not understand what was happening in the field: it looked to him as though Tuvia's forces were disengaging in order to move to the canal zone. In the light of these reports, I contacted Southern Command. Angrily, I pointed out that the plan agreed on was not yet being implemented where Sharon's forces were concerned and that the ensuing delays would adversely affect my division's crossing operation. Over and over I called Southern Command, but to no avail.

Shortly before dark, the Egyptian pressure on Gabi was intensified, and at 1750 hours Dovik reported: ''I am looking at the area between Televizia and Tirtur. It is being heavily shelled by the enemy. Gabi is holding his ground, but it looks like the enemy has not given up at this stage. If we pull Gabi out, there will be no one left there. It might be a good idea if you contacted Southern Command HQ as well as your neighbor [Sharon].'' Gabi then said he was concerned about the Egyptian infantry who were advancing toward him. He requested more artillery support, including illumination shells to light up the battlefield. When the pressure abated, about 1800 hours, I told Gabi to continue to hold the area but to pull back forces on a rotation basis for restocking until being replaced by Sharon.

After I informed Southern Command of the delay, Gonen tried to contact Sharon; however he could not find him, so he spoke with Sharon's chief of staff. Then General Elazar himself stressed to Sharon that he had to replace Gabi with all possible speed. But by now the deterioration in relations between Sharon and his superior officers had become evident, and they found it difficult to impose their authority over him. Even before the ''council of war'' on the morning of the seventeenth, Sharon had ''smuggled,'' as he himself put it, ten tanks to the west bank. In response, Bar-Lev forbade Sharon to transfer any more tanks and emphasized that any such action required the approval of HQ. Later that morning, at 1015 hours, Sharon complained to Gonen that he was ''being held on a short leash.'' Gonen replied that a situation estimate was underway, following which Sharon was likely to be allocated forces and given missions that would be to his liking. Following the council of war, on 17 October Bar-Lev had suggested that Oded or Ben-Ari be posted to Sharon's HQ in order to keep him informed of Sharon's activities. When Dado arrived at Southern Command HQ that day, Gonen pointed out to him that Sharon had in fact lost control of his division during the night crossing and that since then all the work had been left to my division. Gonen went on to say that in the wake of the decisions taken at the ''council of war,'' he had ordered that Amnon (of Sharon's division) replace Amir Yoffe, and he had even so directed

Amir personally (again bypassing Sharon, though this was of doubtful effectiveness, of course).

At 1600 hours, following my complaint that Gabi was not being replaced on the contact line, Gonen tried to contact Sharon but couldn't find him on any of the radio nets. At the same time, Gonen heard the report that Tuvia was moving toward Lakekan. In an atmosphere of suspicion, Gonen ordered Sharon's chief of staff to halt Tuvia's brigade and to have him return to securing Hamadia and the Akavish and Tirtur roads. However, it later emerged that there was a misunderstanding, and that it was not Tuvia's entire brigade that was moving toward Lakekan, but that Tuvia was going there personally in order to get his orders from Sharon.

At 1645 the chief of staff contacted Sharon concerning the operation of his division and the need to replace Gabi in the Akavish sector. Dado and Sharon agreed that there was no need to capture Missouri that night, but that it was essential to maintain a good bridgehead, to which end Sharon must keep the Akavish and Tirtur roads open. Sharon said that in his opinion the Tirtur axis was not essential for the bridgehead, "but if you want me to open it, I will open it!" (In point of fact, Sharon's remark was astonishing. For not only was the Tirtur Road needed to advance the roller-bridge, but also to hold off the Egyptians' Sagger-missile units that were operating toward the Akavish Road.) Sharon added that "tomorrow morning Southern Command will have a secure bridgehead" and that another force should be prepared to hold the bridgehead so that he could cross as soon as possible to the west bank.

Following the "council of war," Dayan accompanied Sharon to the bridgehead, and at 1730 hours, he arrived back at Southern Command HQ. A tense conference began. Dayan remarked that the Egyptians neither saw nor understood what was happening on the battlefield. Turning angrily to Dado and Bar-Lev, he said: "The option you asked for from the cabinet is now in your hands. With every hour that passes the Egyptians will organize better."

Showing some discomfort, the chief of staff replied: "I have ordered Bren to move, and Arik told me that he would replace Bren within minutes."

Dayan: "Replace or not replace, they have to speed to the bridge, the bridge is ready for a crossing."

Bar-Lev: "The division of the HQs, as decided on, is now causing time to be wasted."

Dado: "Arik is physically incapable of moving now, and it would be a mistake to move him."

Dayan: "This morning we said that Bren would cross the bridge at about 1600."

Bar-Lev: "That depended on his armored battle against the enemy armor [the 25th Brigade]."

Gonen: "Bren is starting to cross, but Gabi is under attack, and Arik still hasn't replaced him."

At 1745 hours Gonen contacted me: "Take half of Gabi's force and move!"

I could well understand the impatience and discomfort: at last we had a bridge, but the crossing continued to be delayed. Already ninety minutes had gone by, and the crossing was still not under way. Sharon, too, asked over the radio: "The bridge is ready, why isn't Bren crossing?"

The main reason for the delay in my crossing was the necessity to refuel the tanks and rearm them, since the entire division had been engaged in intensive, prolonged fighting. Despite the many difficulties involved in getting supply convoys through via the blocked Akavish Road, my logistics officers had succeeded in bringing supplies to the Caspi axis. Only Ze'ira's and Lapidot's battalions had even partially restocked. Aryeh's and Natke's brigades moved to fill up as soon as they disengaged from the battle against the 25th Brigade, but by the time they pulled back and organized for restocking, it was already quite late. My forward command post was the first to replenish, but unfortunately at 1745 hours the process had just begun. The area was being shelled; the explosions were everywhere seemingly searching us out in the dark. Even though the shelling was ineffective, it was still dangerous. We ignored it, but it still slowed things down, as did the darkness. The supply-laden vehicles were on the road and could not get to the tanks. And even when the tanks were able to draw near the vehicles, the conditions ruled out any quick replenishment.

Had Gabi's brigade been able to disengage around noon — as had in fact been agreed on at the council of war — it would have been ready to move across as soon as the bridge was ready. Then, by the time Gabi's brigade was across, the rest of the division would have completed its replenishment and been ready to cross as well. My repeated warnings to Southern Command HQ that commenced even before the battle with the 25th Brigade had been to no avail. Now the consequences were apparent to all: the bridge was ready, but there was no one to cross.

The conference that took place at Southern Command HQ with Dayan's participation did not provide a sufficiently in-depth appraisal of the actual situation. The real problem was not to get tanks across quickly, but to transfer formations ready for prolonged combat in order to launch an offensive and penetrate deep into the other side. The only brigade not involved in battle that day, Haim's brigade with its thirty-eight tanks, was in fact already on the west bank, but it, too, had no fuel. Had we crossed immediately, we would have had to wait on the west bank until the supply vehicles could cross, and then we would have had to replenish under an artillery shelling. Such a move would have been unwise and risky.

Nor was replenishment of fuel and ammunition the only preparation we had to make prior to any crossing. We had to reorganize and regroup. Along with the brigades, I had to send across artillery units as well as elements for evacuation and ordnance support. The pressure exerted on me was relentless. At one point, Gonen radioed to say that if I didn't set out the mission would immediately be given to Sharon. The implied threat stung me. I couldn't help thinking that it would have been more useful for Gonen to press Sharon to release Gabi at the time agreed on. At about 2000 hours Tuvia deployed in a broader sector, so that Gabi could be disengaged and move to reorganize. Now under the conditions of the duny terrain and the darkness, it would take him at least two to three hours to stock up.

CHAPTER TWENTY-FIVE

18 October: WE CROSS AND LAUNCH THE BREAKTHROUGH

A t 2130 hours I ordered the replenishment halted and directed that the tanks set out even with "stomachs" only half full. I noted the order of movement and the route to be followed. I had decided that we would move in the open area south of Akavish, from the area of the Kishuf hills toward Lakekan, which was on the shore of Bitter Lake, and from there on the Lexicon Road through the Nahala axis to the bridge, which was at Matzmed. The division was led by a small scout force followed by my forward command group, then Gabi, and finally Natke. Aryeh's brigade was left on the Caspi Road as the Southern Command reserve. (The following day, Aryeh was again told to position himself around Tassa to deal with any possible breakthrough of Second Army forces into our territory.)

The division's night movement, though steady, took time and was accompanied by an incessant flow of queries from Southern Command: How far are you? When will you cross? Finally at 2240 hours, we reached the bridge.

Abruptly the entire landscape changed. In the light of an almost full moon, the calm sparkling water of the Suez Canal was revealed. The canal was spanned by a large, strong bridge. There was no enemy shelling; the scene was still, silent. By the bridge I met Jackie, Sharon's deputy. Gripped by excitement, I radioed my forces: "The

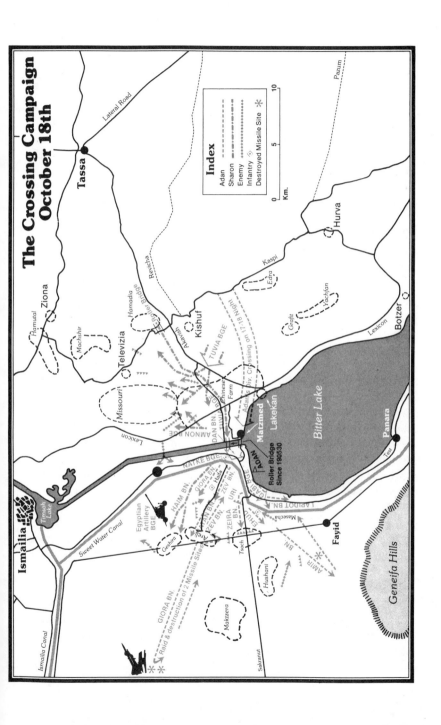

great moment has arrived, and we are crossing to Africa. The bridge is a magnificent sight, and it is waiting for your speedy arrival.'' Just then I felt my knee being struck by something hard from inside the Zelda. Bending down, I found myself looking into the eyes of my driver, Moussa. "General," he said, "have a shot of whiskey — the bottle's open." Now that's what you call a crew. I held the bottle high and raised my voice for the entire crew to hear: "To the breakthrough into Africa! Friends! We've come a long way so far, and it won't be much longer before we break the enemy! *L'chaim!*" The bottle was passed from hand to hand. Spirits were high in the Zelda. I then contacted Southern Command and told them, in rather florid language, that I was already in Africa and my forces were in the process of crossing the canal.

Gonen called me to say that until morning we were to remain within the bounds of the bridgehead. He asked how things were going, and I told him the crossing was very impressive. I also took the opportunity to remind him that Amir Yoffe's battalion was to have been returned to me long ago, but that Sharon was not releasing it, even though it was fully replenished and waiting to cross. Gonen's reply made my blood boil: "You'll get Amir's battalion back only in the morning." This appeared to be acquiescence to Sharon's refusal to release the battalion. I didn't let the matter go; I argued with Gonen and demanded explanations. I got a typical reply which by now made no impression on me: "Circumstances don't permit me to explain — I'll explain everything after it's all over."

I was obstinate: "I have to organize and prepare my forces for the breakthrough during the night."

Pressed, Gonen said, unwillingly: "All right, I'll give Sharon the order." Whether he actually issued the order I don't know, but at 0320 hours it was explained to me that Amir's battalion was securing Sharon's forward command post and that it was impossible to release him. The situation was absurd. In addition to his own units, my two brigades — engaged in a lengthy crossing operation — were also stationed quite close to Sharon's forward command post. Finally, at 0420 hours Sharon gave the long-awaited order to Amir. But some time would pass before Amir crossed and caught up with his brigade, which would launch its attack without waiting for him.

As soon as I reached the west bank I wanted to carry out some reconnaissance, so I would be able to orient my brigades into the staging area prior to our attack at dawn. Astonished that there was no one to meet us on the west bank, I contacted Jackie and within a few minutes Colonel Haim, already a veteran on that side of the canal, showed up. We were happy to see each other. Haim climbed onto my Zelda, and we set out for the Deversoir airfield. To the left were one-story white buildings; the gaps and fissures in them — the results of shelling — were plainly visible in the moonlight. We advanced on a limestone road with tall casuarina trees on either side, a green, closed area so different from the white seemingly endless dunes in which we had been fighting until now.

As Haim was briefing me on the area and relating his experiences in raiding the missile sites, the pastoral calm was suddenly shattered. The bridgehead area came under intense, heavy shelling. Within minutes, some of the scouts on the jeeps accompanying the forward command group were hit. In the meantime, Gabi's brigade began crossing, and I asked Haim to dispatch his scouts to guide Gabi on the Test Road to the southern zone of the bridgehead.

The heavy barrage began to have its effect; an irritating series of disruptions afflicted us. Gabi reported that after his third tank had crossed, the bridge had snapped and the tank was stuck on it. It was 2345 hours. I contacted Jackie, who was responsible for the bridgehead area. His reply: "We're checking it out." And then that it would take some time to repair the bridge; he did not know how much time. In the meantime Gabi's brigade would continue to cross on the Gilowas. This change meant that Gabi's tank column would have to move from the approach to the bridge to the point from which the Gilowas were launched, a few hundred meters to the north. Jackie sent scouts to lead Gabi's forces.

The heavy shelling continued unabated. I turned back toward the bridge zone, keeping the forward command group vehicles close to the buildings. The shelling intensified, becoming totally hellish with artillery shells, and worse, Katyusha rockets exploding all around us — ear-splitting blinding fireballs, sparks flying all about, the smell of an iron foundry. Our fear and concern for the men now crossing was growing. At 0006 hours (18 October) Jackie still didn't know how

long it would take to repair the bridge. The "professionals" hadn't
yet arrived. Nine minutes later he reported that the bridge could be
repaired, but there was still no time estimate. The division was stuck.
Who knows when we'd be able to cross — and only five hours of
darkness left! Suddenly I noticed two bridge-laying tanks not far
from my command post. A piece of luck! I recalled the techniques we
had demonstrated for the senior command staff at the Ruafa'a Dam
on how to bridge a small gap. I informed Jackie and Gabi that I was
sending them bridge-laying tanks. But now the crews of those tanks
could not be found. Dovik went to look for them in the heavy shelling. Finally they were located and Israel, Haim's deputy, set out with
them for the bridge. A bridging operation under an artillery barrage
is no easy matter. And time was running out.

Gabi's tanks were crossing on the Gilowas, but I had had Natke's
brigade halt in a far-off waiting area near Lakekan, so they could
wait their turn out of range of the shelling. New problems arose. The
barrage was nothing short of volcanic, so the gaps between the tanks
had to be increased. A tank driver that tried to move a tank onto one
of the Gilowas wasn't careful enough, slipped and almost sank the
vehicle but was towed out. At 0500 hours one of the Gilowas took a
direct hit and sank. Now Gabi reported that the tanks that had already
crossed were waiting on the other side for Haim's scouts to lead them
to the staging area. Haim said he had dispatched the scouts and that
they would get there momentarily. The artillery and Katyusha barrage
raged on. I made efforts to activate our artillery and requested
Sharon's division also to direct counterbattery fire at the enemy, but
there was no letup in the Egyptian shelling. Haim's scouts had not yet
arrived, but I couldn't hold Gabi up any longer on the bank of the
canal, so I oriented him by radio to his forming-up area.

At 0135 hours we got some good news: one of the bridge-laying
tanks had bridged the gap, and the bridge was once more ready for
traffic. Gabi diverted part of his force to the bridge, so he was now
crossing on both the bridge and on the Gilowas. Gabi's brigade completed its crossing at 0235 hours, and I called up Natke, who had
been waiting at Lakekan. Until he arrived at the bridge there was
again nervousness and frantic radio calls: Where are the tanks? The
bridge is free and no one is crossing!

Natke's force began crossing at 0315 hours. Fortunately, the artillery barrage had ceased. By 0515 hours my division was across the canal with a strength of two brigades — some seventy tanks in each — and a self-propelled artillery battalion. The brigades arrived at the staging area; the brigade commanders met with Haim's battalion commanders for an update, and just then the shelling recommenced.

Dawn would be breaking in just fifteen minutes, and we had to launch our westward breakthrough. We had come a long way, I reflected, from the time the crossing operation went afoul. In forty-eight hours of persistent, stubborn fighting, my division had managed to open the road to the bridgehead, push ahead the rafts that enabled a bridge to be constructed, and repulse the counterattacks from both north and south, while inflicting heavy casualties on the enemy. We were able to remove the pressure on the east bank, we crossed and were about to penetrate to the west. But what had the enemy managed to move up against us on the west bank?

Sharon's forces were to have seized a bridgehead on the west bank up to the Havit Road, but in fact they moved only up to the Sweet Water Canal. This enabled the enemy to move reinforcements close to the greenbelt and into overgrown areas on the belt's western edge. Our information, as we were about to break out of the bridgehead to the west, was fragmented. From what I heard from Haim and from what the brigade commander heard from his battalion commanders, Egyptian infantry had been spotted in the area, and the noise of tanks had been heard during the night, but overall the line of contact was characterized by artillery shelling and the absence of frontal enemy pressure. In fact, when Haim's raiding force had moved into areas farther to the west, the Egyptian defensive positions of Tsach, Maktzera, and Arel had been empty. But two days had passed since then. We received information that the enemy was speeding armored reinforcements from the east, the south, and the north, but that these had apparently not reached the canal yet. We expected a fairly easy breakthrough from the greenbelt with armored engagements at road junctions and in the open terrain. But the reality was different.

Because of the renewed shelling and the lack of time, I decided not to summon the brigade commanders to me but to issue the orders for the breakthrough to the west via the radio. Natke would break through on my right (the north) by crossing the Sweet Water Canal on a Bailey bridge, penetrate westward on the Haifa axis across the Abu Sultan camps, capture Arel — which is about 4 km from the Sweet Water Canal — and continue southwest to Maktzera. To my left, Gabi would move along the Test Road, cross the Sweet Water Canal on the stone bridge toward the Sakranut Road, capture the Uri Stronghold and the Tsach position, then speed southward to take up positions on the Geneifa Hills. On his way, he would leave behind armored infantry and some tanks to secure the zone of operations opposite the Fayid Airport.

Daybreak at 0530. The brigade commanders reported that they had issued orders to their battalions and were waiting for my go-ahead. After holding them back a bit in order to complete coordination with the division artillery, I gave the order to attack at 0545 hours. Full of zest, Gilad radioed: ''Natke, Gabi: hail the Saggers on the way!'' I noted their high spirit.

Reports of our canal crossing began to reach the Egyptian high command on the afternoon of the sixteenth, following Haim's armored raid and Mrs. Meir's statement in the Knesset. Immediately orders were given to the Second and Third Armies to counterattack and destroy the bridgehead on both banks — though so far the main effort had been made on the east bank. From about noon on 17 October the Egyptian high command grasped the scope, and apparently the intention, of our assault. Sadat and Ismail-Ali again contacted Second Army HQ and ordered the annihilation of the IDF bridgehead at any price. To that end, the Second Army was reinforced with the 23rd Tank Brigade from the 3rd Mechanized Division and with the 150th Paratroop Brigade — both of which belonged to the reserve forces of the Egyptians' GHQ. As the two brigades moved eastward to the front from Cairo, they were photographed from the air on the afternoon of 17 October — the photograph being interpreted in Tel Aviv. The paratroop brigade would subsequently reach the greenbelt south of Ismailia, while the tanks and armored personnel carriers of the tank brigade would deploy opposite the crossing zone on the Aida Plains. From the south, the Third Army dispatched the 2nd Tank Brigade of its 4th Division toward the bridgehead. The 207th Tank Battalion of that brigade had already reached a point near the Sakranut axis, on which Gabi was to break through, and waited on two roads — Test-43 and Masecha — in the greenbelt. From the north the Second Army dispatched a tank battalion (probably from the 23rd Mechanized Division) that advanced through the northern section of the greenbelt, ready to take up positions north of the Haifa axis on the earth ramparts around the armories in the Abu Sultan camps.

After allocating one artillery battalion for direct support to each brigade, I opened up with a concentrated artillery shelling, and then the brigades commenced their breakthrough moves across the small bridges spanning the Sweet Water Canal. Gabi ran into difficulties immediately. At 0605 hours he reported: "We have broken out to a junction opposite Uri." And three minutes later: "One of my tanks was hit by a Sagger." At first, Natke's attack seemed to be going well. Natan's battalion broke through on the Haifa axis, encountering only very light resistance. Its main problem was getting through the mud near the railroad tracks; there Natan left four tanks behind that had lost their treads, and crewmen and ordnance personnel labored to repair them. The rest of the battalion sped on. When they reached an earth rampart 800 meters in front of Arel, the enemy responded with an artillery shelling and by moving up tanks. A battle ensued, in which fifteen Egyptian tanks were knocked out of action. At 0700 hours Arel was captured. We found large stores of equipment there, mostly mobile amphibious bridging gear.

Meanwhile, the rest of Natke's brigade followed behind Natan's battalion and was moving inside the Abu Sultan camps. Here in the northern section were empty hangars for warplanes protected by high earthen barriers. Many of the buildings in the compound were half destroyed. Natan's battalion was followed by Natke's forward command group, and then came Ze'evik's battalion. At 0627 enemy tanks opened up from the barriers. Natke reported: "Something to the north. Everyone who goes by there gets hit. Two of my tanks were hit and are burning. I'm directing artillery fire there."

It was a very uncomfortable situation. We were caught in an enemy ambush from the flank, at a range of 600–800 meters, and two tanks had been hit with the first burst of fire. Ze'evik's tanks immediately took up fire positions and a firefight began. Even though the Egyptian tanks were operating from excellent, barely visible positions, a few of them were hit at once. The battle was quickly decided, thanks to the speedy action of Giora's battalion, which had been outside the killing ground. Natke had ordered Giora to change course and attack the enemy ambush from the flank while moving to the north parallel to the Haifa Road. When Ze'evik continued to advance toward Arel, he ran into withering fire at the junction of Haifa-34, apparently from commandos. It was 0630 hours, and it was becoming clear that it was going to be very difficult to break out of the covered bridgehead area. Natke reported: "Rough going here. We hit some Saggers and other antitank weapons, but it's slow going."

And Gabi radioed: "Two hundred meters from the stone bridge there's an entrenched enemy position that doesn't let us lift our heads. Three of our tanks have been hit by RPGs."

Along with my forward command group, I was then positioned on the Test Road in Gabi's tank column. Because both sides of the road were cultivated and marshy, difficulties of deployment arose, and the brigade was positioned on the road in one very long column. Through my binoculars I could see that in the greenbelt zone, and in and around the many buildings there, Egyptian infantry troops were running about, shifting from position to position. We were coming under sniper fire. The front commander, Bar-Lev, came over the radio and asked for a report. I briefed him on our static situation. Bar-Lev: "Do you have contact with Haim?"

I replied in the affirmative and Bar-Lev said: "Locate him and get help from him."

I told Bar-Lev that I would also need some top infantry troops and requested that he direct brigade commander Danny to assist me. Dovik contacted Danny and then set out to bring a company of paratroopers. I asked Natke for his infantry troops, but he informed me that he had dispatched his armored infantry support to the Haifa junction, where a short-range battle was raging.

Natke's situation, while far from comfortable, was immeasurably better than Gabi's, since Natke's quick breakthrough and his capture of Arel gave him a position that dominated the area. In addition, the way in which Natke had extricated himself from the tank ambush showed that he was overcoming his difficulties while inflicting losses on the enemy. He still had one problem to the rear: the Haifa axis remained blocked, and fighting would be required to mop up the enemy forces operating from within and around the buildings there.

Gabi, however, was still stuck on the Test Road, the entire brigade unable to break out of the greenbelt. To assist Gabi, I ordered Natke to leave a small contingent at Arel and move the rest of Natan's battalion up from the north toward Tsach and Uri, thus pressing the enemy blocking Gabi from another direction. Natke asked for a delay, as he was involved in a firefight; he would immediately dispatch Giora's battalion in a flanking movement so that he could join up with Natan and the two battalions could attack Tsach together. Up to 0930 hours reports came in that Natke was engaged in a difficult engagement. Enemy tanks arriving from the direction of Maktzera attacked the battalion at Arel, and most of them were destroyed. Natke reported that just as he had overcome the tank ambush he ran into antitank ambushes on the Haifa axis. He was engaged in combat, tanks of his were being hit, but he was also hitting enemy tanks. He had many casualties, whom he was evacuating. Natke said he was now concentrating armored infantry forces, and he was certain he would overcome the enemy.

Meanwhile, at about 0800 hours Dovik returned with Nudelman's paratroop company from Danny's brigade. Gabi briefed them, issued orders, and coordinated forces for the breakthrough across the stone bridge. Just as Gabi was about to launch an attack toward the Uri position, enemy tanks attacked him from the south, from among the trees. The tanks at the head of the column, near the blocked stone bridge, exchanged fire with the Egyptian forces. They hit some enemy tanks, but some of our tanks also sustained hits. The threat on our southern flank continued; again and again Egyptian tanks sallied out from there to operate against us. I did not like the situation in which dozens of Gabi's tanks were idling in a crowded column on the Test Road, waiting for the breakthrough to Uri that was being delayed by the tank raids on our flank. I thought that even though it was not our intention to move south on the Test Road, it would be worthwhile sending some tanks in that direction in order to catch the enemy from the flank. I issued the requisite order to Gabi, who sent Lapidot's battalion to do the job. Very quickly the 207th Tank Battalion was knocked out of action, half its tanks ablaze, the rest mired in the mud and abandoned.

Now that the threat from the flank had been disposed of, the attack on Uri could begin. Under cover of artillery fire and direct trajectory fire by tanks, the paratroopers charged toward Uri, along with Gabi's Zelda-borne scout company. In a twinkling they took the position. The paratroopers began mopping up the trenches while Gabi's troops continued operating from their Zeldas. The commander of this unit, Maj. Mark Yames, who charged with his men, was killed; the paratroopers had two killed and five wounded. The objective was ours, and Gabi's brigade could now cross the bridge. However, because Tsach dominated Uri — and on Tsach were dug-in tanks and an abundance of antitank guns and missiles — Gabi's brigade, after crossing the stone bridge, could not advance westward but was forced to disperse among the trees in the greenbelt. I told Gabi to wait: I intended to attack Tsach in coordinated divisional strength using his and Natke's forces. To that end, though, I had to coordinate between Natke and Haim.

At 0615 Sharon had already ordered Haim to advance toward the Nefisha bridges on the Ismailia Canal, but Haim replied that he was short of fuel. When I reported to Bar-Lev on our situation, he suggested that I attach Haim to take part in our efforts on the west bank. We gave Haim fuel and ammunition, and I committed him on Natke's north flank toward Geshira. Haim set out at 0820. One battalion moved northwest reaching Orcha, where they destroyed fifteen enemy tanks. From there the battalion was ordered southward, to help Natke, who had already taken Arel but was still fighting on the Haifa axis. On the way, they destroyed Missile Site 6321 and a number of tanks. The battalion now linked up with Haim, who with the second battalion had already reached Geshira while capturing an artillery site with thirty-six abandoned guns. I now told Haim to secure the area toward Arel, since Natke was about to leave it and attack Tsach. However, it now emerged that Haim was getting orders from two division commanders. Southern Command made it clear that Haim was under Sharon's command but told Sharon to leave him at Geshira, to secure the zone of operations.

At 1120 hours Natke reported that he was ready to move with two battalions from Arel to Tsach. I held him up in order to complete preparations for a coordinated divisional attack, Gabi's brigade from the east and Natke's from the north. I had the division artillery shell Tsach, but I soon had to stop the attack. The Tsach position dominated the open areas and was well fortified — even the tanks there were dug in — and both Natke and Gabi had tanks hit. Battalion commander Natan, of Natke's brigade, was wounded in one eye but refused to be evacuated; he continued to command the battalion from a stretcher in his command vehicle. Gabi, trying to bypass Tsach from the east, sent his battalions south into the greenbelt and its fringes, but five of his tanks were hit, and he remained in the greenbelt. I reported the situation to Southern Command and requested Aryeh's brigade, which was serving as the Command's reserve force. At 1315 hours I was informed that this request was approved and that Aryeh had set out from Tassa to link up with us.

It was clear that the Tsach position was preventing our breakthrough into open terrain. I asked for air support but was told that the antiaircraft missile batteries in the area made this impossible.

I suggested that we raid the surface-to-air missile batteries in order to open the skies for the air force, and this idea was approved. I told Haim and Gabi to send one battalion each deep into enemy territory in order to attack the missile sites. When Haim said he was just about out of fuel and ammunition, I reassigned his part of the mission to Natke. Natke, too, was short of fuel and ammunition, so I told him to refuel the raiding tanks from the tanks that would remain at Arel.

In aerial photos the antiaircraft missile bases were seen to consist of a large mound of earth covering a bunker housing two vehicles that held the fire-control instrumentation. In the center of the mound was the antenna, and around it could be seen four open circular positions.

When Gabi received the order to raid the missile sites with one battalion, he contacted Lt. Col. Amir Yoffe: "I want to assign you the task of attacking two missile bases."

Amir's reply: "With pleasure!" Amir Yoffe was a battalion commander in the regular Armored Corps; before the war he served on the teaching staff of the School of Armor. Amir was a hard fighter and had earned the reputation of being a "tiger." His men, who cursed their luck in being sent to his battalion during peacetime, now thanked their fortune for such a fine leader to guide them.*

Gabi's planning was meticulous. He dispatched Ehud's battalion

*Amir Yoffe was decorated with the Medal of Valor. He was later killed in a road accident.

southward to replace Amir, and he also forwarded one company to isolate the area between Tsach and the raiding force. Amir's battalion set out at 1500 on the Havit axis headed by a scout unit. When he arrived within firing range of the missile site, he deployed two small companies to secure himself, one to the west and the other to the south toward the Faid Airfield. Destruction of the control center's antenna from a distance of 3–4 km was a relatively easy task for the tank gunners. The Egyptians responded by firing antiaircraft missiles in inaccurate flat trajectory fire and also tried to move tanks out from Tsach — but those were blocked by the company Amir had dispatched there. Meantime, the tank force assaulted the site and destroyed it. Due to the shortage of fuel and to increased enemy pressure as tanks of theirs appeared from the west, I decided to forego a raid on another missile site further to the west. Amir returned slightly before nightfall. At the same time, Giora's battalion, from Natke's brigade, penetrated about 20 km westward and destroyed two missile batteries. Because of a shortage of fuel, he barely made it back to Arel, with some tanks having to be towed by others.

These raids had a major impact on the battlefield, though we would not know this until the following day. As a result of the raids, the Egyptians decided to move back some other forward missile batteries, thus enabling the air force to attack Tsach the following day and assist our advance.

When Natke committed one of his battalions as a raiding force deep into enemy territory, he also had to solve some problems in his rear: to mop up the Haifa axis, which served as the sole connecting route between his forces at Arel and the bridge on the canal. Until he cleaned up that road, we would not have an axis on which to move additional forces or the capacity for supply and evacuation. Natke had very little armored infantry, and most of it was already fighting to mop up the Haifa axis. Ze'evik's armored infantry company had sustained heavy casualties, among them the company commander, his deputy, and three platoon leaders. The best description of the fighting comes from those who took part in it directly; the sergeant-major of the armored infantry company:

"I was in a Zelda with our company commander, Mandy, an engineering officer, a communications sergeant, and an officer named Kafri, who had just been released from hospital after being wounded in the battle against the commandos at Baluza. A sergeant named Yamini and a machine gunner named Gamzo were also in the Zelda. On our way to evacuate the crew of a tank burning due to a missile ambush, we entered a manned Egyptian stronghold. We came under terrific fire and continued until we found concealment near two buildings, close to a water tower. But we soon found that our 'hiding place' was right under the nose of Egyptian RPGs. They hit us with no trouble, and I remember that the explosion threw me inside the Zelda. For a few moments I lay stunned and seemingly blind. I thought it was death.

"When I regained consciousness, I jumped out and found a hiding place in a building. I saw Mandy there. Yamini lay outside, crying for water. Mandy rushed to the Zelda to get a jerrycan. Suddenly I saw him collapse. An Egyptian was standing a few meters away and firing. I shot and killed him, but Mandy was dead. In the adjacent building I saw Kafri, wounded. He couldn't get out of the building because the Zelda was blocking the entrance. I was in a crater in the sand. An Egyptian carrying a missile ran by me. I shot him. He was hit, but he managed to throw himself behind the water tower. I had eight bullets left. By then, Kafri was out of the building, and he reached me; he had ammunition and grenades. Another three soldiers, who had managed to get out of a disabled tank, joined us. All of us were wounded. The Egyptians kept trying to get close and finish us off. Once some of them actually reached us, but one of the crewmen who was outside wiped them out.

"We waited four hours for help. No one came. Only toward evening medics showed up with stretchers and evacuated us under fire. But they didn't find the crewman who had wiped out the charging Egyptians. It emerged that after he had killed them he lost consciousness and fell down among three Egyptian corpses. At night he awoke, got up and started to walk without knowing where he was going. Finally, he met up with another unit, and they took him to a medical checkpoint."

Another soldier, Benny Carmel, relates: "In the bitter fighting all that day at the Haifa junction, my half-track was hit by an RPG as we were charging an enemy position. The explosion knocked me into the half-track, wounded in one hand and in my belly. The driver, who was seriously wounded, managed to open the door and get out.

The deputy company commander, who was with us, said to me: 'I'm going to die.' The company sergeant, who was also wounded, said: 'I've had it.' The Egyptian position raked us with fire. The deputy company commander fell out the back door, dead. The sergeant died sitting beside me. I was the only one alive in the half-track. My right hand was in bad shape. Luckily I'm left-handed and that hand was only lightly hit. I managed to throw five grenades at the enemy, who were about 20 meters away. The Egyptians fired another RPG at the half-track: the fuel tank was hit and began to burn.

"I gathered up my remaining strength and jumped out. A few dozen meters away I saw a small knoll with a bush by it; it was the only imaginable hiding place, and I ran there. An Egyptian soldier who spotted me began running toward me to cut me off. By the bush we met face to face. Even though I had only one good hand, I fired first and he fell dead. I lay down behind his body, which now served to conceal me. Now I found that I was in fact inside the Egyptian position. I was being fired at from all directions. The knoll and the Egyptian's body stopped the bullets. Men of my company were lying about 60 meters away, but they were pinned down by the withering fire and couldn't get to me. Between them and me lay a soldier named Max Giler, a new immigrant from England. He had a light machine gun and kept firing at the Egyptians, who from time to time tried to get to me. The men kept throwing him loaded magazines and he kept firing without letup, and so he saved me from the Egyptians.

"At one stage of the battle, Egyptian artillery shells started landing on the position. They were intended to hit us, not taking into account that the position was still manned by Egyptian troops. My condition worsened. I was losing blood all the time, and I began to suffer from dehydration. Clouds of flies hovered above me and walked over me. I had one piece of gum. I broke it into sections and every time I would take another section. For me, that was my 'iron ration.' While I was lying there helpless, I saw a few Egyptian Sukhoi planes and right above them one of our Mirages, which was swooping down on them. Two of the Egyptian planes exploded and fell to the ground.

"Then a Zelda pulled up close to me. I waved my hand at them, they opened the rear door and pulled me in. Just as we began to move the machine gunner fell on me, a bullet through his head. As we were turning the Zelda exposed itself broadside and was hit by an RPG. Immediately it started to burn. The heat was terrible. I got out through the top hatch, jumped down, and ran toward a building, where our men were. I jumped through a window into the building. Besides the wounds in my stomach and hands, my face was scorched. I lost my eyesight for twenty-four hours. I was given first aid. On the stretcher next to mine lay Kafri, who had been pulled out of the ambush into which he had fallen that morning. From him I learned that Mandy was dead and that in fact not a single officer of the armored company had survived. When I heard that Mandy was dead, I couldn't stop myself, and for the first time in the war I broke down and cried."

Around noon, I asked Southern Command for infantry reinforcement, and I was given a paratroop company from Uzzi's brigade. They joined Natke's brigade, where a paratroop company under Weiner was already fighting. Natke also sent Ze'evik back with tanks to support the armored infantry and the paratroopers who were fighting side by side. The enemy fought obstinately, and the battle raged for many hours, but gradually, after nightfall, the enemy broke and scattered in all directions. The Haifa axis was clear. Within hours, more of our forces would advance on the road, westward, deeper into Egypt.

CHAPTER TWENTY-SIX

INTERVENTION OF EGYPTIAN AIR FORCE

At noon, my forward command group was deployed among the buildings in the greenbelt not far from the stone bridge across the Sweet Water Canal. On my flank and not far in front of me, most of Gabi's forces were positioned; his forward forces were positioned about 2 km in front of us at Uri. Defense Minister Dayan joined my forward command group to observe the fighting.

For two days now, there had been intensive air activity above us. The Egyptian air force had gone into action about noon on the sixteenth, and this had enabled our planes to operate, since when the Egyptian aircraft were in the skies the surface-to-air missiles were not fired. A substantial part of our air strikes were aimed against enemy ground forces in the Chinese Farm and Missouri areas, but they had not had much effect. Some sorties were directed at radar and missile battery sites. But most of the air activity took the form of air battles above us. On the sixteenth and seventeenth, twenty enemy aircraft were shot down, while we lost six planes. Now, on the eighteenth, the Egyptian Air Force sought to hit our bridges in a concerted and brave, though largely senseless, effort. A wave of twenty fighter planes came over to attack our bridges. Many were shot down by antiaircraft fire while others were downed in dogfights. The air combat took place right over our heads, and we watched it with great interest. Every time a burning torch spiraled earthward, we literally held our breath until we received verification that it was Egyptian.

The air activity hit its climax when suddenly, from our rear, two slow, low-flying MI-8 helicopters passed overhead from the direction of Bitter Lake. One of them dropped a barrel, which fell about 60 meters from my Zelda and about 20 meters from Dayan, who was wandering about the area, scraping at the ground looking for antique shards. The barrels, which were meant to act as napalm bombs, failed to work, but our ears were deafened by the sound of the automatic-weapons fire that burst out all around us. All the machine gunners on the tanks and Zeldas, all the soldiers — including those of the forward command group — who had machine guns or rifles were firing like madmen. And the two giant helicopters were hit, plummeting to the earth and exploding among Gabi's tanks. It was an unbelievable spectacle. From this act of suicide we could only conclude that the Egyptians were in desperate straits. We were witness to many of the sixteen planes and seven helicopters downed that day. We lost six aircraft.

With evening, I assembled the division for reorganization and preparation for the next day's fighting. To secure our night organizing, Gabi deployed Lapidot's battalion on a forward line near Uri while also maintaining forces in the greenbelt far to the south, so that we would be able to infiltrate forces on the route opened up by Amir. Most of Gabi's troops moved about 1-2 km to the east, deploying in night bivouac along the Test Road. Natke's brigade — except for the battalion that fought on the Haifa axis — also encamped for the night in the Arel area.

Since the beginning of the crossing operation, some seventy-two hours earlier, I hadn't slept a wink. So I looked for a night bivouac spot for the forward command group where I could plan the next day's activity quietly and maybe even get some rest. As we were moving back along the Test Road, I saw a gleaming white patch on the lake shore, and I directed the driver to move there. We descended on to the sand. Suddenly at the very last second the Zelda ground to an abrupt halt as we all shouted: "Moussa! Stop!" At that moment we had seen that we were entering a minefield. The Zelda had stopped just 20 cm from a mine. I held my breath, we were all silent, as tension ran high. Gilad directed Moussa to move back out exactly on the path on which we had entered. Slowly, very slowly, we backtracked. After emerging successfully, we moved into the center of one of Gabi's battalions and positioned the forward command group there for the night.

Throughout the eighteenth, while my division was fighting on the west bank, Sharon's division was engaged on both banks. His mission was to extend the bridgehead northward on both banks: on the east bank to capture the Chinese Farm and Missouri and on the west bank to take the ramparts in the greenbelt toward the north. The capture of these objectives was intended to eliminate the threat on the Akavish and Tirtur roads and so remove enemy artillery fire from the bridging zone. He also was to mop up the area where the Egyptians could station their forward observers to direct fire toward the bridges.

On the east bank, Sharon had gained some objectives. So battered were the Egyptians' 16th and 21st Divisions in the fighting on 15, 16, and 17 October, that they preferred during the night of 17–18 October to evacuate most of their forces from the Chinese Farm. In the morning (of 18 October), when Tuvia's brigade began making its way northward from the Tirtur line, it was surprised to find so little resistance. Immediately engineering units began clearing the Tirtur axis of mines, so the roller-bridge could be towed to the canal. At 1100 hours the road was declared open, the bridge began to be towed about an hour later, and with nightfall it was positioned about 1 km north of the unifloat bridge. (By this time most of the Gilowa craft had been hit and had sunk.) The roller-bridge was floated at about midnight and from the morning of the nineteenth was available for ongoing traffic. It was decided that vehicles moving westward would cross on the pontoon bridge, while those returning eastward would use the roller-bridge.

When Tuvia's brigade began moving northward from Tirtur, Amnon's brigade also went into action on the northern rim of the bridgehead (on the Shick axis), and in the face of light resistance, they captured the buildings of the Chinese Farm. However, the further northward advance of the two brigades ran into enemy resistance from Missouri. Both brigades were understrength, and the line of contact was stabilized about 1 km north of the Chinese Farm structures and toward the east.

While Sharon's division thus had some success on the east bank, it had no comparable achievements on the west bank. Danny's brigade, which was holding the bridgehead, was heavily shelled throughout the day. Noticing concentrations of Egyptian infantry and armor on the east bank moving across the canal on rafts to the west bank around the Saruk area, they adjusted our artillery fire on the enemy troops. They also secured the bridges and the area around them. Thus at the end of the eighteenth, Danny's brigade was holding the same positions it had held that morning. Haim's brigade, however, which had destroyed an enemy artillery brigade as well as enemy tanks, was holding new positions in the Geshira area.

The partial expansion of the bridgehead and the breakthrough to the west — which had been blocked in its initial stage — were discussed before noon that day at Southern Command. The most important decision taken was to immediately move additional forces to the bridgehead. In line with the precrossing summation, it was decided that Aryeh's brigade would return to my division, Uzzi's brigade would join Sharon's division, and General Magen's division would be split in two. He, with eighty tanks organized in two reduced brigades, would move from his sector in the southern part of the east bank to join the offensive effort on the west bank; while the rest of his division would be reorganized as part of the forces operating under Col. Israel Granit (the "Granit force"). His mission was to stay on the defensive on the south of the east bank.

Dayan arrived at Southern Command HQ from his visit to the west bank at 1730 hours and conferred with the staff there (also present were deputy Chief of Staff Israel Tal and Major General Yariv). Dayan knew that Kosygin had been in Egypt since the sixteenth, trying to arrange a cease-fire, and he was concerned over the attrition of the Israeli forces. Dayan focused the discussion on possible future situations: what ground disposition was required on the southern front in the event the fighting would soon terminate? At 2030 hours the Southern Command staff convened and decided to organize the forces for the continuation of the operation according to the *Abirei-Lev* Plan: my division would seize the Geneifa Hills, destroying missile sites on the way. Sharon's division would be split, with a force under his deputy, Jackie, which with Tuvia's brigade on the east bank and Danny's brigade on the west bank, would hold the bridgehead. Sharon himself would cross the canal along with Amnon's brigade, attach Haim's brigade and a reconnaissance unit to his forces, and would attack southward on my west flank, up to Mount Ubaid. Magen's division would station itself about 15 km west of the bridges, in the center of the operative forces on the west bank and serve as a reserve force.

The preparations implicit in these decisions began while we were still fighting and went on into the night. Aryeh's reduced tank brigade left for the bridge (leaving one battalion, Artzi's, at Ziona opposite Hamutal). Magen's division, made up of two small brigades, set out from the Gidi and Mitla passes. When they drew near the bridges, they found the approaches to them blocked, and the bridgehead under intense artillery shelling. Our supply convoys were also speeding there. They all found themselves in "traffic jams," stuck for lengthy periods, and under fire. Aryeh's brigade was given crossing priority and began moving across on the uni-float bridge and on Gilowas as well. As they were crossing, one of the Gilowas sustained a direct artillery hit, and two tanks sank before their crews could get out. All those who witnessed this were severely jolted. Now only one Gilowa remained, and Aryeh continued to move tanks across on the bridge only. Following Aryeh's brigade, the divisional artillery crossed and then the first brigade of Magen's (47) supply convoys braved the shellfire. It was only after half the night had gone by that the first supply convoys began to cross.

The job of refueling and loading up with new ammunition was no easy one. Natke's and Gabi's brigades, which had in the morning broken out of the proximate area of the bridges and were in fairly distant night bivouacs, took only a little shelling, and that mostly inaccurate. Aryeh's brigade, however, encamped for the night at the Deversoir Airfield, was heavily shelled. The supply convoys on the roads to and from the bridge also came under concentrated shelling. There were many casualties among the logistics personnel, and control difficulties grew. Every time the shells started landing near the convoy vehicles, the drivers would leap out and scatter in every direction, trying to take cover as far as possible from the trucks loaded with fuel and ammunition. Reassembling in the dark was difficult and complicated.

Had it not been for the logistics officers from division and brigade HQ and from division logistic supporting units, we would never have managed to move. Staff officers at all levels now had to show not only planning and coordination ability but also leadership under fire. There is no doubt in my mind that under the extreme conditions that prevailed that night and the following day at and around the bridgehead area, it was only the "follow-me" type of leadership that ensured we did not come to a standstill for lack of fuel and ammunition or for want of someone to repair the disabled tanks or to evacuate the casualties.

Due to all these circumstances, the supply convoys reached the brigades far behind schedule. The area was narrow, the crowding great, the shelling an impediment. In Aryeh's brigade, fifteen men were wounded while restocking. Fearing to assemble all his officers at one point to issue orders, Aryeh moved from one battalion to another to give his orders, and the battalion commanders did the same with the companies.

Dawn was about to break, and the three brigades were still refilling. We were compelled to start out later than we had planned, but at least all the supplies had arrived and were being taken on. With dawn, Magen's division advanced along the Haifa axis. Magen met with Natke, was updated, and continued toward Maktzera.

Four days and nights had gone by since the beginning of the crossing operation. We had undergone a lot but had managed to cross, consolidate ourselves, expand the bridgehead, and mass forces for the breakthrough westward. In breaking out of the crossing zone the previous day, we destroyed two battalions of tanks that tried to attack us from our northern and southern flanks. The coming morning would see the division breaking through to the southwest. I now had three armored brigades — about 170 serviceable tanks — and I hoped at last to break through into flat extensive terrain and begin to conduct mobile warfare. To my right, Sharon's division would advance, and Magen would support us as a reserve force. The time had come to vanquish the enemy!

And what was happening on the other side of the hill?* While we were completing our preparations for the breakthrough southward, the night of 18-19 October was a sleepless one for the Egyptians, and

---

*Description of events in the enemy camp is based on Egyptian sources, including captured material.

a dramatic struggle was unfolding among the top war leadership. At about midnight the Egyptian war minister contacted the president of Egypt and asked him to come to Bunker No. 10 — urgently. When Sadat arrived, he found his generals in the midst of a tense debate stemming from a deep difference of opinion: Chief of Staff Shazli was demanding the return of the forces now on the east bank of the canal, while War Minister Ahmed Ismail-Ali was strongly opposed to such a move.

Taking part in the conference, which had been called by Shazli, were also the commanders of the air force, of the antiaircraft command, and of the artillery corps, Generals Hussni Mubarak, Muhammad Ali Fahmy and Muhammad Mouhi a-Din al Mahi, respectively. On 16 October, Shazli had been dispatched to the front to see to the annihilation of the "small Israeli pocket" on the west bank. Upon his return, on the eighteenth, he explained that this was no small pocket but that there was a major breach in the Egyptian lines through which substantial Israeli forces were now flowing. Shazli had tried to coordinate the counterattacks of the Second and Third Armies and had been witness to their failures, first on the seventeenth on the east bank and then on the eighteenth on the west bank. The attempts by the Egyptian Air Force to hit the Israeli bridges had also failed, and our raids on the missile sites increased Shazli's worries even more.

It was Shazli's fear that the road to Cairo was now open to us and that there were very few forces between the Egyptian capital and Israeli armor. This was the background to Shazli's convening the conference and his suggestion that the Egyptian formations be recalled from the east bank to the west. If this were not done quickly, he asserted, not only would the breach not be sealed, but worse, Cairo would be in danger, and the Third Army was liable to be encircled and destroyed. Ismail-Ali was against this approach, averring that a withdrawal of Egyptian forces from the east to the west bank would cause a total collapse. He perceived that once the Egyptian soldiers began to move back, it would be virtually impossible to stop them. He recalled General Amer's order to retreat in 1967 and the debacle that had ensued.

Relations between Ismail-Ali and Shazli were even more strained because of the differences that had emerged between them from the beginning of the war. When Shazli saw the Egyptian armed forces' surprising success in the initial stage of the campaign, he had urged that this success be taken advantage of and the offensive momentum be continued. But Ismail-Ali, sticking to the original plan, insisted that the "operational hold" phase be introduced. Nor had Ismail-Ali forgotten that when, under considerable pressure, he had given the order to attack, the Egyptians had sustained a crushing failure. So he was now more convinced than ever that he, not Shazli, was right. (My own view from the professional military aspect is that Shazli was right in both instances: when he called for a continuation of the attack momentum at the beginning of the war, and now, when he demanded that steps be taken to prevent the encirclement of the Third Army. But Ismail-Ali had intuition and a profound understanding of the "soul" of the Egyptian soldier — understanding which often is more important than professional military know-how.)

The two presented their divergent views to Sadat, who decided in favor of Ismail-Ali. Shazli had to resign. He was replaced by the chief of operations, General Gamasy. The Egyptian public knew nothing of all this.

Between Sadat and Ismail-Ali there was complete understanding. Following the stormy conference, the two remained behind for a tête-à-tête in which Ismail-Ali explained that a cease-fire was not only desirable but vitally urgent. It was far from easy for Sadat to consent to a cease-fire. Since the beginning of the war he had rejected many such appeals, mainly from the Soviets. The latter were concerned about the situation of the Syrians, who had lost 1,200 of their 1,800 tanks. It was the Russians' apprehension that the IDF would rout the Syrians and then mass all our forces for a decision on the Egyptian front. From the beginning, Russia pressured the Egyptians to launch an offensive on their front, so as to ease the IDF pressure on the Syrian front, and at the same time they suggested a cease-fire. However, the Syrians — despite the severe pounding they had taken — did not want a cessation of hostilities, preferring to wait for the arrival of Iraqi and Jordanian reinforcements for their beleaguered forces. Sadat, too, rejected all approaches aimed at achieving a cease-fire. He was approached on this matter on 12 October by the British Ambassador to Cairo, and on 12 and 13 October by the Soviet ambassador. The two told Sadat that the Americans had brought pressure to bear on Israel until it had, unwillingly, agreed to a cease-fire at the present positions. Sadat replied angrily: "Egypt will not agree to a cease-fire while its forces are advancing."

Soviet apprehensions grew following the failure of the Egyptian attack on the fourteenth. The Russians perceived that the tide of the war was liable to reverse itself and that the Arabs could face another disaster such as that of 1967. Soviet Premier Kosygin arrived in Cairo in the afternoon of 16 October. Over the following two days, he was unable to convince Sadat to agree to a standstill cease-fire. According to Heikal, a few hours before Sadat was called to Bunker No. 10, Kosygin showed him aerial photos taken from a Soviet satellite that showed a substantial number of Israeli tanks on the west bank. Even then Sadat was adamant in his refusal.

Beginning on the fourteenth, and with even more intensity on the fifteenth, many of the Egyptian formations were under strong Israeli pressure. However, their reports were imprecise and made it difficult for the Egyptian high command to get a faithful picture of what was happening. Even when they grasped the fact of our crossing operation, they thought that only a small pocket, soon to be wiped out, was involved. Now, very late, it was becoming clear to Sadat that the situation was extremely critical. The Egyptian president understood that he had no choice; he must prevent a military catastrophe by political means, so he agreed to an unconditional cease-fire at the present positions. The next morning (19 October), Kosygin departed Egypt with Sadat's consent to a cease-fire.

Syrian President Assad, Sadat's partner in the war, was about to get a surprise. When Sadat's message was brought to him, on 19 October, he found that his Egyptian counterpart had already given his consent to a cease-fire. To justify his move, Sadat explained that after fifteen days of fierce fighting, not only against the Israelis but against the Americans as well, he could not allow the destruction of the Egyptian Army for the second time in this generation. Therefore he had agreed to a cease-fire.

Assad was shocked. He had many reasons for complaint against his Egyptian ally. The Syrian president had undergone some very difficult days since the war began. Since 8 October his army had taken a fearful pounding, suffering tremendous losses in manpower and materiel. We had captured another substantial area of the Golan Heights and now were poised not far from Damascus. The Israeli Air Force had bombed Syria's logistic infrastructure heavily, setting fuel reservoirs, power stations, and ports ablaze. Throughout the period when we were hammering the Syrians, the Egyptians were in their "operational hold" phase. Repeated Syrian requests for the Egyptians to renew their pressure were to no avail. The Egyptians said they were acting in line with the agreed plan, and it was now time for the "operational hold." For their part, the Syrians retorted that it was their understanding that the Egyptians were to reach a line 100 km east of the canal (the Nahal Yam–Refidim–Abu Rodeis–Mitla-Gidi line) and only then go into the "operational hold" stage. Now, without so much as consulting with his ally, Sadat was informing Assad that he had already decided and agreed to a cease-fire.

Assad, then, was seething with anger, but not being one to act rashly, he sent Sadat a moderate message. The Syrians, he asserted, were in a terrible situation, but despite the heavy price they were paying their spirit was not broken, and they would go on fighting. Now that reinforcements had arrived from Jordan and Iraq, plus arms shipments from the USSR, the situation was stabilizing. Assad called on Sadat to stand fast in his difficult situation, expressing his confidence that if he did so the Arab reinforcements would arrive, so that ultimately — with obstinacy, sacrifice, and steadfastness — the victory would be achieved. Sadat did not accede to Assad's request, and a rift developed between them.

Thus it was that in the early hours of 19 October the seed was planted that would result in the cease-fire — though we knew nothing of this. Sadat's problem now was would the cease-fire come into effect soon? Could his forces hold out until then?

CHAPTER TWENTY-SEVEN

CRITIQUE OF THE CROSSING OPERATION

The crossing operation was far more complex, difficult, and prolonged than we had surmised when planning it. According to the *Abirei-Lev* 2 Plan, Southern Command intended to seize a base for a bridgehead on both sides of the canal and construct two bridges — all this during the first night and using Sharon's division only. My division was then to join the fray fresh and cross on the bridges in the predawn morning. During the first day's fighting, the two divisions were to break out of the greenbelt and destroy enemy forces there, advance southward and secure the zone of operations on the Ismailia Canal bridges, and capture the wide area extending from the central Sweet Water Canal in the north, Mount Ataka in the south, the Vada'ut Road in the west, and the Suez Canal itself in the east. For capturing Suez City and mopping up the canal bank and the lakes area, another twenty-four hours had been allotted.

It is always difficult in the planning stage to estimate how much force and time are required to complete a mission. Nonetheless, the plan as laid down appears to have been overly optimistic with respect both to the time that would be needed and the troops to be provided for its completion. Sharon's division was reinforced, but one of its tank brigades was assigned to tow the bridging gear. The division was given the task of seizing the Chinese Farm and Missouri, taking control of both banks of the canal, and consolidating a base for a bridgehead — and, of course, to bridge the canal. Against Sharon were deployed the 16th Infantry Division and the wounded 21st Armored Division.

When we began to plan the crossing operation, on 12 October, I suggested both Sharon's division and mine join in capturing the east bank bridgehead area: Sharon's division would attack from the direction from which in fact it did attack, while my division would come from the Havraga sector southwest toward Mifras. My suggestion was turned down, mainly out of the desire to leave my division fresh. Taking into consideration the small forces we had at our disposal, this was a well-considered notion but one steeped in optimism. Sharon, who at first supported my idea, did not insist on it, and neither did I. Today, with hindsight, I regret that my suggestion was not accepted. Since I had to wait until the bridges were completed, it would have been better to attack with two divisions. Admittedly both divisions might take heavy losses, but I assume that we would have mauled the 16th and 21st Divisions and then reached the canal in a far broader sector. As a result of the decision to assign the bridgehead mission to one division only, we were compelled to confine the crossing sector to just 4 km.

This restriction contradicted the generally accepted rules for crossing operations. Indeed, one of the conditions for success in such an operation is to push the enemy back — including his artillery and at the very least his forward observers — to a point where he cannot fire at the crossing site. While it was hoped that Sharon's division would accomplish this, the order itself — recognizing the difficulties — called on him to push the enemy back only to a point (about 4 km) from which it would not be able to employ flat trajectory fire against the bridging zone.

Nor was the time allotted for completion of the entire mission realistic. The smaller the forces and the more missions spread over a large area, the more likely it is that more than forty-eight hours will be required. It's usually easier to estimate the timetable for the first phase. I think the estimate for the bridging phase during the first night was realistic, at least with respect to the plan for constructing the bridges. The intention to push the bridging gear and the crossing force ahead at an early stage was practical, even if the fighting at

Amir and Missouri were still in progress. In my opinion, responsibility for the disruptions that occurred in pushing the equipment ahead rests primarily with Sharon, who did not control the roads in his sector.

On 15 October, Sharon found that the crossing preparations were not proceeding as they should. Haim called to report that the roads were blocked and about half the uni-floats had not arrived. He requested that the division take charge of opening the axes and suggested that the crossing operation be put back twenty-four hours. Sharon took this under consideration, but his feeling that one could not rely on the "authorities" — they were liable to have a change of mind about the crossing operation — led him to decide that the risk was worthwhile. Using this train of thought, he recommended to Bar-Lev that the operation proceed as scheduled; I regret that the latter gave his approval.

One could argue that any postponement would have imperiled the entire operation, as the Egyptians might have surmised our intentions. This was a minor risk, since our aircraft controlled the Sinai skies, and all our preparations were being made well to the rear. Moreover the Egyptians were busy licking their wounds from the drubbing they took in their abortive offensive of 14 October. What is obligatory for a complicated mission such as a water-crossing operation is to move all the necessary equipment up, see to it that there is order on the access roads, and place the crossing gear near the head of the advancing column. Because the operation was not postponed, it became counterproductive. When the Akavish Road was opened up in front, the heavy rafts were stuck in a traffic jam in the rear; then, when the shock of surprise wore off, the road was closed again. But during the night of 15–16 October, and throughout the sixteenth itself, the Egyptians had not yet grasped that a crossing operation was in progress, nor had they located the crossing site. By the time the rafts were brought to water's edge, thirty-six hours after the start of the operation, construction of the bridge had to go on under concentrated shelling.

Not only did Sharon recommend that we launch the crossing campaign before we were completely ready, but it would appear that his plan itself was defective. One entire tank brigade, Haim's, was necessarily assigned to tow and secure the crossing gear. After getting the equipment to the water, the brigade was to cross at once and join in the fighting; but in the first stage it was precluded from any combat. In this light, it is difficult to understand why all of Tuvia's reduced brigade was assigned to carry out a diversionary move to the east. Not only was Tuvia's brigade too large a force for such a mission, but the area for the diversionary move was remote from the main sector. This ruled out in advance any possibility that Tuvia could provide support in the main effort either to reinforce it or exploit the momentum of the assault. Amnon's brigade, strengthened to four tank battalions and three reduced battalionlike infantry forces, was given the entire burden of the fighting in the first stage. While Amnon penetrated from the south through empty territory and his breakthrough into the enemy's rear was correctly predicated on surprise, the plan called for him to fight every which way from the Lexicon axis: west to Matzmed and the canal, up to Mifras, northeast to Amir and Missouri, east to open up the Tirtur and Akavish axes, and south to secure the zone of operations. His sudden appearance in the enemy's rear enabled all these attacks to be simultaneous, advantageously exploiting the inherent surprise. But to hope that a single brigade commander could control all these expected engagements in divergent directions was pretension bordering on delusion.

A fourth brigade, Danny's paratroops, was to wait for the Akavish Road to be opened from west to east and then move to the canal and cross to the west bank. Fortunately, the Akavish Road was opened without difficulty, but had we encountered problems, Sharon would not have had nearby reserves to force its early opening. Even within the framework of Southern Command's intention of maintaining my division fresh, it was a mistake that we were not given a task such as making the feint to the east. Had this been done and had Sharon kept Tuvia's brigade as a reserve by Kishuf, he could have opened Akavish and Tirtur and also assisted in the capture of Amir and Missouri. It would have been preferable had Amnon's brigade operated west of Lexicon only, with Tuvia east of Lexicon and both of them moving from south to north. And even then it would have been better had Southern Command placed me in reserve.

Some of Sharon's planning mistakes showed themselves in the implementation stage. Fortunately the crossing area on both sides was free of the enemy. Thus Danny had no problems when he seized the west bank, nor did Amnon have to make an effort there. But when fighting broke out simultaneously at the Tirtur-Lexicon junction and north of there (initially south of Usha and then close to the Shick axis), Amnon had to hold up his northward advance in order to press at the Tirtur-Lexicon junction. Sharon wanted to support Amnon but had no nearby reserve, so he ordered Tuvia — who was then east of Missouri — to terminate his diversionary mission and attack westward instead. The result was a waste of power in a remote area, with Tuvia being worn down without any compensating benefit to Amnon. In the meantime, Sharon arrived at the Matzmed yard, placing him 3 km east of the Tirtur-Lexicon junction. That crossroad continued to be a vital objective that had to be captured to open the Tirtur axis and move the roller-bridge up. But instead of lending himself to that main effort, Sharon busied himself with transferring tanks and units to the quiet west bank, while attaching a battalion from Tuvia's brigade to Amnon and later a battalion from Haim — both of which were some 10 km to the east — so that he would coordinate an attack from east and west. Amnon himself had already been engaged for hours in organizing a cohesive force out of the fragments of his battered units, and again and again he sent small forces into action piecemeal. All the attacks from west to east failed, with losses to our forces. Amnon's obstinacy and steadfastness are noteworthy, but in the end, while he did capture the junction, he did not open the Tirtur Road. Sharon's decision to impose the entire burden of the fighting on Amnon — a burden beyond the capacity of one man — had to have been wrong.

There is no doubt that Sharon's division was in a difficult situation. It fought fiercely and bravely but was badly worn down. Its achievements that night were a basis for going on but did not create conditions that would permit us to transfer massive forces to the west bank and take advantage of our initial success before the enemy could recover. Fortunately the enemy reacted slowly at first, not realizing that a full-fledged crossing operation was in progress but believing, perhaps, that this was an attack on the 16th and 21st Divisions. Even when an armored task force carried out raids deep into the west bank and when Israel's Prime Minister declared this in the Knesset — even then the Egyptians responded very slowly.

The raid on the missile sites was carried out too soon. Its results were excellent in themselves, but the Egyptians were thus alerted about the crossing sector. This kind of raid can be very positive when executed immediately before a breakthrough of forces from a bridgehead base, before the enemy can rush troops to the crossing sector. In this case, however, the raid took place before we had bridges, even before we knew when we would have them. Fortunately the Egyptians reacted slowly, but they did mass forces in the crossing area.

In contrast to what was planned, Sharon's bridgehead troops consolidated themselves on the east bank of the Sweet Water Canal instead of deploying on the Havit Road. Admittedly, this deployment afforded the troops greater security because they were positioned behind a canal 10 meters wide, but by doing so they allowed the Egyptians to move within the greenbelt on the west side of that canal. Because this area was closed and difficult to cross, the Egyptians were able to impede our breakthrough from the bridgehead base. Had Sharon's forces held the outskirts of the closed greenbelt, they would have had more information on the enemy massing against us.

At about noon on the sixteenth, attempts were made to employ tank battalions to open the Akavish and Tirtur roads, but these brought no results. The problem was a tough one: fighting against enemy tanks that were operating in concert with infantry equipped with Sagger missiles. Our attempts to advance were halted, with losses. Personally I felt badly because of our deadlocked situation — stalemate. Even the operation of Uzzi's paratroopers in night combat didn't improve my feeling; I felt that we had become stuck and lacked the capacity to advance.

In retrospect, I perceive things differently. The decision to push the rafts ahead following a kind of reconnaissance fire patrol proved itself. It also seems to me now that the fighting of 16 October was no less important. That cautious combat, although it did not get the road open at once, bore fruit the following day. Because we fought cautiously and patiently, we did not fall into the missile trap; we broke all the counterattacks from the north and opened the Akavish Road. When my division moved that night, we left a weakened and drained enemy behind. The ability to fight continuously and persistently, which we demonstrated by moving in the paratroopers, permitted us not only to transfer the bridging gear, but also to fight more fruitful armored battles on the morning of the seventeenth.

I have a different feeling about our ambush against the 25th

Brigade, equipped with T-62 tanks. I was among the developers of the armored-ambush technique. This had originally seemed impractical and virtually unusable, since tanks raise dust and smoke and can be heard for miles around. In order to lend realism, I would emphasize that a "leap-ahead ambush" was what I had in mind. Moreover, I stressed that the larger the formations, the greater the distance from which the "leap-ahead" should begin. It was the ambusher's problem to come up with a sufficiently large killing ground to take in all or most of the enemy force. True, there were also elements of luck in our successful ambush — first and foremost, the enemy's unsecured advance. In addition, the killing ground looked like it had been created just for this purpose: a plain, closed on one side by a lake whose shore was mined, dominated by sandy hills that raised no dust. This apparently helped hide the movement of the one battalion we dispatched near Lexicon in the morning. Natke pushed in the second battalion only after fire contact was made. The timing of Aryeh's assault, as he closed off the enemy's rear, did not require precise coordination. He was even a bit late, although that was an outgrowth of his distance from the battlefield when he was reattached to us and of the difficulties of movement on the Pazum dune road. It was a smooth battle, just like an exercise. In this hard and protracted war, these were successful hours.

The breaking of the Egyptian armored assaults — directed uncoordinately at the access corridor to the bridges from the north and the south — along with the movement of the rafts and the subsequent construction of the bridge permitted the division's crossing. Sharon thought that Southern Command was dragging its feet, that the crossing should have been made earlier. The Gilowa craft were in his hands, and on the sixteenth the crossing zone was not harassed by artillery shelling. Nonetheless, his request to transfer more tanks on the Gilowas was disapproved. Southern Command insisted that armored divisions not cross without a bridge and a well-secured bridgehead. I believe this was right, because the Egyptians had stronger forces on the east bank than those on the west. Had we transferred major formations to the west, the Egyptians might have cut off our corridor to the crossing site. At any rate, HQ had to take that into account. I recall the threat posed to the convoy column loaded with fuel and ammunition, bumper to bumper on the Akavish Road with no possibility of getting off. Had our forces not been deployed there, the enemy could have attacked from the north and caused a disaster.

When I reflect on the crossing operation and on the immense gap beween what was planned and what actually took place, I think there are lessons to be learned. The campaign began without sufficient preparations and was accompanied by mistakes in planning and execution; it evolved into a stalemate. Against this background was the demand to go ahead with the crossing as though everything were "just fine." Had we done so, I believe we would have only compounded our mistakes. The enemy's mistakes sometimes balance one's own, and it's possible to succeed even when mistakes are made, but there is no guarantee of this. For myself, I'm glad that Bar-Lev prevented the crossing. It's best to leave the mistakes to the enemy.

Our crossing turned out to be very difficult. The Egyptians fought stubbornly and bravely. Our soldiers fought heroically. Even though we made mistakes, we fought with greater thought, while the Egyptians reacted slowly, with a lack of imagination.

Now, following four days and nights of fighting, we were able to concentrate forces on the west bank, and orders were issued for the breakthrough west and south. The men were busy getting the tanks ready. Dawn was about to break on a new stage in the war.

PART V

ENCIRCLING THE THIRD ARMY

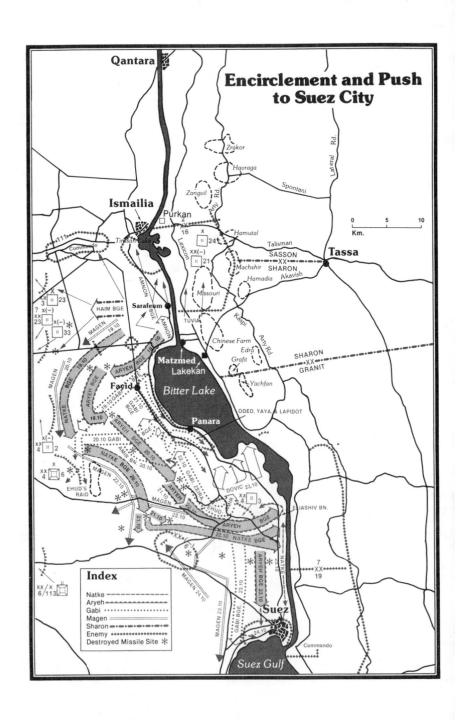

Encirclement and Push to Suez City

Qantara

Ismailia

Purkan

Tassa

Suez

Bitter Lake

Suez Gulf

Index

Natke	-------
Aryeh	━━━━━
Gabi	•••••••
Magen	═══════
Sharon	━•━•━•
Enemy	＋＋＋＋＋＋＋
Destroyed Missile Site	✳

CHAPTER TWENTY-EIGHT

BREAKOUT TO THE AIDA
PLAINS AND SEIZING
THE GENEIFA HILLS,
19-20 OCTOBER

A t dawn of 19 October we were to break deep into enemy territory. Two divisions were to push south toward Suez, while the third was to position itself as a reserve force near Maktzera. But things developed differently, and it soon became apparent that we were again subject to changes and delays.

With morning, Magen's division moved along the Haifa axis via the Arel position, was updated by Natke, and continued to its deployment point at Maktzera. Sharon was supposed to have moved southward with two reduced brigades. However, he recommended that the plan be changed, and Southern Command agreed that his division not be split but remain to secure the bridgehead and expand it northward. My division's departure was delayed. When I awoke at dawn, I found that we were still not prepared for action. Gabi's brigade was the closest to being ready to move out, having completed about 80 percent of its replenishment process. Lapidot's battalion, deployed opposite Tsach, had not yet begun restocking. Aryeh's was beginning to take on fuel and ammunition, while Natke was still awaiting the arrival of the supply convoys, hoping they would get there within a half-hour.

I was angry. Even though I knew the delays came from the Egyptian shelling of the narrow bridgehead, I found it hard to accept the idea of "useless hours." I ordered the brigade commanders to have one battalion replenish completely before the others began so that it could set out immediately, with the others catching up later.

The Egyptians had pulled back their missile batteries following our raid on the missile sites the previous day. When our planes began attacking Tsach, at 0600 hours, they no longer encountered antiaircraft missile fire.

At 0620 hours Gabi moved out with two battalions, followed by the forward command group. Natke's first battalion set out at 0715 hours and Aryeh, with two battalions, at 0820 hours.

According to the information we had, we were about to break out into an area with many missile sites, artillery battalions, and a few defensive positions; but we did not know how many mobile armored forces we might encounter. The previous day Gabi, Natke, and Haim overcame battalion defenses at Uri, Arel, and Geshira. Today we would have to deal with the battalion disposition at Tsach, a reinforced battalion alignment at Hushani, and an artillery brigade position at Maktzera. The previous day we destroyed the 207th Tank Battalion of the 2nd Tank Brigade south of Uri, and a tank battalion from the 23rd Division north of the Haifa axis. We knew that in the Ridan al-Hamah area, about 30 km west of us, three tank brigades were deployed (the 23rd Tank Brigade from the 3rd Mechanized Division in the Matzlema zone, the 116th Mechanized Brigade from the 23rd Mechanized Division near Rama, and the 35th Independent Tank Brigade between Matzlema and Rama). What we did not know was how far they had advanced and when we would meet them.

The division's mission was to destroy missile bases and seize a foothold on the Geneifa Hills. According to the plan, we were to break through on two axes. Natke's brigade would move southward from Arel toward Maktzera and from there via Mitznefet to the Geneifa Hills; Gabi's brigade would tie down Tsach (which dominated the Havit junction) though without capturing it, infiltrate southward through the greenbelt, and move on to the Havit axis south of Tsach. Then, leaving a blocking force near the Fayid Airport, they would turn west to the Aida Plains and charge toward the Geneifa Hills. Between and behind these two brigades, Aryeh's brigade would be ready to support each of them.

When Gabi set out at 0630 hours, Ze'ira's battalion took up positions and fired at Tsach. Under cover of this fire, Ehud's battalion moved to Havit-43, where it deployed to secure the operational zone toward the south while engaging the Fayid Airport with fire. Ehud set fuel tanks ablaze and destroyed radar, waiting for enemy tanks that were expected from the south. Following Ehud's battalion was Amir Yoffe's, with only nine tanks. Amir reached Havit-42 at 0800 hours and then turned west toward the western edge of the Geneifa Hills near the Vada'ut-Vitamin junction. Following him were Ze'ira's and Lapidot's battalions, the latter having completed taking on fuel and ammunition at Uri in the meantime. When the three battalions passed the Havit axis and turned west onto the Aida Plains, they deployed in a broad formation and began a full-speed gallop. The scout company was on their southern flank, securing the charging battalions from the Geneifa Hills.

Aryeh's brigade began moving south at 0820 hours, following Gabi's brigade until Havit-42, where it turned west toward Hushani, south of Maktzera at 0845 hours. Natke moved his first battalion out from Arel toward Maktzera at 0715 hours. Within forty-five minutes he was reporting contact with Missile Base 6218, then a battle with enemy tanks and Saggers. Natke said he was gaining the upper hand, with some enemy tanks hit and some abandoned whole. Natke's two other battalions finished replenishing and set out at 0935 hours.

My forward command group was advancing with Gabi's brigade. As we sped across the Aida Plains and I saw the broad fan-shaped formation of Gabi's and Aryeh's battalions racing across the flat terrain, my heart skipped a beat. It was as though the armored forces, which had fought so hard to break out of the greenbelt, had achieved the prize of the freedom to maneuver they so much wanted. For the moment, I could breathe with relief. Soon enough we would run into problems.

The division was deployed over an immense expanse that was flat and lacking distinct features of terrain, which caused orientation difficulties. Moreover, the dust clouds raised by the tank columns blanketed the entire area, creating observation problems and fear that some dust clouds might be enemy movements.

We began the arduous task of coordinating movement and sectors, of making changes where required and of mutual identification. The missile sites that popped up here and there on the plain — some of them active, others dummy — helped us orient ourselves. The firefights with the units defending the missile sites were generally quick and decisive. Our tanks encountered infantry troops and were fired on by antiaircraft weapons. We lit a lot of fires, mainly by hitting the radar antennae at the missile bases. But even though resistance was light, it was sufficient to cause uncertainty; the radio calls for identification and for coordination were frequent.

At 0900 hours Natke reported that he was engaged with a serious enemy disposition north of Hushani, between there and Maktzera. At about the same time, Aryeh reported that he was in combat with enemy forces south of Hushani. The battle for the Maktzera zone became the division's main engagement. That area contained an Egyptian artillery brigade with dozens of guns, reinforced by tanks and infantry. Natke, who ran into the artillery when he was with his leading battalion, waited for his two other battalions to arrive. On his northern flank was Dan, of Magen's division. While Natke and Dan were examining the possibility of a joint attack, Natke's own tank gun took a direct hit, and his operations officer was wounded. Another fifteen minutes passed before Natke ordered a charge against the enemy forces, but not before he and Magen had asked me over and over whether it was not in fact Aryeh who was firing at Natke. Finally, Natke was convinced that it was the enemy and deployed for attack. However, Magen was not so persuaded, and Natke carried out the attack on his own. The terrain was flat and open and dotted with fleeing Egyptian troops. Natke's tanks overran the artillery, and the locality was captured.

In Ze'evik's battalion two tanks were hit. Standing in the turret of one of those tanks was a young platoon leader — my neighbor and young friend of whom I was so fond — Ilanon. It was just four days ago, on 15 October, that I had talked with him next to a tank from which I had been addressing the men prior to the start of the crossing operation. In the last days of his life he had gone through a lot. On 18 October, as he advanced on the Haifa axis, his battalion was waylaid by an Egyptian infantry and tank ambush. The three tanks ahead of him were knocked out, but he managed to break through and reach Arel. Just before nightfall, a tank company was sent back to the inferno of the Haifa axis to help our infantry mop it up. Ilan's tank was among them, and he fought until the job was complete. The company commander now wanted to return with all his tanks to Arel, but the paratroopers asked that one tank remain behind to stay with them. The commander would not agree to this request. Ilanon volunteered and then convinced his commander to let another tank stay behind with him. The next morning — the nineteenth — he returned to Arel smiling. Then on the way to Maktzera his tank stalled, so he switched tanks and went on. He fell in the brief battle at Maktzera. I did not learn of his death until 22 October.

While Natke and Aryeh were busy on both sides of Hushani, Gabi's brigade continued to advance. At 1020 hours he arrived at Vada'ut-50 and began climbing the Geneifa Hills. To improve my observation of the battlefield, I stationed the forward command group on one of the peaks, about 1.5 km from Amir's battalion. It was about 1100 when Natke overcame the artillery between him and the plain where the rest of the division was fighting. I ordered him to move westward, past the Vada'ut Road, designated as the boundary between Natke's and Gabi's sectors. All this time I kept reminding the brigade commanders that our main task was to destroy as many missile sites as possible. Aryeh, simultaneously with his attack toward Hushani, sent forces to attack a missile site 6 km west of the division. Gabi, who was now holding the northwest corner of the Geneifa Hills, saw armored concentrations lined up against him; nonetheless, he carried out the order concerning the missile bases. He sent out a tank patrol with Zeldas and jeeps to knock out the missile sites on the nearby peaks. The increasing amount of black smoke rising into the sky attested to the location of additional bases destroyed by our forces.

At 1130 several dozen enemy tanks could be seen on Mount Um-Katib and in the Mitznefet area. (This was the 2nd Tank Brigade of the 4th Armored Division, which had already lost its 207th Battalion when we decimated it south of Uri.) I decided to have Gabi's and Aryeh's brigades attack the enemy forces together and ordered Aryeh to move westward toward Vitamin-51. However, on second thought I came to the conclusion that to launch a concentrated attack on the enemy armor deployed in the hills before us would require a coordinated divisional offensive that would eat up precious time. This would halt our rapid progress and reduce the surprise and momentum of our attack against the missile sites. Deciding, then, to push on without letup into the Geneifa Hills and to continue destroying missile bases, at 1220 I told Aryeh to change direction, move south, climb the hills, and penetrate eastward to Vitamin-40 to wipe out the missile sites located deep in the hills.

Having ensured continuation of the thrust against the missile bases, I now turned to line up an attack against the enemy tanks of the 2nd Egyptian Brigade. I ordered Gabi, already engaged in combat, to concentrate his forces. Natke's brigade would be employed on the northern flank and in the rear of Mitznefet, west of the Vada'ut Road. The orders were issued, the brigades began moving, and the forward command post requested air support as it began to concentrate artillery fire.

Meanwhile, the forward command group also saw action. Around noon, the spectacle of air battles above us recurred, with many MIGs being shot down. As we were deep in enemy territory and far from the bridgehead area, we saw pairs of MIGs swooping in from the south above the hills, flying very low and headed for the bridges. One pair of MIGs passed right over the forward command group. Before I could say a word the machine gun on my left let loose with a deafening volley, followed at once by the other vehicles. I was far from pleased with this burst of fire, initiated — as it happened — by my driver, Moussa. We were a small cluster of vehicles, and any fire was liable to draw unnecessary attention to our presence. Indeed, the two MIGs were now circling around, heading back toward us. Now everyone was firing like mad. Then four bombs detached themselves from the planes and arced toward us. Sudden fear — what to do — stay in the Zelda or jump out and look for shelter? Some jumped; most stayed in the vehicles. Tension was high as the bombs made their seemingly interminable descent; would they hit us? Luckily, they missed, landing in a wadi behind us. But the Egyptian planes made another turn and began diving at us. Sharp bursts plowed up the ground and then four rockets were fired; heart-stopping fear, numbing tension, explosion, smoke, and at once the shouts: "Medic! Medic!" Two soliders of the forward command group were wounded. A second later we saw one of the pilots bail out and a white parachute open. Moussa claimed that he was the one who shot down the plane but, of course, many besides him had joined in the firing.

When the pilot was brought back by jeep, we found him to be a tall good-looking man of about thirty. He looked pale and was in pain. After seeing to his wound, we questioned him. He said he was not aware that Israeli forces were operating on the west bank of the canal. His mission had been to bomb the bridges. He had, it was true, seen many vehicles below him, but he had not imagined that they were IDF vehicles. It was only after he noticed our firing that he turned around, circled above us, and recognized the vehicles and armor as Israeli. The fact that the pilot had not known of our progress and that above us large-scale air battles were taking place in which more and more enemy planes were being downed were encouraging signs. The disarray in the Egyptian camp was growing.

That afternoon, I went through another experience which was the lot of many of my troops when they raided the missile bases. From time to time reports came in that the Egyptian defenders of the missile bases were firing huge surface-to-air missiles at our troops, although this flat trajectory fire was inaccurate, and they had so far not hit any targets. Not far from us, one of Gabi's patrols was operating against a missile site that was already afire. Suddenly a huge missile was fired at them. It passed above them and curved its way at us. With a tremendous explosion it luckily hit the ground about 400 meters in front of us.

Although my division had penetrated successfully into enemy territory, one problem remained unsolved. Until Tsach on the Havit-Sakranut axis was captured, our supply convoys would have no available open route. Since Magen's division was to capture Tsach, I contacted him to ask when he planned to attack. Finally at 1445 hours, he informed me that his men had captured the position in an operation from the north and the west.

During this time Natke was moving westward, dealing with missile sites as he came across them. At 1410 hours one of his battalions — Giora's — was destroyed from long-range Missile Base 6214, which was situated 2 km west of the Vada'ut Road. The Egyptian soldiers there had not fled, and as Giora's force drew close to the site, they were suddenly fired at with Saggers and RPGs. Within seconds three tanks were hit, including Giora's, with many soldiers hurt. The evacuation vehicle which rushed in to pick up the casualties was also hit. The lightly wounded helped the badly hurt, and scout jeeps arrived at the scene to take the casualties out to the battalion medical station. From there they were flown by helicopter to a hospital in the rear. This brief clash changed the entire disposition of the battalion. Two men were killed and sixteen wounded, including the battalion commander, Giora, a deputy company commander, and the intelligence officer. Command of the battalion was assumed by Major Micha. When the war broke out he was a company commander; six days ago he was made a deputy battalion commander, and now he became a battalion commander. Two of Natke's three battalions were now being led by company commanders. Lieutenant Colonel Natan, who was wounded at Arel, refused to be evacuated; he was continuing to advance with the troops while lying on a stretcher in his Zelda, the battalion being led effectively by Captain Nitzan. Now a similar situation arose in Giora's battalion.

Just at this time Southern Command informed me that Magen's division would replace Natke and Gabi, so they could continue their penetration deep into the Geneifa Hills. I therefore decided that we would continue to press on in line with our original aim, so canceled the attack on Mitznefet. I directed Gabi to continue maintaining contact with the enemy until he was replaced, thus securing our rear while we advanced into the hills with Aryeh and Natke. Two hours went by from the time of the announcement until Natke's brigade was actually replaced; nonetheless, the two brigades managed to position themselves in the hills before dark. Aryeh's brigade, which advanced from north to south, had many difficulties in finding passages on the steep cliffs, but finally they managed to ascend a peak and encamp above Vitamin-44. Despite the short time they had before nightfall, they were able to destroy another six missile sites in the hills on both sides of the Vitamin Road. As night fell, Natke's brigade bivouacked at Vitamin-47.

After dark, Gabi's brigade also camped for the night. However, while Aryeh's and Natke's brigades would spend the night in the heart of the Geneifa Hills, Gabi's battalions deployed along the Uvda axis, which became the division's supply route for that night. Lieutenant Colonel Baruchi's armored infantry battalion, whose half-tracks were unable to advance on the Revicha Road, moved along the Akavish Road when it was opened and now crossed the canal to join Gabi. Baruchi's battalion replaced Ehud's at the Fayid Airfield, so that Ehud could move west and link up with the brigade. The division's logistical and engineering elements made their way to Havit-42.

My forward command group was positioned in a small valley along the hills, about 2 km east of one of Gabi's battalions. Two of Aryeh's tanks, which had been delayed due to malfunctions and were looking for Aryeh's bivouac, were now attached to the forward command group to help secure our small force. We put up the side tent, opened up the table, unfolded the maps on it, and began the task of collecting the reports needed to sum up the day of fighting that had just ended. In the course of the day we had penetrated about 35 km southwest, sped across and mopped up the Aida Plains up to the Vada'ut axis, and gained a substantial foothold on the Geneifa Hills — all this while defeating an enemy artillery brigade and destroying missile sites. We had casualties in all the brigades, but only Giora's battalion had been badly mauled. Now we had to replenish and prepare to continue our southward penetration.

It looked like the supply problem was going to be a major one. The area of the bridges was being heavily shelled throughout the day so that the convoys were having a hard time crossing. Fortunately, the capture of the Tsach position would enable traffic to move on the Sakranut Road, but southward from there the convoys would encounter desert zones and fields. The radio nets were humming with communications concerning supply problems. I took the opportunity to contact Southern Command for an update on what was happening on the rest of the southern front so I could broadcast my daily news bulletin to the men.

Sharon's division was to have attacked westward parallel to my division but was ultimately — according to Sharon's recommendation — left at the bridgehead in order to mop it up and expand it northward. At 1032 Sharon contacted Southern Command saying: "I pressed you to penetrate deep into Egypt, but now I think we should mop up both sides of the canal, and then perhaps continue doing so toward the north."

At Southern Command, Uri Ben-Ari opposed the mopping up, saying it would involve many casualties, while Gonen favored the idea, particularly the capture of the Egyptians' ramparts on the west bank. From here they would be able to support Tuvia's brigade as it mopped up the east bank. As it turned out, Gonen was disappointed when his hopes for the mop up of both banks of the canal were not realized. That afternoon, at 1710 hours, he gave his frustration exaggerated expression when he declared: "Sharon's division did nothing today."

In fact, on 19 October Sharon had less than one hundred tanks operating in three brigades, along with two reduced paratroop brigades. Tuvia's tank brigade, with forty tanks, was deployed on the east bank. As it sought to advance toward the north it was blocked by missile fire after having moved just 1–2 km. Amnon's tank brigade, which also included armored and infantry scout units, crossed to the west bank and captured the Orcha area, 2 km north of Arel. The brigade was involved in some hard fighting at the Vardit-Nura junction, and after suffering some losses, consolidated itself there. Haim's tank brigade, which was at Geshira, advanced 4 km westward to Vardit-37. Uzzi's paratroop brigade mopped up about 3 km in the greenbelt, moving north to a point opposite Saruk. Danny's paratroop brigade made no advance at all. Summing up, on the average Sharon's division succeeded in expanding the bridgehead about 2–3 km toward the north.

Magen's small division, which captured Tsach, operated in close cooperation with me. In order to coordinate our moves, we would enter each other's radio net from time to time. I found it pleasurable to listen to Magen's net. I could virtually feel his movement on the battlefield, sense the pace of his armored activity.

On the evening of the nineteenth a conference was held at Southern Command with the chief of staff to determine the objectives for the following day. It was decided to press on with the breakthrough along the same lines originally laid down. Sharon's division would continue to mop up both banks of the canal toward the north. My division would move southward toward Suez City and cut off the Asor and Sarag roads linking Suez and Cairo. Magen's division would remain a reserve force and would replace Gabi's brigade by Mitznefet and by the Fayid Airfield, so that Gabi's could join the division for the southward effort.

Around midnight, in a conference held in Tel Aviv on the war aims for the twentieth, the chief of staff summarized these plans. A few hours earlier, the prime minister informed the defense minister and the chief that United States Secretary of State Kissinger was expected to leave for Moscow, so that Israel might have just three days of combat left before a cease-fire was imposed. The defense minister discussed the matter with Bar-Lev. The overall aim was clear to all, but no one was certain we would succeed in taking Suez City in that period of time. The General Staff issued orders to carry out some territorial "grabs," but the main effort was directed toward expanding the west bank breakthrough to the north and the south. The director of Military Intelligence stated that the Egyptians were transferring large forces from the east to the west bank, with just 40 percent of their tanks now on the east bank and the remainder already on the west bank. It appeared that the Egyptians had ceased reinforcing their deployment on the east bank in order to prevent an IDF breakthrough to Cairo as well as the encirclement of their two armies. By now, a force equivalent to three reduced armored divisions and one reduced infantry division was deployed in a broad arc around our forces on the west bank.* These Egyptian forces were ordered to contain our troops in the "pocket," to continue the intensive artillery barrage on the bridgehead, and to harass us with commando raids and "tank-hunters" in the greenbelt and among the Geneifa Hills.

Many questions now arose: having broken through to the west, would we be able to break the enemy? Or would the enemy succeed in wearing us down and in halting our advance? Was a cease-fire in fact imminent?

After a quiet night's sleep I awakened at 0400 hours to find that

---

*Egyptian forces were deployed opposite our troops as follows: North of the bridgehead, in the greenbelt, was the 150th Paratroop Brigade reinforced by a commando battalion; in their rear was the 118th Mechanized Brigade from the 23rd Mechanized Division positioned to defend the outlying areas of Ismailia. To the south, in the greenbelt and in the Egyptian camps along the breakthrough zone, was the Palestinian Brigade reinforced by a Kuwaiti infantry battalion and by the remnants of the tank battalion from the 2nd Brigade; to their rear was the reduced 3rd Tank Brigade from the 4th Armored Division. The Egyptian forces defeated at Tsach, Maktzera, and Hushani had retreated westward and had joined the three armored brigades that were defending in a broad arc from the greenbelt in the north to the Geneifa Hills in the south (the 23rd Tank Brigade from the 3rd Mechanized Division, the 116th Mechanized Brigade from the 23rd Mechanized Division, and the 35th Tank Brigade). West of the Geneifa Hills was the 4th Armored Division, its 2nd Tank Brigade deployed at Mitznefet and its 6th Mechanized Brigade at Bolognia. South of the Geneifa Hills was the 6th Mechanized Division, which deployed its 1st Mechanized Brigade in the Aghroud camps and its 113th Mechanized Brigade near Mount Ubaid.

our supply convoys were again delayed at the bridgehead and that we would, in consequence, be late in pulling out. I ordered one battalion from each brigade to be sent out at once, without waiting for all the supplies to arrive. At 0440 hours I ordered that Gabi should continue to engage the enemy at Mitznefet until he was replaced by Magen's forces; in the meantime, he should raid missile bases in the vicinity toward the south. Natke would advance on the Seria Road, eliminate the missile sites on the ridge to the south, and then cut off the Asor Road. Aryeh, moving on the Evra axis, was to destroy the missile sites on the northeastern ridge line and would then go on to capture the Odeda and Metzila camps.

By about 0730 hours Natke's and Aryeh's brigades were advancing in full strength. By noon, Aryeh's forces destroyed three missile bases (Numbers 5620, 5621, 5622). They then continued along the eastern ridge of the Geneifa Hills and demolished three more sites — 5323, 5423, 5421 — at the same time engaging the tanks and armored infantry that were securing the bases. Natke's brigade made its way toward the southeast, reaching Asor-62-63 and destroying Missile Base 5321 on the way. The Egyptian traffic flowing on the Asor Road showed that they were still unaware that our troops had reached that area; Natke destroyed many enemy vehicles that continued to go by for many hours. Natke dispatched two battalions southward to the highest hill in the area, on which Missile Base 5121 was located. Giora's battalion quickly seized this dominating site without a battle; the missile base had been abandoned intact and was in perfect working order. In the meantime, the enemy began to shell the site and to concentrate tanks on the Ro'i axis (the Cairo-Suez railway line) south of the hill. I told Natke to move southward to the Ro'i and Sarag (Cairo-Suez Road) axes. The Egyptians would try time and again over the coming few days to win back Hill 5121.

Gabi's brigade, while maintaining contact with Mitznefet, sent Ehud's battalion southward. West of Bolognia they engaged the enemy in battle. Of Ehud's twelve tanks one was hit by a missile, but the Egyptians began fleeing by the hundreds, and three more missile sites were destroyed (5317, 5416, 5617).

Around noon, there was a slowdown in the advance of the brigades and in the destruction of missile bases. Finally the brigades came to a total halt deep in enemy territory because of enemy resistance.

My forward command group was following Aryeh's brigade. I was looking for a peak that would afford me observation of both the flat strip between the Geneifa Hills and Bitter Lake and the valley through which the Seria and Evra axes ran. It was on these roads that our forces moved to the Asor axis and to Odeda and Metzila. As we were advancing, Dayan arrived by helicopter and joined me in my command Zelda. As we continued, we passed several captured missile sites. We stopped to tour one site and have some photos taken. These bases were well fortified and organized. Four round, open sandbag positions were spread equidistant on a circle of about 100 meters in radius. In each position was a missile-launcher, some still containing missiles. In the center was an artificial mound with a fortified bunker containing two huge covered vehicles where the electronic instrumentation was located. Above the mound was a rotating antenna. Reserve missiles were stored close to the site. The missiles themselves were very impressive: long and sleek. Some were still packed in long cases. Bodies of Egyptian troops were scattered over the area, equipment was thrown all about, and the only living things were bony dogs, howling as though to say: What are you doing here? Where have our masters gone?

Since 16 October Dayan had visited our forward command group every day. We were pleased to see him, and Moussa would make coffee for the visitor, who already knew all the members of the forward command group. Dayan would update me concerning the other sectors and give his views about my operations and objectives, though he was always careful to stress that these were "ministerial" opinions and not to be seen as intervening with the orders coming through regular command channels. Dayan's aide would leave us newspapers, so we could see how our activities were being reported on the home front. The defense minister would usually stay for something over an hour, following the fighting from the command vehicle. As he left he would say: "See you tomorrow somewhere else."

At about noon the Fayid Airfield fell to a force from Magen's division that was operating together with a paratroop company which had been attached to him. I thought a situation assessment was called for at this time.

The division had penetrated deep into the south: Natke was already across the Asor axis, and Aryeh was close to Metzila. Both were reporting increasing enemy resistance. The farther southward we penetrated in the Geneifa Hills, the greater were our logistics problems. The supply and evacuation routes traversed nearly impassable areas. The division needed a paved road! There were three parallel north-south roads, all of them in the flat stretch between the Geneifa Hills and Bitter Lake. These were Havit, which ran through the Egyptians' military camps; Masecha, which passed through the greenbelt along the southern Sweet Water Canal; and the Test route, which ran along Bitter Lake.

The entire plain was dotted with military camps and villages and covered with areas of vegetation and mud. That is, it was a zone which would lend itself to defense and pose problems for armored forces. I did not want to open the road through continuous fighting from north to south — the direction in which the enemy was deployed for defense. On the other hand, we needed a paved road, and to clear this one would require north-south combat. I decided to opt for advance within the Geneifa Hills, while looking for paths by which to breach the flat strip from the flank. I ordered Gabi to reinforce Natke and Aryeh with one battalion each from his brigade and then open the Havit Road. Gabi ordered Baruchi and his armored infantry to advance southward from Fayid, while he — with Ehud's and Lapidot's battalions — moved eastward along the Vitamin Road with the aim of breaking through to Havit from the flank. They would cut it off while capturing army camps and then move southward toward the area where Aryeh's brigade was operating.

The afternoon hours were difficult. Natke was given Ze'ira's battalion (from Gabi's brigade) and deployed it on Hill 5121. Ze'evik's battalion was dispatched southward toward Sarag and reached Ro'i; en route he destroyed Missile Site 5020. Then he began hitting, from long range, the dozens of enemy vehicles that were moving along the Sarag Road. When he was blocked, he asked for air support, pointing out: "Traffic is heavy — it's a golden opportunity." However, the air force was apprehensive about attacking there because there were still four missile sites operating around Suez City. Aryeh was also brought to a standstill after he sustained losses in a hard battle with tanks and missiles, and he was now under artillery fire. It was the 3rd Tank Brigade from the 4th Armored Division that managed to block him near the southeastern peak of the Geneifa Hills north of Metzila and at the exit point from the hills to the area of the camps near Odeda.

Following Natke's and Aryeh's brigades, the division artillery battalions advanced before noon, deploying around Evra-60 with units of 155mm howitzers and 160mm heavy mortars. At once they adjusted their fire and wiped out an artillery battery at Dakdekan-52. I had already contacted Ben-Ari that morning to complain: "I don't understand. More than twenty-four hours have passed since I suggested that you secure the area east of Bitter Lake and enable me to deploy an artillery battalion there which would assist me from the flank. Do you prefer that I bring it across via the bridges? You know we are barely able to get ammunition across."

Ben-Ari: "Who is stopping you?"

"Your artillery officer has vetoed the idea," I told him.

Following an internal clarification of the matter at Southern Command, the problem was solved.

Gonen: "Okay, we'll locate for you at Lexicon-267."

"I'd prefer it at 275," I said. (Near Botzer.)

"Can't be done, it's being held by the enemy," Gonen came back.

"What about 269?" I asked.

"Could be," Gonen replied.

Southern Command then stationed a 175mm artillery battalion there which, with its greater range, improved our artillery support.

Gabi, too, ran into difficulties. The moment he moved from the Vitamin to the Havit axis he encountered tank and missile fire coming from entrenched positions at Havit-49. Lapidot's battalion, which was covering the advance, managed to knock out six enemy tanks, but when Ehud's battalion launched its assault it was stopped, and he took losses. Two tanks and one Zelda were hit; six soldiers were killed — among them the armored infantry company commander, Dvortzki — and a number of men were wounded. We tried again, this time with air support and with an attempt to penetrate to the rear of Havit-49. To that end, I gave Gabi back Amir's battalion, which had earlier been attached to Aryeh and was now positioned on the eastern ridge of the Geneifa Hills to the rear of Aryeh's brigade. I suggested to Gabi that he have Amir move on the Lampa Road, on the enemy's flank and to his rear. This was a steep, winding, barely passable road, and I was hoping that the enemy would not expect us from that direction. But the Egyptians were waiting. Within minutes three of our tanks were ablaze, with four crewmen dead and three wounded. It was only with the greatest difficulty that Amir managed to evacuate his casualties and reclimb the hill.

It was dark by now. Another day of fighting was over on which the division had advanced about 20 km southward. In the course of our advance, we destroyed many missile bases, cut off the Asor Road, reached Ro'i, and cut the Cairo-Suez railway line. Nonetheless, we felt we had been blocked toward the end of the day and that we would have to fight even more resolutely the next day. The division moved into its night bivouacs. Because we had a considerable number of casualties and the evacuation routes were long and bumpy, we asked for air evacuation. But we were told we would have to wait until morning for the helicopters to arrive.

As the brigades settled down for the night, they were dispersed over a large area. Natke's brigade, with some fifty operable tanks, was positioned at Missile Base 5121 and at the Asor-Arish junction. Aryeh's brigade, with just two battalions and thirty tanks, was at the top of the Agon Road, in front of Metzila. (The third battalion — that of Artzi — had been holding Ziona since the fifteenth of the month. Southern Command had now released it, and it was making its way to the brigade, where it was expected the following day, thus increasing the brigade's strength to about fifty tanks.) Gabi's brigade, also with some fifty tanks, was in the main bivouacked around Vitamin-43, except for Baruchi's armored infantry battalion at Fayid. The forward command group was at Missile Site 5621.

At Southern Command discussions were held during most of that day — 20 October — to plan the continuation of the fighting. Bar-Lev clearly defined the two necessary conditions, as he saw them, for the development of the southward effort: to expand the access corridor to the bridgehead northward on both sides of the canal and, second, to capture and operate the Fayid Airfield as a logistical base for the southward advance. Magen's division had in fact taken the airfield around noon that day. As regards the expansion northward of the bridgehead, while Sharon gave the impression that he aspired to "leap" far ahead (at least that was Dayan's impression, according to his autobiography), his ability to do so was in inverse proportion to his ambition and to the capabilities of his greatly reduced division.

Sharon wanted to get the bridges on the Ismailia Canal and seize them quickly, but things went slowly. His division worked to mop up the area with the assistance of air support; their progress was steady but slow. By the end of the day his forces were still far from the bridges. Amnon's brigade was committed northward on the west bank, moving with one battalion from Orcha into the greenbelt and capturing the ramparts at the Tov A position. A second tank battalion of twenty-five tanks arrived from Lakekan, was reinforced with a reconnaissance force, and dispatched to seize the bridges across the three branches of the Sweet Water Canal on the Havit Road. However, the battalion managed to seize only two bridges — at Havit-29 and 1 km north of that point.

Infantry and paratroop forces also engaged in mopping up operations to the rear and on the flank of Amnon's brigade. All told, Sharon's division cleaned out some 3–4 km to the north. Toward the west, Haim's brigade deployed along the Vada'ut Road, at the Vada'ut-Arzal junction, and at Maktzera. On the east bank, Tuvia's brigade advanced a little northward until it had control by fire over the Usha Road. It was assisted by tank fire from Amnon's brigade, which was deployed at Tov A. Tuvia's attempts to advance in the Missouri sector were blocked, and our expectations that the Egyptians there would collapse did not materialize.

In a second conference held that evening at Southern Command, it was decided to place emphasis on the southward expansion. Sharon's division would be "tautened" and would be given the Mitznefet sector. This would free Magen's division to move south, replace forces from Natke's brigade at Asor and Ro'i, and secure the zone of operations to the west. These moves would enable my division to concentrate all its forces to the east and to the south. It was also decided that Sharon's division would continue to press northward, especially on the east bank.

At 2300 hours Ben-Ari awakened Sharon to inform him: "We have completed the plans for tomorrow. We don't want you to cross the [central] greenbelt area. Tomorrow the stress will be on Missouri. You'll get all the air support you want."

Ben-Ari then contacted me, saying: "Your mission is to open the Havit bottleneck, fight along the Asor axis, and capture Metzila — as long as that doesn't involve breaking your neck. If things are tough, destroy missile sites with artillery fire."

Far to the north, in Tel Aviv, the conference that began at 2030 hours at GHQ was held under the looming shadow of an imminent cease-fire. The chief of staff asserted that he would not stop our forces on the west bank from advancing northward and southward, but we must be ready at any time to shift eastward in order to close the enemy within a pocket against the lakes and to place the emphasis on annihilation of enemy forces. The main air force effort would be made on the east bank in the hope that the planes would help Granit and Sasson rout the Egyptians there. But none of these intentions concerning the east bank were to find concrete expression, either in the written order issued by the Operations Branch or, certainly, in the field. Sasson's and Granit's troops were now too weak to carry out large-scale operations, and our main forces were now on the west bank. Dado's directives to retransfer troops from the west to the east bank were not translated into unequivocal orders. The actual orders issued were for all the divisions to continue operating on both sides of the canal. The question was what would we be able to achieve before a cease-fire was imposed?

CHAPTER TWENTY-NINE

21 October: OPENING THE HAVIT ROAD

E ver since we had crossed the canal, my forward command group had been separated from my main headquarters not only during the daytime fighting but also at night. Since 19 October the main headquarters was deployed at Caspi-55, while the forward command group would generally deploy alone for night bivouac, secured by a jeep company. On the night of 20–21 October the forward command group bivouacked at a captured missile site (5621) on the eastern Geneifa Hills.

The forward command group was unique. While the division commander and his staff officers would be replaced every few years, the drivers and communications personnel were reservists who served for many years as a permanent team. Except for the group's communications officer, Captain Gabi Komisar, who was now in the final stages of completing his doctorate in electronics at the Haifa Technion, all the others were workers from town and country (kibbutz). This team had been serving together for some twenty years, had taken part in exercises and gone through wars together. I was personally acquainted with the team from the time I was operations officer in this division in 1958 as a lieutenant colonel. In the 1967 war the team was General Tal's forward command group. A highly cohesive unit, when they were not called up for an exercise for a long period, they would arrive together at Armored Corps Headquarters to volunteer for reserve service.

Gabi Komisar was their commander. Galamidi, a radio operator, was the joker, always laughing at everyone including himself. He was a bank clerk who had a short time before gone into the electrical goods business. Another radio operator was Weizman, an economist who worked for the Education Ministry in Jerusalem.

The most colorful member of the group was my driver, "Big Moussa," who lived on a kibbutz in the Negev. He liked to hunt and would bring his rifle to every exercise so he could go out and bag us some game for our bonfires at night. He always had everything with him you could think of: cooking oil, onions, salt, plates. He could even improvise a field shower from captured equipment if we needed it. He was a superb driver, one of those who make you feel that if the vehicle wouldn't move under its own power, he would push it where it had to go. However, in order to preclude any such contingency he was helped out by another kibbutznik, Giora, a driver and a first-rate mechanic.

There were some in Israel who called the Yom Kippur War "the war of the fathers and the sons." Those of my generation, who had fought as youths in 1948, were now taking part in their fourth or fifth war. Meanwhile their sons had reached military service age and were also fighting in this war. Just a couple of kilometers in front of my forward command group, a young officer was fighting — Moussa's son. A recent graduate of an officers' course in the Armored Corps School, he was in Amir's battalion. His battle indoctrination had begun on 6 October, near Mifreket. At first he fought as a platoon leader, but as the war went on and took its toll, he was promoted to the post of operations officer in the tank battalion. During the fighting, Moussa would put on earphones and monitor his son's radio net.

Sometimes when he had the opportunity in the evening, Moussa would hop over for a visit, and when he returned he would relate the arguments he had had with his son. Moussa would question some of the orders he heard his son issue over the radio; his son would then see fit to remind him that he was an officer while Moussa was just a sergeant who knew nothing of tactical doctrine. After the fighting ended, while we were still in a state of cease-fire, Moussa — who was already over forty — asked to attend a tank commanders' course and an officers' course. Permission was granted on condition that he continue to serve with the forward command group.

When I awoke just before dawn of 21 October, Komisar approached me to say: "Bren, the radio nets are quiet now, why don't I connect you with your home? Usually the lines are jammed but right now I can do it, with the help of the radio-telephone."

It was 0400 hours, the stars were just beginning to fade. Komisar handed me the phone and said, "It's ringing." From the other end I heard the pleasant voice of my wife, Miriam, say "Hello." This was my first direct contact with the home front in Israel. Miriam had had many messages from me via persons who had arrived at the front and then returned back north. From them she knew I was well.

She also knew that the war was bitter and terrible, but as a general's wife, expressed confidence that the IDF was in control. Nor was this an easy thing to do. No one had expected that the IDF would have difficulties in deciding the war. Indeed, the IDF itself was not prepared for a prolonged war; all its means and methods were adapted to a short conflict.

The machinery for dealing with losses vis-à-vis the civilian population — reporting to and attending to the families — simply could not cope with the numbers involved. In many instances, neighbors and friends knew of casualties, when the family had as yet been given no official or authoritative report. Among the many reasons for this, besides the IDF being generally not organized for it, was the incessant disruption in the chain of command because of the high casualty toll among officers. The "administration" was neglected because the main effort had to go into the terrible effort to ensure that we could, first and foremost, go on fighting.

Moreover, Jewish religious law states that a person may not be declared dead unless two witnesses could testify that they had seen him die or unless identifying marks were found on his person, such as the international identification card carried by the soldiers, or a dogtag. But there were cases when tanks blew up with their entire crew inside, and the raging fire destroyed any identifying mark, even the dogtags. Moreover, because of the many replacements among the crews in the wake of casualties, there could be no certainty, sometimes, as to the composition of a particular crew. Another problem was that many tanks — especially in the war's initial stages — had been abandoned on enemy territory, sometimes with the crew still inside. Even though their comrades were certain that there had been no survivors, many of these men were declared missing in action because no one had actually seen them die.

Israel is a small country, and when letters didn't arrive and no phone calls came from the front, the families began seeking out people who had access to information from the battlefield. Many approached Miriam in this regard: "My son is in the Armored Corps, but I don't know where he is fighting." Or, "My son is in your husband's division, and I haven't heard from him for ten days." Miriam would contact my secretary, who had remained in the rear, and she would try to get the information requested and pass it on to my wife.

The son of one of my top ordnance officers, Lieutenant Colonel Razon, was seriously wounded. His son was serving in the paratroop battalion that had fought between the Tirtur and Akavish roads on the night of 16–17 October. At the same time, Razon, the father, was working to repair the broken roller-bridge. When he completed this task he was informed that his son had been wounded and evacuated to a hospital in the rear. Razon was given leave to visit his son, but he refused to go and continued to extricate and repair tanks in my sector. It was only when the cease-fire came into force that he went to see his son. The son of my supply officer served as a young platoon leader in my division. Two days before his father was to arrive with a supply convoy he was killed. The father looked for his son but was given evasive replies to the effect that his son had been wounded and evacuated to the rear.

In the afternoon of 21 October I was contacted by Southern Command to be told of Nahum Sarig, an officer admired by those under him. He had been my brigade commander in 1948 when I served in the Negev Brigade. Nahum had come to the southern front in order to take one of his sons home. He had six, all of whom were officers in the Armored Corps. Hardly a year went by when Nahum did not show up at the graduation ceremony for the officers' course in the Armored Corps School to see one of his sons graduate. This war was cruel to him: two sons were wounded and a third was killed. According to IDF rules, when one brother is killed in action all the other brothers must be taken off the battlefield. One of Nahum's sons was commanding a platoon in my division not far from my forward command group. I contacted Gabi to ask whether he could spare the young officer, and Gabi replied that he understood my intent. The young Lt. Eyal Sarig was brought to my Zelda in a jeep.

It was a difficult moment — most of all for young Eyal, who was abruptly pulled out of a tank that was engaged with the enemy and sent to the division commander. He looked thin, exhausted, worn out, but I at once recognized the distinctive features of the Sarig tribe. I recalled the expression on his father's face, twenty-five years earlier, in the desperate hours of the besieged Negev. I don't know what the young Sarig's heart was telling him, but I felt that I must not talk in circles. I told him straight out that two of his brothers were wounded and a third was dead. He bit his lip and said not a word. I sent him in a helicopter to Umm-Hashiba, where his father was waiting. I returned to my command vehicle immersed in thought. It was some time before I picked up the microphone to resume command.

Miriam told me that our daughter, Netta, who was eighteen, phoned home from time to time from the Gaza Strip, where she was serving. Our son, Omer, also called home, to say that unfortunately he was not taking an active part in the fighting because he had completed a course just three months earlier and had not been able to finish his training. This was not true, of course. Omer was involved in the fighting but had wanted to calm his mother so she wouldn't worry. Moreover, one day after the war, Omer asked me about a certain event in the fighting, which made it clear that he was among those who had given my division considerable support.

What eased Miriam's days during the war were the daily gatherings at our house of classmates of our sixteen-year-old daughter, Talila. They hoped, no doubt, that at the home of a general they would be able to learn "what's going on." They were a fine, cheerful group who during the morning worked at digging trenches and building bunkers. In the afternoon they met in our yard. When I called home at 0400 on the twenty-first, Miriam woke up Talila, too, so I could exchange a few words with her. I told them both that the worst of it was behind us and that we were about to wrap things up. I then called my parents in Tel Aviv and gave them regards from Africa. The phone calls were a moving experience. For a time I continued to think about my family, whom I had for so long pushed out of my thoughts. Now I missed them terribly. I found it hard to go back to thinking about running my division.

Our heavy losses were leaving their mark on morale in the rear and were having a definite effect on decisions at the front. The heaviest losses had been sustained during the first days of the war and mainly by our small regular army that had been called on to repulse the charging waves of an enemy that vastly outnumbered them. The longer the war went on, the greater our losses were. Now after two weeks of fighting, we considered and reconsidered each step in terms of how many losses it was liable to cause. The phrase ''charge ahead carefully'' became very common, despite its internal contradiction.

It was dawn of 21 October, and the division engaged the enemy. We had already received reports at 0400 hours that elements of the 4th Armored Division and the 6th Mechanized Division were preparing to attack our forward forces. Natke and Aryeh were given advance warning to this effect and directed to prepare their forces for defense and to throw the enemy back. So when troops of the 113th Mechanized Brigade attacked Hill 5121, they were repulsed. At about 0700 Natke and Aryeh began to move forward against growing tank and missile resistance and under heavy artillery fire. Aryeh sought to push forward to Metzila, while Natke moved along both sides of the Asor Road. Natke had to direct part of his effort toward the south because his flank was attacked from Missile Base 5122 and from across the Sarag axis. Around noon, forty enemy tanks, accompanied by infantry, attacked the 5122 site and reached its very center but were thrown back by Ze'evik's battalion with the help of Ze'ira's battalion. At 1100 we had hit fifteen Egyptian tanks and had five of our own knocked out. By 1300 we had destroyed the 5121 site and had hit another ten tanks, but our progress was slow. Because of the threat from the south, Natke was pressing toward Sarag as well.

At about 1100 hours Bar-Lev, accompanied by Deputy Prime Minister Yigal Allon, arrived at my forward command post. I reviewed the situation for them, and we spoke of our immediate objectives and the general lines of development in the fighting. Bar-Lev and I now got into a dispute that would continue until noon of the following day. Bar-Lev was against my advancing southward to the Cairo-Suez Road (Sarag). In his view, I should move from two directions to the southern edge of Little Bitter Lake, to Zidon — both eastward along the Asor Road and southward on the flat strip of the camps along the Havit Road. I thought it preferable to advance to Sarag, both in order to close off Mount Ataka, thus encircling the Third Army and to open further room for maneuver to outflank the enemy now fiercely defending the Asor Road. The argument ended in a draw; we decided to come back to it later. In the meantime Gonen called and told Bar-Lev that he was having trouble with Sharon, both in connection with the attack on Missouri and as regards transfer of the amphibious battalion. As they conversed, I was able to speak with Yigal Allon. I was very pleased to see my old Palmach commander here. Before he and Bar-Lev left, he gave me a pat on the shoulder and asked whether I was aware that the fate of the entire campaign rested to a large extent with me. To tell the truth, that was what I myself felt. I smiled and said, "Everything will be okay."

As we pressed forward slowly in Natke's and Aryeh's sectors, we were also engaged in heavy fighting on the open flat strip between the Geneifa cliffs and the lakeshore. Despite the unfavorable terrain for our tanks — the camps with their many buildings and the mud of the greenbelt — and despite the enemy's resistance, we brought about some concrete achievements. Gabi's brigade was fighting here, and he also had forces to the north, near Fayid. Baruchi's armored infantry battalion, to which a tank company was now attached, advanced on the Havit Road. To his right, between the road and the Geneifa Hills, Artzi's battalion was making its way to Aryeh's brigade, and I placed him also under Gabi's command temporarily. The two battalions were attacking southward, with air support in front of them. They were coming under heavy missile fire from among the buildings in the camps, where tanks — some of them dug in — were also hidden. Progress was slow, with many vehicles hit and men wounded, but by noon we reached Havit-48 so we were able to open a supply line to the division up to the Havit-Vitamin junction. This shortened and improved our line of communication to the rear.

Now I was informed by Southern Command that in the afternoon I would be getting two more battalions in order to mop up the Test and Masecha roads to Zidon. At 1400 the divisional engineering battalion would arrive to open up the Test Road, and around evening an airborne infantry battalion code-named Marak would arrive to open Masecha. I attached both battalions to Gabi's brigade and then asked Gonen also to attach the battalion equipped with armored amphibious vehicles taken in the 1967 war to my division. I explained to Gonen that in view of the need to mop up the greenbelt by means of a frontal assault, I wanted to employ the battalion as well as amphibious elements to outflank the enemy in the rear via Bitter Lake. Gonen was persuaded by my reasoning, but I doubted whether he would succeed in transferring the battalion, which was operating under Sharon's command — though not in amphibious missions.

At 1400 hours I had to make a situation reassessment. Magen had not yet arrived to replace my forces near the Asor Road. Natke and Aryeh were shuffling about exchanging fire with the enemy but not advancing. Gabi, who was fighting in the flat plain, now had seven battalions — after I had attached four battalions to him — but not all of them were being employed. I decided to widen Gabi's sector, giving him also the entire eastern ridge line of the Geneifa Hills including the Agon axis and the Metzila area so that he would fight to open the roads on the plain while his forces advanced both on the plain and on the ridge dominating it from the west. This move would enable me to push Aryeh and Natke closer together and so intensify our pressure in the narrower expanse of Asor and Sarag. I also directed Artzi's battalion to move to link up with its original brigade, Aryeh's.

In the afternoon the going to open the Havit axis grew rougher. As Baruchi's and Artzi's battalions approached the Havit-Vitamin junction, Gabi added Lapidot's battalion in a flanking movement via the Vitamin Road. Thus as Artzi and Baruchi moved in from the north and Lapidot from west to east, the pincers were closed. But the fighting in the built-up area of the camps caused considerable problems and losses. In Baruchi's battalion, half the tanks and half-tracks had been hit, and Artzi's battalion also had losses.

Later that afternoon, Lapidot, Artzi, and Baruchi launched a southward assault and took Havit-49. On their way, five tanks of Artzi's battalion hit mines. Among those killed was the battalion commander. Artzi was about twenty-eight. Ever since we had launched our crossing operation, he had been left to block the Tassa-Ismailia Road near Ziona. For every one of those six days he had not ceased asking his brigade commander, Aryeh, when he would be able to rejoin the brigade and take part in the offensive. At last he was called back to the brigade, and at the very end of his first day on the offensive — when he had led his forces so well — he fell in action.

Now on the northern edge of the flat shore strip, the Marak battalion, commanded by Yaya, began its advance. This was a regular *Nahal** paratroop battalion that had been deployed in strongpoints on the Golan Heights at the outset of the war. When the Syrians had burst through, they remained cut off but had thrown back Syrian infantry and tank attacks until they were rescued in the wake of the IDF's counterattack. I was told that they were to arrive the previous night, but it was only in the afternoon hours of the twenty-first that they had shown up and were immediately placed under Gabi's command. A full three days were to pass before Gabi would have the opportunity to meet the battalion commander, Yaya, face to face. To the east of the Marak battalion, which was moving on the Masecha Road, the divisional engineering battalion now advanced on the Test Road. By nightfall, all the battalions were aligned on the Masecha-49 line.

Gabi's two other tank battalions — Amir's and Ehud's — operating on the Geneifa ridges, were to replace Aryeh near Metzila. They spent the morning in replenishing and when they arrived to replace Aryeh, they found him engaged in combat and joined in to help him. At the request of Aryeh and Gabi, who did not want to carry out a replacement move during battle, I agreed to postpone the change of sectors until the following morning.

At 1630 hours I asked Ben-Ari for urgent air support: "We are blocked by two rows of mines; one tank company has hit the mines. Opening of Havit Road is critical. Request air support."

Ben-Ari's reply: "The air force is busy in the attack on Missouri. Its capture is more crucial."

At 1720 hours Bar-Lev called, and I briefed him on the results of the day's fighting: the opening of the Havit Road, the throwing back of two Egyptian attacks on Missile Base 5121, the difficult fighting

---

*The *Nahal* is a paramilitary corps whose members combine military service with working the land, usually in border settlements.

around Asor, Sarag, Ro'i, and Metzila. I estimated that in the course of the day we had destroyed some fifty enemy tanks, several artillery batteries and many antitank units.

"Well done!" Bar-Lev exclaimed, and Dado added his words of praise.

Again I got into a lengthy argument with Bar-Lev concerning the Sarag axis. I said I was adamantly against a frontal attack on the Asor Road, explaining that I needed room for a flanking movement and that I would advance carefully, in a "trial-and-error" style.

To which Bar-Lev replied: "I know you. You'll patrol, make an attempt, go cautiously, and in the end you'll break through. We don't need all that."

"But all day I was in fire battles," I told him, "unable to conduct mobile warfare. I want to outflank the enemy in order to collapse the center."

Bar-Lev: "The Air Force will help you overcome resistance on the Asor Road."

"Sure," I said, "today they helped, too — in bits and pieces and at long intervals."

Bar-Lev: "Tomorrow it will be different. We are going to use artillery fire and aerial attacks to destroy the last of the missile bases around Suez City. Okay, Bren, have some supper, think about it, we'll call back in an hour and conclude things." Still a draw.

It was on that day, 21 October, that the differences between Sharon and Southern Command reached their peak. It will be recalled that during the night Sharon had already received an order from Ben-Ari to capture Missouri. At that time his division was deployed on both banks of the canal: Tuvia's brigade on the east bank with forty tanks, and the main part of the division, Amnon's and Haim's brigades — with some eighty tanks — along with Danny's and Uzzi's two small paratroop brigades on the west bank. Sharon's main aspiration was apparently to reach Ismailia. Even though Southern Command's order had placed the emphasis on capturing Missouri, Sharon did not make any serious preparations in that direction. On the morning of the twenty-first, when Bar -Lev left to visit my forward command group, it was Gonen who maintained contact with Sharon. At 0853 hours Sharon asked Gonen if he could get tank and artillery reinforcement. Gonen explained to him that no reinforcements were available, and he would have to make do with what he had. Sharon replied that the artillery he then had would be needed to capture the area south of Ismailia so that the Missouri mission would be adversely affected.

Gonen: "Determine your priorities, either go for the city or for Missouri — I'm interested in Missouri."

To which Sharon said: "It makes no difference, I don't have enough artillery or enough ammunition." Sharon went on to show prolonged and detailed interest in what was happening in all the other sectors, all the way to the Budapest Strongpoint in the north.

Their conversation ended with Gonen saying: "The main problem is Missouri. If you take Missouri the entire situation on the front will be altered."

And Sharon: "Okay, we'll try to do it today."

At about 0900 hours the chief of staff arrived at Southern Command HQ and explained that the main effort had to be made on the east bank: to launch a massive air attack first and then to coordinate a combined operation by Sharon against Missouri and by Sasson against Hamutal and Machshir. Following this, Gonen again contacted Sharon, at 0842 hours, telling him — this time in unequivocal terms: "You must transfer your main effort to Missouri — even if you have to shift all of Amnon's brigade and part of Haim's there. We must capture Missouri."

Sharon: "What about Hamutal?"

Gonen: "Sasson is operating there, we'll coordinate a sector boundary."

Sharon: "All you need is to have the air force attack there without letup."

Gonen: "The air force is already attacking. Are you directing their sorties? If not, do so, and keep them at it for another two hours. Then attack with your forces."

Sharon: "All right, see you."

At 1015 hours, in another conversation, Sharon said: "Lots of air attacks there. H hour set for 1400 hours."

At about noon, Bar-Lev landed at Sharon's forward command post, after Dayan had already been and gone. In his book, Dayan relates that Sharon was furious that Southern Command had forbidden him to bypass Ismailia and advance northward and instead had ordered him to carry out a pointless attack on Missouri, which would cause many losses. At all events, Bar-Lev discussed the attack with Sharon and they agreed that H hour would be set back to 1430 hours. At 1515 hours the attack had not yet commenced, and Gonen demanded of Sharon that he attack and not wait for any more air support.

Forces from two brigades did attack — and failed. A force of reduced battalion strength from Yoel's brigade in Sasson's division attacked Hamutal, while Tuvia's reduced brigade attacked Missouri. Apparently, the air bombing from high altitude had not brought the expected results — had in fact proved largely ineffective — and both of the too-small attacking forces encountered fierce resistance. Yoel, who had a tank company and an armored infantry company, was forced to withdraw from Hamutal-west but remained on Hamutal-east. Tuvia, who was reinforced with five tanks only, attacked with forty-one tanks and withdrew with just nineteen tanks intact. Some hit mines, others were hit by tank fire or missiles. The brigade lost twenty-four men killed or missing in action, including eight officers. Tuvia remained on the Lexicon-Usha axis.

While the attack on Missouri was at its height, Dayan and several generals arrived at Southern Command HQ to discuss continuation of the campaign in light of the approaching cease-fire. The chief of staff arrived from the northern front, after the first Israeli helicopters had landed on recaptured Mt. Hermon. Dayan arrived directly from my forward command group and Bar-Lev from Sharon's forward command post. Gonen was already there. According to his book, Dayan convened this session in order to determine priority of action among three major objectives: an operation against the Third Army on the east bank toward Suez City and against the southern edge of Bitter Lake; or against the Second Army on the east bank around Missouri; or Sharon's suggestion of a northward advance on the west bank while bypassing Ismailia. Dayan did not share Bar-Lev's and Dado's view that Sharon's opposition to capturing Missouri stemmed from subjective Sharon-type calculations but rather accepted Sharon's views as an objective military evaluation. At the same time, Dayan expressed his own view: "I do not consider myself qualified to veto an operational decision which was wholeheartedly

supported by both the southern command and the chief of staff. . . .
As far as Arik's proposal to advance northwards is concerned, it was
rejected. The chief of staff did not support it and I do not think it is a
good one either. It will make things more difficult for the enemy but
it will not bring about the destruction and defeat of the Egyptian army. . . ." Dayan went on to explain the difficulties that such an
operation would impose on our forces and concluded: "We have to
establish a front line as compact and operational as possible."

Following the failure of Tuvia's attack on Missouri, another
sharp dispute broke out between Sharon and Southern Command
which demanded that Sharon attack the objective again that night.
Sharon retorted that he had been against the original attack — which
had cost much blood — and that this was certainly not to be
repeated. Bar-Lev pointed out that Sharon was supposed to have
transferred forces from the west bank but instead had made do with
reinforcing Tuvia with just five tanks, thus sealing the fate of the attack.

When Dayan returned to Tel Aviv that evening, following the
conference at Southern Command HQ, he was called at 2200 to the
prime minister's office. Mrs. Meir informed him that the United Nations Security Council was slated to convene at 0300 Israeli time to
decide on a cease-fire. Dayan informed Bar-Lev and the General
Staff of this development. In his talk with Bar-Lev, Dayan urged that
Granit advance on the east bank in order to reach the canal opposite
my forces which were pushing toward Zidon so that we would be able
to bridge the canal south of the lakes as well. In the wake of the new
information concerning the imminent cease-fire the General Staff
met in conference, and this was followed by intensive activity at
Southern Command HQ. Ben-Ari radioed instructions to all the division commanders concerning containment of possible Egyptian attacks and attainment of final objectives. I was to get to Zidon; Granit
was to link up with me from the east bank; Sasson and Sharon were
to repeat the attack on Hamutal, Machshir, and Missouri.

At 2337 hours Ben-Ari tried, unsuccessfully, to speak with
Sharon. He was sleeping and no one could wake him up. Ben-Ari implored that Sharon be given coffee or a hard drink or that water be
brought so he could wash his face. Ben-Ari said that what was in-

volved were the most important orders of the war to date. He wanted to inform Sharon that he should expect an attack by two armored brigades from the west.

Gonen tried his luck: "Where is Jackie?"

"At the bridge site."

And again: "Where is Gideon [Sharon's chief of staff]?"

"At Tassa."

Finally, Gonen spoke with Hillel, the communications officer: "Do you happen to know if orders were issued to attack Missouri tonight?"

Hillel: "Yes, I'm just about to send a message to Tuvia on this."

Gonen: "What time is H hour set for?"

Hillel: "It hasn't been determined." And then he added: "Sharon isn't yet aware of the problem — he's sleeping."

Finally, at midnight, contact with Sharon was made and Gonen asked him: "Do you intend to reinforce Tuvia?"

Sharon: "Absolutely not!"

Gonen: "Then I say reinforce him!"

Sharon: "That's out of the question!"

Gonen: "Bear in mind that this will be failure to carry out an order!"

Sharon: "Well, really, don't bother me with things like that."

Now Bar-Lev took the receiver: "Well, Arik, not at night — at first light. . . . That's impossible. . . . Transfer Amnon's brigade. . . . Arik, there's no point in us talking all night. . . . It's part of an overall plan."

After midnight, the phone rang in Dayan's office. On the line was Sharon, who asked the defense minister to intervene to have the attack on Missouri canceled because this would be a pointless erosion of forces. Dayan then called General Tal, Dado's deputy, and requested that either he or the chief of staff check out the matter and issue the necessary orders: "We can't just ignore this kind of appeal from Sharon. If necessary, I'll intervene, too," Dayan said.

Tal then contacted Gonen and convinced him to change the order to attack Missouri into an option to do so. If Sharon wants to attack, let him; if not, not! This of course meant the effective cancellation of the attack on Missouri. When I learned of all this I was astonished: at Sharon, whose heavy sleep prevented him from hearing orders and who, upon awakening, had bypassed both the front commander and the chief of staff to take his case directly to the minister of defense; and at Dayan and Tal, who had also bypassed Dado and Bar-Lev on such an important matter.

There is no doubt that 21 October was a very disappointing one for HQ. On the east bank the situation had not been improved. On the contrary, the attacks on Hamutal and Missouri had resulted in heavy losses and had failed. Sharon, who had refused to transfer forces from the west bank, had not done much there either. Amnon's brigade had taken some Egyptian ramparts, but overall Sharon's division had advanced no more than 2–3 km that day. Magen's division had remained in place, while decimating an Egyptian tank company that had advanced to the Vitamin-Uvda junction. My own division, too, had made little progress in the zone south of the Geneifa Hills (toward Metzila and Odeda). Nonetheless, the groundwork had been laid for the next day's fighting, which might turn out to be the last of the war. The Fayid Airfield had been restored to use and supply-bearing transport planes were already landing there. In addition, the Havit Road was now open as a supply and evacuation route, enabling new troops to be sent in to strengthen the southward assault.

In the conference held in the afternoon at Southern Command HQ, only Gonen backed my suggestion that our attack be developed toward Mount Ataka in order to complete the encirclement of the Third Army. All the others — the defense minister, the chief of staff, the southern front commander — apparently feared to bite off much more and favored an attack toward Zidon. It would be no easy matter for me to get to Zidon. From Metzila I would have to advance 25 km eastward in the face of enemy resistance; and from the north I would have to push some 25 km southward along the flat shoreline strip through army camps and villages from Havit-49 to Zidon, and about 35 km through the heavy growth of the greenbelt on the Test and Masecha Roads. Moreover, the terrain was rough, and the enemy was still resisting stubbornly.

Our supply convoys making their way southward after dark on the newly opened Havit Road soon ran into enemy ambushes, and fuel trucks were set ablaze. During the night we continued to mop up the built-up areas we had passed through and which we had thought to be free of enemy troops. I could take some consolation in the fact that all the preparations for the coming day were now in high gear. The battalion formerly commanded by Artzi was on its way to Aryeh's brigade, and Ze'ira's battalion — which was now operating in Natke's brigade — was ordered to return to Gabi the following day. By that time the sector boundaries would be improved, and our forces opposite the key areas of resistance augmented. I expected the better dispositions and the concentration of forces to make their mark in the next day's fighting.

CHAPTER THIRTY

22 October: GENERAL ASSAULT BEFORE IMPOSED CEASE-FIRE

The report concerning the anticipated cease-fire was not long in reaching me since Ben-Ari contacted me several times during the night. Southern Command wanted me to attack via the shortest route eastward toward the canal, through Metzila and Odeda. But I insisted on an attack via the Sarag axis as well. This would enable me to cut off the final supply artery to the Third Army, to cut off the Suez-Cairo Road, and also give me more space for maneuver so I could outflank the enemy, too, and not just push ahead with a frontal attack. My plan was finally approved at 0450 hours.

Meanwhile, at 0215 hours I had contacted my brigade commanders concerning the forthcoming cease-fire. I urged them to fill up with fuel and ammunition quickly and to prepare for the final push of the war. But once again problems arose. Magen's division, which was to replace Natke's brigade and take responsibility for securing the zone of operations to the west, had not yet arrived. Moreover, not only would we not be able to get close air support from first light, but the division artillery would be employed to destroy the final missile sites still operating near Suez City, far to the south. The hope was that these missile bases would be out of action by 0700 hours, and then I would be able to get artillery and massive air support.

Activity got underway at 0510 hours. "All Karish stations, this is Karish. Good morning, over."

"Natke here, over."

"Aryeh here, over."

"Gabi here, over."

"Karish here. Today is Monday, 22 October, the eighteenth day of the war. On this day the Levites would chant in the Temple: 'And you shall strike the Egyptians and pursue them to the end.' Strike them thoroughly and quickly. Should it come to pass that you do not hurry, you will not finish the task! Ready for orders, over." The brigade commanders reported that they were ready. My orders were as follows:

Gabi would launch a pincer-movement attack. Half his brigade would move from north to south along the Bitter Lake shoreline strip and half from west to east on the Agon axis to the Havit axis, making a flanking movement at the southern extremity of the Geneifa ridge and then bursting through northward to the lake plain and from there to the north in the rear of the Egyptian forces. Aryeh would attack from west to east along both sides of the Asor Road. Natke would move south on the Sarag Road, turn east, move along Aghroud and go on to attack on the Akel Road, operating south of Aryeh. I went on to define the brigade boundaries: in the final stage of the fighting they would extend from the west bank of the Suez Canal south to Bitter Lake, as envisaged by Southern Command. The division's tank strength remained stable at about 175 operable tanks. While we had sustained some losses in the past few days, we had also received some repaired tanks and even some reinforcements.

Natke had three battalions, though not one was under its original commander. Assaf's battalion was now commanded by Lieutenant Colonel Ze'evik; Giora's was under Major Micha; and Natan's was commanded by Lieutenant Colonel Guy. Aryeh's third battalion — that commanded by Artzi, who had been killed the previous day — was on its way to join him. Aryeh now asked me to let him have Major Yitzhak, who had been my aide when I was commander of the Armored Corps and was with me now in the forward command group. It was hard to let Yitzhak go; he was a young, efficient officer who was of great help to me. But I did not want to deprive the battalion of a commander who on the basis of his past military record would do a good job, and I did not want to deprive Yitzhak of the opportunity to command a battalion. Regretfully, I parted from him and summoned my previous aide, Major Yehuda, from the rear. He arrived the following day and went right to work. Ever since the days of defense on the east bank, Gabi's brigade was organized in four small battalions — those of Lapidot, Ze'ira, Amir, and Ehud — as well as Baruchi's armored infantry battalion and some small armored infantry companies within the tank battalions. Since the previous day Gabi also had two more battalions attached to him, Yaya's paratroop battalion and the divisional engineering battalion. This reinforced brigade was now operating on two axes, along the flat canal strip and the Geneifa ridge line which dominated that strip.

Later we learned of the enemy's fighting that day from captured documents of the Third Army. Against us were positioned forces from the 4th Armored Division and the 6th Mechanized Division, as well as Palestinian and Kuwaiti troops stationed in the camps on the shoreline plain along Bitter Lake. During the night of 21–22 October the Third Army had already issued orders to destroy the fuel reservoirs at Panara, disperse tank-hunting commandos along the traffic axes, block our routes of advance with minefields, and deploy artillery forward observers who would adjust concentrated fire on our forces. In addition, reserve forces on the west bank were to be reinforced by a tank battalion from the 22nd Tank Brigade. Most important of all, they were to launch counterattacks at dawn on the key terrain features we were now holding: Missile Base 5323, on the Geneifa Hills, and Missile Base 5121, which dominated the area between the two major roads, Asor and Sarag.

The Egyptian forces had problems during the night in nearly all their sectors, disrupting some of the missions assigned by the Third Army, particularly in the flat area where their camps were located. A number of trucks loaded with mines were hit and abandoned. Three jeeps from the Third Army's fuel section that were en route to blow up the fuel reservoirs at Panara were destroyed, and the supply officer was wounded and taken prisoner.

A thick fog now hung over the ground, especially in the low places. Gabi reported that he had dispatched engineers to clear the

Test, Masecha, and Havit roads of mines coincident with first light. At 0400 hours Gabi's forces on the plain near Havit-49 came under a dense artillery barrage. Our division artillery countered by directing fire at the enemy batteries. At about 0500 hours the orders of the Third Army — about which we then knew nothing, of course — began to be carried out in each of our brigade sectors. In Gabi's sector fire contact was established between Lapidot's tanks at Havit-49 and Egyptian tanks and Sagger units. A number of enemy tanks were hit, and the attack was driven back. In Aryeh's sector Missile Base 5323 was attacked by two assaulting echelons. The first consisted of a commando battalion that sought to approach our position under cover of darkness. Its attack was repulsed, and the enemy left many bodies and some prisoners behind in his retreat. The second echelon, made up of tanks and armored personnel carriers from the 1st Mechanized Brigade, commenced its attack at first light.

In Natke's sector, Missile Base 5121 came under attack. Two battalions from the 113th Mechanized Brigade advanced from the east, from the Aghroud camps. Leaving their tanks and armored vehicles behind, their infantry moved on foot for the assault. Simultaneously, a mechanized battalion with a commando company and a Sagger-launching company made their way from the south on the Arish Road. From the west a tank battalion from the 4th Armored Division was also advancing toward Hill 5121. By this time, Natke's battalions were already moving southward, except for an armored infantry company reinforced by a tank platoon that had been left to defend 5121. The forces on 5121 spotted the enemy forces deploying for attack from the east and alerted the brigade. Natke urged his troops on, and Ze'evik's battalion just managed to reach the hill at the last moment and join the forces that had been there during the night. A fierce battle ensued. The Egyptians' charging infantry was thrown back, and they left many dead in the field behind them.

Even as the battle for 5121 was at its height, Micha's battalion, deployed south of Asor, observed the waiting tanks and armored personnel carriers of the second assault echelon east of 5121. He reacted quickly, and very soon the scene was lit up by fires as eight enemy tanks and about 20 armored vehicles were set ablaze by our gunners. Natke's report was not long in coming. At 0702 hours he told me: "We really gave them a royal screwing!" In the meantime, Guy's battalion was making its way on the Arish axis to Sarag. At 0708 hours we stopped Guy at Arish-64, according to an order from Southern Command. From the west a tank battalion from the 4th Armored Division was approaching. In the ensuing engagement a few enemy tanks were hit, and the rest backtracked to the west. Continuing on his way southward, Guy reached Arish-66 where he encountered the mechanized battalion from the 113th Brigade. A hard battle developed, with the enemy launching many Sagger missiles.

The brigades began requesting artillery and air support for their advance, but both elements were busy until after 0830 hours destroying missile bases near Suez City. The battalions continued to press forward, but their progress was slow. Requests for support became more and more frequent. At Southern Command there was no awareness of the operational significance of breaking the enemy's counterattacks. Our rate of advance seemed insufficient to them and began to cause concern. First Uri Ben-Ari and then Bar-Lev himself urged me to let up on the southward pressure and concentrate my entire effort toward the east.

"Natke's maneuver is really sharp," Bar-Lev said, "but I'm afraid that by the time he gets to Sarag, we'll have to orient all your forces to Zidon, and who knows what's waiting for us on the way?" I explained to Bar-Lev that our main effort was taking place along the Asor Road, with Gabi pressing from the north and Natke from the south in order to try to ease the pressure on Aryeh. I also pointed out that I wanted to cut off the last road from Suez City, and it would be illogical to leave it open. Bar-Lev concurred and told me he was urging Magen to get to the sector as fast as possible so he could secure it toward the west and release all of Natke's brigade for an attack eastward. At 0800 hours Magen's division arrived and began to replace Natke's forces which were securing to the west.

With morning I had moved up with my forward command group to the hill on which Missile Site 5123 was located so I could have a commanding view of the battlefield. While I was still on my way there, Aryeh called me to say: "I'm not sure that the remnants of the unit whose attack we broke didn't flee to the missile base you're going to. I'm sending my scout unit to mop up the place. It's a fantastic site — you can see all of Asia and Africa from there." It was truly a superb observation point. Only rarely does one have the opportunity to command from a position where the combat can be viewed like a play. From here I could observe nearly the whole divisional battlefield. To my left I had a bird's-eye view of the shoreline strip, on which I could see the enemy's artillery batteries and tanks deployed, some of them dug in. To the north we saw Lapidot's tanks advancing and firing, with the armored infantry following behind. In Aryeh's and Natke's zone of operations, black palls of smoke lifted into the air from wounded vehicles. We could make out the line of enemy tank positions and the deployment of our own tanks. But in the area of fissured hills our advance was still delayed because small enemy forces were still operating among our brigades, giving rise to apprehension that our troops were firing on one another. Using radio coordination and colored smoke, our units identified one another, and so we were able to spot the enemy units that were still acting as a wedge between Aryeh's and Natke's brigades.

Beginning at 0900 we received artillery and air support. For the first time I was able to allocate planes to each of my brigades at the same time, and, generally, in a continuous manner. It soon emerged, however, that the process of engaging the ground targets was a slow one. The planes circled high overhead, first to identify our forces and then to locate their targets, and finally discharged their bombs. Nonetheless, the cumulative effect of the sorties began to have its results.

The situation of the Third Army commander was far from easy, but he did his best. Contacting the commander of the Palestinian Brigade directly, he ordered it not to withdraw. He ordered the 19th Division — whose 22nd Tank Brigade was stationed on the east bank near the bridges — to dispatch a tank battalion to the village of Geneifa, promising it the support of the division artillery. He also tried to coordinate among all the forces engaged against us. However from his subordinates he got only bleak reports. At 0805 hours the commander of the 256th Mechanized Battalion, which was fighting on the flat strip, informed him that the Israelis had attacked with planes, antitank weapons and tanks, destroying his antitank means; the remnants of his battalion had withdrawn and joined the Palestinian Brigade. This battalion commander added that we were attacking and flanking him incessantly and that the radio set of his artillery liaison officer was out of commission so that he was unable to halt us. Fearing that he was in real danger of being totally cut off, the Third Army commander ordered his troops to stand firm because this line was a vital one. He promised to send tanks out to help; every request would be met. He then reported to the deputy chief of operations on the fate of Battalion 256. Then he ordered the 19th Division to dispatch a tank battalion from the 22nd Brigade in order to prevent us from employing tanks from the Geneifa peaks.

The headquarters of the Third Army was located in deep bunkers close to km 109 on the Cairo-Suez Road (at Sarag-70), not far from where Natke's forces were pushing ahead (at Sarag-Arish). The situation soon became worrisome to the army commander, and he ordered the commander of the 6th Mechanized Division to dispatch a battalion from the 113th Mechanized Brigade in order to defend Third Army Headquarters. He summoned the commander of the 22nd Tank Brigade to him and directed the commander of the 4th Armored Division to attack our forces with tanks on Hill 5121 and on the Arish Road. In addition, the Third Army commander instructed a senior officer to coordinate with the 1st Mechanized Brigade and then personally join the commando company that was to operate against Natke's tanks. Meanwhile, reports of IDF advances and requests for permission to withdraw kept arriving from many units. At 0904 hours, Third Army reported that the enemy was attacking the entire zone of operations of the army as well as its headquarters in strength from the air; the communications system had been hit and his control capacity damaged. The 7th Infantry Division, east of the canal, also reported that it was being hard hit from the air.

At about 0900 hours Magen's forces deployed to replace Natke's troops in securing the zone of operations westward. But instead of taking up stationary positions, they began advancing southwestward and seizing missile bases. Southern Command informed Magen that Ran's small tank brigade was on its way to reinforce him.

In my division, movements to increase the mass of forces according to the new sectors were just being completed. Aryeh left the entire Geneifa Hills to Gabi, and his three battalions were now operating in the Asor Road sector. At the same time, Gabi was also stepping up his southward push toward Asor. At 0930 hours, as our brigades advanced in all sectors, there were incipient indications of an enemy retreat. Gabi's scout company, at an observation point high in the Geneifa Hills, reported that the enemy was evacuating his positions north of Panara (Havit-50). He had Lapidot speed there, and the site was captured. In the course of the day this reconnaissance company would, besides its observation activity, assist in adjusting artillery fire and in locating ground targets for air strikes from its high position overlooking the entire expanse from Suez City in the south, the bank of the Canal to the east, and the Ataka and Aara mountains in the west. As Aryeh and Gabi continued to press from the Geneifa Hills, they found that the Egyptians were beginning to flee from Hill 5124. Slow but constant advance — movement and fire, movement and fire — was under way along the entire divisional sector.

At about 1000 hours, Dayan landed by my forward command group and joined me in the command Zelda. As usual, he accepted a cup of coffee from Moussa. From our observation point we could see, on the edge of the Panara camps (at Havit-52) about a dozen Egyptian tanks deployed behind earth ramparts and waiting to engage Lapidot's battalion, which was advancing in their direction.

Over and over our planes attacked the Egyptian tanks. Their crews could be seen evacuating the tanks, running off, and then returning. The same was the case with the antiaircraft units (23mm guns) that were deployed near the tanks. The Egyptians' staying power was surprising. We sustained casualties in most of the battalions. I suggested to Gabi that he dispatch tank battalions into the Geneifa wadis to the rear of Havit-52, but the scout company was unable to locate any passes through the hills. Lacking any alternative, in an attempt to help Lapidot, Gabi ordered Amir Yoffe's battalion — which was positioned nearby — to open fire from high up downward against the enemy. Every tank crew member knows that it is easier to fire from down to up than the opposite. The depression angle of the tank gun is limited, so to fire downhill the tank must move forward a bit down the slope, thus exposing not only part of its turret but sometimes even the hull. From down below effective tank and artillery fire was opened up on us. The forward command group's vehicles quickly moved alongside the stone buildings in the military camp. Some of the men took cover inside the structures, among them Lt. Avishai Ben Zvi, who was attached to the forward command group and who was killed in this exchange of fire.

Dayan was still in my Zelda, so I decided temporarily to relinquish my unlimited observation position. I directed the vehicle to a nearby trench that the Egyptians had dug for vehicles. A CBS TV crew that was present in the area — the men were wearing bulletproof vests — were now able to interview Dayan with smoke and explosions as the proper background. Dayan stayed about an hour. He reiterated the great importance he attached to our reaching Zidon before the cease-fire went into effect. We were still about 25 km from that destination, but even though our progress had been slow if steady, I told Dayan that "the mission will be accomplished!"

I based my assessment on two factors. First, we were now getting close support from the air force, which was increasing in intensity moment by moment; I assumed that this air support would soon bring about a cumulative effect which would leave its mark on the battlefield. And the second factor was the terrain. Although for the time being we were still fighting in a hilly area whose wadis and slopes facilitated both the enemy's retreat and his ability to delay us, I was absolutely determined — the moment we pushed the enemy off the present broken terrain and reached the extensive plain between the hills and the canal — to cover the last 15 km in an all-out charge.

Meanwhile, Egyptian reinforcements had arrived to engage Lapidot's tanks which were advancing between Panara and Kabrit. He was attacked by MIGs, and three of his men were wounded. We could see Egyptian tanks moving northward from Suez City (these were from the 22nd Brigade, which had been transferred back from the east bank of the canal). At 1044 hours Gonen called to find out what was happening on the Sarag axis. Ben-Ari also intervened to offer his view that I should push Natke to take Odeda. However, I still held to my view not to evacuate the Sarag axis, and I suggested that I move from the Sarag Road to Odeda via the Akal axis. The enemy was continuing to beat a slow retreat on both sides of the Asor Road, and now he had to pull back his artillery. Eliashiv, from Aryeh's brigade, spotted this and began sniping at them. Gabi's scouts located a team of Egyptian artillery forward observers at Hill 5324, very close to where the forward command group was, and took them prisoner. Enemy resistance continued to weaken.

Just at this time the Third Army commander contacted the commander of the 1st Mechanized Brigade and found that the commander of the 113th Mechanized Brigade was there too. Lashing out jeeringly at the latter, he said: "Your artillery is already employing flat trajectory fire and is almost encircled — and you're 13 km to the rear." (Actually, half of his artillery had already been destroyed.)

After ordering the two brigade commanders to move forces up at once to contain us, the Third Army commander contacted the Egyptian minister of war, saying: "Sir, the situation is fluid, the enemy is breaking through. The commander of the 113th Brigade is behaving like a frightened rabbit and is at the HQ of the 6th Division at km 109 [near Natke and Aryeh] 13 km from his units. Enemy tanks are annihilating his artillery. . . . Unfortunately, I have to deal with liars. The brigade commander is not leading his men through the wadi but is sitting at km 109. . . . May God ease our burden!"

At the same time (1130 hours) some interesting discussions were under way on our side. Bar-Lev contacted me once more to ask for an explanation. He was unable to understand Natke's movement toward the Sarag Road. In Bar-Lev's view Natke's entire brigade should be pushing toward Odeda. I told Bar-Lev that one of Natke's battalions was already moving toward Odeda and that there was no room for more tanks in the Asor sector because all of Aryeh's brigade was already there too.

Said Bar-Lev: "That reminds me of a joke I heard from Yoske Geva [General Geva was the commander of Central Command from 1960 to 1966] after he returned from a visit to the German Army. Geva had asked a German general how he had managed to deploy one thousand tanks in a very narrow sector. The German officer's reply: 'What's the problem? If you can't get them in widthwise, you get them in lengthwise'." We both laughed.

"Do you get my point? Maybe you should direct Natke straight to Odeda without any unnecessary flanking movements to wrap up our main problem. There are still five hours of daylight left — let him move!"

An uncomfortable situation. I had had differences with Southern Command since Bar-Lev's visit to my forward command post on the morning of the previous day. Moreover, since 0705 hours that morning, Ben-Ari, Gonen, and Bar-Lev had contacted me to urge me over and over to stop pushing toward Sarag. The move south may be examined from two greatly different aspects. The first was the operational aspect, cutting off the Cairo–Suez City Road, which was in fact the last supply and evacuation axis left to the Third Army. The consideration to get to that destination was within the sphere of responsibility of Southern Command. If they were against my initiative, should I not yield the point? On the other hand, it seemed to me that the reason for their opposition was that they were not sure I would fulfill the declared mission of reaching the Suez Canal whereas I was certain that I would. So I regarded my adamant attitude as justified.

The second was the tactical aspect. If we did not move southward, we would have to launch a frontal attack with no flanking capacity. I despised that kind of warfare. Lacking any alternative, this was how I acted on the flat plain, but here I could expand the sector and employ a "lever" from the flank.

But all in all there were just five hours of daylight left. Perhaps the time had come to concede the point. Dovik, my deputy, suggested that we keep pushing southward. I decided to make one final try: "Natke, can you deploy additional forces toward Sarag?"

Natke: "Negative!"

"Then leave a blocking force at Sarag and move eastward with two battalions. Move the third battalion in gradually." Natke found this hard to believe, but after hearing my explanation he began to carry out the order.

At 1215 hours the pressure eastward hit a peak. Aryeh advanced to a point 2 km from the Akal-Asor junction; Natke was deployed north of the Aghroud camp (about 2 km north of the Sarag-Akal junction); Lapidot of Gabi's brigade had reached Havit-52 where he encountered a minefield that blocked his advance; and Amir's battalion was fighting on Hill 5324 at the Metzila position. But among all these encouraging reports some grimmer news arrived from Natke's brigade. Micha's battalion, which was moving in the center of the sector north of the military camp around Missile Base 5122, was caught in enemy fire from behind and suffered casualties. Under cover of artillery shelling and smoke bombs — and with the help of Ze'evik's battalion that Natke rushed to the site — Micha managed to extricate himself.

At 1210 hours the Third Army's forward command post announced that they regarded it as pointless to continue to deploy in a forward zone and employ units wastefully in its defense. This was followed by an argument among the Egyptians. Apparently, the 19th Infantry Division was not ready to let the 22nd Tank Brigade go, since this was liable to result in the loss of the eastern bridgehead. But the order was given to move the brigade westward. (To which the Third Army commander remarked: "If I move to the east, who will guard us from the west?")

At 1235 hours I coordinated a two-brigade attack on the Akal-Asor junction; Natke to move in from the south and Aryeh from the east. In the meantime, the artillery was moved up, and I was making preparations to get strong air support against the junction. Our air force liaison officer, who operated within the forward command group alongside the artillery liaison officer, was Lt. Col. Shmuel Kislev. He had done first-rate work since the war began, but now he was outdoing himself. He seemed to know the entire air force and was able to find common language with all the pilots and, no less important, with me and with the liaison officers in the brigades as well. Calmly, efficiently, he requested and distributed squadrons to the brigades, and when things got crowded above us, he sent planes to bomb the greenbelt and even east of the canal.

Meanwhile, even though only a small detachment from Guy's battalion was blocking the Arish-Sarag junction, a real drama was taking place at Third Army HQ at km 109. For hours now, the Third Army commander had been fearful that the Cairo-Suez Road (Sarag) would be cut off. He was constantly complaining to the minister of war that the enemy was making air attacks relentlessly, that he had no more Strella missiles left, and that he urgently needed his own air umbrella. He had also complained about the behavior of the 113th Brigade commander. He now contacted Kabil, commander of the 4th Armored Division, to inform him that the enemy had cut off the Cairo-Suez Road and that he was in effect encircled, while Kabil was "outside." Imploring Kabil, he said: "You are under my command. Why are you against . . . I tell you that the army is being encircled, the road is not in Arab hands. . . . You must open the Suez Road, issue an order to the 6th Brigade. . . . I am giving you a clear order. The enemy is moving in my direction. . . . Now that he has captured km 109, the Third Army reserve is you!" (Actually, our forces were closing in on the site but had not yet taken it.) At 1245 hours he pointed out to the minister of war that units from the 4th Armored Division, which was under his command, had not heeded his order to attack from the west and open the Cairo-Suez Road. He requested the war minister personally to order this attack. At the same time, the Third Army commander informed the commander of the 19th Infantry Division that the enemy had cut off Highway 12 (Sarag) at km 109 so that the division no longer had a supply route.

It was just then that we had let up our pressure to cut off Sarag. The blocking detachment from Guy's battalion was reporting thousands of Egyptian troops fleeing westward, as they abandoned their vehicles on the road, circled southward into the field, and then returned to the road. Meanwhile, at 1315 hours, Aryeh's forces captured the Akal-Asor junction and sped into the plain.

In fact, when I had stopped Natke's southward advance and had ordered a massing of forces for the assault eastward, the Third Army commander went out to reconnoiter the Sarag Road at km 109. At 1520 hours, when the Egyptian war minister tried to contact him, he was told that even though the Third Army commander had been warned that the area was crawling with Israeli tanks, he had nonetheless decided to go out and see for himself what was happening. The Egyptians were surprised — and delighted — when we broke off our southward push and turned to the northeast. It was the deputy commander of the Third Army who was the first to realize that this "retreat" was not as simple as it looked, since it was logically at odds with what the IDF should be doing in the face of an imminent ceasefire — namely, expanding the area under its control and destroying the maximum number of enemy forces — not relinquishing its achievements. However, the reports of our air activity against the canal bridges along with our abrupt shift on the ground soon brought the Egyptian officer to the realization that the Israelis were probably planning an assault toward the canal. The deputy Third Army commander relayed his evaluation to the chief of operations, General Gamasy, and asked for urgent air support.

The Egyptians dispatched Libyan Mirage aircraft to the front, and they attacked Gabi's forces on the Havit Road. Our advance continued. I pressed the brigade commanders to move up and deploy the maximum force in order to step up the pressure on the enemy. The division artillery operating on our bank had already been moved up to the Agon area. Together with my operations officer, Gilad, I planned the final assault order on a map. It was getting close to 1400 hours, and we still had 20 km to the Suez Canal. Studying the map, I saw that the planned objective, Zidon, was located deep in the green-belt. However, 4 km south of Bitter Lake, the Sweet Water Canal assumed an arc shape and approached the Suez Canal at a point named Kilo. At a point named Mina, 3 km south of Kilo, was another rampart situated where the Sweet Water Canal was still very close to the Suez Canal.

It was my conclusion that to seize these two objectives would be easier in terms of the terrain; we would not get entangled in heavy undergrowth. I inferred that to take the alternative objectives south of Zidon was consistent with the spirit of my orders, and in fact went beyond the mere carrying out the letter of my orders. At 1400 hours I radioed: "Commanders to the set for orders. Over!" Aryeh was to capture Zidon, Natke would take Kilo and Mina, while Gabi would open the Havit axis with a pincer movement, from the north on that axis and from the south from the Agon Road. More time was taken up in clarifying to the brigade commanders their sector boundaries to a depth of 15 km on a flat, open plain lacking any distinctive terrain features. Summing up, I stressed that the hour was late and that we must burst through in an all-out charge in a fairly narrow sector and reach our objectives before the cease-fire took effect.

While the brigade commanders were making final preparations and passing on the orders to their battalion commanders, Ben-Ari called from Southern Command to inform me that they had learned that an Egyptian commando force was about to block the Vitamin axis to the west and to the east. Ben-Ari wanted me to operate against the roadblock on the east side, while Magen would deal with that in the west. I was entirely caught up in the imminent breakthrough to the canal, and now suddenly I was being handed some small and bothersome mission somewhere about 30 km to the rear. Ben-Ari promised to land an infantry company for us at Vitamin-40, commanded by Lieutenant Colonel Hisdai. They were to land within thirty minutes. Ninety minutes later Southern Command informed me that Hisdai's force was not yet ready and that the helicopter landing would take place in another hour or two. Fortunately, the Egyptian threat to cut off the Vitamin axis did not materialize. At 1430 hours,

Bar-Lev directed Magen to deploy his forces to ensure that the Vitamin Road remain open to the west, while the Sarag Road remained closed and cut off to the south.

The division's forming up for the final assault was taking time because we still had to carry out mopping-up operations of the positions near the Akal-Asor junction, at Odeda, and around the Akal-Havit junction. These sites were located at the points of egress from the hills. East of the line of junctions, a divisional deployment and a rapid charge across the plain was possible. An hour went by: mopping-up operations were continuing. At 1500 hours I announced over the radio: "It has just been reported by Radio Cairo that Egypt has agreed to accept a cease-fire. It will come into force in less than three hours. We have to hurry!" The brigade commanders passed on the news, urging their battalion commanders on — but another hour passed, and my nerves were starting to get the better of me. All the brigades were engaged in combat with enemy infantry and tanks; mines were holding us up; we were taking casualties.

Finally, at 1600, the division commenced its charge. At once there were problems. We had to leave a force behind to secure the junctions behind us; these were vital positions (Akal-Asor and Akal-Havit), and the enemy must not be allowed to recapture them in a counter-attack from the south. I asked Magen, who was assisting us by securing the zone of operations to the west and to the south, for forces to replace ours. At 1618 hours I suggested to Gonen that Magen close off the Sarag Road, which we had been compelled to leave under pressure from Southern Command.

Gonen radioed to ask whether I was planning to get to Zidon by evening. I replied: "I'll get there for sure! The only question is how long it will take. For instance, we are not getting air support just now because they are busy in a mass air battle with Mirages."

Gonen pressed me: "So far, you've been a pretty good pusher! Give one more push and get to Zidon and Lituf."

I asked Gonen whether an order had been issued for a cease-fire at a certain hour.

"Not yet!" he replied.

And I said: "Do me a favor, don't be in any rush."

At 1658 hours the deputy commander of the Third Army reported to the commanders of the 4th and the 6th Divisions that their allies from Libya, who had been piloting the Mirage aircraft, had bailed out south of Fayid and should be rescued. (Some of them were picked up by our forces.)

At 1700 — at last, a feast for the eyes. The division was speeding across the plain in a broad, deep structure. The sun was at our back, but vision was obscured by the many clouds of dust raised by the charging tanks. The reports were coming in fast and furiously, mentioning a thousand and one code names, so that it was hard to follow them. Thousands of Egyptians, I was told, were fleeing every which way but were not throwing down their arms. The question was to fire at them or not? I was familiar with this problem from the 1967 war: the Egyptians would surrender but did not know that this had to be accompanied by throwing down their arms. They would raise their hands, still bearing their rifles. You needed strong nerves. We had no interest in preventing surrender and in arousing resistance that would only end in more casualties — mainly on their side but to us as well. The order: be on the alert; don't be quick to open fire; try to show them how to surrender.

The air force now announced that it was ceasing its operations due to darkness. A pity; they did a wonderful job.

The division was now deployed across an immense expanse. Gabi's pincers were about to snap shut. He was now taking a huge army camp — the Geneifa camp — where thousands of Egyptians wanted to surrender, but we had no time to take prisoners. Aryeh and Natke continued to push eastward. Only Gabi's brigade was taking a few prisoners. Yaya's battalion had reached only the Panara camps, which he was mopping up; he was still lagging behind.

At 1730 hours I instructed Natke and Aryeh not to enter the closed areas of the greenbelt but to send in only small detachments which would make their way to the canal. The brigade commanders were extremely busy in coordinating and directing their battalions. Suddenly an excited radio call came from Natke: he had left a company from Ze'evik's battalion to supervise the repair of disabled tanks around Hill 5121 in our rear, and the enemy was now attacking there. I contacted Magen, who said he would rush troops to the site at once. This was what it meant to be comrades-in-arms, I reflected. It was good to have Magen adjacent to my division. He was efficient, active, and cooperative.

At 1851 hours, with just a minute's worth of grains left in the United Nations' hourglass, Bar-Lev called to ask what the situation was. "The dark caught us in the middle of our charge, but we pushed on. It was bold, messy, glorious. The area is dotted with the fires we set. At Zidon we have reached the water and within minutes we'll be at the water at Kilo and Mina too. I've ordered the men to take control of all the ramparts they find."

Bar-Lev: "Okay. In another two minutes the cease-fire is supposed to take effect."

"Repeat, please," I said, "I can't hear you." (Apparently my ears did not want to hear that particular message.)

At the same time, Magen — informed by Ben-Ari that the cease-fire was in effect — reacted by asking: "Are you sure it's today?"

Ben-Ari: "It's a shame, but yes!"

Earlier, Ben-Ari had relayed many messages concerning the cease-fire. He told me that two infantry companies would be arriving by helicopter so that they could be stationed at Mina and Zidon. (They actually arrived late.) Ben-Ari also passed on instructions for our troops' behavior during the cease-fire. The next day there was to be no further advance southward, but we would have to mop up the area we had captured and achieve territorial continuity between Kilo and Zidon and between Kilo and Mina. Ben-Ari also suggested that I dispatch forces to the top of the ramparts to open fire, so that the Egyptians could see we had taken that area before the cease-fire came into effect. Now Bar-Lev radioed: "If they don't shoot at us, we won't shoot at them. If they open fire, of course we'll respond."

Already at 1725 hours, the commander of the Third Army informed all his forces that on the basis of a resolution of the United Nations Security Council and with the consent of the Egyptian government, fire would cease at 1852 hours at the order of the commander in chief of the armed forces; this, provided the enemy (us) honor its commitment and also cease firing. All the commanders, he added, were responsible for securing their troops and guarding the area in their hands. The minister of war also contacted his subordinates to explain that immediately upon the cease-fire, the troops must reorganize in order to strongly defend the bridgeheads of the two armies. The war minister was in fact impatient for the cease-fire to come into effect, and so, I assume, were many other Egyptians.

We accepted the cease-fire with very mixed feelings. It had been imposed because it was advantageous to the Egyptians — not just advantageous, in fact, but actual salvation for them. On the other hand, there was no doubt whatsoever that the people of Israel, from its leaders to its ordinary citizens and soldiers, were heartily sick of this bloody struggle. We knew the toll the war was taking.

Personally, I was not anxious for a cease-fire that cut us short in midcharge. I remembered the terrible days we had endured at the beginning of the war, and I was eager to settle accounts with the Egyptians. I felt they had not yet "got what they deserved" and that this kind of ending — an incomplete one — boded ill for Israel in the political campaign that would now commence. My blood boiled at the thought of the superpowers and the Security Council being unable to agree on a cease-fire as long as the Egyptians didn't want one. I felt furious, not only over the fact that when the Egyptians wanted a cease-fire it was declared at once, but also at our own leadership, which had not been able to get its way at least to the same extent as Egyptians — who had just thumbed their noses at the world, both in launching the war and rejecting many proposals for halting it until they were good and ready.

One way or the other, I did not believe the cease-fire would be observed. There were too many complex problems in the field and too many Israeli and Egyptian troops intermixed.

At 1801 hours the Third Army commander reported to the chief of operations that a number of enemy tanks had penetrated from Shalufa toward the passages on the Suez Canal and that the enemy was also attacking the Geneifa camp. Deployed in these camps was an infantry battalion from the 1st Brigade of the 6th Division. An aide to the Third Army commander checked with the 6th Division's operations officer about the fate of the 20th Infantry Battalion with which contact had been lost. While he was deciding that Colonel Balal would go into the area as a liaison officer to find out what had happened, the Geneifa camp commander was on the phone to the Third Army deputy commander. The latter ordered the camp commander to hold on but was told that the battalion was already wiped out and that about 35 Israeli tanks were moving about inside the camp.

When the cease-fire order was relayed to the 19th Infantry Division, it replied that they had spotted Israeli tanks in the El-Abid camp (one of the Geneifa camps) and had opened artillery fire on them. Contradictory orders continued to be given. At 1851 hours, the Egyptian General Staff told the deputy commander of the Third Army personally to order the unit commanders to hold their fire. He replied that he himself had read out the cease-fire order to the commanders in the field and had told them that the enemy (us) had undertaken to observe the cease-fire. But at the very same time the Third Army commander was ordering the 6th Division commander at all costs to prevent enemy tanks from reaching the Cairo-Suez (Sarag) Road.

As soon as the cease-fire was declared the question of what to do about the many Egyptians who were in the field between and near our units arose. An order had come down that there was to be no further advance southward, but the area we were holding should be mopped up and prisoners taken. Between Panara and the southern tip of Bitter Lake (Zidon) was a pocket that had not yet been cleaned out. I did not know if there were Egyptians there, and if so, how many. I was apprehensive that the camps and villages, the roads and hills, the wadis and the various buildings and armories were still aswarm with enemy soldiers whom we had not managed to round up.

Orders were now issued on both sides to maintain a high state of alert and to deploy for night bivouac with maximum security precautions. Of course, with regard to the IDF this meant organized units, whereas the Egyptians now had disorganized fragments of a disintegrating army alongside units that continued to exist whole. The Third Army was ordered to transform night into day, and they used illumination flares across the entire expanse to show us that they were watching us and following our movements — and perhaps also to quell somewhat their own extreme nervousness.

Not much time passed before the Egyptians violated the cease-fire. At twilight, Eliashiv's battalion from Aryeh's brigade had arrived near the greenbelt close to the southern Sweet Water Canal. Just as they moved into the greenbelt zone a company commander, Lt. Kobi, was shot and killed by an Egyptian sniper. The battalion continued to advance, reached Zidon, and took the rampart on the canal bank. Darkness made the vegetation look like a jungle and shrouded the greenbelt's swampy areas. Fierce fire was directed at them from all sides; the battalion had to evacuate its position and move northward. Eliashiv scouted the area, found a level place, and deployed his battalion there in two columns for the night. Whispering seemed to be heard and then silence. Fifteen minutes after the cease-fire came into effect, withering fire opened up on the bivouac from every direction. The initial blast hit many of the men and set tanks and Zeldas ablaze. It emerged that Eliashiv had deployed his bivouac right in the center of a huge Egyptian position (of the 7th Division) that was defending the Suez Canal passages in its zone. Eliashiv gave the order to open fire. Under its cover the men evacuated the dead and wounded, and then Eliashiv ordered them to follow him northward. The swampy terrain was rough going in the dark, but finally they found and crossed a bridge across the Sweet Water Canal and moved out of the greenbelt to the west — only to run into mines. Nine of the battalion's eighteen tanks as well as two armored personnel carriers were left behind, but all the casualties were evacuated. Three hours later the battered battalion linked up with its brigade, which was encamped outside the greenbelt.

Now came a report that the division's main headquarters group had been caught in an intense artillery barrage while crossing to the west bank and had suffered many casualties. There was plenty of work awaiting the main headquarters. It would have to activate all the logistical units concerned with evacuating tanks to the rear and provide heavy technical maintenance for all the division's vehicles. We would have to repair disabled tanks left along the course of our advance, as well as those tanks which — despite the damage done to them — were able to continue.

When I got the news of the mauling the main HQ group had taken, I gritted my teeth. It looked like the cease-fire was not being observed. There was much confusion in both the division and at Southern Command. The more I tried to get things clarified, the less certain I was of what would happen the next day. I decided that it would be best to prepare for another day of fighting because the chances were good that there would be more cease-fire violations.

My forward command group was encamped on the Geneifa Hills, the staff working hard to collect reports on the disposition of forces and preparations for the next day. We had to replenish our fuel and ammunition during the night — no simple task because the troops were so widely dispersed — and prepare to take thousands of prisoners. We already had hundreds of POWs, among them officers up to the rank of lieutenant colonel.

Utterly exhausted and tense in anticipation of the coming day, I reflected on the day of fighting that had just ended. It had been an extraordinary day in which the entire division with all its battalions had been engaged from morning to night. In the final two hours we concluded with a spectacular tank charge, a major assault by all the division's forces in a very broad and deep formation. It was the first time we had carried out a classic charge in this filthy war that had already gone on for seventeen days straight. Well, it was a fine finish. We had destroyed many dozens of enemy tanks, though we, too, had suffered losses, unfortunately.

I contacted Southern Command to ask what had taken place that day in Sharon's sector. Tuvia's brigade had engaged Missouri in a long-range fire fight. Just before the cease-fire came into effect the Egyptians launched a Scud surface-to-surface missile containing two tons of explosives. No one knew where it was aimed, but it had exploded in Tuvia's zone, killing seven soldiers. Amnon's brigade had exchanged companies with Uzzi's and Danny's brigades, and the mixed task forces had fought toward the north, generally reaching points proximate to the central Sweet Water Canal. Sharon even ordered Amnon to enter Ismailia, but Amnon replied that he hardly had any forces left, and the order was unrealistic. When Sharon's troops did try to enter Ismailia, they were halted at the sewerage plant, a few kilometers south of the city. Haim's brigade had expanded northward, reaching the Vada'ut-Nura axis. The general feeling in Sharon's division was that they were just worn out.

Scanning the map, I saw that we had achieved the aims set by Southern Command for the day's fighting and had captured an extensive area, from the central Sweet Water Canal to Zidon. The Third Army was falling apart. The division was still operating well. Was this really the moment to stop? Would there really be a cease-fire in effect on the twenty-third?

CHAPTER THIRTY-ONE

CLOSING THE RING: 23 OCTOBER

The first night of the "cease-fire" was a very tense one for me. The cease-fire itself had in fact been violated almost as soon as it came into effect when half of Eliashiv's tanks had been knocked out, an incident that was followed by firing in various zones. The summation for 22 October was: thirty-two tanks, three Zeldas, five half-tracks hit; five men killed, forty-eight wounded. Nor did this take into account our casualties in the rear when the main headquarters group came under shelling. I was particularly annoyed because I was unable to grasp exactly what the higher echelons wanted. I had several times pointed out to Southern Command that the cease-fire was not being observed in practice, but I had not managed to get a clear order beyond the original directives: "No further southward advance!"

I was to retake the rampart by Zidon, from which we had been dislodged after the cease-fire came into effect, and I had an okay to carry out the mopping-up operations required to obtain territorial continuity between the forces. I could hardly believe it: I wanted to complete the encirclement of the Third Army come hell or high water — but the order was just not forthcoming! It was only natural that the cease-fire was not being observed, given the complicated state of affairs in the field, and of course we were permitted to open fire in self-defense. But these exchanges of fire would go on for only so long before the situation was stabilized and quiet reigned on the battlefield. Was this what the high command wanted?

There can be no doubt that many commanders of all ranks felt as I did. When Magen had radioed to Gonen asking him if he might not somehow have made a mistake about the timing of the cease-fire, Gonen had replied: "We in the army take orders. It was the Government of Egypt that decided to launch this war, and the Government of Israel that decided on the cease-fire. And we in the army accepted both orders."

Dayan writes that on the following morning (23 October) at 1000 hours he convened an extended conference in his Tel Aviv office with the participation of, among others, the chief of staff, his deputy, the commanders of the air force and of the navy, and the director of Military Intelligence. The subject under discussion: quick consolidation to keep hold of the area in our possession so that we would be able to withstand the coming nerve-wracking months of negotiations. Dayan relates that those present did not believe that there was any real intention of maintaining the cease-fire. He said he pointed out to them that the sides had accepted the cease-fire not because of the authority of the United Nations, but as a result of the intervention by the two superpowers; it would be best if all acquiesced in the fact of the cease-fire.

I found myself in considerable inner turmoil. I was never one to disregard the responsibility and decisions of the echelons above me. On the other hand, I thought, was this not the time and were these not the circumstances in which certain decisions could be taken only on the battlefield? If I were to decide to respond to fire against me not only with fire of my own but with fire *and* movement, would all levels not welcome such a decision? I recalled that in 1967 Dayan had ordered the IDF to halt 10 km short of the canal, but the IDF had nonetheless reached the banks of the canal. And when the cease-fire had come into effect on the Golan Heights, on 10 June 1967, the then commander of the northern front, Dado, had managed to position forces by helicopter on many of the hills in front of our ground troops — and as far as I knew, Dado hadn't been too meticulous about consulting his watch. After pondering the matter for some time, it was with a heavy heart that I came to the decision that we would have to finish off the job the next day.

At about midnight I informed Gonen that since the cease-fire was not being observed, I was going to continue fighting on the following day (23 October). I added that I did not expect the cease-fire to be enforced. Nor could I interpret Gonen's reply as a negative one, and I did not press the matter further. As far as that went, conversations at all levels were ambiguous: Maintain the cease-fire, but . . . should the enemy violate, etc. . . . Well, the enemy had already done that. I had no doubt that they would continue to do so.

The two infantry units that were to have reached me earlier that evening did not show up, and I was told that they would be arriving only the following day. These were Lieutenant Colonel Hisdai's paratroop battalion and Major Ivan's mechanized reconnaissance battalion. I planned to mop up the area we had captured, hoping that the enemy would violate the cease-fire, thus leading to an expansion of the fighting so we could complete our task of encircling the Third Army. I assigned three brigade sectors: Natke would mop up the west bank of the Suez Canal from Mina north to Bitter Lake. Aryeh would mop up the area opposite Little Bitter Lake and capture Zidon and the Kabrit peninsula (Tanganyika and Margalit). Gabi would clean out the remaining section from Great Bitter Lake and capture the Tangier and Syracuse points. I expected problems. The division sorely lacked infantry forces, and the tanks were not adapted to fighting in the marshy and overgrown terrain of this zone.

In the southern section the task was to seize the ramparts and engage the east bank with fire. Many pockets of resistance and fragments of enemy units were located in the many camps of the two northern subsectors. In my briefing I stressed that few tanks should be sent into the greenbelt zone of dense vegetation; the tanks would do better to cover the infantry troops from outside that area and support their advance from behind. After the area had been mopped up by the infantry, the tanks could move in to take fire positions. But who would do all this combing of the greenbelt when we were so short of infantry? In addition to Baruchi's armored infantry battalion in Gabi's brigade and Yaya's battalion of airborne infantry, Hisdai's force (no more than one hundred men) and Yossi Yoffe's battalion from Danny's brigade in Sharon's division were now also on their way to join us. I decided that Gabi would send Yaya to join Natke; Hisdai's force would be attached to Aryeh; and Yossi's battalion to Gabi. The division engineering unit was still busy clearing the roads of mines, but when they were finished, they would be given an infantry assignment.

"At 0620 hours Gilad radioed to all the brigade commanders: "All the Egyptians around you are to be taken prisoner."

Gabi: "You're talking about millions."

Ten minutes later, Natke reported that the Egyptians had opened up with tank fire and requested artillery support. Gilad told all the brigade commanders to be at the ready. Natke was hesitant and suggested that we check to see if the Egyptians were firing at Aryeh too. Intervening, I gave him a verbal roasting: "Keep calm and stop worrying about other sectors. The enemy has opened fire, and we are responding. If they have opened fire on you, fire back. Take up positions and fire back! Don't make me any armistice here — fire back and go into action!" I reported to Southern Command and requested air support.

When the fighting resumed all the infantry battalions were still on their way to the division, so we went into combat without them, with just the little armored infantry and the many tanks we had. The morning hours were marked mainly by our taking prisoners. They flowed in from all directions while fighting broke out at a considerable number of places. The Shalufa position, which completely dominated the flat plain below and even the other side of the canal, was a huge and well-defended fortification; but after the Egyptians there put up resistance initially, the site fell to Aryeh. The fighting in the military camps and in the villages was more of a nuisance than a burden. But we still sustained casualties, and the need for caution slowed down our pace.

Since we had little infantry, the armored infantry units had to carry out the combat and mopping-up operations in the closed and agricultural areas, and some tank crews had to serve as jailers for the many POWs we were rapidly collecting. Indeed, within a few hours we had some forty-five hundred prisoners, including many officers. Later, the division military police arrived to guard the field jails and begin transferring the prisoners to the rear. The shortage of manpower compelled us to come up with some original rules of our own.

We appointed Egyptian prisoners as commanders of the convoys of POWs to lead them on foot to the temporary detention areas. They were very bewildered and upset, still living the traumatic moment of a prisoner who is uncertain whether he will reach the prison alive or be shot by some nervous soldier on the other side. Eventually we placed them on captured Egyptian vehicles, formed them in convoys, and took them to the central detention areas on the Havit Road.

One scout jeep that was leading such a convoy drove too fast and only five of the eight convoy trucks were able to keep pace with him. When the jeep crew noticed that three trucks were missing, they stopped to wait for them to catch up. When the trucks arrived, an Egyptian officer in one of them began shouting excitedly: "Is that how you lead prisoners? It's scandalous; it's irresponsible! You could have killed us!"

The young lieutenant in the jeep didn't get upset but replied, with a thin smile: "Knock it off — what chutzpa! Just say thank you that we're taking you to prison, and if you don't want to be killed, your driver had better keep up with me." On that day and the next, the division took over six thousand prisoners. There were many civilians in our zone of operations, but to our surprise they seemed unaffected by what was happening around them and simply kept working their fields. Where in the world did they get their unshakable confidence that nothing would happen to them? I only hoped that our POWs were also being treated in the same way.

At 1020 I picked up an encouraging sign. Gonen informed Dovik that Magen's division was to advance southward in order to complete the encirclement of the Third Army. Our mission was to continue mopping up but also to serve as a reserve for Magen. Shortly thereafter, at 1055, Gonen found that Magen had some difficulties. Magen's task so far had been to defend toward the west, and he was deployed along a very extended line from Vitamin-Vada'ut to Sarag. Thus, while Gonen wanted Magen to begin his move at 1300 hours, the latter informed him that he would be able to get underway only at 1500.

At 1220 Gonen contacted Magen and me to change his earlier decision. I would attack first, and Magen would move in after me and operate on my west flank. We were to begin at 1400 hours. I received this order with no little enthusiasm. At last we were going to complete the encirclement of the Third Army — that is, to cut off two and a half divisions with thirty thousand men, along with about three hundred tanks and a similar number of artillery pieces. But this would be no easy task. The entire division was totally engaged in fighting and in taking prisoners. My forward command group went into intensive activity to prepare the attack. We decided first to disengage Gabi, who was operating more to the north, or rear. I directed Aryeh and Gabi to meet in the field so that Aryeh could take over Gabi's sector. While they were still coordinating the move, Natke radioed to inform me that one of his battalions had by mistake reached the edge of the greenbelt at a point too far to the north — in Aryeh's sector. Natke asked that I alert Aryeh to this so as to preclude any firing by Aryeh's forces at this battalion in the belief that it belonged to the enemy.

An idea crossed my mind: Since one of Natke's battalions was already in Aryeh's sector, what if I were to expand Natke's zone of operations by giving him Aryeh's entire sector, and so pull out a second brigade — Aryeh's — for the southward attack? I thought it over: Fine, Natke would get Aryeh's sector, but then what of Gabi's sector, which Aryeh was to have received? Encirclement of the Third Army was more important than the mopping-up of the greenbelt. It was essential to have two brigades take part in the southward push, but to leave Natke on his own in a sector of 25 km dotted with Egyptian army camps in which were still many enemy troops and where the greenbelt was alive with resisting enemy forces — that would be an unreasonable move. Improvisation, that's what we needed. Well, my deputy, Dovik, was no mean fighter. Dovik was then in the field, helping Gabi absorb the newly arrived infantry troops. I called Dovik to tell him that Gabi was about to move southward and that he — Dovik — should take his armored infantry and the airborne infantry as well as the divisional engineering unit and assume responsibility for Gabi's sector. Dovik said he would be pleased to do so and requested only that I dispatch to him officers and vehicles for a small forward command group.

My staff officers were working with much exhilaration. Gilad was attaching and detaching infantry and armored infantry battalions from brigade to brigade, coordinating sectors, and updating the brigade commanders on the changes of forces, sectors, and missions. My division communications officer, Leibel, was perspiring freely. A very hefty man weighing in at about 220 pounds, he was an efficient

staff officer, possessed of energy, initiative, and organizational ability. Above all, he excelled in human relations, knowing how to get the
most out of his men. He may not have looked the combat type, but
now he was running about among the vehicles of the forward command group, splitting it in two in order to build a second command
group for Dovik: an operations officer, an assistant intelligence officer, an assistant artillery liaison officer, a communications officer.
Time was pressing; we wanted to move out to the south as soon as
possible.

In the meantime, Gabi's and Aryeh's brigades were pulling out of
the greenbelt and from the area of the camps, deploying on the Pach-
Havit axis in a line 8 km wide. Aryeh would attack on the left (the
east) and Gabi on the right (the west). I had already designated a
bombing line south of the Mina-Sam line, and our planes were now
ripping the area apart. We requested special aerial treatment of
Missile Base 4925. According to the information we had received, the
Third Army's forward command group was located there. Gabi was
instructed to search them out during his southward assault and try to
take the generals there prisoner. Just as Gabi and Aryeh were about
to move out — at 1500 hours — I radioed them to say that when
seven tank battalions were charging ahead in a relatively narrow sector with massive air support, we expected them to reach the Gulf of
Suez before dark.

Magen's forces had also been engaged in combat since morning.
The Egyptian forces to the west tried to break through to the east
along the Asor and Sarag roads, but Magen's forces contained them
and inflicted heavy casualties on them. Gonen informed me that
Ran's brigade from Magen's division — which was deployed on Akal
— was to join our attack, assaulting from the west. We spent some
time coordinating sectors, but in the end their assault was delayed
because they were waiting to be replaced at Mitznefet by Sharon's
forces, who were late in arriving.

So it was just my two brigades on the charge, and once again
there was the pleasurable sight of columns of dust-raising tanks
rushing across the plain full speed ahead. We had to cover about 20
km of open terrain which, while it seemed to be flat, was in fact marked
by low hills, many wadis and was crisscrossed by connecting trenches. It
was really surprising to see that the Egyptians were dug in "Through

the length and breadth of Egypt.'' On many hills we still saw the radar installations of the missile sites. At many of the defensive localities there were concentrations of vehicles, some camouflaged, others in motion. We saw few enemy tanks in the field. Hundreds of Egyptians were killed in our assault, and thousands fled in every direction; we had no time to stop and take them prisoner. Gabi's and Aryeh's reports spoke of much military equipment being abandoned by the fleeing Egyptians: artillery batteries, SAM-2 and SAM-3 missiles, vehicles of various types, and even tanks. Even as those forces were speeding southward, excellent reports kept coming in from Natke and Dovik as well; there, too, things were proceeding apace. The Kabrit Peninsula had been mopped up, and we had captured some fifteen PT-76 amphibious tanks. The Third Army forces on the west bank seemed to be in an advanced state of disintegration.

But now some difficulties arose on Aryeh's left flank. Even before we had launched our assault, Aryeh had expressed apprehension over the greenbelt, which at this point extended as far as the Havit axis. It later emerged that the Egyptians' 19th Infantry Division had transferred a Sagger missile company westward during the night, and they were now letting loose at Aryeh. Even though Aryeh had been moving — as decided when the original attack order was given — fairly far from the woods of the greenbelt, some of his tanks were hit, and his pace was slowed. I ordered Natke to step up his southward advance through the greenbelt in order to cover Aryeh's flank; he gave it a try, but the essence of his operation was a mop up on foot, which is a slow process. Ultimately, Aryeh reached only the Shalufa Airfield, 10 km north of Suez City, but Gabi pushed on farther to the south.

About an hour after dark the encirclement of the Third Army was complete. Gabi had reached the Suez Gulf, taking the fertilizer plant on the outskirts of Suez City. Great news! Now even if a genuine cease-fire should come into force, we would have improved conditions, not only for the cease-fire per se, but also for the total decimation of the two Egyptian divisions — the 7th and the 19th — trapped on the east bank, should the fighting resume. Gonen now radioed to inform me that Magen would push southward and storm the Port of Adabiya. I contacted Magen, who was still far behind us, to explain to him where our forces were deployed. An hour went by and still no sign of him. I called him again to suggest that since he was moving through an area my division had already taken, why not use his lights to illuminate the way? He agreed, and suddenly we saw hundreds of lights come on and pierce the darkness far to the north. At 2300 hours Magen's forces passed through Gabi's lines, shut off their lights, and continued southward to capture the Port of Adabiya and deploy a few kilometers to its south. The following morning Israeli Navy boats entered the port. Now the Third Army was encircled, blockaded, locked in tight. The twenty-third of October — the eighteenth day of fighting in the war — was over. Would it be the last day?

No new orders had been received from Southern Command. I assumed that two main possibilities were now open: either to maintain the cease-fire, in which case I still foresaw fighting in the greenbelt zone necessary to complete our mop up there and extend the area under our control; or, to continue the annihilation of the trapped Third Army, which would mean our recrossing to the east bank of the canal. On the previous day we already had been directed to search in the Egyptians' crossing area for an intact bridge or one that could be repaired.

At about midnight, I instructed the brigades to prepare for and plan another day's fighting. Gabi would encircle Suez City in a broad arc extending from the Gulf north to the Havit Road. The other two brigades would mop up the greenbelt while being on the alert for the possible seizing of an Egyptian bridge. Aryeh's brigade, which was encamped north of the Shalufa Airfield, would carry on with its advance to tighten the encirclement of Suez City up to its outskirts and would then turn eastward to mop up the southern part of the greenbelt on both sides of the Eitza Road, from "Red" in the north to Eitza-88. Natke's brigade would continue mopping up the greenbelt north of "Red."

While the division was planning its coming moves according to my guidelines, General Headquarters and Southern Command were evaluating the situation while also awaiting the resolutions to be adopted by the Security Council, scheduled to convene at 0100 hours Israeli time. Following a consultation between the chief of staff and his staff officers, the trend that emerged was to tighten the noose around the Third Army to prevent its being supplied by sea. Thought was also given to some last-minute capture of positions. Missions assigned were, for that night, the capture of Ayun-Moussa, on the east side of the canal, and the landing of troops on Mount Ataka the following day. The taking of Mountain Ataka was important, and Dayan had been recommending it for several days now; but Bar-Lev, fearful for the fate of the attacking force, was objecting to such a move. Now that our forces had reached the foot of Mount Ataka, Bar-Lev withdrew his objections. At 2330 hours Gonen contacted the chief of staff to say that in his estimation Ayun-Moussa was too strongly held, and we should not attempt to take it. He added: "We might enter Suez City tomorrow morning, if it's empty."

Gonen then directed his staff: "We have to clean up the west bank and capture Suez City, provided it's empty." The guideline was passed on to Gilad, who in turn relayed it to Gabi and Aryeh.

Some time later, at 0130 hours (24 October) Ben-Ari radioed to inform me of my missions for the coming day: To mop up the entire divisional sector and seize all the ramparts in the area of the greenbelt in my sector, to cut off the water pipes from the west bank and from the Suez City suburbs to the Third Army forces on the east bank, and to capture Suez City "provided it does not become a Stalingrad situation." In reply I requested an intelligence update on the city. This I was given at 0550 hours, and the information was more or less what we already knew. In the city were a commando battalion that was holding the island of Port Ibrahim at the southern tip of the Suez Canal, the remnants of the 4th and 6th Divisions — apparently the equivalent of two mechanized infantry battalions — that had retreated there after being pounded by our forces over the past few days. We also knew that the 19th Division had transferred an antitank missile company from the east bank, which had already operated against Aryeh that afternoon.

Suez City was in the past a city of about a quarter-million inhabitants, but since the War of Attrition it had been a ghost town. Port Ibrahim was built on a sandy island southeast of the city and was connected to it by a jetty some 600 meters long and 15 meters wide on which were a road and a railway line. South of the city, along the Gulf of Suez, were various industrial plants, such as oil refineries, fertilizer plants, and an oil port. The densely built downtown area ran along both sides of the Cairo-Suez highway — the Sarag Road —

and the railway and consisted of buildings of two to five stories as well as some high-rises. Sarag, the main road, traversed the city in a southeasterly direction all the way to Port Ibrahim. Along most of its urban section it consisted of two lanes divided by the railway line that was protected on either side by a concrete strip 30 cm high. Not far from the outskirts of the city, and through it, ran the Sweet Water Canal, which was bridged on the Sarag and Pulhan roads.

The city was not empty, but we envisaged the collapse of the Egyptian forces there based on our experience of the mass surrender of the past two days. Therefore, I assumed that we would encounter no particular difficulties in capturing the city. The renewed cease-fire was to come into effect at 0700 hours, and our instructions were that anything not captured by then would be included in the mop up that would afterward have to be carried out in order for us to gain full control of the area we had taken. The main problem I faced was to deploy very quickly to carry out the attack.

A proper attack requires considerable preparation. In this case, all my infantry was separated and far from the tank brigades that were bivouacked near Suez City. (Most of the division's infantry forces were with Natke and Dovik, cleaning up the greenbelt and the Bitter Lake area, guarding prisoners, and seeing to captured materiel. They were spread out over the greenbelt and from the Panara camps to the Kabit Peninsula.)

The division now had some 175 tanks, about 60 in each brigade. In almost every tank battalion there was a reduced armored infantry company operating on armored personnel carriers or half-tracks. Our artillery strength consisted of two battalions supporting us from Havit-78 and an intermediate battalion operating from the east bank (at Lexicon-269).

We began hasty battle preparations — mainly regrouping. The forward command group issued orders to concentrate the infantry and have it set out at once southward to the brigades. Ivan's mechanized reconnaissance battalion, mounted on fifteen BTR-50 light-armored vehicles captured in 1967 and numbering 150 soldiers, finally arrived. At midnight the battalion was attached to Natke in order to help with the mopping up of the greenbelt. Baruchi's armored infantry battalion was detached from Dovik and moved toward Gabi's brigade, camped west of Suez City. Yossi's battalion, with 160 men, had joined the division the day before and had been placed under Dovik's command; now it was on its way to link up with Aryeh's brigade. Yossi's men were mounted on three buses and on nine captured "Topaz" amphibious armored personnel carriers. These vehicles were wholly improvised: Gabi's brigade had readied them for movement and had even put some of Yossi's qualified drivers through a "course" on how to drive them. The paratroopers had then hastily put together weapons and communications systems on these vehicles. Another arrival, at midnight of the previous day, had been Lieutenant Colonel Hisdai's force. He, along with eighty paratroopers mounted on two half-tracks and three trucks, had joined Aryeh's brigade.

The entire operation was in the nature of a last-minute, grab-what-you-can action. Since the second cease-fire was due to commence at 0700 hours, I decided to launch our attack at dawn, without waiting for the infantry to arrive, so that when the cease-fire did become effective, we would already be engaged, and it would take time — perhaps even some hours — until the troops could hold their fire after completing the mop up of the areas under their control. By then we would be holding all or most of the city.

At 0520 hours I gave the order. The attack would be opened by a large-scale preparatory air bombardment. Under its cover and that of an artillery barrage as well, the brigades would advance and form up with their attached infantry at the edge of the city. For Aryeh's brigade, this approach meant a southward advance of 8 km while capturing and mopping up the army camps situated north of the city. Only then would the two brigades burst into the city, with the Zer Road being their sector boundary. Gabi's brigade would move in from the west, take the industrial zone and push forward on the Pulhan Road, along the northern shore of the Gulf of Suez all the way to the oil port. Aryeh's brigade would move in from the north-west along the Sarag Road to capture certain key intersections in the city. The second echelon of Aryeh's brigade would then penetrate into Port Ibrahim along the connecting causeway while getting fire support from the first echelon that was on the gulf shore. Natke's brigade was to mop up the 24 km of the greenbelt, principally toward the south, and be on the alert to seize a bridgehead to the east bank if he found one intact.

The infantry battalions moving to link up with the tank brigades found the going rough. The area was not yet entirely free of enemy troops, and the fact that they were, in part, using enemy vehicles — even though these had been marked with identifying flags — increased tension, the men fearing they would be fired at by mistake by their own forces. Progress was further slowed because they hit mines and were fired on by Sagger missiles.

At 0600 hours Defense Minister Dayan had already landed at my forward command group. From him I learned that United Nations observers were on their way to the front and that the air support would stop at 0700 hours. The morning mist did not lift until 0630 hours, so that of the entire massive bombardment we had planned only four squadrons had managed to carry out sorties — a pretty poor softening up.

By 0830 hours, Aryeh's brigade had advanced southward while cleaning out military camps on its way to the city's outskirts. Resistance was light, though two tanks were hit from Sagger ambushes. Yitzhak's and Eliashiv's battalions stormed and mopped up camp after camp. Just outside Suez City, at the Sarag-Havit crossroads, Eliashiv overcame SV-100 tanks and antitank guns that were firing at him from between buildings. Thus he held the outskirts of the city preparatory to the attack into the city itself. Aryeh now had to await the arrival of the infantry.

While Aryeh was mopping up the city's approaches in his sector and awaiting completion of the preparations for the penetration, Gabi's brigade had also moved into action. It encountered no real resistance and moved into the industrial zone. Gabi's attack began at 0820 hours, moving along the Pulhan Road the moment Baruchi's armored infantry battalion arrived. First, the brigade's scout company, commanded by Dudu, crossed the small bridge over a branch of the Sweet Water Canal, securing the nearby area while at the same time seizing and cleaning out a few buildings.

Gabi's artillery support set a number of fuel tanks ablaze at the refinery, and thick black smoke and intolerable heat disrupted Gabi's operation. he immediately called off his artillery. Amir's battalion crossed the small bridge, passed through a suburb of villas, reached the oil port, and took up positions on its breakwater; from here he engaged Port Ibrahim and its connecting causeway with fire. Ehud's battalion moved in after Amir to sweep through the housing quarter of the industrial zone — with Baruchi's armored infantry mopping up behind him — until they reached the sector boundary at the Zer Road. Lapidot's battalion remained behind to secure the rear and hold all the road junctions west of Suez City, while Ze'ira's battalion covered from the northwest.

Since Gabi's brigade had successfully penetrated into the city encountering only very light resistance, I spurred on Aryeh, who had not yet completed his preparations for the move into the city. Yossi had in fact sped on ahead of his men and had met with Aryeh at 0700 hours. Aryeh explained his plan: Yitzhak's and Eliashiv's battalions would provide covering fire for the penetration from a broad sector on either side of Sarag, which would be the penetration axis. Initially, Aryeh had wanted to have the paratroops lead the attack into the city, but when he saw that they were delayed — and he would still have to brief them and have them complete hasty attack preparations — he suggested, and I agreed, that Nahum's tank battalion would lead the attack, his force to include both tank and armored infantry companies. Nahum's battalion would be followed immediately by Yossi's infantry and then Hisdai's force. (Aryeh had earlier directed Yossi to meet with Hisdai and attach him to his battalion.) The advancing column would be closed by the brigade's scout company on Zeldas.

The column was to press ahead without stopping while firing in all directions, and its mission was to seize three road junctions: that of the Sarag Road with the Sweet Water Canal; that of the Jema al Arba'in Mosque (henceforth, the Arba'in junction); and the junction of the Sarag Road and the causeway leading to Port Ibrahim (henceforth, the triangle junction). Simultaneously with this action, Gabi's brigade was to advance on the Pulhan Road up to the Zer Road and from there cover the breakthrough into Port Ibrahim. Only then would Yitzhak's and Eliashiv's battalions move along the Sarag Road to Port Ibrahim. When Yossi's battalion at last reached the outskirts of the city, all that Aryeh could do was offer him two maps and delay the breakthrough for thirty minutes, while Yossi briefed his men and issued his orders.

At 0930 hours Aryeh reported: "The picture is not yet clear.

There are tanks and antitank weapons among the buildings; we are engaged in combat. At this stage I'm holding up in order to get some more artillery support.''

Gabi also reported antitank fire from among the buildings. From the greenbelt, Natke radioed that he was exchanging fire with the east bank and had taken many casualties; he was at Havit-88.

"They aren't giving up, they are still fighting," he said. I spurred Natke to extend himself southward in order to assist in the effort against Suez City.

By now Aryeh had completed his preparations for the penetration into the city. Yitzhak's and Eliashiv's battalions were providing covering fire, the artillery was shelling the intersections. The attack began at about 1015 hours. Nahum's battalion, which was leading the column, had twenty-one tanks, seven Zeldas and eight half-tracks. They were formed as follows: eight tanks, followed by the Zeldas, more tanks, then the half-tracks and the rest of the tanks closing the line. Up to the Sweet Water Canal at the entrance to the city the battalion advanced while returning fire at the low buildings on its flanks. The column extended over about 2.5 km. As they moved deeper into the built-up zone, the buildings on their flanks were of six and seven stories. The low concrete wall on either side of the railway line made it impossible for the tanks to move from one street lane to another.

When the column reached the Arba'in junction, it came under a withering blast of fire. Simultaneously it was hit by flat trajectory fire from guns, antitank missiles, hand grenades thrown from balconies, and by bursts of automatic fire leveled at them by Egyptian soldiers who suddenly leaped out from the buildings. Within minutes nearly all the commanders were hit. In the entire battalion only four officers were left who could function; all the rest were slouched over in their turrets, dead or wounded. Control of the battalion was lost, the radio net jammed by too many cries for help. Some of the hit tanks had come to a halt, and the others could barely get by them. Some of the tanks and armored personnel carriers turned down side streets, some made it back, others were never again heard from or seen. Despite the chaos, battalion commander Nahum was able to revive some of the radio nets and contact radio operators or drivers who assumed command of their tanks. He managed to lead the column forward while returning fire in front and to the sides. The battalion reached the triangle junction (Sarag-95) near the causeway extending from the gulf shore. By now the battalion had suffered eighteen killed and about forty wounded. Two burned-out tanks remained on the penetration axis. At Sarag-95 the battalion halted in order to begin evacuation of the casualties and to pull hit vehicles off the road. Throughout they continued to fire in all directions.

Yossi's paratroop battalion, in its nine Topaz light armored personnel carriers and its three buses, was moving in Nahum's wake but was unable to keep pace. At the Sweet Water Canal crossing, a gap of 400 meters had opened up between the two battalions. When fire was opened on Nahum's battalion, Yossi ordered his men to dismount from their vehicles to begin fighting on foot. Aryeh's deputy, Carmeli, at once directed Yossi to have his men reenter their vehicles in order to catch up to Nahum's battalion. But precious time was lost until the battalion remounted and began moving again. Now when they reached the Arba'in junction, they encountered dense fire. Three soldiers were killed instantly and others wounded. Yossi — who was himself among the wounded, having been hit in the leg when his command vehicle came under antitank fire — ordered the men to evacuate the vehicles and take up positions in nearby buildings.

About 200 meters south of the Arba'in junction the local police station was located in a rectangular two-story building surrounded by a stone fence 80 cm high. Initially, Yossi's men took over the yard of the police station, as a young company commander named Dudu took command. He had the men mop up the lower first and then the upper story of the building. Twenty or thirty frightened policemen, who were huddled together in one of the rooms, were ordered to evacuate the premises. The wounded men were moved inside on the first floor, while the rest of the men were stationed on the second floor, and lookouts were positioned to cover all directions. Yossi's men quickly took two more nearby buildings. The wounded battalion commander continued to advise Dudu, though he would lose consciousness from time to time during the day. Dudu made certain that the troops did not fire indiscriminately so as not to run out of ammunition; nor did they have much drinking water. Several radio sets were brought into the building from the abandoned vehicles, but the first attempts at communication failed due to the screening effect caused by the many buildings in the area. Finally, Dudu went out to the yard where he at last succeeded in contacting Aryeh's artillery unit and also Aryeh's headquarters.

The police station was surrounded by buildings of four and five stories, from which there was relentless sniping; hand grenades were thrown and several attempts to storm the police station were even made. One of the assaulting Egyptians was shot right at the entry to the room where the wounded men were lying. The besieged battalion was informed of attempts by armored columns to link up with them and get them out. At first they were certain that this would be accomplished in short order, but the hours dragged by and still there was no link-up. The battalion's artillery liaison officer adjusted the artillery fire around the police station, and this proved their most effectual defensive measure.

When Yossi's force came under fire and his men abandoned their vehicles, he ordered those of his troops who were moving in the buses to evacuate them and to join Hisdai's force. Hisdai had already had his men dismount from their vehicles even before they reached the Sweet Water Canal. Aryeh's deputy, Carmeli, tried to get them to reboard. But when Hisdai heard of Yossi's encounter, he again abandoned his vehicles, and the men began moving by foot toward the Sweet Water Canal. Just as they crossed it, they came under fire, and Hisdai ordered them to take up positions in nearby buildings. Carmeli's small forward command group was hit; Carmeli himself took a bullet in the head and was evacuated to the rear. The brigade's intelligence half-track was seen turning into one of the side streets — and then it disappeared forever; all nine officers and sergeants in it were declared missing in action.

At the rear of the breakthrough column was the brigade's scout company, moving in seven Zeldas. They, too, were pounded by enemy fire and within seconds had suffered sixteen casualties. The company managed to get back.

At least a half-hour passed before Aryeh was able to renew communications with his forces in Suez City. Far more time would go by until the units were able to describe their locations and explain what had happened to them. The picture that Aryeh formed was that the column was scattered all along the Sarag Road, with Nahum's battalion at the triangle junction on the shore, Yossi's battalion besieged in the police station at the section junction that was to have been captured (the Arba'in junction), and Hisdai's force — along with part of Yossi's men — at the Sarag-Sweet Water Canal junction. But not only were these junctions far from being taken and mopped up, the forces themselves were trapped and besieged and had some seventy to eighty casualties with them.

At about this time, thinking of the possibility of seizing an Egyptian bridge, I was on the move to Shalufa Hill, from where I could have excellent observation of both the greenbelt and the east bank. The reports I received at 1100 painted a bleak picture. I immediately requested renewed air support. The approval was given, but Aryeh was not absolutely certain of where his men were and was afraid to have the city bombed. Having no choice, we began bombing Port Ibrahim. While this caused terrible outcries among the command battalion, it did not help relieve the pressure on our besieged forces. Aryeh was later able to pinpoint the location of his men so that we were able to bomb other parts of the city as well.

At 1130 I decided to try to ease the pressure on Aryeh's brigade and perhaps also to break the Egyptian resistance in the city by bringing in forces from Gabi's brigade along the Pulhan Road to the downtown area. At noon, Ehud's battalion reached the triangle junction and met up with Nahum. I now directed Gabi to send in his armored infantry battalion and place it under Aryeh's command. Soon Baruchi reached Nahum, who was still busy evacuating casualties and pulling out vehicles. Baruchi was able to move out most of Nahum's casualties along the Pulhan Road. Now Nahum and Baruchi consulted on how best to employ the armored infantry battalion. At first the soldiers dismounted from their half-tracks in an attempt to clean out the Cleopatra Hotel, the highest building in the area. In parallel, some half-tracks were moving on the Sarag Road to evacuate casualties. The briefing to the soldiers for the capture of the Cleopatra Hotel as well as other high buildings in the area consumed a lot of time — and their capture did not bring about any concrete results. The battalion was then called down from the buildings and sent to move, while firing, on two side streets parallel to the Sarag Road to the west, in the hope that this would cause an Egyptian collapse and enable a link-up with Yossi's forces. I don't know how many casualties the movement-and-fire action caused the enemy, but

Baruchi's battalion soon had twenty-three casualties, because the enemy had no trouble hitting soldiers in the open half-tracks. The battalion was forced to pull back to the triangle junction and from there to the Pulhan Road and out of the arena of fighting.

When I ordered Gabi to rush help to Aryeh along the Pulhan Road, I also concluded that we were liable to deviate from our order of taking Suez City provided it did not entail a costly battle — if, as Ben-Ari had put it, it was not a "Stalingrad situation." The question was how to halt the attack and extricate the trapped men without taking even more casualties. I ordered Aryeh not to send any more forces into the city except to help in the rescue of the besieged troops. Aryeh decided to make one more attempt at a link-up by sending Yitzhak's battalion along the Sarag axis. But as soon as the leading company crossed the Sweet Water Canal, it came under heavy antitank fire: Yitzhak's tank was hit, and he himself lightly wounded. The battalion was called back.

Meanwhile, Natke was fighting in many places in the greenbelt and was firing at the east bank near a point where he had found a bombed Egyptian bridge that we thought we could repair in order to send tanks across it, even though this kind of bridge required slow, cautious movement. Dovik was still busy mopping up and organizing our control of the area of the Kabrit Peninsula and the camps. I now had Dovik move over to Aryeh to assist in the evacuation operations. I also directed Natke to dispatch Ivan's mechanized reconnaissance battalion along with a tank company to the northeast corner of Suez City (to Eitza-88) where he would come under Aryeh's command. They would try to penetrate into the city from a new direction — the northeast — and link up with Yossi to evacuate his casualties.

Ivan had arrived from the center of Israel at around midnight of 23 October, with fifteen BTR-50 light armored vehicles (captured in the 1967 war), and before dawn of the twenty-fourth he was fighting in the greenbelt south of Shalufa under Natke's command. Shortly after he went into action, one of his vehicles took a direct hit from a tank on the east bank, and all the men in it were killed. Some of his other vehicles were evacuating casualties. When he got Natke's order — at noon — to join the battle of Suez he set out with less than 150 soldiers on the nine armored vehicles he had left, along with five tanks Natke had given him. He left two tanks behind to secure his rear at Eitza-88 and from there he began to advance along the Eitza axis — it was now 1415 hours. The two lead tanks failed to turn off to the Sarag Road but continued to move instead on the Eitza axis. Ivan himself did turn on to Sarag, firing without letup in every direction, while himself being fired on and sustaining casualties. According to Aryeh's arrangements, Ivan was to look for chairs along the side of the road — chairs thrown out of the windows of the police building by Yossi's men serving to pinpoint and identify our troops. Ivan failed, however, to notice the chairs. In the meantime, the two erring lead tanks had corrected their course and turned onto the Sarag axis; but even though they passed by Yossi's force, they did not spot it. Ivan and his tank company, who were now moving west on Sarag in order to exit the city, suddenly noticed — amid all the exchanges of fire — soldiers from Hisdai's pinned-down force. Ivan left the tank company with them, while he himself moved to Sarag-91 where Aryeh's forward command group was located.

As a result of Ivan's foray, Aryeh now had precise and verified information concerning the location of the besieged paratroopers. At Aryeh's order, Ivan, along with the Zeldas of the brigade's scout company, returned at 1600 hours to attempt a rescue of Hisdai's trapped men. Ivan's force returned within fifteen minutes. At first the men of Aryeh's forward command group thought he had failed, but it quickly emerged that the mission was accomplished. This breakthrough, too, demonstrated that armored personnel carriers were the most suitable vehicles for fighting in a built-up area. They charged in, each Zelda firing its three machine guns like mad in every conceivable direction — including upwards. Within minutes Hisdai's men had placed their sixty casualties on the Zeldas, and the force broke out again. The evacuation was a success, with only six wounded men, for whom there had been no room, now remaining with Hisdai.

Just 3–4 km north of Suez, on the Sarag Road, Aryeh's medical company was deployed. Close by it was a second such company that Dovik had brought. Near them helicopters landed for a quick evacuation of the wounded. About 140 men were treated at these field hospitals, and it was thanks to the treatment they received and to their quick evacuation that most of them survived.

It would be dark within a half-hour, and still the basic situation remained unchanged. We had many forces within the city, some of them stationary and besieged, others mobile but standing their ground and firing. I had to decide what to do next. I was worried that nightfall would exacerbate the situation of the tanks in the city, and I decided to pull out those forces that could be moved out. The battalions moved out westward on the Pulhan Road — Ehud's, Baruchi's, and Nahum's forces, with Amir's battalion as rear guard.

Still trapped and besieged in the city were Yossi's and Hisdai's forces. We were confronted with a real dilemma now; should they be ordered to try to filter their way out by themselves? That would be a very high-risk move, the more so since they had wounded men to see to. What about another attempt at an armored breakthrough to evacuate them? A nighttime penetration into a built-up area is a highly complex operation, and any such attempt would have to be postponed until morning. But I had received reports that the enemy was now mining the road and setting up obstacles on it, as well as positioning antitank weapons. I decided that they should try to extricate themselves during the night. If this failed, we would employ armored forces again the next day. I issued the appropriate order to Aryeh.

In my mind's eye I pictured the extrication of the men of the strongpoints. Of those who had dared, most had made it. But one needed luck. The operation would be relatively easy for Hisdai, complicated for Yossi. Nearly all of Hisdai's casualties had been evacuated already, and he was just 2 km from our lines. He made his preparations during the day and began his pullout under the cover of darkness and artillery support. He moved out led by a strong advance guard. The wounded men were in the middle of the column, and he led a strong rear guard. In line with advance coordination, Yitzhak's tanks lit up the sky with spotlights. After crossing the Sweet Water Canal on a bridge and on a smaller bridge intended for a water pipe, Hisdai and his men reached our lines at 2030 hours.

Yossi's ninety men, among them twenty-three wounded, were besieged in the city center, 4 km from our lines. Yossi himself was unconscious most of the time. Lieutenant Dudu, who had assumed command, saw no possibility of getting out because he was so deep in the city. He thought it would be far simpler to wait for daylight to be extricated by an armored force. Aryeh tried to convince him to move out on his own, but his efforts dragged on and on and nearly broke down altogether. Finally, with great unwillingness, he agreed and said they would try to slip out of the city toward our lines in small groups. However, Aryeh rejected this, asserting that they must make the attempt as one group that could both carry the wounded and defend itself, fighting its way out if attacked. Now Lieutenant Colonel Hisdai took the microphone to carry on with the persuasion efforts. He himself had just made it out a short time before, and he was acquainted with Dudu; their conversation was fruitful and resulted in the drawing up of a plan for organizing the force and for a route of escape.

In the meantime, Gonen contacted Dudu directly and was told that he was being called on to move out on his own, whereas he would rather wait until the following day so as to be rescued by an armored column. Dudu explained his difficulties to Gonen, and Gonen accepted his point of view. Now Aryeh called me to explain that after hours he had managed to convince Dudu to pull out, and then Gonen had intervened and spoiled the whole matter. I contacted Gonen and made it clear that we well understood Dudu's apprehensions and were well aware of how complex this extrication effort would be. I went on to ask Gonen whether he was aware of the rescue efforts that had been made during the day and of their cost in blood. Gonen now changed his mind, called Dudu again, and — with the aid of an aerial photo — tried to pinpoint his location and guide him in an exit route. But Dudu had no such map, and Gonen's explanations seemed to him complicated and abstract. Meanwhile, battalion commander Yossi had regained consciousness and after hearing Dudu's report said he favored moving out by night. Aryeh's unequivocal order to commence the pullout within ten minutes provided the final impetus. Dudu called all the soldiers in the adjacent buildings to him; stretchers were brought from the armored personnel carriers outside the police station.

At about 0230 hours, under cover of artillery, Yossi's men moved out toward the north. Just two of the wounded men were carried on stretchers; all the rest, including Yossi who was wounded in his foot, walked, supported by their comrades. They moved along a side street north of and parallel to Sarag, passing Egyptian units — but they were not fired on. Leading the column was an advance guard, which reconnoitered the way; in the middle were the wounded, who were accompanied and secured; and finally came the rear guard. Dudu himself ran back and forth along the entire length of the column, checking the wounded men and ascertaining that the force was moving as one unit. They crossed the Sweet Water Canal on the small railway bridge north of the highway bridge, and at 0445 hours linked up with Yitzhak's battalion.

The officers at all levels who were following their progress with bated breath could now breathe more easily — but the price we had paid for the fighting in Suez City was appalling: 80 killed or missing, about 120 wounded and evacuated.

While Gabi and Aryeh were fighting in the city (24 October), Natke's battalions were engaged in trying to complete the mopping up of the greenbelt toward the south from Bitter Lake to the suburbs of Suez. At dawn the members of Natke's forward command group were having coffee around a bonfire at their encampment by the Shalufa Airfield not far from the greenbelt in an area considered to be empty of enemy troops. Suddenly a burst of automatic fire and antitank missiles slammed into the group, wounding the deputy brigade commander, Haike, and half the staff officers. Immediately the scout company charged into the greenbelt, killing dozens of Egyptians. But Natke was now left with a very depleted staff; we had to round up officers and improvise a new command group for him.

This incident illustrates the problem we faced in our fighting in the greenbelt that day and in the days to come. Time and again we encountered Egyptians in areas we had thought mopped up. Some of them were hiding in the dense vegetation; some took cover in bunkers that we missed in our rapid combing operations; some even swam across the canal from the east bank. In addition to the two battalions that were already holding the Zidon and Kilo-Mina zones, Natke employed Ivan's mechanized reconnaissance battalion vis-à-vis the south. When that battalion was dispatched at my order to join Aryeh, this meant that the sector of Ze'evik's battalion was widened. Natke's only infantry forces were Yaya's battalion and the armored infantry "Banana" company.

Two armored personnel carriers — one from Ivan's unit and one from "Banana" company — had been hit by tank and antitank fire from the east bank. So it was not only a problem of concealed men, tanks and antitank weapons in the greenbelt, but also one of coping with fire from the other bank. Some of the hidden tanks were destroyed with relative ease, but dealing with the infantry units was far more difficult and called for caution and patience. Nonetheless, Natke's men were deployed along the entire southern greenbelt (at Lima, Red, Seter, and Leset). The Egyptians' behavior was inconsistent, not to say contradictory: on the one hand there were officers and men who swam across the canal to give themselves up, while others continued to put up resistance — and there were instances in which Egyptian officers fired at their own soldiers who were trying to surrender to us. Our search for a bridge proved fruitless. The bridges we did find were either destroyed beyond repair or folded up on the east bank. Natke had fifteen killed and about thirty wounded. Most of the greenbelt was in his hands, but it was still dangerous to wander about there, as from time to time the Egyptians would suddenly open fire.

Company commander Major Brick from Assaf Yaguri's battalion was one of the few tank personnel who had not been hit or taken prisoner when it charged the Hizayon Strongpoint on 8 October. In the intervening two weeks, Brick had gone through quite a bit. What he related of his experiences on the last day of fighting, 24 October, well illustrates what we had to cope with in the greenbelt: "We were moving toward the road junction. To our right were impassable swamps and on our left was the earth rampart with openings toward the other bank. My tanks were moving behind the paratroops. At one point I got a report of a tank in motion 400 meters from us. While the tanks in front of me moved aside, I remained exposed and the tanks fired at me. What I remember from that moment is smoke and being thrown in the turret. I shouted to the driver over the intercom to shift left fast. There was no reply. Then I realized that the driver was dead. Immediately I gave an order to abandon the tank. Only now did I notice that the cupola had been hit — I came out alive by a miracle, with just a few light wounds to add to those I already had. From a nearby half-track I ordered one of my tanks to approach. Its crew got out and my crew (except for the driver, who had been killed) got in. This was the seventh tank I had been in during the war. The six previous ones were all hit and I had to replace them."

Although wounded, Brick was not evacuated and continued to

command the small tank company. Paratroopers were dispatched to eliminate the enemy tank from up close, and at the same time our artillery opened up. Brick's force continued to advance along the road, constantly being fired at from the openings in the rampart.

All that day, while my division was engaged in Suez City and in the southern greenbelt, Magen's division fought across a very broad sector. During the morning they mopped up the Port of Adabiya area, destroyed enemy tanks, and took over the port. They took 1,200 prisoners, among them officers from the Red Sea Headquarters. West of there, Magen's division held and stabilized our western line of contact from the Vitamin-Uvda junction through Missile Sites 5518 and 5519, which were opposite Bolognia, up to the Sarag-Arish junction at km 101 from Cairo. By then, Magen's division had already been reinforced by Fedale's mechanized brigade. The division's main battle took place at the Aghroud camps close to the Akal-Sarag junction. Natke had already attacked this area from the north on 22 October until we had been pressed by Southern Command to halt that assault in order to speed eastward. There were still Egyptians in this pocket; the bunkers there housed the command posts of the Third Army and the 6th Mechanized Division, and some thirty enemy tanks were still active there. Magen moved reinforcements to the area from the Adabiya zone. He attacked in the afternoon with effective air support and captured the camps and bunkers at about twilight. Many of the Egyptian troops fled southward and westward, bypassing the small force stationed at km 101. Also on that day, helicopters landed Israeli forces on Mount Ataka, and these were placed under Magen's command.

Sasson's, Granit's and Sharon's forces were already maintaining the cease-fire, and now Magen's and my division also joined the cease-fire, since we held an immense expanse on the west bank as well as about a third of Suez City. We now had to get ready to receive United Nations observers who would try to get between the opposing sides to stabilize "cease-fire lines" the next day. At the same time, we prepared fully for the possibility that the enemy would resume the fighting.

The morning of the twenty-fifth found us with Gabi's brigade alone holding the section of Suez City that we had captured, Natke's brigade holding the greenbelt, and Aryeh's brigade engaged in a brief reorganization prior to being given the southern half of the greenbelt from Natke.

The United Nations observers arrived. Here and there some skirmishes occurred, and we all wondered whether the United Nations staff would succeed in stabilizing the cease-fire. We were in for a surprise. When the observers moved between our lines and the Egyptian lines on the Sarag Road in Suez City, scores of Egyptian soldiers burst out of the buildings and ran toward our tanks, shouting and cheering and waving their arms. They apparently felt that they had just had their lives given them as a gift. They soon surrounded our tanks and embraced our embarrassed soldiers. Following this spontaneous display, their commanders arrived to take them back across the lines, and they disappeared from sight. Things were different in the greenbelt; when the United Nations observers showed up there, Egyptian soldiers suddenly popped up at our rear and demanded that our lines be moved back. Now the observers were embarrassed and bewildered, not knowing what to do. However, our resolute stand led to the lines being drawn according to our forward positions.

The cease-fire was now established, but would it hold? After all, the Third Army was cut off, and we knew that there were some two thousand casualties there as a result of our air strikes of the past few days. We had cut off their water and fuel pipelines. We had taken huge reservoirs of fuel and ammunition. They were besieged! Unquestionably, we held the power of life and death over the entire Third Army. That was a real bargaining card!

It had been a long road for the division since 7 October. Starting out from Baluza in the north, after eighteen days of fighting we had reached Suez in the south. Surprised, we had been badly bruised — but not broken. We gritted our teeth and fought back, accumulated strength, attacked, and forced the enemy to ask for a cessation of hostilities — though it was unfortunate that a cease-fire had come into force before we finished the job.

CHAPTER THIRTY-TWO

REFLECTION AND REASSESSMENT

I shall begin by discussing the battle of Suez City first, before turning to the overall campaign of encircling the Third Army, which brought us from the area of bridges to the Gulf of Suez and km 101. In my view, the capture of Suez City could not have contributed to the encirclement operation itself, and I do not accept Dayan's outlook (as stated in his autobiography) that the taking of the city would have led to the surrender of the Third Army. Although I was an active partner to the decision on the thrust southward and on completing the Third Army's encirclement, I did not initiate the conquest of the city because I envisaged that the encirclement would be achieved without it. However, when the order was given I made no objection, mainly because the taking of the city would have strengthened our control along the entire length of the Suez Canal in my sector and rendered even more total the cut-off of the Third Army on the east bank from water sources. Moreover, the mission was not necessarily to conquer the city but to attempt it. If it went well, we would press on; if not, we would leave it. It should also be borne in mind that the conquest of Suez City was not our only task for 24 October. The division was charged with completing the capture and mopping up of the west bank, in particular the entire length of the greenbelt, and to seize the ramparts in my sector; to cut off the Third Army's water sources, some of which were in the eastern suburbs of Suez City; and, above and beyond all this, to try to seize a bridge and gain the capacity to cross to the east bank.

Our success in the battle to conquer the city was only partial, and our losses were heavy. But it is not only for this reason that this is a subject worth going into; the day's events also offer lessons concerning armored fighting in a built-up area. The order stated: "To capture Suez City, if it does not become a Stalingrad situation." This formulation contained a highly untypical and very exceptional reservation vis-à-vis a military mission; and, I must admit, I understood it very well. The spirit of the order was that in the light of the signs of disintegration of the Third Army — signs that were visible in the field the previous day — Southern Command assumed that the city could be taken without entanglement in a battle. I also found this an acceptable assumption. We had suffered hard losses in this war, and if the nut proved too hard to crack, we would forego it — that is how I understood the order.

Even given these assumptions, the question was, were we capable of carrying out the mission? To this there is no cut and dried answer. Not only were we tense and tired after seventeen straight days of fighting, but we faced many concrete problems of which the main one was the lack of infantry in the intended zone of combat. It would take time to move the infantry from the Bitter Lake area to Suez City and to attach it to Aryeh's and Gabi's brigades — and time was just what we did not have. The cease-fire was imminent. The dilemma of whether to accept the mission or to reject it, in view of the considerable difficulties it presented, I solved in the fighting spirit that characterized the division throughout the war. Certainly there were difficulties — but with an effort we could overcome them. And it was in this spirit that the brigade commanders once again responded to the tasks given them.

In retrospect, I regret that the mission was assigned, and even more that I did not object to it. The reason is simple. We were very sensitive to more casualties, so it would have been better not to try to take the city, especially in light of the fact that its conquest could not have altered the strategic situation.

The capture of a city is always a complicated operation. A city offers many advantages to a defender, enabling him to put up stiff resistance in house-to-house fighting. So the conquest of a city always involves a good deal of fighting, takes time, and results in substantial losses. Armored forces are not the most suitable ones for the conquest and mopping up of a built-up area. The enemy can seal off streets with relative ease and hit combat vehicles from short range. Nonetheless in the Armored Corps we had dealt with the subject of capturing built-up areas — though this had been mainly in the realm of theory — including tactical exercises without troops. Live-ammunition training and exercises were limited due to the lack of suitable sites (built-up areas) for training.

The general lines on which armor usually copes with a built-up urban area are based on several phases. First, bypassing the city while cutting off all the traffic routes connecting it with its environs. Then encirclement of the city while taking the positions dominating its outskirts and, if possible, also buildings inside the city. In the following phase, armored columns break through into the city, moving on parallel streets and scattering fire in all directions while staying on the move. The aim of the movement-and-fire is to defend the advancing column, sow destruction, inflict losses on the enemy, and — most important — to undermine his confidence in his ability to resist and paralyze him. The armored columns move directly to the key objectives: to the main government buildings, the broadcasting stations, to high buildings that dominate their surroundings, and to the major intersections that control traffic routes within the city. Following the takeover of these intersections, armored columns continue to roam about the streets, still bent on destruction and shock. Then on to the neighborhoods or the blocks of buildings where pockets of resistance are pinpointed; these are rooted out and mopped up by infantry in house-to-house fighting. It was with very similar techniques that the IDF took Gaza in 1956 and 1967; and Nablus, Ramallah, and Jenin in 1967. The conquest of East Jerusalem in 1967 was, however, different. That operation began with infantry troops engaging in house-to-house fighting with support from just a few tanks; and it concluded with the rapid breaking of resistance as armored columns moved in from the north.

The ability to employ armor in this manner within a city requires training and knowledge of the techniques of producing fire upwards and in all other directions, as well as the capacity to maneuver and overcome street-blocking obstacles. In practice, the grouping of the force is a combination of tanks, armored infantry, and combat engineers in the smallest possible units — to the point of being able to advance in a column consisting of one tank, one armored personnel carrier, followed by another tank, another armored personnel carrier, etc. If the streets are wide, movement is in pairs or platoons (trios) of tanks and armored personnel carriers, alternately.

In order to conquer Suez City — "provided there is no Stalingrad situation" — we thought we would employ the armor technique of bursting in while firing all around in order to produce a shock effect. We believed that a massive aerial bombardment, over a few hours, along with a sustained artillery barrage, would prepare the ground for the armored breakthrough. The cumulative effect of all this would, we thought, lead to the surrender of the city.

But things developed differently. Even though the basic combat preparations were made under pressure of time, the basic elements of the divisional plan existed. The city was cut off — its encirclement from outside had been completed that morning — and tank battalions dominated its outskirts. Because of the heavy morning mist, however, the air force commenced its bombardment late and had to break it off early — within a half-hour of its start — because of the formal cease-fire. This was of course a mistake that enabled the Egyptians to recover, the more so as the brunt of the artillery barrage did not land on the city itself but supported Aryeh in the capture of the camps north of the city. Nonetheless, the indications were that the city could be taken in the face of light resistance only. Gabi, who moved in first, encountered virtually no resistance, and no movements or preparations for combat were sent from Aryeh's direction.

Because of the Sweet Water Canal, which runs through the west of the city, Nahum's tank battalion moved in only along the main street. His mistake was in not breaching the low concrete fence which ran along the middle of the street. Had he done so, he would have been able to deploy across a wider area, thus enabling better fire production to the front, mutual covering fire, and better maneuverability. Nor was the combination between tanks and armored infantry — though there was grouping of forces within the advancing battalion — good enough. The optimal grouping would have been tank, armored personnel carrier — tank, armored personnel carrier, etc., rather than in companies (even if small ones) of tanks and armored infantry, alternately.

The major weak point of the attacking forces lay in the infantry troops who were rushed to the division. These infantry forces were neither equipped for nor trained in combined combat with armor. Not only were Yossi's and Hisdai's forces not organic to the division, but they themselves consisted of companies that had joined up on the battlefield, without being acquainted with one another. Their training led them to aspire to fight on foot, and this was given greater impetus by the fact that they were moving on buses and trucks, rather than on armored vehicles. And even those who were mounted on captured armored vehicles lacked the installations that enable firing through movement. In short, neither their equipment nor their vehicles, neither their training nor their inclinations fitted them for armored action — and, in fact, in the field they had soon separated themselves from the armored forces.

This was an unsuitable force that was committed hastily on the basis of assumptions that did not materialize. The trouble was that once it became apparent that the mission could not be accomplished as easily as had been thought, the intended disengagement was far from simple to achieve. The armored forces that were caught could, despite their losses, make their way out. The infantry forces dispatched to accompany them, however, even though they were among the IDF's best fighting men, were unsuitable for combined-armor combat. And when they were caught, their extrication became a difficult task, entailing many losses. Once again the weak point of the lack of balance in the structure of the IDF was demonstrated: the armored operation was affected precisely at its weakest link, i.e., absence of properly equipped complementary forces. Thus in the actual — not the assumed — circumstances, an armor-type operation was unjustified, while an infantry-type action was impractical within the framework of the forces and within the time and the space at our disposal.

To draw lessons from the battle of Suez concerning the ability of a combined armor-infantry force to capture a city in the face of tough resistance is difficult because we called off the attack when it became apparent that we were encountering hard enemy resistance.

The fact that the armored columns did in fact pass through the city in the face of resistance attests to the technique's latent potential. But clearly we did not have good, well-trained armored infantry, and two hundred paratroopers are a negligible force for this kind of mission. The faulty cooperation between these two elements only detracted from the effectiveness of the forces.

When I move from the Battle of Suez to the attempts made close to the cease-fire of 22 October — by Sharon to enter Ismailia from the direction of the purification plant, by Eliashiv to capture the rampart opposite Zidon, by Sasson to take Hamutal — I find that they all have a common denominator. The attempt to "grab" something at the last minute without a proper concentration of forces and without adequate preparations results in failure. Most of these attempts were undertaken hastily in the wake of time constraints the source of which lay in the favorable consideration we gave to political demands by the superpowers (via the United Nations). I cannot help thinking that if we had ignored these constraints and had taken the time we needed for preparations, if we had pounded the city from the air for a few hours, if we had taken the time to concentrate more infantry forces, to plan the battle and issue orders and give briefings, and to move up our artillery and have it employ flat trajectory fire as well — we would have enhanced our prospects of conquering the city. As it was, we did not maintain the cease-fire and did use the air force — but now it was to help get our forces out.

In a battle of advance and pursuit, many targets and areas are taken in a trial-and-error method. This is part of the art of war; sometimes it works, and sometimes it doesn't. Are we to conclude, then, that it doesn't pay to try for last-minute "grabs"? Undoubtedly it is best to refrain from them, and well-prepared operations are always to be preferred. At the same time, anyone who foregoes such "snatches" is also foregoing taking advantage of his success and is reducing his achievements. I'm afraid that proponents of the "art of war" will find it difficult to give an unequivocal answer to this question. That is why battle theory also holds with trial and error, with pursuing an evolving opportunity. Had we not acted in line with this, the map of Israel would look different today.

Six days and nights passed from the time we crossed the canal until we completed the encirclement of the Third Army. The planners of

Operation *Abirei-Lev* 2 had allotted thirty-six hours for the task. Moreover, had hostilities in fact ceased on the evening of 22 October, the mission would not have been carried out in full. Did we fight tardily? It was the inner perception of the IDF high command that when the tide of war turned against the Egyptians and in Israel's favor, a cease-fire was more likely to be imposed so that the enemy would have to be vanquished quickly. But in this war, that perception was blunted because of the repeated proposals for a cease-fire that were rejected by the Arabs and because of the prolonged and even nature of the fighting. In addition, there was the feeling that this time the "rules of the game" had changed, that the superpowers would not impose an early cease-fire.

It was against this background — the prevailing perception was that we had time — that maximum emphasis was placed on slow and careful fighting. And there was ample reason for this. The number of casualties grew higher and higher, units declined in strength, and there were no fresh reserves. So it was that orders came down from above along the lines of: "Charge cautiously," "No more breakthroughs," capture the target if it does not entail "busting your ass," "Conquer Suez City, provided it is not a Stalingrad situation."

The spirit and underlying conception of orders such as these led me not to press and spur my subordinate officers. The division's average rate of progress was 20-30 km a day. Only twice did we deviate from the "charge cautiously" directive: on the afternoons of the twenty-second and the twenty-third, when we launched classic armored assaults in broad, deep, powerful formations — on the twenty-second toward the canal and on the twenty-third toward the Gulf of Suez — because we knew we were in a race against time. Despite the enemy's stubborn resistance and despite the "cautious charges," we attained the pace that we did thanks to the armored style of fighting. Whenever we could, we left a part of the force to pin down the enemy, while we bypassed him with the main part of the division to penetrate into the enemy's depth in order to destroy "soft" targets, mainly missile sites. We moved in very deep at an early stage, reaching and cutting off roads from Geneifa and Suez to Cairo. We developed the fighting in the maneuverable expanses, to reach and crush the camps and clean out the greenbelt. Nor did we hesitate to leave behind enemy pockets — in the camps and in the greenbelt — to be mopped up at a later date. We tried to use the flanking approach whenever we could, but when we had to we attacked frontally.

Magen's tactics were similar to ours. His division was small — usually he had only some eighty tanks — and for much of the time he had a defensive mission, to secure the zone of operations toward the west. But Magen never stopped initiating moves, never stopped requesting offensive missions, and — most important — he never missed an opportunity to attack either during defensive tasks or in the last few days of the war, when he was reinforced and received offensive missions. He was able to extract the maximum armored potential from his forces.

Sharon's mode of operation was entirely different. After the crossing, Sharon's progress was limited to 3-5 km a day. His strength consisted of two small paratroop brigades and three reduced tank brigades, averaging eighty to one hundred tanks. (One of these brigades was positioned on the east bank of the canal.) Sharon also had difficulties that stemmed from differences between him and Southern Command on how to employ his division. They pressed him to develop his main effort toward Missouri, while Sharon wanted to make for Ismailia. But the truth is that his ambitions were disproportionate to the tank strength at his disposal. His pretensions lacked any realistic basis. And alongside the objective difficulties, Sharon's military tactics must come in for criticism.

He did not employ the armored forces he had correctly. He concentrated most of his efforts against the closed terrain of the greenbelt, generally in frontal attacks (except for the attack on Orcha). Had Sharon attacked the greenbelt through an indirect approach, he could have captured the Ismailia Canal bridges at Abu Suweir — where the greenbelt is very narrow — moved in an armored force to destroy the airfield there, and taken the other bridges from the rear. That move could have been accompanied by a chopping up of the greenbelt into a number of pockets, thus enabling the paratroopers to mop it up slowly, with the support of few tanks.

There is, then, a major contradiction between what Sharon's division accomplished and what was hoped he would do. How are we to account for this? Sharon's unreasoned employment of his forces is only a partial explanation. To this must be added the fact that the crossing operation decimated Sharon's division, and it never managed to recover from that blow. From a strength of 230 tanks, Sharon was reduced to about 100 — and these he had to employ on both banks. Had he recognized his limits, however, and made correct use of his tanks, he could have done more, as Magen did, with just 80 tanks. But Sharon preferred to put up the front of a vigorous and aggressive commander — though this was inconsistent with his division's capabilities — and thus created a situation that also became his motto after the war: "Had they [i.e., Southern Command] only permitted me . . . From the very outset of the war I wanted to cross, but they wouldn't let me. . . . When the crossing operation began I asked to transfer tanks to the west bank [when there was as yet no bridge] and again they prevented me. Later, I wanted to attack Ismailia — and once again they did not let me." And more to that effect. All these claims were well absorbed by the public. One hardly heard any claims concerning all the missions Sharon was assigned and did not carry out, or those he carried out at a slow pace that was totally disproportionate to his pretensions.

The IDF's plan called for the main effort to be concentrated on the west bank toward the south: to seize territory, destroy enemy forces, encircle the Third Army, and thus to alter the military balance and create the conditions for the defeat of the entire Egyptian armed forces. Did we implement correctly the "concentration of force" principle to achieve our main objective?

Southern Command decided, on the evening of 18 October, (consistent with the plan and objectives of Operation *Abirei-Lev 2*) that my division would attack southward toward Suez, while Sharon's division — with two brigades — would also attack southward, to my right (west). Sharon's third tank brigade and his two paratroop brigades were to remain at the bridgehead under the command of Sharon's deputy, Jackie. In addition to the two southward-moving divisions, Magen's reduced division was due to arrive and station itself as a reserve force at Maktzera with the aim of assisting either at the bridgehead or with the two divisions, according to how the situation developed.

Sharon was apparently not enthusiastic about splitting his division in two. That evening he succeeded in convincing Southern Command that his division should remain intact in order to defend the bridgehead and expand it northward. In my view, Southern Command was wrong to consent to this because the new plan meant that fewer forces would be committed in the main effort. It was subsequently decided that Magen would move south instead of Sharon, but this was not exactly the same thing. First of all, Magen had to expend too many detachments to secure the zone of operations westward; and secondly, his move southward was delayed because it was contingent upon his forces being relieved by Sharon's division. Furthermore, because Sharon's division was not split, Southern Command did not incline to take any of his forces for the main effort. In my opinion, the bridgehead could have been expanded northward with one tank brigade and the two paratroop brigades — and had it emerged that these forces were insufficient, another two or three tank companies could have been brought in from Sasson's and Granit's forces.

The question of the concentration of forces and of the pressure of time became more acute from 20 October, when Kissinger left for Moscow. The Government and the IDF high command were apprehensive that a cease-fire was imminent. There was still time to transfer forces from the east to the west bank in order to expedite the attainment of the designated objectives. But when Fedale's brigade and Emanuel's battalion were at last dispatched to join Magen, it was already too late.

Since no steps were taken to concentrate more forces on the west bank or measures taken to transfer forces from the east to the west bank in time — and because the pace of advance was as I have already described — the approaching cease-fire led to the problem of final lines we should strive for. Dayan, Dado, and Bar-Lev were all of the view that in order to hold comfortable lines, I must cease moving southward toward Sarag and instead seal off the area around Zidon and mop up the territorial continuity we would then have. My proposal — to close off the area toward Mount Ataka — was not accepted.

Fortunately, hostilities did not cease on 22 October, and we were able to complete our mission. Because time was running out, the decision was taken to try to make some last-minute "snatches" on the east bank too. Granit was given the task of driving a wedge toward Lituf, with the aim of linking up with the forces and thus enabling us to bridge the canal south of the lakes also. Sharon was to attack toward Missouri and widen the narrow corridor into Africa, this in coordination with

436 ENCIRCLING THE THIRD ARMY

Sasson, who was to attack toward Hamutal and Machsir and from there westward to the canal between the Timsah and Bitter lakes.

Sasson's and Granit's forces were too weak, however, and they did not concentrate enough forces, so that in fact nothing materialized from all these last-minute efforts. This development shows that it would have been preferable to concentrate more forces in the direction in which we had achieved initial success, that is, to have them join the main effort of a southward push on the west bank aimed at the total encirclement of the Third Army. But it was precisely then that Sharon suggested an attack on Ismailia, a purposeless move that would not have achieved any concrete strategic advantage but would certainly have diverted forces from the main southward effort.

When the time was short and the work still plenty and the Southern Command sought to activate the divisions to attain the final goals before the cease-fire, differences of opinion emerged between Southern Command and myself, in addition to the ongoing dispute between Sharon and Southern Command.

Differences at the operational command level usually stem from differences in the observation point and in the situation assessment. Such differences are natural and "permissible," provided that the resulting actions and inactions do not conflict with discipline. For about twenty-four hours I stuck to my view against Bar-Lev, Gonen, and Ben-Ari, all of whom insisted that I concentrate all my forces in an effort to reach Zidon and forego continuation of my push southward. Before dawn on 22 October, Southern Command gave its unwilling approval to my move, the argument having gone on without any clearcut decision being taken. But even obstinacy has a limit, and when the front commander determined, at noon that day, that I must halt Natke's southward thrust, I was compelled to agree — even though I remained convinced that the decision was a mistaken one.

The debate between Southern Command and Sharon was different in nature. Sharon did not want to carry out the order to capture Missouri, preferring instead to advance toward Ismailia. When he first received the order from Ben-Ari, he did not so much as hint at any objection. It was only the following day that Gonen found that for Sharon, Missouri was a secondary objective. Following the arrival of the chief of staff at Southern Command HQ, Gonen told

Sharon unequivocally that priority was to be given to taking Missouri and that the forces from the west bank were to be returned to the east bank to that end.

Sharon's reply: "Fine." But he went on with his activities on the west bank. This then is, first, ignoring orders and then ignoring the spirit of an order. Then when Southern Command ordered a second attack during the night to try to capture Missouri, Sharon reacted first by ignoring the order, then by refusing it, and finally by going directly to Dayan, thus bypassing both Bar-Lev and Dado.

I am well aware that a commander at the operational level could face the intolerable situation of being confronted with the dilemma of either to carry out an order against his conscience or to refuse to fulfill the order. In my view, military discipline does not afford the right to appeal against an operational order to a higher authority and certainly not to bypass the top echelons of army command. The choice facing a commander who arrives at such a situation is either to warn the higher echelons of his reasons for objecting to the mission and then to carry it out as best he can; or, in very extreme situations, to refuse to carry out the order and face the consequences; or to resign. This affair attests to the difficulties caused with regard to Sharon personally and is no indication of the situation within the IDF as a whole. On the Golan Heights, too, the campaign was a bitter one, but no such crises of command occurred there.

In five days of fighting (19–23 October), up to the unsuccessful attempt to take Suez City, the division covered about 100 km in which we fought against fresh formations of the 4th Armored Division and the 6th Mechanized Division. We destroyed about thirty missile bases, hit some two hundred tanks and many armored personnel carriers, threw back counterattacks, stormed infantry and armored formations that were holding army camps and entrenched positions, mopped up infantry troops in the greenbelt, and succeeded in encircling the Third Army — taking thousands of prisoners and capturing a great deal of military equipment. Most of the burden fell on our shoulders. We were able to stand up under it thanks to the support of Magen's division and the spirit of cooperation between us. Moreover, in the final two fighting days Magen's division was reinforced, and its operation on the battlefield was effective, leaving its mark on the southern and western borders of the salient we now held.

Cooperation with the air force also tightened and contributed greatly. We destroyed most of the missile bases, and in return enjoyed
close, massive air support that was of tremendous assistance to our
fighting in the last two days.

At any rate, the firing stopped. The front was quiet. The two armies faced each other tensely. The Third Army was surrounded, its
fate sealed even without fighting. All this meant that the situation
could not go on like this. Things were unstable; there had to be some
imminent shift. I did not know what exactly was going to happen.
What was clear was that I had to prepare the division urgently in case
the fighting resumed.

PART VI

CEASE-FIRE TO DISENGAGEMENT

CHAPTER THIRTY-THREE

FRONTLINE ALERT AND TRAINING

O n 25 October the firing ceased and United Nations observers began demarcating the cease-fire lines. But the campaign was not yet over. On the surface, the front would henceforth remain quiet, while the main effort shifted from the military to the political sphere. Even during the days of political activity, preparations continued in both armies for resumption of the fighting should the diplomats reach deadlock. Moreover, not many days would pass before the Egyptians and Syrians would commence artillery barrages aimed at wearing us down and weakening our staying power. The "situation in the field," the military situation as frozen at the end of the fighting, reflected the IDF's operational superiority. On the northern front, the IDF held a larger salient than before the fighting began, as well as the peak of Mt. Hermon (nearly 500 square km of enemy territory); and we held a broad, deep salient on the west bank of the Suez Canal on the southern front (some 1,600 square km). The Syrians had been totally repulsed from the Israeli-held Golan, while the Egyptians held only two shallow bridgeheads east of the canal, one of which was completely surrounded and the other threatened with the same fate. (The two Egyptian bridgeheads totaled nearly 1,200 square km.)

In the air, we had gained sweeping control in both arenas, and the enemy's antiaircraft defenses had withdrawn far into the rear of their territory. The Third Army was besieged and at the mercy of the air force and the threat of Israeli armor.

By our estimates, the enemy's dead totaled some 15,000 — of these, 11,000 Egyptians. Their wounded numbered about 35,000, of whom some 25,000 were Egyptians. In our hands were over 8,000 prisoners, most of them Egyptians. The enemy had lost some 2,300 tanks — about 1,000 of them on the Egyptian front — and about 500 artillery pieces. We, too, had many casualties: 2,222 killed in action on the two fronts, 5,596 wounded, and 301 of our men taken prisoner, of them 232 held by the Egyptians. Half of our casualties were from the Armored Corps, including many officers. Nearly every Israeli tank was hit during the war, but most of them were repaired — the majority in the course of the fighting — and ultimately only some 400 of our tanks and 25 artillery pieces were "wiped off the books."

When the fighting stopped, we had about 400 tanks on the west bank against about 250 Egyptian tanks. This situation would change in a matter of days. During the fighting, expeditionary forces from Iraq and Jordan had already arrived on the Syrian front, and now an inter-Arab force began to be organized in Cairo that consisted of a Libyan tank brigade and an Algerian mechanized brigade. In addition, Soviet arms deliveries, which had already begun flowing into Syrian and Egyptian seaports and airfields on 9 October would have their effect. Less than a month after the cease-fire, the Egyptians would have a renewed force of some 1,000 tanks on the west bank. Within three months of the cease-fire, they would have more tanks than they had when hostilities began; and of this number, some 1,500 were deployed against our forces on the west bank in the sector south of the Ismailia Canal.

On the Israeli side, too, the buildup of strength got under way as soon as the front was quiet and continued relentlessly. The number of tanks we received was far smaller than what the enemy had, but with an effort we managed to maintain the traditional balance of forces.

The problems we faced in strengthening our armed forces were far more complicated than those of the enemy. For war materiel, we had three sources. First, supplies from the United States. The initial planes of the American airlift began landing at Lod Airport on 14 October, and now heavy equipment that had been sent by sea began arriving at the front as well. Secondly, we captured enemy tanks, artillery pieces, and ammunition. Thirdly, tanks of ours that had been badly hit underwent major repair in workshops in the rear and were returned to active duty.

More serious still was our manpower problem. As noted, over half of our casualties were men of the Armored Corps, and now we badly lacked tank crews to operate the tanks that began to accumulate. The only way was to train new teams — and fast. But how to do this when all our armor was dispersed over the fronts and on high alert? The cease-fire seemed to be a very shaky thing, and there were apprehensions that the enemy was planning a major offensive to wipe out the "Israeli pocket." The enemy had even launched a "war of attrition" expressed by artillery fire, and we, too, were planning offensive operations in the event the fighting was resumed.

This then was the situation that characterized the prolonged period between the cease-fire and the disengagement of forces. Broad political activity in which the superpowers, and particularly the United States, were involved continued. We also continued to comb the areas of the greenbelt and the camps and to improve our hold on the west bank while making plans and preparations in case the cease-fire would be violated.

We began by examining our options for creating a canal-crossing capacity in our present sector so that we could move to the east bank and destroy the surrounded 7th and 19th Divisions there. However, close to midnight, 2 November, I was ordered to cross on our own bridges to the east bank with a part of my division. At midnight, Dado arrived at my forward command post to inform me of a discussion with the defense minister as to who should be assigned the task of attacking the encircled divisions. He told me that Dayan had said that he didn't care who got the assignment as long as it was my division. While this was flattering, I expressed my disappointment that the order meant I had to split the division, leaving part of it on the west bank. The chief of staff accepted my suggestion of a different allocation of forces, and soon the entire division set out. We were well organized and well oiled, and the move to the east bank was carried out at "armor pace." Before daylight we had completed our disengagement and covered the 50 km to the bridges. Soon we were on the east bank again, en route to the staging areas to prepare for the attack, now set for the fourth or fifth of November. The enemy had not even noticed our departure from the sector. We were replaced by other forces, under Magen's command. Magen was given responsibility for the entire southern section of the west bank. In addition, another force had now arrived in Sinai and was deployed to defend the narrow corridor to the bridgehead on the east bank. Sharon's division was now wholly on the west bank.

The division began intensive combat preparations. We carried out patrols and observation; we planned, issued orders, even held exercises. But the order to attack failed to come.

I felt that we must not waste time. The fighting had terminated. I had to look at the situation not only as a division commander but also, again, as commander of the Armored Corps, and find solutions for manning the tanks and restoring our armored formations. This was also an opportunity to train armored infantry reservists in combat from armored personnel carriers and to tighten cooperation between tanks and armored infantry. The process of training proficient tank crews and commanders of the various levels is a lengthy one and requires an entire school program. When the war broke out, the training system had been disrupted as everyone joined the fighting formations. All the teaching personnel were still at the front in a state of high alert. Yet the war could resume in another day, another week, or perhaps a month. And if it did begin anew, we must be at maximum strength.

My experiences in all of my country's wars dictated to me the need for constant and realistic training whenever the troops were not occupied in actual combat. This was especially relevant when I was a young company commander in the Negev during the War of Independence in 1948 where I had to assimilate many new recruits who had just come from refugee ships. Later the lesson was repeated to me during a period in 1955 when I was a reservist battalion commander called to a point near the Egyptian border to guard against a possible enemy attack. Ever since those times I have had a rule. One can and must create the conditions for effective training even at the front.

That must be the solution now, too, in November 1973. Even though we were on high alert, we had to train ourselves and train new crews. Since we could spare neither instructors nor tanks, I decided that each tank crew would take a new crew and train it on the spot. In this way I was able to make use of all the tanks and all the officers in the division. Initially they would train on our tanks, and when we got new tanks, they would continue on those. There was no choice. We would train on tanks loaded with ammunition and at the same time remain on high alert. The fighting might resume at virtually any moment.

We worked out an "austerity" program and engaged in only the most essential elements in each training phase so as to advance to the following phase and arrive at the ability to run a tank as soon as possible. True, the training might be faulty from a professional point of view, but an emergency situation obligated emergency training.

So the brigades deployed and spread out, seeking training areas. Training tents went up, aids were improvised, and school began.

Armored Corps HQ dealt with sending us reinforcements. We received mostly yeshiva students — wonderful boys! But we had a problem: Time was our most precious commodity here in the field — the fighting was liable to be resumed momentarily, and we had to engage in a speedy buildup. Therefore we wanted to train seven days and nights a week — including, that is, the Sabbath. I put the issue to the yeshiva students. Their response: In Jewish law, the duty of saving life overrides the Sabbath laws. Who are we, they said, to judge the situation. "If you, the commander, assure us that you will weigh matters carefully and then you give us an order to train on the Sabbath — then train we will."

Tanks were arriving, reinforcements were flowing in, the division's training system was growing and branching out. It had to be extended to other divisions as well.

CHAPTER THIRTY-FOUR

GENERAL TAL TAKES COMMAND

B ut in the meantime, on 9 November, changes which were to have a major effect on all spheres of activity in the Southern Command area took place in the front command. Former Chief of Staff Chaim Bar-Lev, who had assumed command of the southern front when the sitaution was at a nadir, and who — despite objective and internal difficulties — had succeeded in leading us to a dazzling victory, doffed his uniform and returned to take up his post of minister of commerce and industry. Defense Minister Dayan also hesitated to leave the command in Gonen's hands, and so he was placed in charge of the Southern Sinai district.

Thus Bar-Lev and Gonen departed simultaneously, and command was given to General Israel Tal (in addition to his post as deputy chief of staff). However, Tal's superiors were apparently disappointed by his approach very quickly, because he was replaced by the end of December. Why? In his autobiography, Dayan writes: "The reason for his replacement — or for accepting his resignation — was not that he was unable to carry out this task. His view concerning our fire policy at that time conflicted with my view. But it was not this which tipped the scales, either; Tal was unwilling to carry out a policy which had been laid down but with which he disagreed. . . . Nor indeed did many days pass before his view against a policy of sharp reactions on our part — when the Egyptians opened fire and advanced in the field — found practical expression in the form of his interpretations concerning 'how to react to what.' I saw no point in ignoring the situation; and I certainly did not want to change a policy which I deemed a correct one.''

Dayan's remarks will, I believe, be better understood if I describe some of the problems and activities we were occupied with during Tal's period of command over the southern front.

During November and December, the Egyptian 7th and 19th Divisions remained surrounded on the east bank, south of Bitter Lake. On the west bank, remnants of the Third Army were absorbing reinforcements.

On our side, too, the buildup of strength continued apace. The decision to attack and destroy the encircled Third Army on the east bank would be carried out when political circumstances permitted. Despite this decision from above, two other proposals were put forward as well. Sharon suggested that we attack the Egyptian forces deployed west of the Israeli salient. Tal was against both the destruction of the Third Army and Sharon's idea. Instead, Tal wanted to transfer my division back to the west bank to join Sharon and Magen in a defensive posture.

As soon as Tal took over command of the front, he ordered me to transfer one brigade back to the west bank. This order conflicted with the mission I had been given and placed me in a delicate situation. Should I carry out the order even if I suspected that by doing so I would be thwarting the intentions of the General Staff? I reached the conclusion that despite the unpleasantness it entailed, I would do well to ascertain whether the General Staff's intentions had been changed. It did not take long before Tal's order was canceled. But Tal did not give up. Time and again he approached the chief of staff and the minister of defense with the demand that my entire division be transferred to the west bank and be placed in a defensive posture. He explained his repeated requests by stating that he was not ready to accept personal responsibility for what was liable to happen should the Egyptians launch an attack.

In my view, the balance of forces on the west bank did not justify the transfer of my division there. Desiring to allay Tal's anxiety concerning our situation on the west bank, in my capacity as commander of the Armored Corps in charge of the training and influx of reinforcements, I gave top priority to reinforcing Sharon's and Magen's divisions stationed on the west bank; this, despite the fact that I believed my own division should have priority, since we were to carry out the main attack.

The notion of transferring my division to the west bank had another aspect as well. It would seriously affect our training and buildup program, since training possibilities on the west bank were far more limited. Magen, for example, who also made serious efforts to take part in the training program, was able to train only fifty crews because he was situated on the line of contact. As for Sharon, he was not too enthusiastic about training at a time like this; he was still thinking mainly about "operations."

General Tal didn't care much for the training idea. We were waiting for certain areas to be declared "fire zones" so we could train there, but the approvals were not forthcoming. When in addition to our differences concerning the operational plans I sought to explain to Tal what effect a transfer to the west bank, where training was virtually impossible, would have on our operational capacity within a few weeks — we would have tanks without crews — Tal's reply was: "There is the danger that we will be attacked on the west bank; you must move there!" Fortunately the chief of staff did not accept Tal's operational outlook and did not give approval for our transfer to the west bank. Thus our "training for the masses" project — which built up our strength — was able to continue. Not much time would pass before our strength in tanks and crews would exceed that of the opening of the war. It is to be regretted that the program was accompanied by still other needless difficulties.

The debate concerning the operational approach we should adopt continued. I could not understand Sharon in this regard. Before the war I had esteemed him as one who was well able to perceive military considerations comprehensively. Could it be that he would prefer an attack on the west bank, which at best would lead to destruction of some enemy forces, to the alternative of achieving that and more by the destruction of the besieged Third Army on the east bank? Moreover, the cease-fire lines were long lines of contact and meant the engagement of great forces on both banks to encircle the Third Army. Thus, its destruction would allow us to shorten the lines of contact and to devote fewer men to holding the lines. In an operation against the Third Army we would be able to make use of our air power in an area where there were no missiles or other antiaircraft weapons. And since we had no intention of advancing any further toward Cairo, would it not be preferable to take prisoners and seize huge amounts of military equipment? And what of the blow to the Egyptians' morale and their prestige that would result from the surrender of their Third Army? I continued to hold my view that Sharon was being swayed by egocentric motives and that he was unable to acquiesce in the fact that another commander held the "fist" that would deliver the main blow, while he was being assigned a secondary defensive task.

At a certain point, Tal changed his original stand and moved to back Sharon's idea. It's possible that he concluded that if Sharon's proposal — to attack on the west bank — were accepted, my division would also be transferred to the west side of the canal. Thus Tal would attain his own objective, which was the reinforcement of the west bank. I continued to oppose the idea, but planning at HQ went on in this direction, and I also had to plan my role in the operation.

Even now, when Southern Command was busy planning an attack on the west bank, Tal continued to raise questions, as he had in the period when he had been apprehensive about an Egyptian offensive. I still remember one evening at Refidim vividly when — following a conference of division commanders — Tal suddenly threw out a question: Did we really think we had the strength to attack the Egyptians? A strange situation was created. The division commanders — Magen, Sasson, and others — calmed their commander: "Talik, when you objected to an attack and were concerned with strengthening our defensive capacity, we could understand that [and some said: 'You were right!'] but now that we have been so greatly reinforced and after we have laid minefields and have fortified our terrain, we are convinced of our capability to attack." The entire conversation revolved around the attempts of the various officers to give Tal a shot in the arm. We seemed to be children trying to boost our father's spirit.

One day, a meeting was scheduled for the division commanders with the chief of staff and the defense minister in which we were to present our plans and report on our operational preparations. As the time for the conference approached, I recalled an "exercise" that Tal liked to recount with no little pleasure. The story went as follows: One day, the late Prime Minister Levi Eshkol, accompanied by the then-Chief of Staff Yitzhak Rabin arrived to visit Armored Corps HQ. Tal, who was then commander of the Armored Corps, was giving Eshkol a talk, with the aid of slides, on the Corps' condition and its buildup of strength. Suddenly Tal broke off to assert dramatically: "Mr. Prime Minister, I want to tell you that the Armored Corps is not prepared for war!" Tal would go on to relate how Rabin began clearing his throat, to go red, express surprise, protest. And Tal went on in his declarative manner: "Mr. Prime Minister, I am responsible for what I say. Our armor is not prepared for war because the stocks of ammunition in the country are too small." Tal would conclude by giving the moral: From that point, more ammunition was purchased and the stocks were increased.

This time, I decided to use the same technique. When my turn came — at the conference with Dayan and Dado — to present my plan, I detailed it at length and concluded: "Mr. Defense Minister, I am convinced that this plan is implementable, but we are not prepared to implement it!" A sudden silence. The defense minister asked: "Why not?" I explained that Tal objected to the operation, was not assisting the preparations, that I lacked the infantry I required, and my forces were split. I was just not getting assistance.

Dayan, somewhat taken aback, asked Dado: "What's going on here? Haven't we decided to attack the Third Army?"

The chief replied: "There is such a decision, but Tal is obstinate and keeps appealing against it."

At this point, Dayan dropped the curtain on the little drama: "Whether he appeals or not, gentlemen, this is a decision by the Government of Israel. Please carry it out."

Nor was this the end of the affair. In view of Tal's objections, the operational plan for attacking the Third Army was presented for approval to the prime minister. Present at the decisive conference were — besides the prime minister and the defense minister — also Ministers Bar-Lev and Yigal Allon; and, from the army, Dado, Tal, and myself. I do not recall the details of the discussion, but I remember being very much impressed by the pointed questions put to Tal precisely by the only person in the room without a military background, Mrs. Meir. The discussion ended with approval in principle being given to the plan.

Besides our preparations for action in the event the political process broke down, we were caught up in a kind of "war of attrition" initiated by the Egyptians and the Syrians — an expression of their confidence that the superpowers would restrain Israel and an expression also of Israel's weakness in that it restrained itself and did not respond as it had in the past. An absurd situation developed, at least on the southern front, where the Egyptians were in an extremely delicate situation. The Third Army was besieged and at our mercy. First of all, we could have warned the Egyptians that if they did not halt the shelling, we would "finish off the job" and destroy the Third Army. As it was, we allowed them to bring supplies through our lines every day. We could at any time have closed off the supply route and prevented them from getting any supplies until a genuine cease-fire was imposed. Such a step would have been more than natural. This is what I had done when the cease-fire first came into force, and it was what Magen had done when the Egyptian shelling began. But now he encountered a furious reaction by Tal, who forbade him to take such action. Moreover, Tal even prevented us from firing artillery after the Egyptians had hit our weak points. Why were we forbidden to fire artillery or even to bomb the Third Army from the air? Tal would permit only counterbattery fire, and even that required his prior approval. Sharon was not impressed by Tal's bans, and in his sector they fired at will. Magen then suggested that we take another of the Mount Ataka ridge lines — one that dominated the Egyptians' artillery deployment — but Tal vetoed this, too. A ridiculous situation developed, which encouraged the Egyptians — who took our restraint as a sign of weakness. Dayan and Dado came to Southern Command HQ for a conference and in the presence of the division commanders explained and ordered an active-fire policy. Tal later told us: "I want to remind you that you are to act solely according to my orders."

As I knew him, Tal was a very complex personality. From conversations with him, I inferred that he was building himself a world view which in my opinion was unjustified. He began to regard himself as standing guard over the peace and thus preventing Dayan from heating up the sector. According to Tal, soldiers from all over the front trusted only him and were asking him to beware of the "trigger-happy" division commanders. In the discussions concerning the disengagement of forces, Tal expressed views that I did not like at all: The IDF, he would say, "really screwed up," so "it deserved to be punished. We ought to withdraw at once, even as far as the Gidi and Mitla passes, then to accumulate renewed strength and attack in another year."

In my estimation, our activity and our military capability reached a nadir during Tal's period of command. On the eastern shore of Bitter Lake was the besieged Botzer fortification, in which about a company of Egyptian infantry and some ten tanks were located. The question was when they would surrender, due to a lack of food and water, but time and again they succeeded in infiltrating supply boats across Bitter Lake. We set ambushes along the lake shore, but they managed to evade us. Opposite our ambushes, at a distance of about 1,000 meters, was a group of small islands. Instead of deploying ambushes there, the islands were just mined, and Tal continued to busy himself with "development" matters: the construction of a tank-bearing raft. Meanwhile, months went by, and the Egyptians at Botzer continued to eat and drink their fill.

Tal's behavior during the weeks when he was Southern Front commander and its effect on events there came as no surprise to me. As soon as I heard from Dayan that Tal was to be given command of the front, I told him that I expected problems and that the result would be an end to initiatives and offensive operations; henceforth, we would move into a state of defense and of passivity. Nor would it take long for Dayan himself to find that I had not just been speaking off the top of my head. My own prior evaluation was based on close acquaintance with Tal and on awareness of the difference between the man as I knew him and his image as formed by the public following the Six Day War of 1967. Subsequently, after I had studied the history of the Yom Kippur War closely, I would find that when he served as deputy chief of staff, too, Tal had adhered to a minimalistic approach, had expressed opposition to our initiatives, and had tended to await enemy moves.

As long as Tal was serving at GHQ, his conflicting views had been confined to verbal statements before decisions were taken. However, when Tal was given command authority over the southern front, his dissent was more than verbal. Dado quickly perceived that not only did Tal disagree with his views, but also did not carry out his or the defense minister's directives.

When I reflect on Dado and those with whom he worked, my admiration for his ability to make decisions, for his strength of spirit in leading the army, grows. At Dado's side was a deputy like Tal, above him was a defense minister who, in the critical situations at the beginning of the war, had a pessimistic outlook. Below him, one of his front commanders fed him optimistic and unrealistic reports. At Southern Command the personal difficulties were renewed shortly after Bar-Lev's appointment, mainly due to Sharon's behavior. When Tal replaced Bar-Lev after the cease-fire, they were exacerbated. Throughout, Dado acted with forbearance and patience. He convinced the Cabinet, and most of the high command, of the soundness of his analyses, and he was able to stand firm against all the pressures to change his decisions.

At times of crisis, particularly in wartime, everyone is expected to outdo himself and exploit his abilities to the full. Some break when the responsibility is intolerably heavy. Even though Dado felt that he was in part responsible for our having been caught by surprise, and despite the erosion in the mutual trust between him and Dayan, and then between him and Tal, he bore the burden of decision-making, preserved his calmness of spirit and clarity of calculation and took the right decisions at the right times. Against the few mistakes to his debit, there is, to his great credit, his manner of command and his indomitable spirit. I shall always remember him as a great commander who led a battered army to recovery and victory.

When Dayan saw his mistake concerning Tal's appointment, he decided to replace him. For three weeks Dado tried to convince me to accept command of the front, but I was not persuaded. Had I been a division commander only I would have agreed, but I was also serving as commander of the Armored Corps. At this time I was totally engrossed in the work of rebuilding the IDF's armored strength, which had been so decimated in the war. I left my division in the hands of my deputy while I toured the armored formations on the southern and northern fronts. It will be recalled that I was to have retired in October, but when the cease-fire came into force Dado asked me to stay on in the regular army. My scheduled replacement,

General Avraham Mandler, had been killed in action. The Armored Corps had been severely battered, losing thousands of men, among them hundreds of commanding officers. I felt that I must remain to reconstruct the Armored Corps.

Meanwhile, the chief of staff kept up the pressure on me. Against my unwillingness to leave the Armored Corps and assume command over the front there arose a new consideration: my feeling that the front was now under the command of a general whose military approach was in the main defensive. As long as the cease-fire remained in force, however, I stuck to my refusal to accept the command. Every time the political process seemed to be breaking down, tension rose in the light of possible resumed fighting. This was the situation at the beginning of January 1974, when we felt we were at the brink; either the forces would disengage or the war would resume. It was my own appraisal that the fighting would recommence, and it was that evaluation that tipped the scales; I agreed to assume command over the southern front.

But my assessment was wrong. Within two days Kissinger had succeeded in bringing the sides to agreement, and I found myself at km 101, engaged in negotiations with the Egyptians concerning a disengagement of forces.

CHAPTER THIRTY-FIVE

MORALE PROBLEMS

W e had reached the negotiations at km 101 in the wake of Secretary of State Kissinger's mediation and pressures. This process was able to get under way by virtue of the IDF's achievements on the battlefield, which had led the Egyptians to request a cease-fire. As the process began, the IDF's attainments and its threatening force were still very much in evidence. Both the Egyptians and the Soviets had to accept the fact that the encirclement of the Third Army had been completed after the first cease-fire was declared because it had been the Egyptians and the Syrians themselves who violated it. But gradually the effect of the war's outcome on the negotiations diminished. Many external interests and pressures play a part in political negotiations. Israeli leaders faced an extraordinarily difficult task for which they had to summon up all their inner resources. Two days only had passed since the cease-fire when we already felt the political pressures being brought to bear on us. We were ordered to allow supply convoys to pass through our territory on their way to the surrounded Third Army. Was it for this we had encircled the Third Army? When had something similar happened? An army, victim of a surprise attack, had paid a heavy price in its fighting and then had achieved the encirclement of a very substantial part of the enemy's forces. Now we had to lift the siege and allow the enemy to receive supplies, without even getting our prisoners back in return.

I expressed my disappointment to the prime minister when at the end of October she paid a visit to my division, which was still on the west bank. It was not easy for me to be critical. I was well aware that Mrs. Meir had to bear a virtually intolerable burden, far beyond any of the other decision-makers in the war. I knew her toughness of spirit and her ability to withstand pressures exerted by world leaders. And I knew also that I myself was not sufficiently informed concerning the hard pressures being brought to bear on Israel in the political arena. I had heard about Soviet threats to intervene and about tremendous pressures on the part of the United States — our only support — not just in the political sphere but also in that of military supplies.

At the same time, I knew that even though the political level had given in to United States pressures and agreed to certain things, in practice the events on the battlefield had led to deviations from these agreements, and that the sides could do nothing but acquiesce to them. Thus it was that we had gone on after the 22 October cease-fire to complete the encirclement of the Third Army. And even after the political level had given its consent for the transfer of supplies to the Third Army, the convoys were held up for two more days without any of the pressure getting to me. It was at my own initiative that this was done: we sent the convoys back because the Egyptians were still engaging in sporadic shooting, and we informed them that as long as the fire did not stop completely, we would not allow the convoys to go through. Having no choice, the Egyptians were forced to restrain their men. I sensed that in expressing my own disappointment and criticism I was expressing also the feelings of my men: "Why did we agree to let them have supplies when they refused to trade prisoners?" It irritated me that we were forced by the Americans to play by the rules of the game according to concepts prevailing among the Arabs — for we were asked not to press the Egyptians and to show understanding for feelings of "Arab honor." Well, why should we not bring them to recognize that for us the exchange of prisoners was such a burning issue that we were not ready to discuss anything until our men were back with us?

Within a few days I would learn that the strength and resoluteness of the leaders is a function not only of the results on the battlefield and of military potential, but also of the degree of support they receive from the public. Among the public there was already a general decline of morale, in the wake of what would come to be called the "earthquake." The nation was in a state of crisis and went through some of the lowest times it had ever known. This was a period of deep unease and discontent in Israel. Public opinion makers began speaking of the *Machdal* — the catchall word for the eve-of-war blunders by the country's military and civilian leaders who had been surprised by the Arabs' attack. It was a result of this public mood of resentment and depression that a commission of inquiry, headed by Justice Shimon Agranat, was set up in November to look into whether there had in fact been such a *Machdal*.

In the press various stories began to appear, such as complaints from General Sharon who, in total contradiction to standing army orders, gave interviews to foreign papers in which he accused his superiors of lack of preparedness and of faulty conduct of the war itself. Worst of all, he spoke of the politicalization of the army. When the war erupted, in October, the country was in the midst of an election campaign. Because of the war the elections were moved from the end of October to the end of December. Sharon himself, it will be recalled, had left the army in the summer of 1973 and had at once entered the political arena. It was he who initiated the establishment of the Likud party, and he was a Knesset (parliament) candidate on its behalf. Immediately after the cease-fire he declared his desire to remain in the army, but in practice he did not relinquish his Knesset candidacy. As noted, he also began giving interviews — against army rules and regulations — complaining, *inter alia,* of politicalization within the IDF. This claim was itself a political one, but by making it Sharon gained a quasi-immunity for unrestrained behavior and violation of military discipline because any attempt to punish him would now be interpreted as revenge taken by the "Establishment."

While the war on the Egyptian front was still at its height, an Israeli professor, Amos Perlmutter, who had been lecturing at a university in Washington, D.C., arrived at Lod Airport. There a military plane was waiting to take him directly to Sharon's division where he joined the community of reporters. From the tenth of November a veritable flood of stories began to appear in the foreign press. The Israeli press, which was bound by military censorship, was very eager to report all it could by quoting these stories from abroad (which, under the rules of the military censorship, it could do). Among the headlines which appeared in the Israeli press: *"Le Figaro* Heaps Praises on Sharon"; "Israeli 'War of Generals' Is Piquant Matter in France"; "Foreign Press, Including Egypt, Plays up Israeli 'War of Generals'." Interviews with Sharon, in the same spirit, were also published in the *New York Times* and the *Los Angeles Times*. On 20 January 1974, a synopsis of an article published by Professor Perlmutter in *Harper's Magazine* appeared in the Israeli media; in this article, Sharon was quoted as stating: "From the first day of the war, politics was more important than military considerations or military strategy. When at last it was decided that the time had come to cross the canal, everyone was busy discussing who would carry out the crossing — which political party would get the prestige. I told them: 'Listen, I am in command of 15,000 soldiers and I have to fight with them now. But in the end I'll screw you all. First I'll cross the canal and screw the Egyptians and then I'll come back and screw all of you, and you'll all have to wear helmets.' "

In Israel a public storm sprang up. The independent daily *Ha'aretz* editorialized under the title, "The Likud Must Draw the Conclusions Concerning Sharon": "Knesset Member Ariel Sharon's recent appearances show all the abhorrent qualities to be found in a public person: arrogance, sanctimoniousness, contempt for law and justice, encouragement to violate orders, fostering of demoralization, lack of reliability. . . . Mr. Sharon's sanctimoniousness virtually cries out from his remark that in his military service he never engaged in politics. His last three and a half months of service demonstrate precisely that there has never been a senior officer who engaged in politics as much as he did. As a division commander, Sharon was surrounded by a court of reporters and sympathizers, gave irresponsible interviews to foreign papers, met with political figures in order to promote a line which his superiors opposed. In one way or another, he never let it be forgotten for a moment that he is a politician who is up for election."

But not all of Israel's opinion molders held this view, and not all of them agreed with the *Ha'aretz* editorial. Writing in the same paper, on 30 January, Professor Amnon Rubinstein, head of the *Shinui* (Change) movement, averred that one should not take account of marginal matters or of the way in which things were said; it would be best to examine the content of Sharon's accusations. Others went so far as to give support to Sharon's claims.

The general mood of frustration over the fact that we had been caught by surprise and had sustained many casualties proved fertile ground for the planting of charges and accusations and made it easier for Sharon to promote his image among the public as the hero who had fought the enemy despite the "harassers" who had tried to hamper him. Other senior commanders were silent — as army regulations required — and by their silence helped create a one-sided picture.

To me, this was the most demeaning period in the entire history of the IDF. The main blame for failure to prevent this unrestrained behavior rests, I believe, with Dayan. The afternoon daily *Ma'ariv* of 25 January 1974 published an article under the headline, "Sharon: Chief Of Staff To Blame For Blunders; Must Be Dismissed At Once." The subheadline said: "Praises Dayan As Courageous, Original — Must Continue To Serve." And Dayan reciprocated. Replying to newsmen and to others who asked what he thought about Sharon's statements and whether he intended to take any measures against him, Dayan said: "No one has ever died from words and interviews."

The evil winds continued to blow from Sharon to the media, from them to the people, and from the press and public at home back to the reserve army that was now on the front. As long as the cease-fire went on without any settlement, the full military call-up remained in force. Tens of thousands of reservists continued to serve; hundreds of persons who had rushed to Israel from abroad in order to enlist now found themselves cut off from their families. Many small businesses were badly hit — some of them were wiped out. Personal and family problems cropped up that made life difficult for the reservists. And in addition to the personal difficulties, the country's economy suffered badly. As the period of full mobilization dragged on, more and more coordination efforts were required. Tens of thousands of workers were absent, and thousands of vehicles had also been mobilized by the army. To ease the burden on the economy and on individuals, we issued temporary leaves, while taking all necessary measures for their quick recall should the fighting flare up again. This was, of course, a complex and sensitive operation that had to be carried out with meticulous scrutiny.

Against this kind of background, it was only natural that there should be considerable grumbling and complaining. To solve the complicated problems required time. One could call for patience until solutions could be found for a part of the problems; or one could — and this was just the style of Sharon's allegations — sound off against General Headquarters for not solving any problems. Sharon put forward issues likely to gain him popularity among his men: Why shouldn't the burden be more fairly distributed? People in the rear must be called up to replace those at the front.

During this period I made it a point to meet with the men for talks from time to time: my deputy met with the supporting logistical units, while I would talk to the brigades. We would collect the men in large groups, hundreds of soldiers, and there in the field under the sky, I would — with the aid of a bullhorn — review for them the political and military situation and reply to their questions. Despite the serious personal difficulties that many of the soldiers were now facing, I did not run into any overwhelming difficulties in explaining the situation. I did my best to give them straightforward surveys without any embellishments, and to the soldiers' credit it must be said that they grasped what I was saying. I told them that we had withstood a difficult war, not only against Syria and Egypt, but also against expeditionary forces from Iraq, Jordan, Saudi Arabia, Algeria, Libya, and Morocco — all of them aided by huge quantities of Soviet arms that flowed in to replace losses. I went on to point out that the war had not yet been decided; it was liable to be resumed. The waiting period was a prolonged one, and if we did not manifest staying power, we would be defeated. I pointed to the example of the British people's firm determination to hold out in the Second World War. To those who put forward difficult problems of economic loss, I did not hesitate to reply by referring to those who had given their lives or would remain incapacitated. I said that while the state had not been prepared to cope with problems that are a result of a prolonged call-up, it was now readying itself for this — by paying compensation and giving loans to the best of a small country's ability. I had no trouble convincing them that the slogan of an "equal burden" was just not realistic. Admittedly, persons who had been released from service were in the rear. But there was nothing new in this; the same had been true of all the serious periods the country had experienced in the past. Of course there was room for improvement, for distributing the burden more fairly, but who could replace a tank-crew member? Or an artillery gunner? It is in the nature of military service not to be distributed equally. There are days when the infantry and armor are called on to do more, and there are other days when the combat troops go home and the quartermasters remain behind to deal with equipment. There are times when the engineers must stay to mine and fortify the lines. It is self-evident that needs are fulfilled according to functional criteria and not by criteria of justice in an equal distribution of the burden. It is the way of the world that some give more to their nation than others; and you are among them, I said to the troops. If you want, you can join the gripers over the lack of equality; but you can, if you want, take pride in your part in and contribution to the saving of the homeland.

Call it "Zionism" if you want — there's no shame in that — and besides, it worked. Even though the period of waiting went on and on, the division's morale remained high, and the men continued to prepare for operations and train new tank crews. In the meantime, we began sending men home on leave; soldiers who departed for home with high morale returned depressed. They thought they had fought a magnificent war, incomparably more difficult than any of Israel's previous wars. But all they found at home were people talking about the *Machdal* and the nation caught up in a depressed mood.

About two months after the cease-fire, after I had assumed command of the front, I visited Sharon's division — he himself had in the meantime left the army following his election to the Knesset. I found, to my surprise, that all the old questions were still being bandied about without having been answered. I found many complaints against a nonequal distribution of the burden, against the lack of adequate economic support for the men, against the early release of persons who had come from abroad, and more in a similar vein.

Here, too, the men tended to respond favorably to my explanations and to show a willingness to understand our difficult situation.

Actually, there would seem to have been sufficient reasons for eroded morale in Israel. The war caught us by surprise and found the IDF unprepared. We had many losses — including many men missing in action — and some three hundred Israeli soldiers had been taken prisoner by the enemy. The war was a prolonged one, and we were unprepared for a brutal, protracted campaign. And not only had the war broken out and been conducted in a way we had not imagined, but it had been accompanied by manifestations attesting that many things were not as they should be. On the front was the fog of battle, which is only natural; but on the home front there was, this time, a thicker fog of war than usual. In line with a decision at governmental level, full information was not passed on to the public at home. The pain at the large number of fallen and missing was overwhelming. Israel is a small country where many people know one another; and the feeling of general sadness was intensified by the shared personal grief of many families. To all this was added the burdensome, gnawing feeling deriving from lack of information and from uncertainty. Egypt's and Syria's refusal to inform Israel of the number of IDF prisoners they were holding or to give us their names increased apprehension and concern over their fate. Tension grew because of the hope that those missing might still be alive — and the dread that they were not. And past experience had led us to be fearful of our enemies' bad treatment of prisoners. Then the enemy launched a war of attrition on both fronts; again we had daily casualties, while we seemed to have acquiesced in this situation. Both the Egyptians and the Syrians — beaten on two fronts — apparently felt confident that the superpowers would prevent Israel from taking any drastic steps in retaliation for a war of attrition; nor can there be any doubt that our restraint here reflected precisely such a state of affairs.

Unquestionably, there was place for the nation's deep discontent considering the circumstances in which the war had begun. There was no lack of signs attesting to serious mistakes that must be corrected. There was place, too, for appointing the Agranat Commission and for awaiting its conclusions. But from this to the depressed spirit — which in itself was weakening our staying power — the way was very long indeed. Unfortunately, we did not surpass ourselves during these weeks to show national maturity. To the press must go a large share of the responsibility for the breakdown of morale.

Correspondents who for years had attached themselves to IDF generals and who had sung the IDF's praises now felt that they had abused their positions and that they had a part in the *Machdal*. Ironically, they sought to atone for what they saw as past mistakes with new mistakes. Many of those who in the past overdid their praise of the IDF now "mended their ways" and turned to writing redoubled criticism. The greatest paradox was that many of those who in the past were led astray by the charisma of the generals now took to firing poison darts at their heroes of yesterday. But even now some sought to hold tightly to those they regarded as superheroes, by winging aloft the slogan painted on one of the vehicles in Sharon's division: "Arik — King of Israel." A long time yet would pass before more and more people would begin to discover that the king might be naked.

Today, in retrospect, one hopes that the people of Israel will examine the crisis of national spirit of those days and will analyze — coolly, soberly, and sorrowfully — what the country experienced in the waning days of the war. Even then there were some who warned of the loss of national sanity, but they were the minority. The then-president, Professor Ephraim Katzir, wrought a storm of criticism when he said, in passing, "We are all to blame for the blunders."* I subscribe to this view. Of course, there are those who are less to blame, but if Professor Katzir's notion were to be taken as everyone's starting point, we would have corrected our mistakes and cleared accounts with those mainly to blame in a responsible and constructive spirit that would have yielded better fruits.

At the same time the judicial commission of inquiry was formed to examine the IDF's preparedness for the war and the conduct of its first days, we in the army also began the process of drawing our own lessons.

*As quoted in *Ma'ariv*, 25 November 1973.

CHAPTER THIRTY-SIX

LESSONS LEARNED

When the firing ceased, and after the plans and preparations were completed for anticipated operations and the task of training aimed at building up our strength was started, we were able to commence the process of learning the war's lessons. We called a divisional conference. The large tent we pitched for the purpose was jammed with battalion and brigade commanders, staff officers from the brigades and the division, and commanders of divisional units. All had gathered for a meeting of comrades in arms who had together gone through a very rough but also very courageous period of fighting.

As I scanned the group before me I thought to myself, all embody unique battlefield stories. As I looked at the brigade commanders I thought of their deputies. They were supposed to deal with the logistical problems of the campaign, but this is not how things had worked out. All three operated as combat deputies, all three were wounded in the fighting. Shilo, Gabi's deputy, had been wounded on 11 October in the battle at Havraga and now returned to us before he was fully recovered. Natke's deputy, Giora, was wounded near Shalufa; his leg was still in a cast. Carmeli, Aryeh's deputy, was still recuperating in the rear from his head wound. And here were the battalion commanders: Assaf Yaguri, who had been released from captivity to an emotional, warm welcome back; Adini, his hand still in a cast; Amir and Eliashiv, who had gone through many tough battles; and Ze'ira, the captain who had commanded a battalion and would soon be promoted to major. As I looked out at them and at others, I thought of the battalion commanders who had fallen in battle: Mulla, Artzi, Dan Sapir, Mark Yames, and the division's physician, Dr. Sahar. Many pictures flashed by in my mind's eye from conversations, exercises, from previous wars.

The conference began with a review of the events and the lessons. Tens of officers — battalion commanders, brigade commanders, commanders of brigade and divisional units — each pinned up his map and described his course of action and the battles he had fought. Each of them noted the lessons learned from the fighting. It was all very interesting, but it soon began to be tiring as well. There were many speakers, and each of them had experienced many battles. We had, after all, fought for nineteen days. Nor was this the first time that officers were describing their combat experiences. The divisional conference was preceded by meetings of this kind within the brigade frameworks; and it would be followed by another conference at Southern Command HQ. The present forum included persons who were very busy — commanders of active units who worked hard and whose time to prepare for such a conference was limited. The various stories were presented, each according to the character of the man relating it. There were those who tended to play down the fierce fighting they had experienced, while others exaggerated their exploits. Worst of all, the men presented events both as they saw them and as they wanted to see them. Much information was lost because of the superficial nature of the conference.

I became well aware of the limited value of these conferences when I read the full report of the Agranat Commission concerning the eighth of October and when I sat down to research the present work and compared my own notes and memories with the studies carried out by the IDF's department of history. I was responsible for eliciting the lessons in my division and later, after I assumed command of the front, in Southern Command overall. I also took part in similar, lesson-eliciting conferences of the IDF high command and of infantry and paratroop officers, where I described my own experiences in the war and discussed the lessons I had drawn from my own vantage point. Today, with hindsight, I realize how superficial all these conferences were. The facts we knew were immeasurably fewer than those that we were, at the time, unaware of.

Nonetheless, there was no choice. As superficial as these debriefing sessions may be, an army like the IDF must engage in quick lesson-drawing, and these preliminary lessons must also be applied quickly, for who knows when we may be called upon to fight again. At the same time, I believe that following this kind of war it would be desirable to appoint one or more commissions, similar to some extent — at least with regard to their authority — to the Agranat Commission. Such a commission would include public figures and retired army officers who could continue to hold hearings for a lengthy period. They would have to inquire into the entire course of a war, and not just into what seem to be blunders. That process would be a time-consuming one, and their findings should then form the basis for a second round of lesson-drawing by the army command.

The war went on for three weeks, a long war by Israeli standards but a very short one by general world criteria. It was a very intensive diversified campaign, fought by armies equipped with the best of modern weaponry. Three thousand tanks were destroyed; hundreds of aircraft were downed. We experienced a wide range of combat situations: defense, offense, mobile warfare, infantry and armor ambushes, commando operations, night fighting, fighting in built-up areas and on mountainous terrain. Obviously, such a war lends itself to lessons being elicited in many varied spheres.

When I arrived in Washington in August 1974 to serve as military attaché, I found that the American army had dozens of officers engaged in learning the lessons of the Yom Kippur War. Tens of thick volumes were produced: tactics, organizational structure of units, changes required in weapons arsenal — all of these were examined. I could not help making the comparison with our own methods. With the Americans, there is a scientific process of data collecting and an effort to adopt an objective approach. I found great esteem for the IDF — at times to the point of envy — admiration for our manner of fighting, devotion, and for our immense military achievements. To the Americans' credit it must be said that this admiration did not prevent them from analyzing the facts meticulously, pinpointing weak points and leveling criticism at several past and present IDF conceptions. I was very impressed by their intellectual openness and their scientific approach in eliciting lessons.

Unfortunately, Israel's security situation permits me to discuss only a few general lessons of the war. I wish to deal with one question that seems to have sprung up full grown from the Yom Kippur War battlefields and to have reverberated around the world: Has the era of the tank passed? No sooner had the sound of the guns faded away than the experts began making their proclamations: "The era of the warplane is over; the tank has lost its place as king of the battlefield." These appraisals were to a large extent based on what transpired during the opening stages of the war, when both tanks and planes suffered substantial losses from missiles which are basically defensive weapons. But if these declarations were correct, how, then is one to explain the Israeli victory, which was achieved by an army whose main strength lay in its planes and its armor?

A considerable part of the enemy's success at the outset of the war came from the difficult conditions the IDF was facing due to being caught by surprise and from the mistakes we made in the wake of that surprise when we acted hastily and with unbalanced forces. When we recovered and moved to counterattacks, the antiaircraft and antitank systems were unable to stop us. At the same time, it cannot be denied that in the Yom Kippur War there appeared effective and relatively simple weapons whose continued development must signal and warn of serious dangers that will be posed in future wars to aircraft and especially to tanks: mines that can be scattered in a twinkling from planes, helicopters, or by rockets to block tanks' avenues of approach; short- and long-range antitank missiles fired by infantry or from assault helicopters; high-precision bombs and missiles that can be fired from afar — from planes, helicopters, various types of launchers, and even from field guns, and which "ride on laser beams" or home in via laser-illuminated targets. Armor's enemies are growing. Will the tank survive on the battlefield of the future?

Every battle, every war, is based on two elements, fire and movement. The tank combines both, and its armor also provides protection against most weapons on the battlefield. The fact that the tank's enemies are growing is insufficient reason to remove them from the battlefield — at least not until effective substitutes are found. At present, I do not see what will replace the tank on the ground. The new assault helicopters do combine fire and movement, but they lack staying power and are incapable of holding or mopping up territory. If the existence of many effective enemies were a sufficient factor for disappearance from the battlefield, the infantry would long ago have vanished from military campaigns. But despite the infantry's high vulnerability to a whole host of weapons, there still exist many battlefield situations in which there is absolutely no substitute for infantry troops. In contrast to infantry, the tank is vulnerable to only a small number of battlefield weapons. The more lethal area weapons become, the greater the importance attached to dispersion — whereas the normal principles of warfare pull in the opposite direction, towards greater force concentration. Under these conditions, the tank takes on enhanced significance. Its mobility, armor, and firepower afford it both protection and the ability to move quickly from situations of dispersion to those of concentration and vice versa. Its qualities allow it to be employed in all forms of combat.

The era of the tank, then, is far from having passed; it will continue to be "king of the battlefield" on land.

Any discussion of the tank's future can be bound up with another question that also found prominent expression in the Yom Kippur War. Although the tank's qualities as a weapons system make it desirable and effective in all forms of combat, the full capability and potential latent in it find their optimal expression in attack. The Yom Kippur War pitted two basic strategic concepts against each other, a defensive strategy versus an offensive one. Israel's security doctrine held that the best defense is a good offense, that the war must be transferred as soon as possible into enemy territory, with the enemy to be vanquished in a lightning thrust. In view of this doctrine, priority within the IDF was given to the Israeli Air Force and the Armored Corps.

The doctrine according to which the Egyptians prepared for the Yom Kippur War held that they must quickly achieve a situation of static battle in which their densely deployed sophisticated missiles systems, in combination with other elements, would shatter the IDF's two main shock components — the air force and armor. The results of the confrontation between the two strategies in the 1973 war are well known. But what of the future? Do new technological developments point to the neutralization of mobility through firepower, hence to the strengthening of defense vis-à-vis offense?

The First World War was the last major conflict in which a similar situation evolved. The development of automatic weapons in general, and of the machine gun in particular, led to firepower gaining the upper hand over mobility and maneuvering capacity. Armor's predecessor, the cavalry, with its horses instead of tanks, was beaten again and again. Infantry charges were also broken. Defense overcame offense, and both sides found themselves engaged in trench warfare, with deadlock and stalemate characterizing the battlefield for four years. Towards the end of the war, the British came up with the tank and the deadlock was broken. The armies regained freedom of maneuver and mobility. Today, with the proliferation of antitank means, the question is whether we are once more facing a situation similar to that of World War I.

I doubt whether the development of all the diversified antitank weapons is drawing us closer to a situation where defense will once more gain the upper hand over offense. It may be assumed, though, that these developments will mean that the blitzkrieg tactics of World War II (and of the battles in Sinai in 1956 and 1967) — when armor exploited its qualities to the full, gaining the shock of surprise — are largely over. Nor am I certain how long the tendency will last to add armor and weight to the tank in order to enhance its passive defensive capacity. It's probable that changes will be introduced, but the way is still open to improve the tank's active defense by adding speed and firepower while reducing weight and size — this to produce more and less-costly vehicles that will continue to leave armor's mark on the battlefield. It is also likely that tanks will be able to be landed from helicopters in the enemy's rear. The growing difficulties will require a more considered combination of elements within the tank, as well as greater balance and cooperation between the components on the battlefield itself, with the aim of maintaining the superiority of offense over defense. For it is ultimately only through offense that the enemy will be defeated.

CHAPTER THIRTY-SEVEN

CONCLUSION

T he entire course of the war was affected by the fact that Israel was caught by surprise; it was the regular army alone which fought against overwhelming odds. This led to situations virtually unprecedented for the IDF: a high casualty rate, men missing in action, prisoners being taken by the enemy, the loss of many combat vehicles. In the wake of the critical situation which developed on the fronts, the first reserve troops to arrive were put into battle hastily, before they could accumulate strength and prepare properly. The results were success on the Syrian front and failure on the Egyptian front, but on both fronts we again paid heavy prices in terms of casualties and loss of equipment. That was the second phase. Henceforth, the IDF would continue to fight at greatly reduced strength while expending great efforts to reorganize and accumulate strength. We also continued to suffer losses against an enemy equipped with greatly superior firepower. One of the characteristics of this war was that the IDF, in its nineteen days of ground combat, fought with far less strength than it had built up over the years to meet the contingency of a war.

In comparison with the forces that attacked us, we were a small army. In formations, warplanes, tanks and artillery pieces the enemy outnumbered us by a ratio of more than three to one. The fact that we were caught by surprise cost us the immediate loss of nearly half of some of our main power ingredients. Moreover, the manner in which the IDF was equipped for fighting precluded our full exploitation of the potential we did in fact have. How, then, did we succeed in halting the enemy, moving within three days to the counterattack on the northern front, destroying most of the Syrian armor and throwing back the Syrians to a point just forty km from Damascus? And on the Egyptian front, to a counterattack within ten days, crossing the Canal, annihilating substantial enemy forces and encircling the Third Army?

Courage, devotion, and high professional standards on land, at sea, and in the air led us to victory. Nor are these mere slogans: their concrete expression was more than evident on the battlefield. It was these qualities which enabled us to take calculated risks. We were confident that any time a small unit would find itself facing an "oversize" mission, that unit would surpass itself and would not disappoint. The needs of the battlefield necessitated many diverse missions and our small army was split and re-split, forcing us to improvise right, left and center. We began the war in Sinai with three divisions and over nineteen days of fighting we suffered losses but at the same time "increased our strength" to five "divisional forces." Were they really forces of a size their name implies? In strength, no; but in terms of missions accomplished, yes.

I have described many mistakes we made. Many of them originated in the attempt to "jump even higher." Mistakes are inherent in any active initiative. However, there is no better yardstick by which to judge the standards and the ability of the IDF than the results of the war itself. Caught by surprise, we were "punished" and badly mauled; but in lightning-fast time, and despite the difficult conditions, we recovered and moved to counterattack. The superpowers halted us on the way to a total devastation of the enemy. Had not Sadat asked — very late but still in time, from his point of view — for a ceasefire, and had the United States not placed all its weight to prevent total victory, we could have achieved that victory.

While caution must be exercised in comparing wars fought in different periods at different places and under different circumstances, it is still worthwhile, in order to gain some perspective, to consider the Yom Kippur War against other wars in which one of the sides was taken by surprise. On 5 June 1967, the Egyptian army was caught by surprise and its fate sealed. Within four days the IDF took Sinai and destroyed most of the Egyptian Army. In the summer of 1941 the Red Army was taken by surprise when the German army invaded the USSR. It took three years for the Soviets to recover and turn the tide of the war, and another year after that to defeat the Nazis. In December 1941 the Americans were caught by surprise when the Japanese attacked Pearl Harbor; two years would pass before the United States turned the tide of the war. Moreover, in all these instances the parties to the conflicts were mobilized and deployed on their front lines. The 1973 attack was a far more serious one for the IDF — a strategic surprise. The main part of the armed forces, the reserves, was not mobilized and was in fact far from the fronts. Yet within days the IDF reversed the tide of the fighting. It is an achievement that speaks for itself.

So concludes my story of the fifth war in which I took part.

I saw my men and commanders in their most desperate hours, when they were barely able to extricate themselves from failed assaults, as they left behind exploding tanks with our comrades whom we were unable to help; and our hearts were filled with grief, with pain and sorrow.

I saw them on the long, hard days when the division came under repeated charges by masses of enemy troops. We were few in number, terribly weary and apprehensive but determined to stand firm no matter what.

I saw them being forged in strength from battle to battle, from fighting day to fighting day. I saw them in situations when the mission was clear and essential but still unattainable; stalemate on the front. A heavy heart; and only our stubbornness, our steadfastness, and our resourcefulness turned the tide.

I saw them as we broke through against stiff resistance deep into enemy territory and onto the wide open terrain where we could maneuver at will and as we destroyed the missile bases and burst into the enemy's camps and mopped them up. I saw them, too, fighting in the greenbelt and in Suez City.

I saw them in the exultation of victory, when we vanquished enemy formations, captured war materiel, took thousands of prisoners, and surrounded the Third Army.

I saw them up close: the tank crew members, the armored infantry men, the paratroopers, the reconnaissance boys, the engineers and the artillerymen, the logistics personnel, the drivers and the radio operators, the ordnance troops and the medics. I saw them up close because we fought as one united body. And when we stormed the enemy and broke through his defenses, our logistics personnel burst through the enemy's fire-barriers and rushed forward supporting the assault echelon with supplies, repairs, and by evacuating casualties.

Many of our comrades in arms fell in the fighting, and we who saw them fall beside us will remember them always, though our hearts grieve at the terrible finality of their deaths. And we who survived, what could we do but go on fighting with even greater will — for them too? The division excelled in its fighting and wrote some magnificent pages in the annals of Israel's armored divisions. How fortunate I was to have the privilege of commanding such a division. I salute all its men and officers!

INDEX

474